Running Rome and

This volume explores the transformation of public space and administrative activities in republican and imperial Rome through an interdisciplinary examination of the topography of power.

Throughout the Roman world building projects created spaces for different civic purposes, such as hosting assemblies, holding senate meetings, the administration of justice, housing the public treasury, and the management of the city through different magistracies, offices, and even archives. These administrative spaces – both open and closed – characterised Roman life throughout the Republic and High Empire until the administrative and judicial transformations of the fourth century CE. This volume explores urban development and the dynamics of administrative expansion, linking them with some of the most recent archaeological discoveries. In doing so, it examines several facets of the transformation of Roman administration over this period, considering new approaches to and theories on the uses of public space and incorporating new work in Roman studies that focuses on the spatial needs of human users, rather than architectural style and design.

This fascinating collection of essays is of interest to students and scholars working on Roman space and urbanism, Roman governance, and the running of the Roman Empire more broadly.

Antonio Lopez Garcia is an expert in Roman archaeology and topography. Since 2022, he teaches archaeology at the University of Granada, where obtained a María Zambrano contract for the attraction of international talent. Recently, he received a Ramón y Cajal grant from the Spanish Ministry of Science and Innovation. Currently, he is directing a research project at the University of Helsinki on Late Antique Rome, which is funded by the Kone Foundation. Prior to his current positions, he was a postdoctoral researcher at the same university within the ERC-funded project Law, Governance and Space: Questioning the Foundations of the Republican Tradition. He was fellow of the Royal Academy of Spain in Rome and obtained a Ph.D. from the University of Florence.

Studies in Roman Space and Urbanism
Series editor: Ray Laurence, Macquarie University, Australia

Over the course of the last two decades the study of urban space in the Roman world has progressed rapidly with new analytical techniques, many drawn from other disciplines such as architecture and urban studies, being applied in the archaeological and literary study of Roman cities. These dynamically interdisciplinary approaches are at the centre of this series. The series includes both micro-level analyses of interior spaces as well as macro-level studies of Roman cities (and potentially also wider spatial landscapes outside the city walls). The series encourages collaboration and debate between specialists from a wide range of study beyond the core disciplines of ancient history, archaeology and Classics such as art history and architecture, geography and landscape studies, and urban studies. Ultimately the series provides a forum for scholars to explore new ideas about space in the Roman city.

Rethinking the Roman City
The Spatial Turn and the Archaeology of Roman Italy
Edited by Dunia Filippi

Urban Space and Urban History in the Roman World
Edited by Miko Flohr

Pompeian Peristyle Gardens
Samuli Simelius

Space, Movement, and Visibility in Pompeian Houses
Michael A. Anderson

Running Rome and Its Empire
The Places of Roman Governance
Edited by Antonio Lopez Garcia

For further information about this series please visit www.routledge.com/Studies-in-Roman-Space-and-Urbanism/book-series/SRSU

Running Rome and Its Empire
The Places of Roman Governance

Edited by Antonio Lopez Garcia

LONDON AND NEW YORK

First published 2024
by Routledge
4 Park Square, Milton Park, Abingdon, Oxon OX14 4RN

and by Routledge
605 Third Avenue, New York, NY 10158

Routledge is an imprint of the Taylor & Francis Group, an informa business

© 2024 selection and editorial matter, Antonio Lopez Garcia; individual chapters, the contributors

The right of Antonio Lopez Garcia to be identified as the author of the editorial material, and of the authors for their individual chapters, has been asserted in accordance with sections 77 and 78 of the Copyright, Designs and Patents Act 1988.

The Open Access version of this book, available at http://www.taylorfrancis.com, has been made available under a Creative Commons Attribution-NonCommercial (CC-BY-NC) 4.0 International license. Funded by University of Helsinki.

Trademark notice: Product or corporate names may be trademarks or registered trademarks, and are used only for identification and explanation without intent to infringe.

British Library Cataloguing-in-Publication Data
A catalogue record for this book is available from the British Library

Library of Congress Cataloging-in-Publication Data
Names: Lopez Garcia, Antonio, 1986– editor.
Title: Running Rome and its empire : the places of Roman governance / edited by Antonio Lopez Garcia.
Description: Abingdon, Oxon ; New York, NY : Routledge, 2024. | Series: Studies in Roman space and urbanism | Includes bibliographical references and index.
Identifiers: LCCN 2023033681 (print) | LCCN 2023033682 (ebook) | ISBN 9781032341774 (hardback) | ISBN 9781032341781 (paperback) | ISBN 9781003320869 (ebook)
Subjects: LCSH: Rome—Politics and government.
Classification: LCC JC83 .R86 2024 (print) | LCC JC83 (ebook) | DDC 320.437—dc23/eng/20231002
LC record available at https://lccn.loc.gov/2023033681
LC ebook record available at https://lccn.loc.gov/2023033682

ISBN: 978-1-032-34177-4 (hbk)
ISBN: 978-1-032-34178-1 (pbk)
ISBN: 978-1-003-32086-9 (ebk)

DOI: 10.4324/b23090

A mi familia

Contents

Acknowledgements	*x*
List of Contributors	*xii*
List of Acronyms and Abbreviations	*xv*
List of Illustrations	*xviii*
List of Tables	*xx*

1 **An Introduction to the Places of Roman Governance**   1
ANTONIO LOPEZ GARCIA

PART I
Theory and Methodology   11

2 **The Administrative Topography of Rome: Mapping Administrative Space and the Spatial Dynamics of Roman Republicanism**   13
JUHANA HEIKONEN, KAIUS TUORI, ANTONIO LOPEZ GARCIA, SAMULI SIMELIUS, AND ANNA-MARIA WILSKMAN

3 **Models of Administrative Space in the Roman World: Between Public and Private**   49
KAIUS TUORI

PART II
The Space of the Magistrate and Politics   77

4 **Legislative Voting in the Forum Romanum**   79
DAVID RAFFERTY

5 **Where's Vestorius? Locating Rome's Aediles**   99
TIMOTHY SMITH

6   Moving Magistrates in a Roman City Space: The Pompeian Model   120
    SAMULI SIMELIUS

PART III
The Space of the Institutions   147

7   The Rise and Consolidation of a Bureaucratic System:
    New Data on the *Praefectura Urbana* and Its Spaces in Rome   149
    ANTONIO LOPEZ GARCIA

8   *Scholae* and *Collegia*: Spaces for 'Semi-Administrative'
    Associations in the Imperial Age   176
    MARCO BRUNETTI

9   Civic Archives and Roman Rule: Spatial Aspects of Roman
    Hegemony in Asia Minor from Republic to Empire   197
    BRADLEY JORDAN

10 Between Private and Public: Women's Presence in
    Procuratorial *Praetoria*   216
    ANTHONY ÁLVAREZ MELERO

PART IV
Displaying Authority Over the Public Space and Religious Space   233

11 From Honour to Dishonour – The Different Readings of
    Columna Maenia   235
    ANNA-MARIA WILSKMAN

12 A Measure of Economy? The Organisation of Public Games in
    the City of Rome and the Development of the Urban Cityscape   251
    JESSICA BARTZ

13 The Administration of the Imperial Property Under Constantine
    in the Light of His Donations to the Church of Rome   270
    PAOLO LIVERANI

14 Topography of Power in the Conflict of the Basilicas Between
    Valentinian II and Ambrose of Milan in A.D. 385/6   282
    JASMIN LUKKARI

PART V
Coda 297

15 Afterword: Space and Roman Administration 299
ANTONIO LOPEZ GARCIA

Index *303*

Acknowledgements

This book is the result of an exchange of ideas among many researchers during the past few years, but it could have never been a reality without the support of many persons and funding from the European Research Council. My first acknowledgements are for Prof. Kaius Tuori for many reasons. To begin he has been a continuous support in my career and in my personal life from the day he offered to me the possibility of embarking on the best job opportunity I have experienced during my career. For his wise counsel in every step I made during the last four years, being a kind of bigger brother, sharing everything he can. I will never have enough good words to explain how significant this honour has been. Also, I want to thank Dr. Taina Tuori, Mai, and the kids for making me feel almost like a member of their family, especially during the dark times of the pandemic.

A special mention to my colleagues and friends of the ERC project SpaceLaw: Dr. Samuli Simelius, Anna-Maria Wilskman, Vesa Heikkinen, and Dr. Juhana Heikonen, who have been the best colleagues one can imagine. Especially, I want to thank Lilian Kiander for her support with the revision of the materials of this volume and the compilation of the index. Also, I am very grateful to the research assistants of SpaceLaw who have been an essential part of our work, including Oona Raatikainen, Mirkka Koskimaki, and Pyry Koskinen, and to the research coordinators Heta Björklund, Kaisu Taskila, and Tuija Von der Pütten for their continuous support with the administrative tasks. Also, I appreciate the support of the colleagues organising the monthly Ancient World seminars at the University of Helsinki (HelRAW), which offer the possibility of debating and sharing new ideas about our research.

I want to thank the current and former members of the Centre for European Studies of the University of Helsinki, especially those from Eurostorie. Many thanks to Dr. Emilia Mataix Ferrándiz for her advice and support with the edition of this volume and for her availability for many other questions.

I am grateful to Prof. Ray Laurence for his support to include this book in the collection "Studies in Roman Space and Urbanism" of Routledge and for offering his encouragement in my career development from the other side of the globe.

Many thanks to Marcia Adams from Routledge for her support and professionality during the process of edition and publishing.

Acknowledgements xi

I am grateful to the Royal Academy of Spain in Rome, and especially to Javier Andrés and Ángeles Albert for their effort in co-organizing the conference "Space and Governance: Towards a New Topography of Roman Administration", although Covid-19 made us postpone it and host it in Helsinki a year later. Again, I want to thank all the participants of that conference for planting the seeds of this volume.

I want to mention my *doktorvater* Prof. Paolo Liverani for his continuous support in my career since 2010, and for offering his contribution to this volume.

I am thankful to Prof. Carlos F. Noreña for hosting me at the University of California Berkeley, where I began writing my contributions to this volume.

Also, I want to thank Prof. Francisco Contreras Cortés, director of the Department of Prehistory and Archaeology of the University of Granada, and Dr. Jesús Gámiz and Dr. José Carlos Coria for their support with my teaching and research visits.

A special mention to the language revisors who worked in some of the contributions to this volume Christopher TenWolde and Robert Whiting.

Finally, I want to mention here my family and all my loved ones, who during most of my career have been deprived of my care for being abroad for very long periods and who always have supported all my projects. Last but not least, I want to thank Mirkka Helkkula and Runo for their care and support during the edition of this book.

I take full responsibility for the editorial choices of this volume.

Contributors

Anthony Álvarez Melero University of Seville, Spain. Is a professor of ancient history at the University of Seville. He did a Ph.D. in History, Art, and Archaeology at the Free University of Brussels and the University of Seville (2010). His research concentrates most on epigraphy, Latin onomastics, prosopography, women in ancient Rome, and Roman social history.

Jessica Bartz Humboldt University of Berlin, Germany. Is a German classical archaeologist, based in Berlin. She did a Ph.D. in Classical Archaeology at the Humboldt University of Berlin. Her research focuses on the study of the political and social structures of ancient Rome, with a particular emphasis on ephemeral architectures during the republican and early imperial period.

Marco Brunetti Freie Universität of Berlin, Germany. Is a postdoctoral fellow at the Freie Universität of Berlin, working on Roman antiquities discovered in the Early Modern Age. He has published articles in renowned scientific journals and was awarded prestigious fellowships by the DAAD Germanic Academic Exchange Service (2019–2020), Bibliotheca Hertziana – Max Planck Institute for Art History (2020–2023), and the Alexander von Humboldt Foundation (2023–2025).

Juhana Heikonen University of Helsinki, Finland. Is a researcher in the SpaceLaw project at the University of Helsinki and the responsible teacher at the Finnish Institute in Rome's architecture student course "Grand Tour". Heikonen's primary academic interests include late antique architecture, history of housing production, and the influence of classical antiquity in Western architecture.

Bradley Jordan University of Oslo, Norway. Is a postdoctoral fellow in the Department of Archaeology, Conservation and History at the University of Oslo. His research focuses on the development of localised political cultures and institutions in the eastern Mediterranean during the transition from Roman Republic to Principate. He has previously held research positions at the British Institute at Ankara and the University of Cologne, after completing his doctorate at the University of Oxford.

Paolo Liverani University of Florence, Italy. Is a professor of Topography of Ancient Italy and Chair of the Department of History, Archaeology, Geography, Fine and Performing Arts at the University of Florence. From 1986 to 2005, he was Curator of Classical Antiquities at the Vatican Museum. He studied Classics at the Sapienza University of Rome with a Ph.D. in 1991 in Ancient Topography.

Antonio Lopez Garcia University of Granada, Spain, and University of Helsinki, Finland. Antonio Lopez Garcia is an expert in Roman archaeology and topography. Since 2022, he teaches archaeology at the University of Granada, where obtained a María Zambrano contract for the attraction of international talent. Recently, he received a Ramón y Cajal grant from the Spanish Ministry of Science and Innovation. Currently, he is directing a research project at the University of Helsinki on Late Antique Rome, which is funded by the Kone Foundation. Prior to his current positions, he was a postdoctoral researcher at the same university within the ERC-funded project Law, Governance and Space: Questioning the Foundations of the Republican Tradition. He was fellow of the Royal Academy of Spain in Rome and obtained a Ph.D. from the University of Florence.

Jasmin Lukkari University of Helsinki, Finland. Obtained a Ph.D in History jointly from the University Helsinki and the University of Cologne in 2023. She specializes in the study of historical narratives in various literary genres as well as cultural identities and discourses of Otherness in antiquity. She is interested in cultural changes and continuities over long periods of time especially from the Late Roman Republic to late antiquity.

David Rafferty University of Adelaide, Australia. Is a Roman historian specialising in the history of the republic. He is currently ARC DECRA Postdoctoral Fellow at the University of Adelaide. After receiving his Ph.D. at the University of Melbourne in 2016, he has published on, among other things, Roman voting, provincial government, and Hellenistic state formation.

Samuli Simelius University of Helsinki, Finland. Is a teacher of ancient cultures in the University of Helsinki, and a post-doctoral researcher in the project Law, Governance and Space: Questioning the Foundations of the Republican Tradition funded by the European Research Council. He has published a book – *Pompeian Peristyle Gardens* (Routledge, 2022) – and research articles about Pompeii and domestic space.

Timothy Smith Regent's Park College, University of Oxford. Is Lecturer in Ancient History at Regent's Park College, Oxford. His research focuses on social relations in the Roman world, with a special emphasis on elections, magistracies, and popular participation in politics. More generally, his research explores how the built environment of ancient cities reflects how people interacted with political elites and engaged with political institutions.

Kaius Tuori University of Helsinki, Finland. Is a professor at the University of Helsinki and PI of the SpaceLaw project. His main field of interest is Roman legal history and its societal and cultural implications in antiquity and beyond. His recent books are *Empire of Law* (CUP 2020) and *Emperor of Law* (OUP 2016).

Anna-Maria Wilskman University of Helsinki, Finland. Is currently working on her Ph.D. in the project Law, Governance and Space: Questioning the Foundations of the Republican Tradition at the University of Helsinki. Her background is in Latin language and Roman literature with a strong emphasis on Classical archaeology and museum studies. Her upcoming dissertation concentrates on the ways especially young Roman magistrates utilized material culture in their political ambitions.

Acronyms and Abbreviations

For Latin sources not considered in OCD: *Thesaurus Linguae Latinae*
For Greek sources not considered in OCD: G.W.H. Lampe, *A Patristic Greek Lexicon*, Oxford 1961.

AE	*L'Année épigraphique*, Paris, 1888–.
CIL	*Corpus inscriptionum Latinarum*, Berlin, Boston, 1862–.
CIL II	E. Hübner, *Corpus inscriptionum Latinarum II. Inscriptiones Hispaniae Latinae*, Berlin, 1896–1892.
CIL II^2/5	A. U. Stylow et al., *Corpus inscriptionum Latinarum II. Inscriptiones Hispaniae Latinae. Pars V. Conventus Astigitanus (CIL II^2/5)*, Berlin, 1998.
CIL III	Th. Mommsen et al., *Corpus Inscriptionum Latinarum III. Inscriptiones Asiae, provinciarum Europae Graecarum Illyrici Latinae. Partes I-II*, Berlin, 1873–1902.
CIL VIII	G. Willmans et al., *Corpus Inscriptionum Latinarum VIII. Partes I-V. Inscriptiones Africae Latinae*, Berlin, 1881–1959.
CIL IX	Th. Mommsen, *Corpus Inscriptionum Latinarum IX. Inscriptiones Calabriae, Apuliae, Samnii, Sabinorum, Piceni Latinae*, Berlin, 1883.
CILSard	F. Porrà, *Catalogo P.E.T.R.A.E. delle iscrizioni latine della Sardegna. Versione preliminare*, Cagliari, 2002.
CJC	S. Demougin *Prosopographie des chevaliers romains julio-claudiens (43 av. J.-C.-70 ap. J.-C.)*, Roma, 1992.
CP	H.-G. Pflaum, *Les carrières procuratoriennes équestres sous le Haut-Empire romain*, I-III, Paris, 1960–1961.
EDCS	*Epigraphic-Datenbank Clauss/Slaby: https://db.edcs.eu/epigr/epi.php?s_sprache=en.*
EDR	*Epigraphic Database Roma: www.edr-edr.it/default/index.php.*
EE VIII	*Ephemeris epigraphica VIII*, Berlin, 1899.
ERPLeón	M. A. Rabanal Alonso and S. M. García Martínez, *Epigrafía romana de la provincia de León: revisión y actualización*, León, 2001.
EyNAstorga	T. Mañanes Pérez, *Epigrafía y numismática de Astorga romana y su entorno*, Salamanca, 1982.
FGrH	*Fragmente der griechischen Historiker.*

FOS	M.-T. Raepsaet-Charlier, *Prosopographie des femmes de l'ordre sénatorial (Ier-IIe siècle)*, Leuven, 1987.
FRHist	Cornell, T. (ed), *The Fragments of the Roman Historians*, 3 vols, Oxford, 2013.
HEp	*Hispania Epigraphica 1989*, Madrid, 2013.
I.Colosse Memnon	A. and E. Bernand, *Les inscriptions grecques et latines du Colosse de Memnon*, Paris, 1960.
ICUR	*Inscriptiones Christianae Urbis Romae*.
I.Ephesos III	H. Engelmann et al., *Die Inschriften von Ephesos. Teil 3: Nr. 600–1000 (Repertorium)*, Bonn, 1980.
I.Ephesos VII/2	R. Meriç et al., *Die Inschriften von Ephesos. Teil 7.2: Nr. 3501–5115 (Repertorium). Beilage: Addenda et corrigenda zu den Inschriften von Ephesos 1–7, 1*. Bonn, 1981.
IDR II	G. Florescu and C. C. Petolescu *Inscriptiones Daciae Romanae. II. Pars meridionalis, inter Danuuium et Carpatos montes*, Bucarest, 1977.
IDR III/2	I. I. Russu et al., *Inscriptiones Daciae Romanae. III. Dacia Superior 2. Vlpia Traiana Dacica (Sarmizegetusa)*, Bucarest, 1980.
IG	*Inscriptiones Graecae*.
ILS	H. Dessau, *Inscriptiones Latinae selectae*, Berlin, 1892–1916.
I.Mus. Burdur	G. H. R. Horsley, *The Greek and Latin Inscriptions in the Burdur Archaeological Museum*, London, 2007.
IRLugo	F. Arias Vilas et al., *Inscriptions romaines de la province de Lugo*, Paris, 1979.
IRPLeón	F. Diego Santos, *Inscripciones romanas de la provincia de León*, León, 1986.
Lanciani FUR	R. Lanciani, *Forma Urbis Romae*, Roma-Milano, 1893–1901.
LP	*Liber Pontificalis*.
LTUR	E. M. Steinby (ed), *Lexicon topographicum urbis Romae*, Rome, 1993–2000 (I, 1993; II, 1993; III, 1996; IV, 1999; V, 1999; VI, 2000), 1993–99.
OLD	P. G. W. Glare (ed), *Oxford Latin Dictionary*, 2 vols, 2nd edn., Oxford, 2012.
PFCR	A. Álvarez Melero, *Prosopographie de la parentèle féminine des chevaliers romains*, Sevilla, 2021.
PIR²	E. Groag, A. Stein, L. Petersen et al. (eds), *Prosopographia Imperii Romani, saec. I. II. III, iteratis curis ediderunt E. Groag et A. Stein*, Berlin, Leipzig, New York-Boston, 1933–2015.
PLRE II	A. H. M. Jones, J. R. Martindale, J. Morris (eds), *Prosopography of the Later Roman Empire*, 2, 1980.
PME	H. Devijver, *Prosopographia militiarum equestrium quae fuerunt ab Augusto ad Gallienum*, Leuven, 1976–2003.
RE Suppl. XII	K. Ziegler (ed), *Paulys Realencyclopädie der classischen Altertumswissenschaft. Supplementband* XII, Stuttgart, 1970.

RIC	H. Mattingly, and E. A. Sydenham, *The Roman Imperial Coinage*, 1, London, 1923.
RRC	M. H. Crawford, *Roman Republican Coinage*, 2 vols, London, 1974.
RS	M. H. Crawford (ed), *Roman Statutes*, 2 vols, London, 1996.
Röm. Staatsr.	T. Mommsen, *Römisches Staatsrecht*, 3 vols, 3rd edn., Leipzig, 1887–88.
SAIE	J. M. Ojeda Torres, *El servicio administrativo imperial ecuestre en la Hispania romana durante el Alto Imperio I. Prosopografía*, Sevilla, 1993.
SCP	H.-G. Pflaum, *Les carrières procuratoriennes équestres sous le Haut-Empire romain. Supplément*, Paris, 1982.
SEG	*Supplementum epigraphicum Graecum*, Leiden, 1923.

Illustrations

2.1	Map 1, Rome, second century B.C.	35
2.2	Map 2, Rome, first century B.C.	36
2.3	Map 3, Rome, first century A.D.	37
2.4	Map 4, Rome, second century A.D.	38
2.5	Map 5, Rome, third century A.D.	39
3.1	Detail of the Altar of the Scribes.	52
3.2	Outline of a portion of the Altar of Domitius Ahenobarbus.	53
4.1	Reverse of denarius of P. Nerva, c.110 B.C.E. (*RRC* 292/1, American Numismatic Society, ID 1944.100.598).	81
4.2	E. Gjerstad's reconstruction of the late-Republican Rostra ('Suggesto J'). From Gjerstad 1941: 125.	89
4.3	Plans of the Temple of Castor and Pollux: Temple Phase 1A and the Metellan temple. From Nielsen, Poulsen and Bilde 1992: 83 and 109.	90
5.1	The Altar of the Scribes.	103
5.2	The coin of Critonius and Fannius.	107
5.3	The tomb of Vestorius Priscus. After Whitehead 1993.	111
6.1	Map of Pompeii with street names. Projected streets with lighter gray.	126
6.2	Wall painting from the Villa di Giulia Felice (II,4,3) depicting a person presenting a young girl to a magistrate.	127
6.3	The locations of the largest and most decorated houses in Pompeii.	128
6.4	Wall painting from house VII,3,30 depicting a person wearing a toga giving bread to another person.	130
6.5	The wall painting of the so-called judgement of Solomon from the Casa del Medico (VIII,5,24).	131
6.6	The lower part of the wall painting depicting the amphitheatre riot. The painting was found in the Casa della Rissa nell'Anfiteatro (I,3,23).	131
6.7	The effect of adding a corner on a Space Syntax analysis. Vicolo del Farmacista is first drawn as a rectangular unit that is enclosed by imaginary lines to the north and south. Second, a corner is added to the same street, which adds three lines to the analysis.	135
6.8	The map used for the Space Syntax analysis.	136
6.9	The best places to be visible or meet people in Pompeii.	138

7.1	Possible locations of the barracks of the *vigiles* and the *urbaniciani*.	152
7.2	Possible locations of the main *stationes* linked to the urban prefect.	156
7.3	Possible locations of the headquarters of the urban prefect.	161
7.4	Possible locations of *secretaria* and *tribunalia*.	164
8.1	From left to right: Ostia, 'Caseggiato dei Triclini'; Herculaneum, so-called Basilica; Velia, *schola* of doctors. Plans based on Zevi 2008, Laird 2015, and Galli 2014.	183
8.2	*Schola* of *dendrophori* on the Caelian Hill. After Pavolini 2020.	183
8.3	Inscription and plan of *collegium Silvani* on the Via Appia. After Della Giovampaola 2008.	184
8.4	Alesia, *schola* of *fabri aerariorum*. After Martin and Varène 1973.	186
11.1	The estimated location of the *columna Maenia*. Based on the interpretation of Coarelli (1983).	240
11.2	The *denarius* issued by L. Marcius Censorinus. Reverse: The statue of Marsyas with a wineskin on his shoulder. The column behind the statue is presumably the *columna Maenia*. Obverse: The head of Apollo.	243
12.1	Funerary inscription of Cornelius Surus (*AE* 1959 147), 55–20 B.C., found in Rome at the Piazzale Labicano, now in Rome, Musei Capitolini, Tabularium, CE 6765.	257
12.2	Coin depicting Head of L. Regulus (praetor) (obverse) and animal hunting scene (reverse). Institute of Classical Archaeology of the Eberhard Karls University of Tübingen, ID1479.	258
14.1	Map of late fourth-century Milan with here discussed places (after Villa 1956: 7; Lewis 1969: 91).	284

Tables

2.1	The radar chart.	34
7.1	Main hypotheses to date about the location of the spaces of the *Praefectura Urbana* within the topography of Rome.	166
13.1	Christian Basilicas under imperial patronage, synthetic view.	277

1 An Introduction to the Places of Roman Governance[1]

Antonio Lopez Garcia

I Introduction

Since the nineteenth century, the study of Roman administration has been central to several disciplines such as ancient history and, more widely, legal studies. The way in which these various disciplines approached this topic made it obvious from the very beginning of the studies that it would be necessary to combine several types of sources. The complex reality of Roman administration requires the use of interdisciplinary and transdisciplinary approaches that can merge the widely scattered information in order to create a comprehensive history of its institutions. In more than a century of studies in the field, the path travelled by several generations of researchers has incorporated new scientific tools and historical methods in combination with the study of the legal corpora and literary sources that have survived to our day. In the early days of the study of the administration of Rome and their dominions, epigraphy constituted the most essential body of evidence, and served as the basis of questioning the orthodox view often illustrated in the legal tradition. The inclusion of archaeology in the formula has since then nuanced many of the initial assumptions made by the fathers of the history of Roman institutions.

However, the development of archaeological practice has been uneven throughout the colossal panorama of the Roman world. In the city of Rome itself, the reconstruction of the ancient topography through the interpretation of the archaeological remains scattered all over the urban landscape has occupied scholars for many decades. The combination of these topographical studies with the quest to identify the spaces of power in the city began more than a century ago, in the days of Rodolfo Lanciani. Nevertheless, this journey has proceeded at different paces in other centres of authority in the Empire, such as the provincial capitals and the late-antique capitals, where the investigations have followed different directions and research on the administrative topography was rarely a priority.

The location of the spaces where the management of the city occurred was always a significant space in the *Urbs*. The footprint of these spaces in the ancient literature was so sizeable that many of the remains of administrative activities in Roman topography were already identified in the nineteenth century. Lanciani, who for instance in 1892 had already discussed the location of the headquarters of the urban prefecture, is an example of this archaeological research tradition.

Scholars coming from the field of legal history took a very different approach. They did not discuss the physical dimensions of the administrative activities hosted in Rome – and throughout the Empire – and they frequently assumed that the physical aspects of these activities were irrelevant. The traditional focus was often on the legal implementation of the activities, without delving into the spatial needs of those systems. In any case, it was the usual lack of communication between the disciplines – archaeology and legal history – that caused a rupture in the reconstruction of these essential spheres of the cityscape.

In the last two decades, some memorable contributions have analyzed many aspects of the Roman administration. These include the volume *La Mémoire Perdue. Recherches sur l'administration romaine* by C. Moatti, *Herrschaftsstrukturen und Herrschaftspraxis. Konzepte, Prinzipien und Strategien der Administration im römischen Kaiserrecht* by A. Kolb, *The Emperor and Rome. Space, Representation, and Ritual* by B. C. Ewald and C. F. Noreña, *Spaces of Justice in the Roman World* by F. De Angelis, and more recently, the monograph *Statio. I luohi dell'amministrazione nell'antica Roma* by F. Coarelli. These books in some aspects complement the work we present in this volume, but the novelty of this contribution is the explicit focus on administrative spaces, incorporating the traditional view of Roman topographers and a variety of spatial theories.

II Theoretical Framework

In recent decades, some trends within the humanities have taken a different approach to interpreting the spaces used for human activities. In this volume, the contributors approach space from several perspectives, using a theoretical framework that ranges from the postulates of T. Hägerstrand and his Activity Space to the Spatial Turn initiated by H. Lefebvre. The combination of this variety of spatial theories with the examination of the archaeological record delivers a new perspective on the study of Roman institutions.

Activity Space is a valuable theory introduced by Hägerstrand in his paper "What About People in Regional Science?" (1970, and earlier in Swedish), which addresses questions related to daily activities and the locations in which they occur, taking a novel approach to understanding the temporal organization and spatial development of human built environments. This theory uses the space-time path to demonstrate how human spatial activity is usually governed by several categories of limitations, such as the restrictions on movement caused by physical and biological factors, the need to be in a specific place at a certain time, or for a certain length of time, and other factors such as the lack of accessibility to a specific domain.[2] The use of this theory has been particularly fruitful in the placement of administrative activities, functions, and places within space-time, with the intention to track these activities and observe their interdependencies over a vast span of time.

This volume also benefits from the Spatial Turn developed in the last decades of the twentieth century. The Spatial Turn proposed a framework in which space becomes one of the most important elements in the study of how social networks function. Geographers, sociologists, urbanists, philosophers, and many other types of scholars have since approached the study of human activities by focusing on the spaces in which they take place. Since the publication of *La production de l'espace* by H. Lefebvre (1974), the humanities and social sciences have dealt more closely with spatial matters. In recent years, this framework has been used by archaeologists as an alternative approach to the study of ancient societies, applying this new lens offered by sociologists to past material culture. This recent change of approach in archaeology looks at the cityscape in a way that differs from traditional topographical analyses; space becomes a productive force, and is viewed as the result of an interrelationship between physical and social networks of meaning.[3] In the last few years, Romanists have often applied this framework to refresh the traditional view of Roman topographers, since it reveals aspects of ancient society that have previously been overlooked.[4]

Studying the topography of Roman administration not only means the study of the spaces in which the management of the diverse systems entangled within the government resided, but also includes the examination of the many components that comprised the official organs of the Roman state. These organs include public, private, civic, and religious elements, and mingle in many different ways, creating an enormous and complex structure. Several attempts to overview the structure of Roman administration have been carried out, with different levels of success, but these efforts have frequently overlooked the importance of some specific aspects due to the aforementioned lack of communication between disciplines. This volume is an attempt to create a channel of interaction between ancient historians, archaeologists, topographers, and legal historians specialized in the Roman Republic and the Empire.

The study of the functioning of the immense apparatus of Roman administration is only approachable through the analysis of the thousands of individual pieces of evidence left by the sands of time. The interconnection of all these traces found in ancient literature, scholiasts, epigraphs, legal codices and corpora, and papyri, along with the remains of material culture, offers a clearer vision of the blurred history of these Roman institutions. We can improve the comprehension of Roman governance by observing and connecting the customs of the people that formed the machinery of the *res publica*, the practical needs of its organs, the display of the institutions in the everyday life of Rome and its centres of power, the implementation of laws to strengthen the management of the city and the Empire, or even the methods used by the establishment to control the populace.

III   The Content

This volume is the result of responding to a set of questions concerning the study of Roman administration, approached from diverse standpoints and by creating a dialogue among the different actors that managed those institutions, in order to deliver a new interpretation of their history. This book explores the transformation of public space and administrative activities in republican and imperial Rome through an interdisciplinary examination of the topography of power. Throughout the Roman world, building projects created spaces for different civic purposes: the meetings of assemblies, senate meetings, the administration of justice, the public treasury, and the management of the city through different magistracies, offices, and even archives. These administrative spaces – open and closed – characterized Roman life throughout the Republic and High Empire, until the profound administrative and judicial transformations of the fourth century.

The work explores in a novel way topics such as urban development and the dynamics related to the expansion of the Roman administration. It accesses some of the most recent archaeological discoveries that connect with themes such as the institutions and spaces of Roman administration, the spaces for the administration of justice and public meetings, the use of private spaces in administration and the imprint of this in the written sources, the movement of magistrates throughout the provinces, the display of authority in the monuments of the city, the residences of magistrates and the elite, their offices, and the archives. In doing so, it also examines several facets of the transformation of Roman administration from the Republican era to the Late Antiquity, considering new approaches to and theories on the uses of public space. This capitalizes on new work in Roman studies that focuses on the spatial needs of humans as users, rather than architectural style and design. Here we find answers to questions such as: Where did the administration work? What were the workplaces of the administrative organs like? How was social status tied to the different levels of administration? The answers to these questions are explored through the lens of archaeology, epigraphy, urbanism, architecture, and art. In this vein, the book examines the performance of the magistrates and other public officials and their use of public and private space.

In order to accomplish this goal, the spatial necessities for the performance of the administration are analyzed through several case studies. The volume is divided into four parts that examine several facets of the spaces of the Roman administration.

The first section explores the creation, expansion, and distribution of the administrative spaces in Rome and its dominions. Chapter 2, "*The Administrative Topography of Rome: Mapping Administrative Space and the Spatial Dynamics of Roman Republicanism*", is a joint contribution of the members of the SpaceLaw Project[5] of the University of Helsinki. The chapter examines diachronically the appearance of administrative centres in Rome from the republican period to the late Empire. Exploring the written sources – literary, legal, and epigraphical – the SpaceLaw Project has tracked the references concerning administrative activities and the recognizable spaces that they occupied within the urban landscape of Rome. The administrative spaces included in this chapter cover the spaces for justice, management offices, archives and libraries, private spaces in which some tasks of the administration were performed, and the places for the representation and display of the officials. The questions treated in this chapter engage topics that have been rarely treated together, such as how large a space was required for the development of some administrative tasks, including the performance of the courts, the spatial needs of the bureaucratic apparatus, and the space required for statal archives, and how the various monuments, magisterial actions, and the city spaces were linked together. In order to analyze these activities, as well as others, as a whole, the Activity Space concept was utilized to measure the spatial behaviour of individuals and activities in time and space. These interrelationships are illustrated through a series of maps included in the chapter.

Chapter 3, "*Models of Administrative Space in the Roman World: Between Public and Private*", dissects the spatial structure of administrative space through the analysis of the different types of activities that took place in the public and private spheres. Kaius Tuori seeks to demonstrate how there are important questions regarding the spaces of administration that have rarely been addressed in the previous scholarship. The chapter explores the administrative processes as functional chains of actions in which different elements use and share domestic places, such as the use of a private domus to host the archives of a magistrate, or open public areas that could be used, for example, to receive people and hold public meetings, or buildings specially designed for some specific tasks of the bureaucratic system, for example for the handling of documents or the storage of money. All of these tasks were essential for maintaining the governance of Rome, but they have never been analyzed jointly.

The second section of the book surveys the spaces used by magistrates for some activities that were crucial to the political side of the Roman administration. Some of the questions addressed in this section are about how the Romans acted during the elections of magistrates and what spaces were used by the aediles, one of the main categories of magistrates; and, lastly, how the magistrates physically moved within the city in their everyday lives. In Chapter 4, "*Legislative Voting in the Forum Romanum*", David Rafferty analyzes how Roman citizens participated in political life, how crowds moved around the spaces during the *comitia*, and how the transformation of the Roman Forum into a political space occurred. He also presents a novel hypothesis on the location of these activities and the use of the space associated with them, challenging the previous theories on the topic. Chapter 5, "*Where's Vestorius? Locating Rome's Aediles*", by Timothy Smith, dissects the written sources in search of the aedilician spaces of interaction. Aediles were very present in civic life, and many of them left an imprint in the urban landscape by carrying out various embellishment activities. They appear in the sources to take part in many different administrative activities, such as trials and grain distribution, but apparently aediles did not have a defined headquarters associated with their office such as other magistrates had in specific locations throughout the city. Chapter 6, "*Moving Magistrates in a Roman City Space: The Pompeian Model*", by Samuli Simelius, offers a novel approach with an experiment to demonstrate the movement of magistrates in a controlled and well-known space such as the city of Pompeii. Considering the information imparted by written sources and the archaeological record, this experiment demonstrates the best street locations to encounter a magistrate or – at the same time – for a magistrate to appear more visible to the public. The author is well aware of the possible problems that such a novel approach can encounter, as well as the difficulties involved in comparing the writings of ancient authors about the city of Rome and its magistrates to a different environment. Despite the difference in contexts, the results regarding the movement patterns produced by Space Syntax and the facts recorded by the ancient authors are surprisingly coincident. The role of private spaces within the context of public administration is fundamental, and this chapter explores some vital elements that must be considered when analysing the topography of a Roman city.

The third section of the book offers four different visions of several key elements used by the administration, both from the public perspective and from the private perspective. Chapter 7, *"The Rise and Consolidation of a Bureaucratic System: New Data on the Praefectura Urbana and Its Spaces in Rome"*, dissects all of the elements that formed the core of what was, in High Imperial and Late Imperial Rome, the main office of the city: the *Praefectura Urbana*. This fundamental institution incorporated thousands of officials, military staff, and slaves who were spread all over the city of Rome throughout a series of subaltern offices that managed activities such as the implementation of surveillance, the maintenance of public works, the construction of infrastructure, the control of food supplies, and the legal jurisdiction over the city and the surrounding territory, among many other tasks. The spatial distribution of all these activities that were managed by the *Praefectura Urbana* is one of the key elements of this chapter, which contains a set of plans that allow the synthesization of all the elements examined in this diachronic study. The chapter summarizes the main theories regarding the spaces occupied by the governmental organs managed by the urban prefect, and includes data that have never been previously analyzed in the context of this institution. In Chapter 8, "Scholae *and* Collegia*: Spaces for 'Semi-Administrative' Associations in the Imperial Age"*, Marco Brunetti zooms in on a crucial aspect of Roman administration: the *publica utilitas* of the *collegia*. These associations oversaw many essential assignments of the everyday life of Romans, such as public buildings and the supply of goods and services. They served as an intermediary between the private contractors and the public administration, and thus the role of the *collegia* must be reconsidered alongside the management of the city. In Chapter 9, *"Civic Archives and Roman Rule: Spatial Aspects of Roman Hegemony in Asia Minor From Republic to Empire"*, Bradley Jordan examines the role of archival spaces in the provincial context. Archives were a critical element of governance, because they served to store crucial information for the administration. This contribution analyzes the phenomenon of the creation of these governmental organs, reconsidering the Greek precedents, the conception of a bureaucratic apparatus in Rome, and the expansion of this model to the eastern provinces to exert control over local communities. To conclude the third section of this volume, Anthony Álvarez Melero presents in Chapter 10, *"Between Private and Public: Women's Presence in Procuratorial* Praetoria*"*, an examination of a fundamental space in provincial administration. This cutting-edge contribution explores the traces of women and non-official members that appear in the epigraphical record, legal sources, and ancient literature. While the presence of women in some official contexts, such as the court of the Roman emperor, has been previously examined by some scholars, the author of this chapter examines how women began to take an active part in the provincial *praetorium*, enjoying some of the same privileges as their husbands, sharing the same space, and sometimes even receiving homages in public in the provincial capital.

The fourth section of the book presents four case studies that explore the relationship of the authorities with public space and religious space. How did the administration deal with the monumentalizing of public areas? What was the symbolic relationship between the magistrates and built space? These are some of the questions explored by Anna-Maria Wilskman in Chapter 11, "*From Honour to Dishonour – The Different Readings of* Columna Maenia". The *Columna Maenia*, located in the Roman Forum, was a socially powerful object for the Romans. The meaning of this place evolved over the centuries, variously appearing in the sources as a place of memory, a working place for the *tresviri capitales* – a fundamental organ of the justice administration – a place of punishment, and many other functions. A different perspective on the use of public space to display power and, perhaps, gain the favour of the citizens was the organization of *ludi publici*. Holding *ludi publici* eventually became a central means to control the city population and improve the governance of Rome. The topic is meticulously analyzed by Jessica Bartz in Chapter 12, "*A Measure of Economy? The Organisation of Public Games in the City of Rome and the Development of the Urban Cityscape*". The public games were a fundamental platform of communication between the political elite and the population that had a considerable effect on the city, but that relationship changed conspicuously between the second century B.C. – when some activities of this kind were limited and the modification of the space was curtailed to prevent large crowds that could potentially interfere with governance – and the first century B.C., when administrators such as the praetors were more and more often the main event organizers, using the games to improve their public images. The impact of this shift in the minds of the rulers on the cityscape is visible in the creation of permanent structures to host public games, starting from the late republican period. In a different direction, administrative display in Roman religious spaces has been increasingly examined by many scholars; in this volume we have two contributions that explore how Roman authorities interacted with the Christian authorities. Chapter 13, "*The Administration of the Imperial Property Under Constantine in the Light of His Donations to the Church of Rome*" by Paolo Liverani, delves into the relationship between the imperial administration and the Church, illustrating how the official authorities used the cult space to increase the goodwill of the Christians – and thus improve governance. The construction of cult basilicas and their ornamentation at the expense of the emperor was a smart political movement on the part of Constantine, but this movement relied on a juridical framework that allowed donations from the public administration to the Church. In this chapter, we see how the emperor manipulated the laws to gain the support of the Church. A very different perspective on the relationship between the Church and the Empire is found in the Chapter 14, "*Topography of Power in the Conflict of the Basilicas Between Valentinian II and Ambrose of Milan in A.D. 385/6*". Jasmin Lukkari dissects the origins of the conflict over the display of civic authority within religious spaces. The redefinition of who had authority over these spaces took place only a few decades after the incorporation of Christianity as the official religion of the Empire. The transfer of this authority from Rome to other centres such as Milan might have had a significant impact on the display of the power of emperors and prefects. The civic administration lost authority over some portions of the cityscape as sacred spaces, and bishops such as Ambrose of Milan were able to limit the role of public administrators, resulting in a rebalancing of authority in Late Antiquity.

IV Background

This collection of essays on the administrative spaces of Rome and the Empire has its roots in the research project "The Public Spaces of the Roman Administration" I ran at the Centre for European Studies of the University of Helsinki within the ERC-funded project "Law, Governance and Space. Questioning the Foundations of the Republican Tradition (SpaceLaw)" directed by Kaius Tuori. The main goal of my research project was the examination of the places occupied by the different institutions that formed the network of the republican system in Rome. The project combined the analysis of archaeological, legal, epigraphic, and literary sources to reconstruct the spaces of power inside the *Urbs*. The complexity of that task led me to narrow the focus to some specific bodies, such as the spaces for the administration of justice,[6] the archives and libraries,[7] and the spaces of the urban prefecture. The collaboration with my colleagues in the SpaceLaw Project in Helsinki produced some significant results when we combined the efforts of our individual subprojects. This fruitful teamwork suggested the possibility of expanding our network of studies on space and Roman administration. Through my participation in several international scientific meetings, such as the 121st Meeting of the Archaeological Institute of America in Washington D.C., the Spatial Turn in Roman Studies held in Auckland in 2020, and the 41st Conference of the Australasian Society for Classical Studies held at the University of Otago (Dunedin) in 2020, I had the opportunity to collect feedback on my own research and open up new paths for collaboration with researchers from all around the globe who have been studying the fundamental elements of Roman administration. Since 2019, in collaboration with the Royal Academy of Spain in Rome, I had been organizing the conference "Space and Governance: Towards a New Topography of Roman Administration", which was supposed to be held in Rome in mid-2020, which unfortunately turned out to be just a few weeks after the advent of the Covid-19 pandemic. The arrival of the virus obliged us to postpone the conference for more than a year, however it finally took place in Helsinki in June 2021. The core of this volume is formed of some of the best papers contributed to the conference, which together with the other outstanding guest contributions helped to shape and complete this book.

Notes

1. This work is part of the project "Law, Governance and Space: Questioning the Foundations of the Republican Tradition". This research has received funding from the European Research Council (ERC) under the European Union's Horizon 2020 research and innovation programme (grant agreement No 771874). This research has also received funding from the Next Generation framework of the European Commission through the programme "María Zambrano" for the attraction of international talent that I have at the University of Granada. I want to acknowledge Kaius Tuori for the support and feedback received, and Christopher TenWolde for the language revision.
2. Corbett 2001: 1–4; Fang 2016.
3. Filippi 2022: 1.
4. Some remarkable contributions in the last few years have successfully approached the reality of Rome through the lens of the Spatial Turn. See, for example Laurence and Newsome 2011; Östenberg et al. 2015; Russell 2016; Filippi 2022.

5 Juhana Heikonen, Kaius Tuori, Antonio Lopez Garcia, Samuli Simelius, and Anna-Maria Wilskman.
6 Lopez Garcia 2021, 2023.
7 Lopez Garcia and Bueno Guardia 2021.

References

Coarelli, F. 2019: *Statio. I luohi dell'amministrazione nell'antica Roma*, Rome.
Corbett, J. 2001: *Torsten Hägerstrand, Time Geography. CSISS Classics*, UC Santa Barbara.
De Angelis, F. (ed.) 2010: *Spaces of Justice in the Roman World*, Leiden and Boston.
Ewald, B. C., and Noreña, C. F. (eds) 2010: *The Emperor and Rome. Space, Representation, and Ritual*, New York.
Fang, F. 2016: 'Activity Space. Obo in Geography', *Oxford Bibliographies*. https://doi.org/10.1093/obo/9780199874002-0137.
Filippi, D. (ed.) 2022: *Rethinking the Roman City. Studies in Roman Space and Urbanism*, London, New York.
Hägerstrand, T. 1970: 'What About People in Regional Science?', *Papers of the Regional Science Association* 24, 6–21. https://doi.org/10.1007/BF01936872.
Kolb, A. (ed.) 2006: *Herrschaftsstrukturen und Herrschaftspraxis. Konzepte, Prinzipien und Strategien der Administration im römischen Kaiserrecht*, Berlin.
Laurence, R., and Newsome, D. J. 2011: *Rome, Ostia, Pompeii: Movement and Space*, Oxford.
Lefebvre, H. 1974: 'La production de l'espace', *L'Homme et la société* 31–32, 15–32.
Lopez Garcia, A. 2021: 'Una corte di giustizia presso il Foro di Traiano? Analisi sulla funzionalità degli auditoria adrianei', *Mélanges de l'École Française de Rome* 133/1, 149–171.
Lopez Garcia, A. forthcoming: 'Fora Litibus Omnia Fervent: The Transfer of the Tribunals in Rome from the Forum to the Courtroom'.
Lopez Garcia, A., and Bueno Guardia, M. 2021: 'Typology and Multifunctionality of Public Libraries in Rome and the Empire', *Journal of Eastern Mediterranean Archaeology & Heritage Studies* 9(3), 247–277.
Moatti, C. 1998: *La Mémoire Perdue. Recherches sur l'administration romaine*, Rome.
Östenberg, I., Malmberg, S., and Bjørnebye, J. (eds) 2015: *The Moving City: Processions, Passages and Promenades in Ancient Rome*, London.
Russell, A. 2016: *The Politics of Public Space in Republican Rome*, Cambridge.

Part I
Theory and Methodology

2 The Administrative Topography of Rome

Mapping Administrative Space and the Spatial Dynamics of Roman Republicanism[1]

Juhana Heikonen, Kaius Tuori, Antonio Lopez Garcia, Samuli Simelius, and Anna-Maria Wilskman

I Introduction[2]

Within the newer studies on space and spatiality as a historical determinant, an often-repeated claim is that physical spaces are reflections of the social framework of the community, a kind of petrified illustration of the values and norms of the society.[3] However, within the study of the spaces of administration and law, this claim is immediately challenged. In the standard works on space, the importance and value of a given feature is observable in the centrality, visibility, and expense apparent in the spaces devoted to it. Thus, the centrality of religion or certain religious cults may be divined in the size and prominence of the place of worship. Given that administration and the law are among the most important features of Roman civic culture and its prime legacies, the spaces devoted to them are disappointing: open spaces, transportable furniture, little or no dedicated room for them.[4] What there is can mainly be described as secondary uses of religious buildings such as temples or transient loci in open spaces such as marketplaces and so forth.[5]

In short, what we are missing are buildings that we can say are the equivalent of a modern administrative office, a court building, or an archive. However, what we do have are many spaces and buildings that have some administrative functions linked to them and which have been given almost modern functions in literature, such as the Aerarium and Tabularium. The purpose of this chapter is to trace and map these administrative functions, actions, and spaces, based on existing Roman sources. Instead of singular buildings and places, it will focus on locations and connections in order to reveal their functional interdependencies.

The aim of the chapter is to produce a diachronic, schematic map of administration as a function of space and time, with a historical analysis of change. It will include various administrative functions, widely understood, beginning with law courts and administrative centres, archives and libraries, the senatorial and equestrian *domus*, and the representations of magistrates in public space.

For the sake of simplicity, we have condensed these into five main chronological points for the map: Map 1. Second century B.C., Map 2. First century B.C., Map 3. First century A.D., Map 4. Second century A.D. and Map 5. Third ccentury A.D.[6] The main sources for these maps are references to various administrative activities in Roman sources. Of these, the most important are written sources,

DOI: 10.4324/b23090-3

This chapter has been made available under a CC BY-NC 4.0 license.

where authors such as Cicero are very prominent. What we have been looking for are references to activities that would have taken place at certain locations and then using that information to provide a place and time marker. Due to the lacunal nature of Roman history, the volume of sources is rather uneven. Evidence of the aforementioned activities and functions is plentiful, whether literary or epigraphic. However, most of it lacks a sufficiently exact location for our purposes. The historical references to administrative activities are indicated with place markers (N = 102), archives and libraries (N = 92), relevant private *domus* (N = 223), and epigraphic data of magistrates (N = 100).

II Method[7]

The theoretical framework of this chapter is based on the notion that, instead of static places, it is more fruitful to track activities that can be located. This ties into an emerging theoretical discussion where the concepts of visibility, movement, and action have been raised as central ways of approaching city space in the ancient world.[8] While the modern notion of administration and bureaucracy relies heavily on the dual poles of office and archive, we hope to bring forward a new way of looking into functioning premodern administrative urban space.

Instead of Lefebvrian analysis of space production this chapter analyzes Roman administration through one branch of Activity Space (AS) research, which partially derives from urban planning research and has later been used in everything possible from transportation to segregation research. AS is a concept used to describe the measurable spatial behaviour of individuals. It is widely used to describe a person's mobility or to identify locations that people are in direct contact with because of their mobility. The modern solutions rely heavily on Geographical Information Systems (GIS) and real time location technologies, such as GPS to produce a mass of information for further data mining.

AS research focuses on the interrelationships between activities in time and space, and the constraints imposed by these interrelationships. Rather than attempting to explain or predict an individual's allocation of time among potential activities in space, this time-geography highlights the factors that restrict an individual's choice. Although often applied to daily and weekly time frames on the urban scale, this time-geography can also accommodate scales as extensive as a person's lifetime, or as in our case, the scale of a ruling class in a timeframe of half a millennium. This chapter focuses on AS, or time-geography, which is an elegant and powerful framework developed by Torsten Hägerstrand and his colleagues at Lund University in Sweden during the 1950s and 1960s, later expanded by several scholars and modern technologies.[9]

Hägerstrand's time-geography is based on the simple notion that everyone deploys certain activities in a certain sequence. In general, we can see a clear pattern in the activities that humans deploy. There are different kinds of patterns based, for example, on life, workweek, or day which show the sequence of activities for a specific time. Individual patterns can be visually presented as prisms. When these come together, they create a pattern cluster. Hägerstrand created this model of a space and time pattern to illustrate how a person finds and navigates his way in space. In his model of time-geography, Hägerstrand used the following assumptions: 1) everything physical has a lifespan, 2) one cannot be in different places at the same time, 3) the tasks of everyone are limited, 4) tasks demand time, 5) movement between activities takes time, 6) only one can occupy the exact same place at one time, and 7) space and activities have biographies.

Our variation of AS research is a very simplified version of Hägerstrand's AS and is improved by a simplified GIS to place administrative activities, functions, and places in space-time, but without any Monte Carlo method-based algorithms of the law of large numbers. The main purpose of the maps is the intention to track the chosen activities' possible interdependence during a period of half a millennium. This means that instead of normal AS research, we do not have different clusters of people doing similar activities at the same time since our clusters (five in total) of AS are the same social class of people, but in different centuries. The clusters are defined by centuries from the second B.C. to the third A.D. The parameters are shown on 250×250 m ($1/16$ km^2) squares in a grid that comprises Rome within the Aurelian Wall. The chosen activities are by no means complete, but they represent the most relevant for this kind of novel research and those which can be located with relatively good accuracy. The first activities are courts and administration. The second set of activities is archives and libraries which we consider to be performing the same kind of functions. The third set is the senatorial and equestrian *domus* that are relevant power bases of the same people who take care of the courts and administration, supposedly also from their *domus*. The fourth set of activities is the inscriptions by or for the previous people. The last variable is the volume of built public space at the end of each century.

We are aware of the inaccuracies our limited data can produce; thus, this approach is a sort of wireframe version of modern AS research. Unlike other AS research our research does not link the different activities as a sequence since we are using this method for other purposes. As a sequence, it could be possible to reconstruct a senator's moving pattern in Rome by Cicero's letters, but it would be hard to apply these movements to a whole class of administration in our long timespan. These present maps are based on the previous work by Heikonen,[10] and they have partially benefitted from topographic contours by the University of Pennsylvania.[11] Most of the built environment is based on *LTUR*.[12]

We have gathered locatable information of the Roman administration's (magistrates, senators, etc.) activities in space to create a *longue durée* AS analysis, which is presented as GIS maps (Maps 1–5) and one conclusive Table 2.1 with a radar chart.[13] This rough model is based on our perception of relevance and sufficient location markers which are subjective. However, moving the criteria markers for recorded activities on our maps would not change their relation to other recorded activities, or above all the chosen data's relativity between the centuries (clusters) our maps display.

In modern AS research the home is often seen as a starting point for various activities. However, as the pandemic has shown us, home is also for work. This was also the case for the Roman ruling classes, as the boundaries between public and private were more fluid. For example, Cicero refers to his real estate from *villae rusticae* to his Roman *domus* in his letters more often than he refers to the exact meeting places of the Senate by name, or other exact places of administration. Hence, this chapter refers to the *domus* as a place of activity. We have left other possible places of administrative activity to lesser notice in our simple model because they would not bear as much relevance to this chapter. However, it would be more than certain, that gatherings at races, games, and baths were important as places of activity in Roman socio-economic affairs. Thus, these have been considered in our maps as a volume that expands in time. Instead of singular points of literary or epigraphic evidence, this volume has been measured very roughly in hectares to give the fifth parameter of Table 2.1 and the table its spatial nature.

III Courts[14]

In the *Dialogus* of Tacitus, the speaker laments the decline of court oratory.[15] During the Republic, a famous orator like Cicero would be expected to wax poetic about virtues and vices, speaking sometimes for hours to a rapt audience of thousands of citizens. The orator was the centre of attention, his rhetorical skill the crucial element of the success of the case. In contrast, during the time of Tacitus, an orator would be confined to a small room, deprived of an audience except for a dour magistrate who would interrupt him and command him to get to the point.

The evidence of the Roman material, when approached in its entirety, paints a very clear picture of the changes taking place. During the Republic, it shows the concentration of courts and administration in the Forum, culminating in the late republican monumentalization and politization of the Forum by Caesar and Augustus.[16] From Augustus onwards, the spaces of justice reflect an imperial dominance, as during the Principate we can see the spread of courts around the city but also their concentration in the hands of the emperor and imperial functionaries.[17]

Our sources on the republican concentration of courts and judicial activity in the Forum Romanum comes to a large degree, but not exclusively, from Cicero.[18] It may be said that for the late Republic, Cicero forms a world of his own, one that is concentrated and focused on the Forum as a place to be seen, act, and be heard. Many other authors mention trials in the Comitium,[19] the Puteal Libonis,[20] the Aurelian Steps,[21] or just the Forum in general, as well as the two seats of the praetors[22] (Map 1: i11). We can thus relatively safely assume that this was not simply a fixation of Cicero's, but rather the concentration of disputes, legal and otherwise, into this relatively small piece of land.

During the mid-republican period, a new architectural type, the basilica, appeared in the Roman Forum. The emergence of this new space seems to have a connection with the development of new judicial practices in the late third century or early second century B.C. Basilicas were the quintessential example of multifunctional architecture in Rome, as they were used for different purposes simultaneously, including judiciary tasks, commercial, financial, administrative, and entertainment activities.[23] During the second century B.C., four basilicas were built in the Roman Forum (Map 2: i11): The Basilica Porcia (184 B.C.), the Basilica Fulvia-Aemilia

(179 B.C.), the Basilica Sempronia (169 B.C.), and the Basilica Opimia (121 B.C.). References to judiciary activities in these spaces are scarce, hazy, and very often indirect, but scholars have speculated widely about their functions.[24]

After the late Republic, the crucial development is the numerical decline in the mentions of judicial activities. The decline is much more pronounced than could be explained by the change in the volume of literature discussing judicial activities or some other development. While we have new types of legal activities, from imperial officials and even the emperor himself beginning to act as judge, the sense of nearly constant discussion of trials is lacking. There are references to trials by authors such as Pliny and Quintilian, who mention how the new Basilica Iulia becomes the seat of the centumviral court (Map 4: i11).[25]

As Cicero mentions,[26] building projects are an immensely useful tool for self-promotion, mentioning in envious terms how enormous projects were realized to bring attention to their makers. It has often been mentioned how beginning with Augustus, imperial power takes over the Forum through new building projects that either replace or revamp most of the building stock in the Forum. In addition to that, the building of the imperial fora brings a whole new level of monumentalization. For the use of law courts and judicial magistrates, only the Forum of Augustus (Map 3: i10) is mentioned as a court of law. Sources such as the *Tabulae Sulpiciorum* and the *Tabulae Herculanenses* mention how the seats of the praetors were moved there.[27]

For the imperial jurisdiction, locations on the Palatine and other imperial properties spread around the city are mentioned. These legal activities led by the emperor mention several types of spaces like the basilicas, the Roman Forum (Maps: i11), the Pantheon (Maps: f8), the Porticus of Livia (Maps: g11), the imperial palaces, and the gardens.[28]

It would appear that the change from a republican notion of justice to an imperial machinery could be seen to follow the course outlined already by the character of Tacitus' *Dialogus*: while the courts continued to function, their role occupied nowhere near the centrality that they had during the Republic. The description of the grandiose oratory and the paid applauders in Pliny are in general outliers; for the most part, law retreats from the public arena, as far as the written sources inform us.

The changes in the judicial procedure in the first and second century A.D. might have affected the spatial needs of the trials, and thus new locations were built to suit the new requirements of the system.[29] The decline of the *quaestiones perpetuae* and the increasing number of *cognitiones extra ordinem* might have affected the spatial requirements of the courts to host a larger number of *iudices*. Quintilian and Seneca highlight that in the Augustan era some orators did not like to address large crowds under the open sky.[30] This may be one of the reasons for the transfer of the courts from open spaces easily accessible to the public to closed venues that were easily defensible from the energic crowds when things went in the wrong direction during the trials. The congestion of the legal system is reflected in several sources of this period. Until the republican period, trials were limited to only some months of the year.[31] The *Lex Iulia iudiciorum publicorum* from Augustan times mentions that trials were suspended during November and December. The reason for that suspension was possibly that open spaces were not always usable during the rainy months of the year.[32] It is likely that the increment in trials led to the extension of the period for trials to the entire year, and, therefore, closed spaces were built to avoid the bad weather conditions of the autumn months.

What is very surprising, considering the enormous volume of building taking place during the first two centuries of the Principate, is the relative dearth of information regarding the activities of the courts. In fact, we have exceedingly little information of what took place in the grand halls and imperial fora that were built by the Roman emperors. What were the imperial halls like the Basilica Ulpia (Map 4: i9), the Basilica of Maxentius (Map 5: i11), or the *Auditoria* of Hadrian (Map 5: h9) for? The sources are unclear about their function, but the hypotheses about their judicial purpose have a great acceptance rate among scholars.[33]

From the Dominate to the late antique period we again have numerous references to the operation of the courts, but they are mainly about imperial courts, especially the court of the city prefect. A new practice of secret judiciary meetings appears in Rome. The *cognitiones* became a secret event in the late fourth century A.D. This new practice was probably a consequence of the insecurity or the fixation on controlling the crowds that until then had still had access to the trials. Late antique sources mention a new space called a *secretarium* that perhaps was the scene of these secret trials (Map 5: i11).[34] Conclusively, we have seen how the spaces for justice changed from the public and open spaces around the Roman Forum in the republican period, to the imperial fora in the early Empire and, finally, to the secluded areas of the *secretaria*.

IV Private Houses and Administrative Processes[35]

Even if the administrative work has a strong spatial connection with public spaces, such as fora and basilicas, it was by no means limited to these. There are several passages mentioning that the work was – at least partly – also done in the private sphere.[36] There is no denying the importance of the public space, but dismissing the private would present a very tortured view of the urban administrative landscape, as much preparation work and many meetings – informal and more formal – occurred beyond the public venues.

Mapping every possible location of administration would be unfruitful, as almost any location could be adopted for this purpose. Consequently, the focus should be in the places where this type of work most likely occurred. Of all the possible private spaces, a house or a lodgement is without doubt such a location. It had a central role in a Roman life – both private and public. However, before starting to map all the *domus* of Rome some methodological notations must be made.

The mapping is mostly executed on the basis of the information of the *Lexicon Topographicum Urbis Romae* (Vol. 2, 1995), with some additions and corrections.[37] The level of accuracy of our maps excludes those houses with very vague locations. In addition, the deduction of the locations of some *domus* are not on a very solid footing, and therefore not every entry is included in this endeavour. The selection of *domus*/lodgement is explained in the following.

Not every house was necessarily used for administrative work – or this function might have had a very minor role – and therefore it is better to narrow down the mapped *domus* to those where this function was likely. The senatorial and equestrian households expectedly belonged to this group. In addition, so did the households connected to the imperial family – such as those inhabited by imperial freedmen – although the link is not perhaps as evident as with the highest strata of the society. Of course, it is always possible that certain individual households of these social ranks had an almost non-existent role in administration, but these are exceptions rather than the rule. The identification of the social rank of the house owner is not always certain in the *Lexicon*. In these cases, we have decided to follow the proposed interpretations, even if the social status might be somewhat debatable. Additionally, there are persons outside these social levels, such as scribes, who were involved in the administrative work.[38] They are also included.

The sources often provide information about private property, but the type of this property remains open. It is uncertain whether the person in question lived, lodged, and worked at the locations reported. It is possible that the property was dedicated to some other purpose, such as a commercial function or perhaps the owner rented it and did not spend much time there. If it seems that the property in question was utilized for this type of function, such as the possible *domus* of Volusius Saturninus, it is excluded.[39] However, the property does not have to be an actual *domus* to involve administrative work. If we can assume that the person in question lived or lodged at the location, it is likely that administrative work occurred there. For example, the nature of *horti* is difficult to define and we cannot be exactly certain what purposes they were utilized for, but it seems likely that they included residential buildings.[40] Consequently, some administrative work likely occurred there. The same conclusion can be applied to other types of property; therefore, we do not have to be certain whether there was an actual *domus* at the location or whether the person in question actually owned the place.

The sources can be divided to three types: literary mentions, inscriptions on lead pipes, and other inscriptions. The late republican houses are mainly located on the basis of the literary sources (Maps 1 and 2). A common problem with the literary passages is that they are not very precise about the location. It was rarely essential for the purpose of these texts to describe the exact location of the houses.[41] However, finding the exact location of the houses is not within the methodological scope of this chapter, but rather finding out the areas where private dwellings of this administrative class were located is, and therefore the vague nature of the locations does not always matter. Many houses can be mapped with a degree of certainty that is sufficient for our purpose – although there are several cases where the degree is too vague and these must be excluded.

The literary sources occasionally reveal several owners of the same house, or a house built in the exact same location that we know had a *domus* before, whereby the exact same location of a house might have several symbols on one map. A good example is the house of Cicero on the Palatine. In the first century B.C., we know of four owners of that house, meaning that on the map the same house has been marked four times on the square with the Palatine (Map 2, j12).[42] This might be confusing location-wise, but for the purpose of mapping administrative activity this works very well, as it highlights the importance of the location.

The question of inheritance of the house is a complex matter to interpret, as noted by Christer Bruun.[43] Many Romans probably lived in or owned the houses of their parents, yet, as Bruun notes, the twists and turns of Roman real estate markets were complicated, and therefore it is often questionable whether the house of a known Roman was the same house where his parents lived. We have decided to include the houses of the ancestors only if the ancient reference suggests that it was the case that the house was also owned by previous generations. This, for example, leaves out the possible *domus* of M. Aemilius Scaurus' father and Q. Hortensius Hortalus listed by Bruun.

The source base changes during the imperial period. The inscriptions become the dominant group to locate the *domus*. On Map 3 – depicting the situation in the first century A.D. – most of the houses are already located on the basis of inscriptions. Nonetheless, the role of the literary sources is not insignificant, although the nature and reliability of many early Christian sources – which also locate houses of imperial Rome – is doubtful and they are excluded.[44] The vast majority of the inscriptions are on lead water pipes – *fistulae aquariae*. In the imperial period, these are the single most important source when trying to locate a *domus* in Rome. Werner Eck has studied them extensively, and he has noted several problems relating to the *fistulae* as sources of house locations. For example, they do not necessarily point to the exact location of the house, but it can be more than a hundred – in the worst case a thousand – metres away from the find spot of the *fistula*. However, Eck concludes that they can tell us the rough region where the *domus* was.[45]

One problem regarding the *fistulae* is that they provide information about a private property, but the type of this property remains open. For example, a lead pipe could direct water to a *domus* but also to a *hortus*.[46] Although, it has already been concluded that the *horti* can also be locations of administrative work, they tended to be so vast that a *hortus per se* cannot be the location of administrative work in our mapping endeavour. However, we can assume that the lodgements in the *horti* were near the find locations of the *fistulae*, and also map these as locations of administrative work.

In Maps 4 and 5, the *fistulae* are clearly the most frequent source of *domus* locations. There are also some located on the basis of the literary sources and other inscriptions, which are the most challenging source group. They are to a certain degree accepted as potential material indicating the location of a Roman *domus*.[47] However, the methodology behind these locations is less than clear. There are inscriptions where the text suggests the location of a dwelling, which function as a straightforward source for house locations, in a way similar to the literary passages. Nevertheless, there are not many of these and usually the findspot of the inscription is considered to be the location of the house. In this case, the inscription would be found – as the scholars express it – *in situ*. Nevertheless, what this phrase actual means is very vague. Most commonly, an inscription is understood to be *in situ* when its find location can be connected to excavation or ancient ruins. If we think about what the phrase means when we do archaeological documentation, this is correct. However, if we think about the *domus* location, it is not so clear that it is actually the same place.

The level of documentation of the inscription findspots rarely offers enough information to conclude that it is where the *domus* was. We are well aware that inscriptions were moved from their original place in antiquity as well as later, which makes this method questionable. Even in those cases where the inscription is attached to the architectural remains, we can ask whether this was the original location of the inscriptions. Romans even moved columns from public buildings to their private houses,[48] so what is the possibility that a single inscription is still in its original place? We can further question whether it is possible that the inscription might have been in the house of a person other than the one to whom it was dedicated. For instance, it was common to have sculptures of *viri illustres* in the private sphere, and it is not impossible to think that freedmen or clients had statues or inscriptions in honour of their patrons inside their houses.[49]

There are a few types of inscriptions that locate something privately owned, such as *terminus* and *cippus*. These can occasionally be at the location of the house, but even in these cases, the information of the find context must be carefully examined before reaching any conclusion.[50] In general, the inscriptions – excluding the lead pipes – can be used to identify *domus* locations only if there is some additional material to strengthen the location, for instance, several inscriptions connected to the same person – or family – found in the same area.[51]

The task of mapping lodgements relating to administrative work results in five maps (Maps 1–5). Two represent the situation in the late republican period, one of the early imperial period, and the fourth represents the second century and the fifth the third century – both also the imperial era. The accuracy selected for the map allows us to locate altogether 223 houses on these five maps: 15 on Map 1, 53 on Map 2, 54 on Map 3, 46 on Map 4, and 55 on Map 5 (some houses feature in several maps). Most are lodgements of the senatorial class (187). The number of the equestrian class (22) is relatively low. The households connected to the imperial family (30) are a bit more numerous than those of the equestrians but clearly fall short of the senatorial. However, they overlap with the senatorial rank, as many houses of the imperial family can also be counted as senatorial.

The *domus* of persons involved in the administration (senatorial and equestrian classes) were generally close to the other locations of administration, as all the maps demonstrate. In particular, during the republican era they are mainly concentrated near the area of the Forum Romanum. However, moving forward in time, locations further away from the centres of administration appear. This might be explained by the transformed structure of the city: it had become larger, and the core was monumentalized, and thus space for *domus* needed to be sought further away. It is also possible that easy access from one's house to the other venues of administration was less and less important during the imperial period. Perhaps both explanations lie behind this development. If we consider that the home functions as the second important venue for administrative work besides the public locations planned for administrative purposes, such as fora and basilicas, this suggests to us that the spatial connection between the core location of the administration became weaker during the imperial era.

V Archives and Libraries[52]

One of the main challenges for understanding the daily labour of the Roman administration is the storage of information. Data produced in the massive bureaucratic system of Rome might have a fundamental role for the implementation of the rights of citizenship, the financial records of the state, and the preservation of the laws enacted by the legislative assemblies among many other functions. Preserving this knowledge, no matter of what kind, was a crucial task and, thus, the creation of suitable spaces for its protection was a requirement for ancient states. Romans were not the first in the creation of such spaces, but they enhanced their performance. Knowledge about the subject is quite limited and interpretations are made based on modern assumptions about what an archive or a library is and what its functions are. In addition to buildings that were used for the storage of information, we have a wealth of material about the publication and storage of laws, decisions, and other official material on the buildings, by posting them in a public place.[53] This is compounded by the fact that the ancient references we have about the archives and libraries in Rome are scarce and incomplete. To these limits we must add the confusion created by the interpretations of the vast historiography about Roman libraries.

The concept of archive and concept of library are often blurred. For most of the republican period we find references about archives such as the Aerarium at the Temple of Saturn,[54] the archive of the aediles at the Temple of Ceres,[55] the archive of the population records at the Atrium Libertatis,[56] the archive with the magistrates' records at the Temple of Juno Moneta,[57] and the archive of the tribunes on the Capitoline.[58] Additionally, we have more controversial information, such as the enigmatic Tabularium,[59] the supposed main archive of the Roman state, and the curious reference to the storage of the archive of the census at the temple of the Nymphs.[60] Ancient historiography clearly shows a distinctive purpose for the archives: the storage of public records (*tabulae publicae*). The appearance of private libraries in the written sources during the early first century B.C.,[61] the creation of the first public library in Rome[62] in the mid first century B.C., and the references about *bibliothecae* that also contained public records or where the stage for some administrative task such as the meetings of the Senate was set, create a complex scene in which libraries and archives are frequently mixed in the sources. Multifunctionality is a frequent feature in ancient buildings, and libraries are one of the most complex types due to the mingling of administrative functions, artistic and scholastic functions, or religious purposes, among many others.[63] The confusion generated by the sources using the term *bibliotheca* when referring to institutions or buildings that contained archival information from the late republican period and the Principate has prompted scholars to evaluate the subject from several viewpoints. The lack of archaeological elements in most of the cases referenced in the written sources does not allow a deep exploration of the topic from the architectural side, but many of the references we have offer some topographical information. Only a few cases such as the Atrium Libertatis do not offer a very specific location, but in any case, the information is clear enough to define an area in central Rome in which the building might have been located.

From the spatial point of view, there are only a few studies that treat the topic with the attention it deserves. Most scholars have focused on the librarian content of the libraries or the architectural features when examining a building located archaeologically. The recent works of T. K. Dix and G. W. Houston[64] make a broad analysis of the libraries in Rome, including some discussion about the spatial aspect of the subject and proposing some exciting theories about the links between the institutions and analysing their presences diachronically. Previously, several scholars analyzed the location of the main libraries and archives in the *Lexicon Topographicum Urbis Romae* individually but unfortunately failed to discuss the interrelations between the institutions.[65]

During the republican period, the archives and libraries converge on a very few spots (see Maps 1 and 2). Most of the places are temples located between the Capitolium and the valley of the Forum with very few exceptions, such as the Temple of Ceres on the Aventine (Map 2: i14) mentioned by Livy (3.55) and Cicero (*Leg.* 3.3.7), and the Temple of the Nymphs burnt by Clodius mentioned by Cicero (*Mil.* 7.3) (Map 2: i09). The archive most referred to in the republican sources is without doubt the Aerarium at the Temple of Saturn (Map 2: h11) which contained laws on bronze tables,[66] the *senatusconsulta*,[67] state fiscal documentation,[68] and a diverse group of other documents such as the *commentarii* of officials, the protocols of elections, and the lists of *iudices*.[69] The Atrium Libertatis has also been frequently mentioned since the second century B.C.[70] The building might have been located just outside the *pomerium*, around the saddle between the Capitolium and the Quirinal Hill (Map 1, 2 and 3: i10). The importance of this archive is due to its use to host the population records and exhibit laws affixed to the building. In the mid-first century A.D., the Atrium Libertatis was restructured[71] and since then included an important library together with the archives of the census, although our information regarding that is not as clear as one would like. The purpose of the library is contested, but its collections might have been so remarkable that Ovid thought that his books were not good enough for inclusion in the Atrium Libertatis.[72] Some scholars link the reconstruction of the Atrium Libertatis and the addition of a library with the project of Caesar to build the first public library of the city that was commissioned by Varro, but never executed.[73] Some years later, Asinius Pollio[74] built a library and put a portrait of Varro inside, perhaps to honour the original commissioner of the project.

Archives might have contained not only space to store tablets or scrolls, but also working space for the clerks who managed the information – *tabularia*.[75] Libraries, being, for example, a place for gladiatorial games, also might have contained space to read the scrolls and a pleasant illumination to allow the reading, but likely also comprised spaces for public lectures like *auditoria* or even pedagogic spaces to host lessons. The most prominent *tabularium* was the Tabularium Publicum located in the foothills of the Capitoline Hill (Map 1: g10), but its existence and function are shrouded in mystery. Only a few sources reflect this institution that might have functioned between the early first century B.C. and the fifth century A.D.[76] This archive probably contained the *tabulae publicae* with the records and might have been linked strongly with the Aerarium at the Temple of Saturn. What would a *tabularium* look like? We can imagine a scene similar to the famous Altar of the Scribes relief from the Porta di San Sebastiano, where several *scribae* work around a table with *tabulae*. Archaeologically, it is difficult to identify a space like the one depicted in the relief and the written sources only mention *tabularia* explicitly in a few cases. Thus, the vision we have about the archives in Rome is very partial.[77] The works of P. Culham[78] and others on the development of the archival practices in Rome during the republican era reflect that even during the late Republic, there were substantial problems within the organization of the statal archives in the city. Ancient authors, such as Cicero or Cato,[79] echo their problems with retrieving information in the precarious collections of the Aerarium due to the lack of proper archives. Possibly, their knowledge about the management, retrieval, and storage of information in Athens made them aware of the necessity of an appropriate statal archive. During the next century, Romans would develop their own statal record offices and, probably, the distinction between the terms "library" and "archive" developed at the same time – when the management of public records and private books became practices much more distinguishable.

Epigraphic and literary sources mention the existence of a library at the Portico of Octavia (Map 2: g10) that might have been intimately linked with the administration and, thus, contain an archive.[80] This library, founded by Augustus, hosted sessions of the Senate and probably had a large room that could host sizeable meetings.[81] The sources are never very clear about the contents of the libraries but leave some footprints about the multiple functions that the libraries of late republican and Augustan Rome might have had. As in the case of the Atrium Libertatis that contained an impressive art collection[82] and a space for public recitations,[83] the references to the library at the Portico of Octavia show a clear multifunctionality. The fire of A.D. 80 destroyed the complex, and Domitian rebuilt the area and likely the library as well,[84] but in A.D. 192 another fire damaged the complex. Septimius Severus and Caracalla reconstructed the Portico of Octavia in A.D. 203,[85] but we have no direct references to the reconstruction of the library in this period.

The third library we know about in this period is the famed Bibliotheca ad Apollinis on the Palatine (Map 2: j12) founded by Augustus between 36 and 28 B.C. next to the sumptuous Temple of Apollo and the Portico of the Danaids.[86] According to Suetonius,[87] there were two different sections in this library: one Greek and the other Roman. Inside the Bibliotheca Apollinis, a statue of Apollo was erected,[88] as well as statues of other poets and orators.[89] Various sources mention that several Senate meetings were held in this library, as well as in the Temple of Apollo.[90] The library was used several times for the meetings of the Senate, the revision of jury lists, and the reception of embassies.[91] Written sources also mention performances involving poetic auditions and declamations in this library.[92] Ovid mentions that this library was open to readers,[93] but we cannot extract any information about either the arrangement of the space or the origins of the readers.

The sources mention other libraries on the Palatine Hill built during the first century A.D. One is the library at the Temple of Divus Augustus, mentioned by Martial[94] and Suetonius[95] – the *bibliotheca Templi novi* or *Templi Augusti* – located between the Palatine and the Capitoline behind the Basilica Iulia (Map 3: h11). We do not have any further information about this library or its contents. The other new library on the Palatine is the one at the Domus Tiberiana (Map 3: i12), mentioned on several occasions in the sources.[96] Aulus Gellius mentions that he conducted philosophical discussions with his colleagues in the library of the Domus Tiberiana, which suggests at least the presence of a space suitable for meetings and academic activities.[97] Unfortunately, the written sources do not provide references to the exact location of this building either.

After the time of Augustus, we do not have much information about the archive/library at the Atrium Libertatis. We presume that, at the time of the dismantlement of the saddle between the Quirinal and the Capitoline, the building disappeared, and its collections were transferred to other spaces. The primitive republican archives, after suffering several tragic events between the late first century B.C. and the first century A.D. might have been reorganized.[98] Perhaps, this reorganization could be visible in the written sources that suddenly stop mentioning those republican archives and only mention the libraries built from Augustan times on.

In A.D. 75, the emperor Vespasian dedicated another library in the Temple of Peace.[99] This library is mentioned several times in the written sources until the fourth century A.D. Its location within the enormous complex of the Templum Pacis (Map 3: i11) has been a matter of discussion among scholars because the building was destroyed during a fire in A.D. 192. D. Palombi locates the library in the hall behind the wall of the Forma Urbis – which has also been linked with the headquarters of the urban prefect – but P. Tucci identifies the library in the great hall towards the Via Sacra corresponding to the current Basilica of St. Cosmas and Damian, which has traditionally been interpreted as a Severan addition. The library appears in the sources until the fourth century.[100] The sources reflect the multifunctionality of the institution, which not only contained an important medical library and a lecture hall,[101] but also a magnificent collection of artworks with masterpieces by Praxiteles and the spoils of the Temple of Jerusalem. If the Temple of Peace was part of the urban prefect's administration it is feasible that the library contained some archives of the magistracy, but beside the speculations of some scholars, there is no evidence of those contents.

The Bibliotheca Ulpia, founded at the outstanding Forum of Trajan, raises some important questions about the use of a library as an official archive (Map 4: i9). This new institution, founded in A.D. 112, is mentioned frequently in the written sources until the mid-fourth century.[102] The Historia Augusta mentions several times that the *libri lintei* and the *liber elephantinus* were in the library.[103] Also, Aulus Gellius mentions that he read a praetorian edict in the library.[104] Some scholars[105] have suggested that the construction of the library in this location was related to the Library of the Atrium Libertatis because the Severan marble plan depicts the word *libertatis* on one of the apses of the Forum of Trajan. Perhaps part of the collections of the second iteration of the Atrium Libertatis – the one refurbished by Asinius Pollio – might have ended up being part of the Bibliotheca Ulpia. Nevertheless, aside from the word depicted on the marble plan, and the ancient *libri* and edicts mentioned in the sources, it is difficult to confirm that assertion. The old library of Asinius Pollio was probably erected in the saddle between the Capitoline and the Quirinal (Map 2: i10), which was removed for the construction of the Forum of Trajan.[106] The Bibliotheca Ulpia complex was composed of two identical buildings with two floors that flanked the Column of Trajan. Niches big enough to host shelves to store the scrolls were placed in the walls of both buildings. The library had high-vaulted ceilings that likely helped to illuminate the interior, creating excellent conditions for the conservation of the scrolls. Sidonius Apollinaris mentions the presence of artwork in this environment.[107] The link of the Forum of Trajan with administrative and judicial activities is well known, and, therefore, it is feasible that the Ulpian Library was linked with these activities in a certain manner, perhaps providing the magistrates archival resources on their progress.[108]

In republican times, aside from the case of the archive at the Temple of Ceres[109] (Map 2: h13), most of the archives were in a relatively small area comprising the temples of the Roman Forum and the nearby Porta Fontinalis (Map 2: i11). In Augustan times, there was a notable expansion of the institutions on the Palatine (Map 2: i12-j12) and the Portico of Octavia (Map 2: h11). During the late first and the second century A.D., we see that there was a dispersion of the archives/libraries toward the imperial fora, but the purpose of the institutions is not very clear. The sources do not clarify whether the republican archives were integrated into the new libraries built from Augustan times on, but the number of archives mentioned during imperial times is quite limited in comparison with the number of libraries that appear. Some scholars have coined the term "imperial libraries"[110] to explain the links amongst all the libraries in the imperial fora and the libraries of the Temple of Apollo and the Domus Tiberiana on the Palatine that might make us think that they were part of the administration because of the environment, or the activities recorded in the written sources. The most important question here is: Can we differentiate between libraries and archives? Often, the sources reflect artistic or scholastic activities within the *bibliothecae* but, sometimes, other sources referring to the same institution offer us a reference to administrative tasks, or the retrieval of bureaucratic information being done. Perhaps the later development of libraries for leisure and entertainment – scholars have some suspicions about the existence of such libraries in the baths of Rome[111] – led to a segregation of the two types of institution from the late first or second century A.D. This naturally happened at the same time that the acquisition of important private libraries by the Roman elites became something common during the first century A.D. Previously, the possession of private libraries seems to be something restricted to some specific republican characters such as Sulla, Cicero, or Lucullus. Clearly, during late antiquity, the number of libraries in the city increased remarkably. The Regionary Catalogues compiled in the second half of the fourth century list a number of 28–29 libraries within the city. This list might be exaggerated or hardly credible, but it seems that libraries became something very popular after the second century A.D. We certainly do not know how the expansion of the libraries from the central area of Rome to the peripheral areas affected spatiality, but we can determine that the administrative libraries – if this is a correct term that encompasses both of the concepts "library" and "archive" – maintained their preeminent position in the imperial fora and on the Palatine during the late imperial era. However, since the catalogues do not mark their exact location or they are not mentioned in relevant literature, they are left out of the maps. The meaning of this expansion of publicly available information is highly contested. Some, like Neudecker,[112] have suggested that the increased publication of information was a conscious ideological choice in the late Republic. However, from the Principate onwards the buildings used for the storage of information were increasingly under imperial control.

VI   Inscriptions as Markers of Administrative Presence[113]

Roman administration culminates in its magistrates. While speeches, trials and Senate meetings have not left archaeological records, officials made a lasting mark on the cityscape through inscriptions, and monuments themselves could serve as meeting points for legal settlements.[114] Rome was filled with statues and accompanying inscriptions. A public commemoration was a high honour, and the Senate and the authorities heavily supervised the desire to erect statues for living individuals.[115] Ancient authors report how this sometimes led to the clearing of the Forum of statues that were not placed there by the initiative of the Senate or the people.[116] Epigraphic monuments not only record the prestige of the individual, but they also express his administrational prowess. In addition to being manifestations of the person's glory and power, they also serve as *exempla*, guiding the elite youth in their career aspirations.[117]

The inscriptions presented in Maps 1–5 are high magisterial inscriptions. The material used in this subchapter is far from perfect. Most are honorific inscriptions, but we supplement the material with other monuments, especially in Map 1, when the total number of inscriptions was lower.[118] Only the inscriptions found *in situ*, or that can be located with relative certainty to the surroundings of the *non in situ* findspot, are included (for the problems regarding the understanding of *in situ*, see earlier).[119] The fragmentary state and dating of the inscriptions create uncertainty and therefore methodological problems. We decided to follow the editors' supplementations and dating presented in the epigraphic corpora. The dating of the inscriptions is sometimes very vague, even covering two centuries. We locate them on the maps based on their earliest possible date. Defining the dates and limits with this kind of work is always somewhat arbitrary. Presenting the inscriptions by centuries obscures the development that would be visible with maps with tighter date blocks. For example, the explosive growth of inscriptions during Augustus' reign does not show in the current maps. Because of these methodological challenges and decisions, the inscriptions presented on the maps should be treated as approximate and considered inspirational for further investigations concerning the activeness and self-presentation of the magistrates through inanimate objects.

Environment played an important role for the statues and inscriptions, and they were used to manipulate the understanding of the past and present.[120] Roman magistrates were exposed to honorific inscriptions and statues already as children, when they accompanied the senators and stayed outside observing the meetings, while affected by the physical environment.[121] The places of administration interacted with the inscriptions.

The link between the physical environment and the monument could also appear in the actual text that records an administrative action. Thus, the inscription became an integral part of the space, recording parts of its history and linking magisterial actions directly to it. Such is the case for example with the inscriptions of the second century B.C., with the inscriptions of Isola Tiberina (Map 1: f11–12).[122] The common feature for the inscriptions on Map 1 is that they are dedications by an active magistrate while in office and with the approval of the Senate. The approval is sometimes manifested textually.[123] The inscriptions are either by praetors or curulian aediles.

The map changes completely when we come to the first century B.C., thanks to the rising habit of erecting objects with inscriptions.[124] The highest frequency of inscriptions follows the epicentres of administrational activeness (especially at the Forum Romanum and Forum Augusti), but they spread farther from the traditional centre, especially towards the east. The most eastern inscriptions (Map 2: o–p) date to the beginning of the first century B.C. and are magisterial inscriptions dictating what is not allowed in the region. Inscriptions inside, but still close to, the city wall (Map 2: m7–8) are honorific inscriptions by individuals for their family members or *patronus*, and are dated to the Augustan era.[125] The contemporary inscription on Map 2: m10 is a possible statue base with two inscriptions for the Claudii Pulchri.[126] Unlike the earlier inscriptions outside the city wall, these inscriptions are in the area of senatorial *domus*, and declare the entire magisterial careers of the honoured persons. Now the focus is more on the person than on his offices, while the inscriptions manifesting certain actions of the magistrates rely on a specific office. In general, the earlier inscriptions of this material first and foremost illustrate what persons *did as* magistrates.[127] Exceptions occur, and the inscription did not always record offices, even though the dedicators held many of them. An example of this is the inscription at the Pyramid of Cestius (Map 2: g18), where his heirs, notable persons themselves, record how they set up statues with the money they acquired by selling tapestries that the aediles declined to put in the tomb.[128]

Inscriptions appear on Map 2 most frequently at the Roman Forum and Forum of Augustus. While those from the Forum of Augustus are quite homogeneous and part of the ideological, heavily curated propaganda programme of Augustus, the inscriptions at the Roman Forum in this dataset are more diverse. A common feature of the inscriptions at this forum is that they often connect to a specific place or a monument, attaching the named magistrate to the place more concretely than easily removable statues. Such examples are the pavement inscription by the praetor L. Surdinus in the area of the praetor's tribunal and Lacus Curtius[129] and the dedication by M. Barbatus Pollio for Iuturna.[130]

The first century A.D. (Map 3) illustrates how honorific inscriptions continue to appear in the central administrative area of the *fora* and the areas of elite *domus*, but also spread to new areas towards the north and farther to the east. On the earlier maps, the scattered inscriptions far from the centre were chiefly records of magisterial actions, such as boundary stones. The more distant stones on Map 3 tend to be honorific inscriptions, perhaps from a domestic context. Some inscriptions linked to office-holding duties still exist, such as the restorations of a *sacellum* on Map 3: m12. In the Roman Forum, the area of the temple of Concordia witnesses inscriptions for a very specific reason: the health and safety of Tiberius (Map 3: i11). These inscriptions date to A.D. 31, namely the year of Sejanus' plot against Tiberius. The two dedicators both donate money and record their offices, but while C. Fulvius names Tiberius first,[131] Q. Coelius sets his own name in larger letters at the beginning of the inscription.[132] This draws the attention of the viewer to Coelius himself. Another example of how honorific dedication was used to highlight the dedicator as well is the fragmentary inscription, possibly commemorating Claudius' victory in Britannia, dedicated by one Sulpicius (Map 3: h11).[133] Sulpicius makes sure to include his *cursus honorum*. In the Forum Romanum, the target of the honour was mostly the imperial family. Therefore, the honorific monument, possibly a triumphal quadriga, for the praetor Silanus, is exceptional.[134]

The higher frequency of inscriptions in the area of today's Largo Argentina (Map 3: f09) is due to the many fragmentary dedications to L. Aelius Lamia by his clients. Likewise, the inscriptions on Map 3: k12–13 are by individuals honouring the entire career of a magistrate. Some inscriptions were reused already in antiquity, such as Map 3: e5, which indicates the location of an inscription recycled already in antiquity. The presence of the magistrates through their texts could be everlasting, but not perhaps the way they originally intended.

Another example of a modified inscription occurs in the second century (Map 4) with h11. This inscription records the action of the republican M. Calpurnius Piso Frugi as a magistrate, but with later restorations by Nerva.[135] With the exception of this, the calendar on Map 4: m10, and the dedication to Hercules in h13, all inscriptions on Map 4 are honorific inscriptions recording the entire, or at least most of the career of the individual. A new high frequency area arises, namely the Forum of Trajan that had replaced the Forum of Augustus as the place of public, state-led honorary monuments.[136] The Forum Traiani was filled with triumphal statues, the heroic Romans who died young, prefects, and especially those noble Romans who died in wars.[137]

Unlike in the earlier maps where the inscriptions farther away were by individuals, the monuments on Map 4: o14 and p14 were public monuments approved by the Senate, one of them with public money, pointing to a non-domestic location.[138] On Map 4: l10[139] and m10[140] the context is possibly domestic, as is the case with g14[141] and f3.[142]

The inscriptions of the third century (Map 5) are all by private individuals, even the single occurrence in the Roman Forum, which is a dedication to Terentia Flavola, Vestal virgin, by her brother Lollianus and his family.[143] The rest of the epigraphic monuments in this data seem to be from a more private context, now especially in the south-western region of the city.[144]

Throughout the times, magisterial, principally honorific, inscriptions appear in or in the vicinity of the Forum Romanum. However, they did not always overlap the other places of administration and archives presented in the maps. Inscriptions spread to a wider area and appeared in multiple contexts, manifesting the actions of a single magistrate, the benevolence of the Senate, the career of the individual, and his connections. All or just some of these aspects could appear in the same monument, expressing the polyvalent nature of epigraphic and especially honorific monuments.[145] They simultaneously told the reader about present and past administration and were directed to contemporary and future generations. The statues in the Forum needed a senatorial decree. Thus, although the Forum was the epicentre of administration, the magistrates could not occupy the space automatically and independently. The Senate and later the emperor had the ultimate power. However, in their own homes, the magistrates and their families could control the space, and the majority of the honorific inscriptions presumably come from the domestic sphere. Honorific inscriptions at the *domus* imitate those in the Forum, but from a more individual perspective. The emperor was not perhaps forgotten, but in their homes, the role of the magistrate was highlighted. The *domus* imitated the Forum more and more.[146]

Another place where the Senate could not regulate the individual's inscriptions was the sacred areas. This chapter excluded the majority of such inscriptions, and we acknowledge that investigating other kinds of materials could offer different results – especially if including the inscriptions known from textual sources but which have not survived beyond antiquity. Once again, it is important to remember that the absence of evidence is not evidence of absence, and different methodological decisions and methodology, such as mapping inscriptions based on their latest possible date, can lead to different results.

VII Public Space as a Volume in Time

To link the activities into the urban space of Roman space-time, public space must be measured and given value. This is in no way a simple task, but we have made a rough schematic sketch of its development as a volume. During this half a millennium, built public space grows and spreads. For this part we have considered the traditional places of public activity, such as the temples, fora, porticos, theatres, tracks, thermae, etc. Of these, the temples, fora, and porticos are obvious. What is less obvious are the theatres, thermae, etc. that are still mentioned as places of activity, not just of passive pleasure. This is especially obvious in the cases of the Circus Flaminia and the Circus Maximus, which were vital places of activity, for example, in triumphal processions and large gatherings, and even revolts. The *naumachiae* are left out. The AS volume presented in Table 2.1 and Maps 1–5 is always the situation at the end of the relevant century. The volume is calculated by land area (ha) but does not include more than one level of buildings. Only spaces exceeding 0.5 hectares are considered. This rough calculation is solely for the purpose of considering the relation between purposefully built public space and their activities.

The "black hole" in this volume of public space is the ca. 10 hectares of palace complexes on the Palatine which has not been considered for reasons of being "private" and an obvious counterweight in the development of the other variables and will be handled in the Conclusions. There has also been discussion of normal streets being stages for administration and public encounter, but these have also been left out. Any open public space is of course public space, but since these are rarely mentioned in the relevant sources, they are considered only as links between the spaces of activity.

The AS volume in the second century B.C. is obviously the smallest. The built public space includes the known temples, the Forum Romanum, and the two *circi* (but without the permanent seating structures). This volume grows in the next century by the new theatres and fora. In the first century A.D, the volume grows by new temples, porticos, fora, the Colosseum, and thermae. In many ways, this is also the advent of the imperial public space, of which we have very little literary or epigraphic evidence. In the next century Trajan's massive public buildings, such as Trajan's Forum, were built. The third century A.D. sees the most impressive public buildings: Caracalla's and Diocletian's thermae. This means that by the end of the century the built public space is somewhere around 105 hectares. These values are very rough estimates, but still vital when trying to find relations between the activities, space, and time.

VIII Conclusions

Our research speaks as much to administration as it does to the preservation of vital evidence for this chapter. Our rough model is not a tell-all tale, but a more schematic approach to understanding the administrative topography of Rome in a novel way. This chapter is a modest look at a wider administrative topography of Rome. In the future, it would be fruitful to add more activities to the model, such as the plebeian councils, the various associations, etc.

Map 1, presenting the period between the middle Republic and late Republic, is the map with the fewest recorded activities (n = 37). However, this gives a context for succeeding centuries and comparing back from the succeeding Map 2, this map seems to be coherent, with the exception that the Senate was more flexible about the chosen places of meetings (Map 1: k15, Piscina Publica). This might also be due to what was then seen as acceptable within the Pomerium. The locations concerning administration are closely grouped around the Forum Romanum (Maps: i11), as are the *domus*. The curious feature, as with all the maps, is the distribution of inscriptions, which generally seem to mostly avoid the other points of our AS research. Do the found locations speak to the individual senators own points of activity or the neighbourhood of their *domus*, which has not left any marker for our maps?

Map 2 shows the heyday of the topography of late Roman republican administration, during the time of Cicero and the early Principate. This map also presents the most active century in AS (n = 174). Compared to the previous map, there is far more administrative activity in the Forum Romanum and the neighbouring Velia (Maps 1, 2, and 3: i10, Atrium Libertatis?) and the new fora by Caesar and Augustus (Maps 2, 3, 4, and 5: j10). Archive and library activities are on the neighbouring

Capitoline (Maps: h10 and h11) down to the Porticus Octaviae (Maps 2, 3, 4, and 5: g10) and the Palatine (Maps: i12). The central points of these activities are surrounded by the *domus*. The highest concentration is on the Palatine. However, the senatorial and equestrian *domus* also start to expand away from the centres of activity to the Esquiline and even farther away. The densest concentration of these *domus* is on the Palatine until during the coming centuries the imperial building projects evict the senatorial and equestran classes to more distant areas. As an exception, the magisterial inscriptions appear both at the location of other activities as well as in the more remote areas of Rome where there is no known evidence of senatorial or equestrian *domus*.

Map 3, showing the situation in the first century A.D., shows many of the characteristics of Map 2. However, there is a recorded decrease of activity (n = 129) especially on the level of archives, libraries, and inscriptions. For the archives and libraries, the Porticus Octaviae and the Palatium seem to have the highest concentrations of recorded activities. The clustering of the *domus* is no longer around the Forum Romanum, but clearly outside it. This also concerns the inscriptions, which do not match with the clustering of the *domus* but are more clearly outside them. Many of the inscriptions on the Campus Martius could also be explained by the fact that the area has not been excavated as thoroughly as the areas were evidence of the *domus* can be found. Or it could also be that the senators had multipolar power bases that differed from their *domus* location. This would not be uncommon even today, or in Roman politics when the senators resided outside the city most of the time, as is already well known from Cicero's letters. Unlike with the other activities, the number of recorded senatorial and equestrian *domus* rises slightly compared to the previous century.

Map 4 shows Trajan's additions to the imperial fora (Maps 4 and 5: i10 and j10), which correlate with the recorded administrative activity. Otherwise, the overall recorded activity is lower (n = 104). The administrative activity is still based in and around the Forum Romanum, and the imperial fora in total seem not to have changed the balance much. All the administrative activities are down by half compared to the first century B.C. The archives and libraries stay on the Capitoline and around the Pantheon. The magisterial inscriptions mostly avoid the other activities, except in the case of the fora and especially Trajan's Forum, which has the highest density of inscriptions. However, the recorded *domus* stay approximately on the same level. The distribution of the *domus* spread wider and thinner. One of the reasons could be that during this period, and especially in the next century, larger and more luxurious *domus* and *horti* were being built.

Map 5 shows activity that has dropped to the second lowest level (N = 73). Administrative activities are reduced around the Forum Romanum and the archives and libraries on the Capitolium. The *domus* are spread on the Aventine, Quirinal, and Esquiline. Combined with Map 4 this gives the topographic picture of senatorial influence, even though it is probable that the *fistulae* give only the ownership of real estate. Many of the *domus* known from archaeological evidence are grander and more luxurious than ever with vast *horti*. Contrarily, the volume of built public space is at its highest.

The late antique development from the fourth century onwards would show shrinkage of the urban fabric and a new appreciation of the Forum Romanum. In the imperial absence, the ruling classes without *Königsnähe* started to mimic republican memorial inscriptions and tried hard to restore the Forum.[147] Many of the second and third century *domus* were converted into churches that partially tipped the balance of power in favour of the early Church, thus creating the later Roman *Sakraltopographie*.

This AS study's radar chart in Table 2.1 shows the spatial development of Roman administration in a nutshell. The obvious results of the maps show a development of the late republican state into an imperial superpower. In the closely knit republican city, its administration and important *domus* are all within a short walking distance from the Forum Romanum, as described by Cicero, where flocks of plebs follow him en route from Forum to home. The early Principate, followed by Empire, concentrates administration on and in the Palatine. However, at the same time the large imperial building projects spread out, but there is close to no administrative record in literature. The growing senatorial *domus* locate farther away from the Forum Romanum.

The inscriptions are a very interesting activity in many respects. Their obvious out-of-sync relationship with the more obvious locations of administration, archives, and libraries and the not particularly obvious locations of the senatorial and equestrian *domus* raise many questions. Were part of these inscriptions in the neighbourhood of senatorial *domus* of which we have no records? Or does their location indicate non-recorded places of senatorial activities? Placing an inscription must have been a very special, well-thought-out, and deliberate activity so there must be some relation to the surrounding public space. The combination of *domus* and inscriptions on the maps would point to a matrix of local influencing except on the Aventine and Caelian. There is already a plethora of research on the Roman *vici* within the 14 *regiones*, so the connection is probably there. On the maps some of the lesser-known public spaces have been added without a corresponding volume. This could be one of the keys to studying the more multipolar topography of Rome's administration on a more local level. The little-known Forum Esquilinum could be one such place along with the Campus Agrippae and its public buildings of which we have little or no archaeological data.

When the Roman administration turned from transparent and recordable republican activities into imperial decrees and edicts without a set space, sometimes delivered outside Rome or by prefects, is very well presented in Maps 1–5 and Table 2.1. The growth of built public space does not correlate with the recorded administrative activity in space or time. The Palatium seems to be the "black hole" of our research, where administration supposedly disappears without a trace. In this sense, the Palatium is in Activity Space terms a non-place since it is necessarily not the place of activity but is only a symbol of activity. As the imperial administration grows, it also seems to transform into something less transparent, even though assuredly more efficient. Records of administration and archives from this period are simply fewer. Topographically, the third-century senators were on their own steep hills, the imperial administration on its own, and the volume of public

Table 2.1 The radar chart

	Courts and administration	Senatorial and equestrian domus	Archives and libraries	Magisterial inscriptions	<u>Public space (ha)</u>	Activities recorded
2nd CE BCE	10	15	6	6	<u>30</u>	37
1st CE BCE	49	53	37	35	<u>50</u>	174
1st CE ACE	20	54	27	28	<u>65</u>	129
2nd CE ACE	20	46	14	24	<u>80</u>	104
3rd CE ACE	3	55	8	7	<u>105</u>	73
TOTAL	102	223	92	100		
UNIT	pcs in literature	pcs in epig. and lit.	pcs in literature	pcs in epig.	vol. Ha, PRC 5	

Source: Author: Juhana Heikonen.

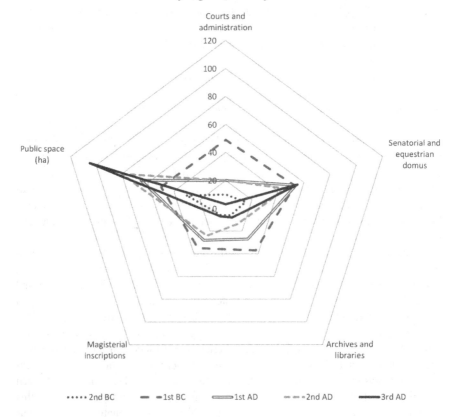

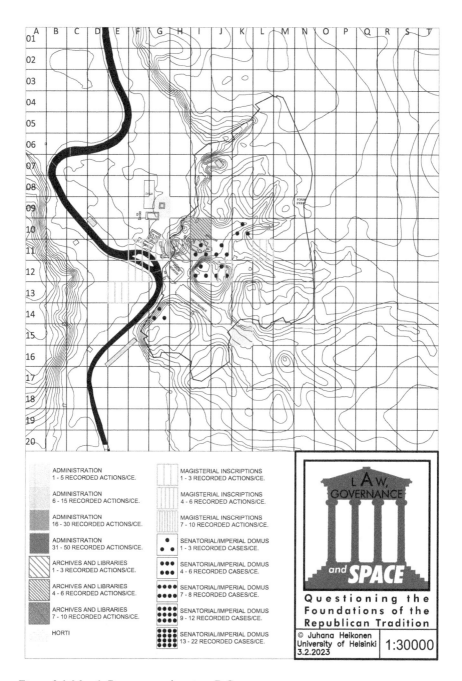

Figure 2.1 Map 1, Rome, second century B.C.
Source: Author: Juhana Heikonen.

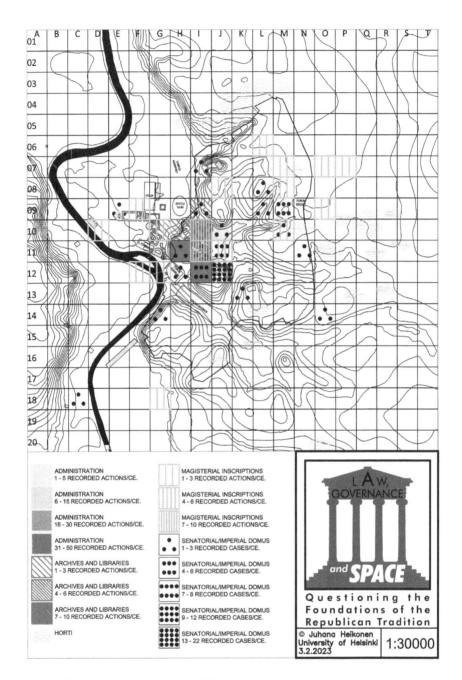

Figure 2.2 Map 2, Rome, first century B.C.
Source: Author: Juhana Heikonen.

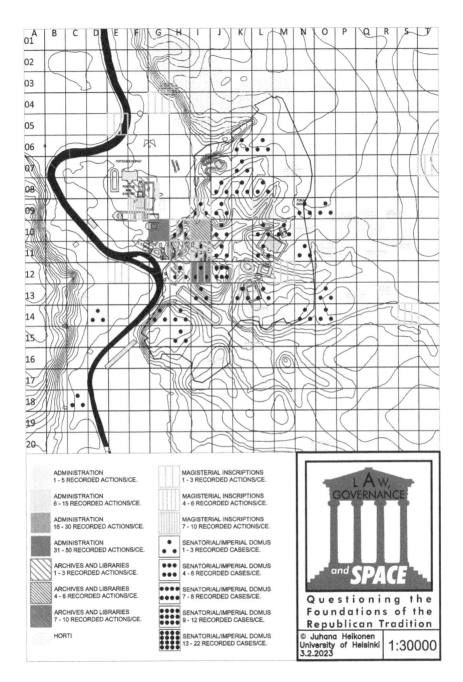

Figure 2.3 Map 3, Rome, first century A.D.
Source: Author: Juhana Heikonen.

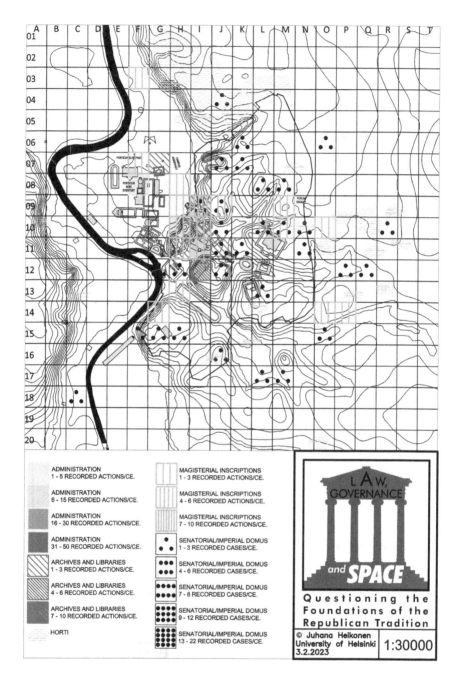

Figure 2.4 Map 4, Rome, second century A.D.
Source: Author: Juhana Heikonen.

The Administrative Topography of Rome 39

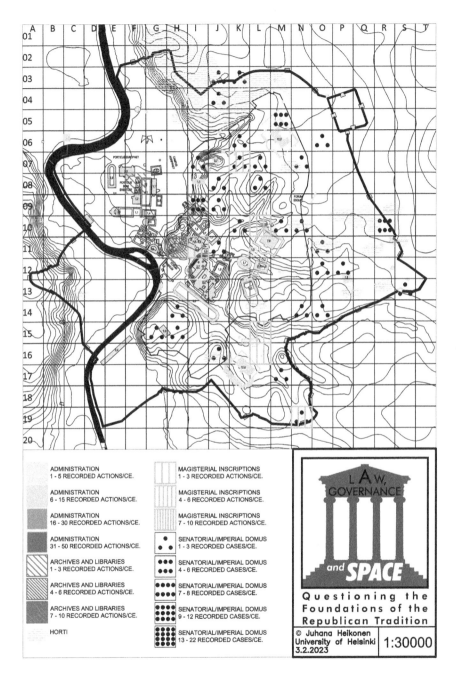

Figure 2.5 Map 5, Rome, third century A.D.
Source: Author: Juhana Heikonen.

space down in the valleys and plains. Two millennia ago, this contrast would have been clearer. This is in complete contrast to the late republican situation and gives considerable room for speculation. The growing distance between the *domus* on the hill and the low-lying concentrations of administration probably points more to lower-level administration "at home and around" than sedan chair traffic jams on the Via Lata. Higher-level administration would take place on the Palatine, or other imperial properties. Both administrations would leave little of literary evidence, except for the inscriptions.

A modern equivalent would be the post-war Stalinist administration that was efficient, but non-transparent in keeping records of its own. At the same time, vast monumental public spaces were built, but with little preserved contemporary literary evidence except for writers like Aleksandr Solzhenitsyn. As in Ovid's case, Solzhenitsyn would be known for his poems and not for *The Gulag Archipelago*.

Notes

1 This work is part of the project "Law, Governance and Space: Questioning the Foundations of the Republican Tradition" (SpaceLaw.fi). This research has received funding from the European Research Council (ERC) under the European Union's Horizon 2020 research and innovation programme (grant agreement No 771874). Antonio Lopez Garcia has also received funding from the Next Generation framework of the European Commission through the programme "María Zambrano" for the attraction of international talent at the University of Granada. We want to acknowledge Robert Whiting for the language revision.
2 Section authored by Juhana Heikonen and Kaius Tuori.
3 This was, however, already pointed out in early works on spatial studies such as Rapoport 1982.
4 The only survey that aims for comprehensiveness is Coarelli 2019.
5 On the uses of temples as administrative spaces, the only major study is still Stambaugh 1978.
6 These maps are also available in colour and full resolution at DOI: https://doi.org/10.5281/zenodo.7716267.
7 Sections VII and VIII and the maps are authored by Juhana Heikonen, who also was responsible for the overall project as the main author.
8 Östenberg et al. 2015.
9 Hägerstrand 1953, 1970a, 1970b, 1973; Hägerstrand and Pred 1967. Hägerstrand's first research (1953) was related to the adoption of agricultural innovation. AS research is usually related to urban planning and research. The ever-widening solutions include for example health, transportation, criminality, segregation, etc. research. For this chapter relevant publications are Järv et al. 2021; Hasanzadeh et al. 2019; Miller 2006; Wilson 2008.
10 Heikonen 2017.
11 D. G. Romano et al., *Digital Augustan Rome*, University of Pennsylvania Museum of Archaeology and Anthropology (http://digitalaugustanrome.org).
12 Steinby 1993–1999.
13 The radar chart is also available in colour and full resolution at DOI: https://doi.org/10.5281/zenodo.7716267.
14 Section authored by Antonio Lopez Garcia and Kaius Tuori.
15 Tac., *Dial*. 19.2.
16 De Angelis 2010b: 137.
17 Ewald and Noreña 2010: 5.
18 The references are spread throughout his speeches, letters, and philosophical works.

19 Dion. Hal. 2.29.1; Liv. 27.50.9; Gell., *NA* 20.1.11; Macr., *Sat.* 3.16.15–16.
20 Pseudacr., *Ad Hor. Sat.* 2.6.35; Hor., *Ep.* 1.19.8; Porphyr., *Ad loc.*; Schol., *Ad Pers. Sat.* 4.49; Fest., P. 448 L.
21 Cic., *Pro Clu.* 93; *Pro Flacc.* 66; *Pro Sest.* 15.34; *In Pis.* 5.11; *De Dom.* 21.54; *Post red. Ad Quir.* 13.
22 David 1995: 376–377.
23 Lopez Garcia forthcoming: 19.
24 For the Basilica Porcia: Syll. 2.747; Plut., *Cat. Mi.* 5.1; Pseudo Aurelius Victor, *De vir. 47*.5; Asc., *In Milon.* 29.3–6; Suet., *Iul.* 78. 2. For the Basilica Fulvia-Aemilia: Plin., *NH* 7.215; Varr., *LL* 6.4; Cens. 23.7. For the Basilica Opimia: *CIL* VI 2338, 2339. For the Basilica Sempronia there are only conjectures about its judiciary functions based on the comparison with the other basilicas or the proximity – its vestiges are underneath the remains of the later Basilica Iulia in which judicial activities are extensively attested. On this matter, see Lopez Garcia forthcoming: 19–24.
25 Plin., *Ep.* 2.14; Quint., *Inst.* 12.5–6.
26 Cic., *Att.* 4.16.8
27 *TH*. 6, 13, 13, 14, 15, 89; *TSulp.* 13, 14, 15, 19, 27.
28 Bablitz 2007: 44; De Angelis 2010a.
29 Lopez Garcia 2021: 154.
30 Quint., *Inst.* 10.5.18; Sen., *Contr.* 9.3.
31 Suet., *Claud.* 23.1; Suet., *Galba* 14.3.
32 Cic., *Verr.* 2.3.77.
33 Coarelli 2019; Lopez Garcia 2021, Lopez Garcia forthcoming.
34 Chastagnol 1960: 252–253; Machado 2019: 34
35 Section authored by Samuli Simelius.
36 On the administrative work in private space relating to juridical matters, see, e.g., Bablitz 2007: 33, 47–48; De Angelis 2010a, 2010b: 1–5, 14–16; Tuori 2010: 64–65.
37 The topic of Roman *domus* and their locations has resulted in several studies. Only a couple of years after the publication of *Lexicon Topographicum Urbis Romae* (Vol. 2), Eck (1997) wrote an article, where he investigated the location of Roman – mostly – imperial *domus*. A year later, Bruun (1998) published an article with some additions and corrections to *LTUR*. De Kleijn (2001: 193–223) has located the stamped lead pipes from the first century to the third century, which she connects with the locations of private property. Noreña (2006: 104) mapped all the *domus* of Augustan Rome, as did Borbonus et al. (2002: 104–117). Carandi et al. (2010) tried ambitiously to locate the houses of powerful persons in Rome, but the study has faced severe criticism; see, e.g., Wiseman 2012. Mundy's dissertation (2018: 353–747) includes a catalogue of *domus* within the Aurelian wall from A.D. 1–500. It only lists the *domus* with archaeological remains, however, meaning in this case that some sort of structure – not just a lead pipe – of a *domus* must have been excavated to be included in this catalogue. Heikonen (2017: 120, Map III, 237, Map V, 240, Table III) has listed and mapped the fourth century *domus*.
38 E.g., house owners with uncertain social status: *Domus* of Aemilia Paulina Asiatica (Lega 1995: 24) and *Domus* of P. Vergilius Maro. It is unknown whether Virgil was equestrian rank, but he had training that includes him in the group of possible administrative workers, although his house likely could be an example of those dwellings where the role of this type of work was very minor. On Virgil, see Horsfall 1995: 8–9. The house of Caesar's scribe Faberius was on the Aventine (Papi 1995a: 95).
39 See Eck 1995a: 216–217.
40 See, e.g., Eck 1995b: 86; Boatwright 1998: 72; Wallace-Hadrill 1998: 1–6; De Kleijn 2001: 256–257.
41 On the problems of locating houses on the basis of the Roman literature, see Eck 1997: 168–169.
42 See Papi 1995b: 90. Although it is not entirely sure that P. Licinius Crassus owned the house, it is very likely, as Papi has deduced.

43 Bruun 1998: 101–103.
44 See Eck 1997: 177 n. 79. Also, other literary sources might occasionally be doubtful, as in the case of the possible *domus Pescenniana* (see, e.g., Eck 1995c: 154–155).
45 Eck 1997: 172–175. Eck has written almost every *domus* entry of *Lexicon Topographicum Urbis Romae* (Vol. 2) if the source of the house is a lead pipe. See also, De Kleijn 2001: 143–146, 148–149, 237–238, Noreña 2006: 103.
46 See De Kleijn 2001: 147; Noreña 2006: 103.
47 See, e.g., Eck 1992: 363–366, 1997: 169–172; De Kleijn 2001: 233–235.
48 See Plin., *HN* 36.2.5–6.
49 On sculpture in private dwellings, see Stewart 2003: 249–259; Fejfer 2008: 89–103. In addition, in the Pompeian context where additional epigraphic information is available to identify possible house owners, it has not been unproblematic to connect the inscriptions on stones with the possible owner. Scholars often disagree on how the person relates to the house; see, e.g., Welch 2007: 569–570; Simelius 2018, 2022: 180–181, 184, 188–189.
50 See, e.g., *Domus* of Q. Marcius Rex (Papi 1995c: 137) where it is doubtful whether the location of the inscription (*CIL* I² 660 VI) can be interpreted as locating the house.
51 E.g., *Domus* of L. Marius Vegetinus Marcianus Minicianus Myrtilianus (Eck 1995d: 138) and *Domus* of Nummii (Guidobaldi 1995: 146–147). A domus of T. Pomponius Bassus (see Eck 1995e: 161–162) can be added to the list; although it only has one inscription suggesting the place, the location is confirmed by literary evidence, as suggested by Eck.
52 Section authored by Antonio Lopez Garcia and Kaius Tuori.
53 In addition to laws, such as the Twelve Tables, being posted in public places (Liv. 3.57.10; Dion. Hal., *Ant. Rom.* 10.57), officials also posted their decisions and other material in public places, for example, the chief pontiffs posting the *annales* (Cic., *De or.* 2.52; Liv. 1.32; Gell., *NA* 2.28.6; Dion. Hal., *Ant. Rom.* 2.74.33). On the posting of information as a combination of publication and preservation, see Corbier 2006.
54 Luc., *Phars.* 3.154; App., *Bell. Civ.* 1.31; App., *Sol.* 1.12; Macr., *Sat.* 1.8; Serv., *Georg.* 2.502; Serv., *Aen.* 8.322; Ascon., *Mil.* 36; Plut., *Ti. Gracch.* 10.6; Polyb., 23.14.5–6; Liv. 3.69, 7.23; *CIL* I² 593.46. On the Aerarium, see Tuori 2018.
55 Liv. 3.55.
56 Serv., *Aen.* 1.726; Cic., *Att.* 4.17.7; Liv., 25.7.12; Liv., 35.10.12; Liv., 43.16.13; Gran. Lic. 28.35; Suet., *Aug.* 29; Isid., *Orig.* 6.5.2; Plin., *NH* 7.115; Plin., *NH.* 35.10; Ov., *Trist.* 3.1.69.
57 Liv. 4.7.12.
58 Plut., *Vit. Cic.* 34.
59 Suet., *Vesp.* 8.5; *CIL* I² 736 = *CIL* VI 1313; *CIL* I² 737 = *CIL* VI 1314.
60 Cic., *Mil.* 73.
61 The first reference to a private library in Rome is found in Plutarch (*Vit. Sull.* 26.1) when he mentions that Sulla owned the famous library of Aristotle.
62 Suet., *Iul.* 44.
63 Lopez Garcia and Bueno Guardia 2021.
64 Dix and Houston 2006.
65 See *LTUR* I: 195–197.
66 Suet., *Iul.* 28; Cic., *Leg.* 3.20.46–48; Serv., *Aen.* 8.322.
67 Joseph., *AJ* 14.10.10; Plut., *Vit. Cat. Min.* 17; Cic., *Leg.* 3.4; Tac., *ann.* 3.51.
68 Plin., *Ep.* 1.10; Plut., *Vit. Cat. Min.* 17; Serv., *Georg.* 2.502; Plut., *Quaest. Rom.* 42.
69 Cic., *Verr.* 2.1.57; Cic., *Phil.* 5.5.15.
70 Liv., 43.16.13; Liv., 45.15.5; Serv., *ad Aen.* 1.726; Ov., *Tr.* 3.1.71–2; Cic., *Mil.* 59.
71 Liv. 34.44.5.
72 Ov., *Tr.* 3.1.71–2.
73 Suet., *Iul.* 44.
74 Plin., *HN* 7.115.
75 Tac., *Dial.* 39.1; Sen., *Dial.* 10.13.4.
76 *CIL* VI 1314; *CIL* VI 1313; Serv., *Georg.* 2.502.

77 P. Culham (1989) proposed that, during republican times, the role of some archives like the Aerarium might have been quite limited and highlighted the role of private magistrates' archives.
78 Culham 1989: 114.
79 Plut., *Cat. Min.* 18; Cic., *Att.* 4. 17.
80 *CIL* VI 2347; *CIL* VI 2348; *CIL* VI 4433; *CIL* VI 4435; Dio 55.8.1, 66.24.2; Mart. 5.5; Plin., *HN* 36.28–29; Suet., *Dom.* 20.1, *Gram. et Rhet.* 21.
81 Dio 55.8.1.
82 Plin., *HN* 36.23–5, 33–4.
83 Sen., *Controv.* 4.*praef*.2.
84 Dio 66.24.
85 *CIL* VI 1034.
86 Vell. 2.81.3; Joseph., *BJ* 2.81; Prop. 2.31.9; Ov., *Tr.* 3.1.60; Serv., *Aen.* 8.720.
87 Suet., *Aug.* 29.3.
88 Schol. Hor., *Ep.* 1.3.17; Serv., *Georg.* 4.10.
89 Hor., *Ep.* 2.1.214–218; Porph., Hor. *Ep.* 2.1.214; Schol., Hor. *Sat.* 1.4.21; Tac., *Ann.* 2.37, 2.83.
90 *Tabula Siarensis*, frag. 2, col. c, 13–14; Joseph., *BJ* 2.6.1.80; Dio 58.9.4–6.
91 Suet., *Aug.* 29.3; P. *Oxy.* 2435; Tac., *Ann.* 2.37; Joseph., *BJ* 2.82; Dio 58.9.3.
92 Schol. Hor., *Sat.* 1.10.38; Calp., *Ecl.* 4.157–159.
93 Ovid., *Tr.* 3.1.63–64.
94 Mart. 22.8.
95 Suet., *Tib.* 74; Plin., *NH* 34.43.
96 Suet., *Dom.* 20; *SHA, Prob.* 2.1.
97 Gell., *NA* 20.1.
98 For example, the fire at the archive of the tribunes on the Capitoline (Plut., *Vit. Cic.* 34) or the fire at the archive of the census in the Temple of the Nymphs (Cic., *Mil.* 73).
99 Joseph., *BJ* 7.158; Gell., *NA* 5.21.9, 16.8.2; *SHA, Tyr. Trig.* 31.10.
100 Amm. Marc., *Rerum gestarum* 16.10.14.
101 Galen, *Libr. Propr.* 19.21, 8.495.
102 *SHA, Tac.* 8.1, *Prob.* 2.1, *Car.* 11.3, *Aurel.* 1.7.10, 8.1, 24.7; Dio 68.16.3.
103 On the *libri lintei*: *SHA, Aurel.* 1.1–10, 8.1. We do not know if these are the same *libri linteii* that recorded the names of the magistrates and were hosted at the archive of Juno Moneta (Liv. 4.7.12). On the *liber elephantinus*: *SHA, Tacitus* 8.1–2.
104 Gell., *NA* 11.17.1.
105 *LTUR* I, s. v. Libertatis (Coarelli): 133–135.
106 Bowie 2013: 243.
107 Sid., *Ep.* 9.16.25–28.
108 Lopez Garcia 2021.
109 Liv. 3.55.13.
110 See for example, König et al. 2011.
111 P. *Oxy.* 3.412, lines 63–68; Dix 1994.
112 Neudecker 2013: 318.
113 Section authored by Anna-Maria Wilskman.
114 As mentioned, for example, *TPSulp.* 19, found in Pompeii: [C(aio) La]ecan[i]o Basso co(n)s(ulibus)/[Q(uinto) Terentio] pr(idie) K(alendas) Febr(uarias)/[Rom]ae in foro Augusto/[ante] statuam Gracci/[ad colum]nam quar/[tam prox]ume gradus/[hora n]ona C(aius) [Camodeca 1984: 63–66.
115 For *cura operum publicorum* in the imperial era, see Kolb 1993.
116 In 179 B.C., M. Aemilius Lepidus cleared the forum of statues and military standards (Liv. 40.51.3); the censors did so in 158 B.C. (Plin., *HN* 34.30) and also later, Claudius (Dio 60.25.2–3).
117 Laurence 2022: 219.

118 We collected the material from the online databases *Epigraphik-Datenbank Clauss/ Slaby* (*EDCS*) and *Epigraphic Database Roma* (*EDR*) by using search words such as *praetor, aedil,* and *quaestor*, but excluded the funerary inscriptions. Because the number of inscriptions increases rapidly during the first and second centuries A.D., we decided to limit the search of senatorial magistracies to the year A.D. 68. The inscriptions dated to the late second century and early third century derive from the material mentioning the *vigintivirate* office that was often included in the senatorial inscriptions. We decided to concentrate on the inscriptions mentioning the *vigintisexviri* because – at least in theory – this also allows us to investigate representations of individuals that had not yet entered the high senatorial offices. Furthermore, it was customary to include the *vigintivirate* in honorific inscriptions. The exclusion of the imperial family allows us to focus on the non-imperial elite.

119 For example, *CIL* VI 39801 (Map 1: f12), although reused in the wall of S. Bartolomeo in Isola Tiberina, is likely to have originated from the sanctuary of the island. However, the original location of movable inscriptions, such as altars, often remains uncertain. Therefore, all the locations portrayed on the map should be approached cautiously.

120 Augustus with his *summi viri* at his forum is a famous example of this. The statues he authorized marked foreign victories instead of domestic conflicts, directing the memory of the audience more towards the glorious past rather than the distressing civil war. In this way, Augustus reinvented the past and affected the present. He decided who should get a statue, and this, according to Zanker, "obviated any desire for self-glorification", or as Stewart remarks, reduced the potential for it. Stewart 2003: 130–131; Zanker 1988: 291.

121 Laurence 2022: 216; Val. Max. 2.1.19.; Tac., *Ann.* 2.37; Plin., *Ep.* 8.14.5–8.

122 *CIL* VI 39801; *CIL* VI 40896a.

123 *Ex senatus consulto*: *CIL* VI 40891 (Map 1: l11), *de senati sententia*: *CIL* VI 110 (Map 1: j12).

124 The habit of inscribing symbols and messages on a non-perishable material goes back thousands of years and is shared by many ancient cultures. Heikki Solin has counted the known republican inscriptions, and it is evident that the numbers grow in the fourth–third centuries before skyrocketing in the second–first centuries, resulting in the "epigraphic revolution" in the Augustan era. Solin 1999: 391–394; Beltrán Lloris 2014: 139–141.

125 Map 3: m7; *CIL* VI 03835 is a *trapezophorum* dedicated by clients for their *patronus*, P. Numicius Pica. Map 3: m8; *CIL* VI 1467 is an inscription for T. Mussidius L.f. (Pollianus).

126 *CIL* VI 1283a-b.

127 In addition to o–p, g12 records a magisterial action. *CIL* VI, 31602.

128 *CIL* VI 1375.

129 *CIL* VI 37068 with comments by Geza Alföldy at *CIL* VI 8.3. p. 4814; Romanelli 1965.

130 *CIL* VI 36807.

131 *CIL* VI 3675.

132 *CIL* VI 91.

133 *CIL* VI 3751.

134 *CIL* VI 41076 with comments by Geza Alföldy, p. 4913.

135 *CIL* VI 1275.

136 Lahusen 1983: 26–27.

137 In this material, for example, *CIL* VI 1377. Trajan's forum was filled, especially during Marcus Aurelius' time, with statues for those who died in his German wars. *SHA*, *M. Aurelius* 22.7.

138 *CIL* VI 41119; *CIL* VI 1444.

139 *CIL* VI 1517.

140 *CIL* VI 31740.
141 *CIL* VI 1333.
142 *CIL* VI 1401.
143 Map 5: i11; *CIL* VI 32412.
144 For the development of the area, see Gozzini 2017 and Bariviera 2017.
145 For the polyvalent nature of visual communication in the streets, see Van Haug and Kobutsch 2022.
146 Pliny the Elder already refers to this when people started to decorate their houses with statues. Plin., *HN* 34.9.
147 Kalas 2015.

References

Bablitz, L. 2007: *Actors and Audience in the Roman Courtroom*, London.
Bariviera, C. 2017: 'Region XII. *Piscina Publica*', in A. Carandini, P. Carafa, and A. C. Halavais (eds), *The Atlas of Ancient Rome: Biography and Portraits of the City*, Princeton, NJ, 375–387.
Beltrán Lloris, F. 2014: 'The "Epigraphic Habit", in the Roman World', in C. Bruun and J. Edmondson (eds), *The Oxford Handbook of Roman Epigraphy*, Oxford.
Boatwright, M. 1998: 'Luxuriant Gardens and Extravagant Women: The *horti* of Rome between Republic and Empire', in *Horti Romani: Atti del Convegno Internazionale, Roma, 4–6 maggio 1995. Bullettino della commissione archeologica comunale di Roma*, 6, Rome, 71–82.
Borbonus, D., Dumser, E., Gallia, A., Harmansah, Ö., Haselberger, L., Kondratieff, E., Morton, T., Noreña, C., Parment, T., Petruccioli, G., Thein, A., Tracy, K., and Varinlioğlu, G. 2002: 'Catalogue of Entries', in E. Dumser (ed.), *Mapping Augustan Rome, Journal of Roman Archaeology*, 50, Portsmouth, 40–275.
Bowie, E. 2013: 'Libraries for the Caesars', in J. König, K. Oikonomopolou, and G. Woolf (eds.), *Ancient Libraries*, Cambridge, 237–260.
Bruun, C. 1998: 'Missing Houses: Some Neglected Domus and Other Abodes in Rome', *Arctos – Acta Philologica Fennica* 32, 87–108.
Camodeca, G. 1984: 'Per una riedizione dell'archivio puteolano dei Sulpicii. III. Empitones con stipulation duplae. IV. I documenti vadimoniali, The archive of the Sulpicii 1–21', *Puteoli* 7–8 (1983–1984), 3–77.
Carandini, A., Bruno, D., and Fraioli, F. 2010: *Le case del potere nell'antica Roma*, Bari.
Chastagnol, A. 1960: *La Préfecture urbaine à Rome sous le Bas-Empire*, Paris.
Coarelli, F. 2019: *Statio. I luoghi dell'amministrazione nell'antica Roma*, Rome.
Corbier, M. 2006: *Donner à voir, donner à lire. Mémoire et communication dans la Rome ancienne*, Paris.
Culham, P. 1989: 'Archives and Alternatives in Republican Rome', *Classical Philology* 84, 100–115.
David, J. M. 1995: 'Le tribunal du préteur: contraintes symboliques et politiques sous la Republique et le debut de l'empire', *Klio* 77, 371–385.
De Angelis, F. 2010a: 'Ius and Space: An Introduction', in F. De Angelis (ed.), *Spaces of Justice in the Roman World*, Leiden, 1–26.
De Angelis, F. 2010b: 'The Emperor's Justice and Its Space in Rome and Italy', in F. De Angelis (ed.), *Spaces of Justice in the Roman World*, Leiden, 127–160.
De Kleijn, G. 2001: *The Water Supply of Ancient Rome. Dutch Monographs on Ancient History and Archaeology*, Amsterdam.

Dix, T. K. 1994: 'Public Libraries', *Ancient Rome: Ideology and Reality, Libraries & Culture* 29(3), 282–296.

Dix, T. K., and Houston, G. W. 2006: 'Public Libraries in the City of Rome: From the Augustan Age to the Time of Diocletian', *Mélanges de l'École française de Rome, Antiquité* 118(2), 671–717.

Eck, W. 1992: 'Ehrungen für Personen hohen soziopolitischen Ranges im öffentlichen und privaten Bereich', in H. Schalles, H. von Hesberg, and P. Zanker (eds), *Die römische Stadt im 2. Jahrhundert n. Chr: Kolloquium in Xanten vom 2. bis 4. Mai 1990*, 2, Köln, 359–376.

Eck, W. 1995a: 'Domus: Volusius Saturninus', in E. Steinby (ed.), *Lexicon Topographicum Urbis Romae*, 2, Rome, 216–217.

Eck, W. 1995b: 'Domus: Cornelia L. F.', in E. Steinby (ed.), *Lexicon Topographicum Urbis Romae*, 2, Rome, 86.

Eck, W. 1995c: 'Domus Pescenniana', in E. Steinby (ed.), *Lexicon Topographicum Urbis Romae*, 2, Rome, 154–155.

Eck, W. 1995d: 'Domus: L. Marius Vegetinus Marcianus Minicianus Myrtilianus', in E. Steinby (ed.), *Lexicon Topographicum Urbis Romae*, 2, Rome, 138.

Eck, W. 1995e: 'Domus: T. Pomponius Atticus', in E. Steinby (ed.), *Lexicon Topographicum Urbis Romae*, 2, Roma, 161–162.

Eck, W. 1997: '*Cum dignitate otium*: Senatorial *domus* in Imperial Rome', *Scripta Classica Israelica* 16, 162–190.

Ewald, B. C., and Noreña, C. F. 2010: 'Introduction', in B. C. Ewald and C. F. Noreña (eds), *The Emperor and Rome: Space, Representation, and Ritual*, Cambridge, 1–43.

Fejfer, J. 2008: *Roman Portraits in Context. Image & Context*, 2, Berlin.

Gozzini, S. 2017: 'Region I. *Porta Capena*', in A. Carandini, P. Carafa, and A. C. Halavais (eds), *The Atlas of Ancient Rome: Biography and Portraits of the City*, Princeton, NJ, 359–374.

Guidobaldi, F. 1995: 'Domus: Nummii', in E. Steinby (ed.), *Lexicon Topographicum Urbis Romae*, 2, Rome, 146–147.

Hägerstrand, T. 1953: *Innovationsförloppet ur kronologisk synpunkt*, Lund.

Hägerstrand, T. 1970a: 'What About People in Regional Science?', *Papers of the Regional Science Association* 24, 7–21.

Hägerstrand, T. 1970b: *Urbaniseringen: stadsutveckling och regionala olikheter*, Lund.

Hägerstrand, T. 1973; 2019: 'The Domain of Human Geography', in R. J. Chorley (ed.), *Directions in Geography*, New York, 67–88.

Hägerstrand, T., and Pred, A. 1967: *Innovation Diffusion as a Spatial Process*, Chicago, IL.

Hasanzadeh, K., Czepkiewicz, M., Heinonen, J., Kyttä, M., Ala-Mantila, S., and Ottelin, J. 2019: 'Beyond Geometries of Activity Spaces: A Holistic Study of Daily Travel Patterns, Individual Characteristics, and Perceived Wellbeing in Helsinki Metropolitan Area', *Journal of Transport and Land Use* 12(1), 149–177.

Heikonen, J. 2017: *San Clemente in Rome: A New Reconstruction of the Early 5th Century Basilica and Its Origins*. Dissertation of Aalto University, published online: https://aaltodoc.aalto.fi/handle/123456789/26564

Horsfall, N. 1995: 'Virgil: His Life and Times', in N. Horsfall (ed.), *A Companion to the Study of Virgil*, Leiden, 1–26.

Järv, O., Masso, A., Silm, S., and Ahas, R. 2021: 'The Link Between Ethnic Segregation and Socio-Economic Status: An Activity Space Approach', *Tijdschrift voor Economische en Sociale Geografie* 112(3), 319–335.

Kalas, G. 2015: *The Restoration of the Roman Forum in Late Antiquity: Transforming Public Space*, Austin, TX.

Kolb, A. 1993: *Die Kaiserliche Bauverwaltung in Der Stadt Rom: Geschichte Und Aufbau Der Cura Operum Publicorum Unter Dem Prinzipat. Heidelberger althistorische Beiträge und epigraphische Studien Book*, Stuttgart.

König, J, Oikonomopolou, K., and Woolf, G. (eds.) 2011: *Ancient Libraries*, Cambridge.

Lahusen, G. 1983: *Untersuchungen Zur Ehrenstatue in Rom: Literarische Und Epigraphische Zeugnisse*, 35, Rome.

Laurence, R. 2022: 'Children and Public Space in Early Imperial Rome', in D. Filippi (ed.), *Rethinking the Roman City. Studies in Roman Space and Urbanism*, London, New York, 213–225.

Lega, C. 1995: 'Domus: Aemilia Paulina Asiatica', in E. Steinby (ed.), *Lexicon Topographicum Urbis Romae*, 2, Rome, 24–25.

Lopez Garcia, A. 2021: 'Una corte di giustizia presso il Foro di Traiano? Analisi sulla funzionalità degli auditoria adrianei', *Mélanges de l'École Française de Rome* 133(1), 149–171.

Lopez Garcia, A. forthcoming: 'Fora Litibus Omnia Fervent: The Transfer of the Tribunals in Rome from the Forum to the Courtroom'.

Lopez Garcia, A., and Bueno Guardia, M. 2021: 'Typology and Multifunctionality of Public Libraries in Rome and the Empire', *Journal of Eastern Mediterranean Archaeology & Heritage Studies* 9(3), 247–277.

Machado, C. 2019: *Urban Space and Aristocratic Power in Late Antique Rome: AD 270–535*, Oxford and New York.

Miller, H. 2006: 'Activities in Space and Time', in P. Stopher, K. Button, K. Haynes and D. Hensher (eds), *Handbook of Transport 5: Transport Geography and Spatial Systems*, Elsevier, Amsterdam.

Mundy, J. 2018: *Domūs and Insulae in the City of Rome: Living Spaces, Design, and Development*. Dissertation of Emory University, published online: https://etd.library.emory.edu/concern/etds/p2676w43m?locale=en

Neudecker, R. 2013: 'Archives, Books and Sacred Space in Rome', in J. König, K. Oikonomopolou, and G. Woolf (eds.), *Ancient Libraries*, Cambridge, 312–331.

Noreña, C. 2006: 'Water Distribution and the Residential Topography of Augustan Rome', in L. Haselberger and J. Humphrey (eds), *Imaging Ancient Rome: Documentation-Visualization-Imagination, Journal of Roman Archaeology*, 61, Portsmouth, 91–105.

Östenberg, I., Malmberg, S., and Bjørnebye, J. (eds) 2015: *The Moving City. Processions, Passages, and Promenades in Ancient Rome*, London.

Papi, E. 1995a: 'Domus: Faberius', in E. Steinby (ed.), *Lexicon Topographicum Urbis Romae*, 2, Rome, 95.

Papi, E. 1995b: 'Domus: Crassus', in E. Steinby (ed.), *Lexicon Topographicum Urbis Romae*, 2, Rome, 90.

Papi, E. 1995c: 'Domus: Q. Marcius Rex', in E. Steinby (ed.), *Lexicon Topographicum Urbis Romae*, 2, Rome, 137.

Rapoport, A. 1982: *The Meaning of the Built Environment*, Beverly Hills, CA.

Romanelli, P. 1965: 'L'iscrizione di L. Nevio Surdino nel lastricato del Foro Romano', in *Gli archeologi italiani in onore di Amedeo Maiuri*, Cava dei Tirreni, 381–390.

Simelius, S. 2018: *Pompeian Peristyle Gardens as a Means of Socioeconomic Representation*. Dissertation of University of Helsinki, published online: http://hdl.handle.net/10138/238264

Simelius, S. 2022: *Pompeian Peristyle Gardens. Studies in Roman Space and Urbanism 8*, London.

Solin, H. 1999: 'Epigrafia repubblicana. Bilancio, novità, prospettive', in *Atti XI Congresso Internazionale di Epigrafia Greca e Latina, Roma 1997*, 1, Rome, 379–404.

Stambaugh, J. E. 1978: 'The Functions of Roman Temples', in W. Haase (ed.), *Religion (Heidentum: Römische Religion, Allgemeines)*, Berlin, Boston, 554–609.

Steinby, E. M. 1993–1999: *Lexicon topographicum urbis Romae*, Rome.

Stewart, P. 2003: *Statues in Roman Society: Representation and Response*, Oxford.

Tuori, K. 2010: 'A Place for Jurists in the Spaces of Justice', in F. De Angelis (ed.), *Spaces of Justice in the Roman World*, Leiden, 43–66.

Tuori, K. 2018: 'Pliny and the Uses of the Aerarium Saturni as an Administrative Space', *Arctos: Acta Philologica Fennica* 52, 199–230.

Van Haug, A., and Kobutsch, P. 2022: 'Visual Communication in the Streets of Pompeii', in D. Filippi (ed.), *Rethinking the Roman City. Studies in Roman Space and Urbanism*, London, New York.

Wallace-Hadrill, A. 1998: '*Horti* and Hellenization', in *Horti Romani: Atti del Convegno Internazionale, Roma, 4–6 maggio 1995, Bullettino della commissione archeologica comunale di Roma*, 6, Rome, 1–12.

Welch, K. 2007: 'Pompeian Men and Women in Portrait Sculpture', in J. Dobbins and P. Foss (eds), *The World of Pompeii*, London, 550–584.

Wilson, C. 2008: 'Activity Patterns in Space and Time: Calculating Representative Hagerstrand Trajectories', *Transportation* 35, 485–499.

Wiseman, T. 2012: 'Where Did They Live (e.g., Cicero, Octavius, Augustus)?', *Journal of Roman Archaeology* 25, 656–672.

Zanker, P. 1988: *The Power of Images in the Age of Augustus, The Jerome Lectures 16*, Michigan.

3 Models of Administrative Space in the Roman World

Between Public and Private[1]

Kaius Tuori

I Introduction

The spaces where Roman administrative activities could take place were remarkably flexible, with valid administrative acts being taken up on the street where petitioners could meet up with a magistrate or even the emperor and a matter could be received or even resolved there and then (Gai. *Inst.* 1.7.20; Suet. *Vesp.* 23.2). This process was called *de plano* by Roman jurists, who discussed what issues could be resolved in this way (*Dig.* 37.1.3.8). What makes this freedom from a place even more surprising from a modern perspective was that there is next to no discussion about where Roman magistrates and officials would normally have worked. This lack of sources has led to an equally surprising dearth of inquiries about administrative spaces in the scholarly literature concerning administration.[2]

The purpose of this chapter is to explore the models of administrative space and the transformation of the spatial dimension of late republican and early imperial Roman administration in the city of Rome. It examines the spaces where administrative activities took place and their implications for the understanding of the workings of administration. Using the findings of the spatial turn in the study of the Roman public sphere, especially the developments in the exploration into concepts of official space, such as the spaces of justice,[3] the chapter seeks to demonstrate how, behind the issue of the spaces of administration, there are important questions about the public and private dichotomy and the role of public administration in Roman society in general.

Earlier studies on administrative spaces have focused on places such as archives or presumptive offices or tribunals.[4] In general, it may be asserted that there are two grand models that have been advanced for the Roman administrative apparatus, the model of the private house and the bureaucratic model. The first, presented by, for example, Peter Eich in the context of imperial administration, supposes that the republican elite *domus* would give rise to the imperial *domus* as the administrative template of the Roman world. The second, most recently outlined by Filippo Coarelli in his new book, locates vital administrative tasks within designated buildings.[5]

The root of the dispute lies in the Roman sources themselves, which give suitable evidence for both theories; authors such as Vitruvius (6.5.1) maintain that the elite house should be equipped to deal with all manner of public administrative events such as trials, while others like Pliny (*Ep.* 1.10.9) relate their personal experiences working in what sounds very much like an office and where he is accompanied by colleagues. What the present inquiry seeks to do is to explore this dichotomy through the various administrative functions and their respective spaces. It maintains that the juxtaposition between the public and private models has no explanatory value when examining Roman sources.

Rather than attempting to locate a specific place or places where the administration would have worked, a matter beyond the scope of a single chapter, as each claim is highly contested, the aim of this chapter is to reconceptualize the spatial dimension of administration. It draws inspiration from the recent distinction between "soft" and "hard" spaces developed in the field of common-sense geography. What it questions is the rigid distinction between the official and the unofficial, the legal and the social, and instead argues for a more nuanced understanding of the activities and spaces. In our case, the crucial point is the abandonment of neat categories of public and private in favour of a procedural understanding of administrative work. What this means is that instead of focusing on simply the built environment (or the "hard" spaces), the chapter explores administrative processes as functional chains of actions in which different elements may take place in domestic places, open public areas and designated buildings.[6]

The main claim of this chapter is that Roman administrative space was structured procedurally, where different functions used public places such as the Forum, while others necessitated confined spaces where both private and public areas could serve the purpose. This continues on and builds into the emerging literature arguing for a more nuanced understanding of the position of the private *domus* and its role as an extension of the public sphere.[7] Earlier works have noted the importance of the private aristocratic house in public life,[8] but connecting activities in public spaces such as the Forum or the Comitium and that of the house is something that has been alluded to but not realized concretely.[9] Thus, while we may distinguish between administrative needs for the work of personnel such as the magistrates or their staff – the need for storage and retrieval of information and valuables and the execution of practical tasks such as the census, water management or the distribution of the *annona* – the administrative processes were interlinked and often extended to them all.

In order to explore this dilemma, we will first examine the various administrative activities, beginning with meeting people and then to the writing of correspondence and where they took place. We will then look into the designation of places for administration. For the specific designated spaces, it is evident that their roots are in those particular instances where private surroundings were not suitable, such as 1) the reception of people in public business, for example, the praetors and their courts; 2) the archival service, for example, the storage and upkeep of the rolls of citizens and their property by the censors or the storage of laws by the aediles; 3) the handling and storage of money by the quaestors; and 4) the large-scale employment of workers for manual labour. Finally, this builds into the understanding of the issues of wealth and status as a component in the administrative process.

II What Model for Administration and Administrative Space?

The older literature on administration presents two stereotypical competing models in the history of bureaucracy in the ancient world: oral and written. The first was the Greek model, which is based on oral, public interactions in the forum or agora. Citizens served in public office for short intervals, but the citizen assembly was a key decision maker and arena for political debate. The bureaucracy consisted of a scribe or two and an archive (like the Athenian Metroon). The second stereotypical model is the Egyptian or Middle Eastern model where the administration was based on written documents. The official acts were recorded, and correspondence was the primary way of communication. Scribes and archives were its defining features. Now that detailed examination of the issues has largely consigned this idealized dualism to the trash heap of history,[10] the question remains: How can one supersede these antiquated models of administration to develop a new model for the Roman administrative tradition?

The model of the private house and the influence of that model is visible throughout the Roman government, but that is far from the whole truth. While in republican Rome that meant simply that magistrates did the bulk of their work from their homes while participating in the public meetings at the Forum, in the provinces the distinction is clearer as the *praetoria* of the provincial administration were modelled after the private house but were quite distinct from it.[11] The most prominent of the examples of the spread of the model, as argued by Eich, is the imperial administration, which grew as a part of the imperial *domus* and the imperial household where the administrative functions are embedded in the framework of the house itself. However, public space carried symbolic value and the functioning of magistrates there formed the basis of the public trust that underlay the republican system.

The investigation of the nature of Roman administration and its relation to space suffers from two ahistorical templates: on one hand the idea of a modern administrative apparatus which worked in public offices and used archives to store information, and on the other the premodern notion of single rule, where the ruler's palace served to collect all administrative functions, both public and private if such as distinction could be made. These definitional distinctions are behind statements such as "No ancient office building and no ancient desk will ever be discovered".[12]

At the same time, in the study of administrative agencies such as the *cura aquarum*, there have been tentative attempts to locate the spaces where their offices were.[13] The big issue here is whether asking where the Roman offices were is asking the wrong question. Many of the suggestions for administrative space have been patently unrealistic, such as placing the administration of the water management of Rome in a corner of a temple.[14]

The Roman administrative tradition fits the stereotypical dualistic model between open spaces and bureaucracies working in offices badly. Especially during the Republic, administration took place over the entire centre of the city. The Senate, the popular assemblies, courts and magistrates had the entire Forum as their arena, but there was little in the way of secluded places. At the same time, the exhaustive Roman style of documentation and the reliance on writing are harder to understand, as there are no distinct places in which to write. Is it possible to make assumptions about the space needed for an administrative staff based on common-sense assumptions or do they contain dangerous modernizing assumptions about space?

The problem has been aggravated by the lack of cooperation from the source material to comply with these modern categories of administration. As the major sources relating to Roman history and thus also administrative space may be divided into two categories, archaeological and literary, we can take each in turn.

What to look for in the material remains or the archaeological evidence is an interesting definitional puzzle. Should one search for something resembling an office room or a desk? Would an administrative space be recognizable through its location or architectural properties? Could we recognize a room where a Roman magistrate and his staff would work? The second issue is that we may not have a complete understanding of the kind of furniture we would find. Roman furniture has largely not been preserved outside the area of the Vesuvian eruption,[15] making the identification of locations for offices an exercise in conjecture on the uses of space in preserved structures.

Our best source for the furniture in use is depictions in art such as reliefs,[16] of which one should mention the famous Altar of Scribes (Figure 3.1) from the reign of Tiberius. It portrays a scene where a seated magistrate, perhaps a curule aedile, is surrounded by scribes. In the centre is a small, low table and on it are five *tabulae* that are the focus of attention.[17] It is clearly from a secluded setting and the arrangement of furniture could easily be from a room or a peristyle. For magistrates, most imagery shows them seated on the *sella curulis*, the symbol of their position as magistrate.[18]

Figure 3.1 Detail of the Altar of the Scribes.
Source: Author: Antonio Lopez Garcia.

Models of Administrative Space in the Roman World 53

Figure 3.2 Outline of a portion of the Altar of Domitius Ahenobarbus.
Source: Author: Antonio Lopez Garcia.

There are also other examples, such as the so-called Altar of Domitius Ahenobarbus (Figure 3.2), which shows a scene which has been interpreted as the census. There are figures, as in the Altar of Scribes, seated on chairs with tablets on their laps. What may be inferred from them is that it is all but impossible to say anything definite about the locations where these activities took place; they may have been in the open air or in a courtyard or in a room. They illustrate the Roman administration's reliance on writing and documentation. Thus, one needs space for writing and drafting documents through dictation, for reading, reviewing and discussing the documents, as well as storing them. Nothing may be said about the specific location, but much about the physical settings that the body of a scribe or a magistrate was surrounded by. The administrative space has distinctive similarities with the libraries of the Roman world, where reading, writing and the storage and retrieval of information were crucial functions.[19]

For the identification of spaces as administrative, epigraphic sources mentioning a *cura* or a *statio* could be seen to indicate a place where the administration worked, but the few known examples are less than conclusive.

The literary sources are equally tricky because there is no real equivalent for the word "office". The term *officium* related more to the magistracies themselves (or rather to the duties included within) than to any physical space, with a few exceptions such as Pliny's (*Ep.* 1.5.11) *in praetoris officio* or *Dig.* 4.5.6 *officia publica*. The terms *secretarium, cancelli, scrinium* or *burellum* are almost exclusively from later sources.[20] Vitruvius does not discuss offices; the administrative buildings he mentions are the forum, the basilica, the treasury or *aerarium* and the *curia*. They are described as meeting places or places for the storage of money, not locations where office work would have taken place.[21] Frontinus is equally silent on administrative places.

The word *statio* was perhaps the closest that one gets to an office or administrative place of work, although it also meant a general place of work or a military guard post.[22] Ulpian mentions *arcarii Caesariani* (cashiers of the treasury) who had their *statio* at the Forum of Trajan.[23] A *statio* is also mentioned in conjunction with officials handling inheritance tax.[24]

In studies on scribes, there are different notions presented about where the physical act of writing took place, from public places to the houses of their patrons. In general, writing and dictation are frequently discussed activities, taking place in homes, in bed (Plin. *Ep.* 5.5) or even while riding.[25]

This issue has major relevance because we know that there was extensive administration going on and thus it would be a fair assumption that there would have needed to be space for it. We know that in provinces like Egypt the *praetoria* that housed the Roman administration were the main locations where provincials would encounter the administrators.[26] But for the city of Rome little is known about this. For the most part, what we have to contend with are educated guesses about the locations where practical issues, such as the water management or the grain distribution, took place. At the top end of the administrative spectrum, Roman emperors would combine their administrative and social tasks, attending to the affairs of the state at the same time as they were preparing for the day in their cubiculum bedroom.[27] The Roman administration's habit of using written documentation and extensive correspondence was known even in the provinces. Documents were drafted, approved, checked, inspected, archived and copied, as markings on documents attest.[28] Where did all this take place?

III The All-Round Gentleman and His *Domus* in the Service of Administration

The modern model of administration is that of a public activity done in a public location such as an office. That model has been recognized as a historical curiosity that came about only with the advent of the modern centralized administration mainly in the nineteenth century. In addition to palaces of rulers, one may draw from the spatial politics of premodern republics, where wealthy officials would run their office from their private residences. Even as late as the nineteenth century, scholars have pointed out how, in diverse cases from Brazilian magnates or British nobility, their public duties were primarily taken care of at home, while grand public meetings would be in public arenas.[29] Would Roman senators or other elite men on the *cursus honorum* have acted in a similar manner? The sources suggest so, pointing to both public activities taking place at home and the lack of public offices. The question is where would the clerks, the minor officials and scribes, who necessarily would not have a suitable residence, have done their jobs, at an office or at the houses of the elite?

The senators and people who were chosen for the upper magistracies were without question people of wealth and high social status. By necessity, they had private income and presumably spacious lodgings in the centre of Rome. During the Republic and the early Empire, these houses were first on the Forum and later immediately adjacent the Forum on the Palatine hill and especially the slope towards the Forum. When one speaks of private houses it should be remembered that these houses were enormous, with some estimated at over 20,000 square meters, four times as large as the largest of the Pompeian houses, the House of the Faun.[30]

Vitruvius writes about how the houses of the elite needed reception areas like vestibules, *atria* or *tablina* (6.5.1). For those whose profession relied on receiving people for consultation, such as "lawyers and orators", their houses "must be more elegant and spacious for the reception of groups of people". The grandest surroundings were needed by the "important dignitaries who hold high office and magistracies and are obliged to serve the state, lofty and regal vestibules, grand atria and colonnaded courtyards should be built".[31] The public functions of the Roman private house ranged from serving as a meeting place to the place where commerce and even trials were held. The public areas of the house such as the atrium functioned as a private forum with a similar social and political significance.[32]

One of the most striking features of the Roman political system was that the leading magistracies were handled on a yearly rotation by people with just general experience of the government of the state. Some of them were recognized as being especially proficient in some fields, such as military matters or law, but that rarely defined them or their career paths. The *cursus honorum* was a general one. Scholars like Michael Peachin have described how Roman officials were, like the later British aristocrats, best defined as all-round gentlemen, people of the nobility who had general experience and could be assigned to almost any spot in the administration and be expected to perform adequately.[33] This view is supported by authors like Vitruvius or Frontinus, who may be seen to embrace the idea of administrative amateurism, entrusting the key administrative posts to the senatorial elite rather than professionals with lower status such as freedmen or equestrians.[34]

Having an all-round gentleman in a post for a year before moving to a new posting was naturally hardly the whole story. Like the early modern British administration or innumerable other similar systems of government, the Roman government relied on the low-ranking specialists, who were more or less on a permanent appointment, to function properly. The senatorial elite would control the state, but the actual work of administration would have needed to be as professional and permanent as the political magistracies were fluid and temporary.[35] In the case of slaves, the word "permanent" had a whole other meaning. When looking at the records of people working in the administration, we find a plethora of these scribes, slaves and other functionaries. Where did they work?

From a modern point of view, the obvious option could be that there would be an office where they had a permanent station. Had such a permanent station existed, we would probably have heard of it, but the only instances known in the sources are the reference to the *statio* of the *arcarii Caesariani* mentioned earlier and a couple of other similar inscriptions relating to tax offices.[36] This reference continues the already noted tendency of a designated space being needed when there was a particular need to receive people, for example, for monetary transactions. The other possibility is that they were assigned to the magistrate and decamped to the house of the new magistrate, where they worked alongside the personal staff of the magistrate in dealing with the business of the magistracy.

If we look at the practical implications that such an arrangement had, there are two major difficulties involved. The first is whether each and every magistrate would have suitable spaces for such a team. The second is what that would mean for suffect consulships and other more limited terms.

To answer the first query, conjecture is heavily involved and relates to the idea of a privatized administration. If no designated space was available for these minor officials, the scribes, messengers or heralds working with the magistrates, they would perhaps meet with their superiors in their homes. The highest officials were quite often senators and thus men of great wealth, who had large estates and town houses for their private staff. What this entails is that the highest officials would be expected to be able to furnish their own spaces, perhaps even to take care of official business with their own resources. Of course, most magistrates simply were required to be wealthy; there were set limits on how much wealth one had to have if one were to become or remain an equestrian or a senator. A similar tendency may be found in the cities around the Roman world, where the local magistrates were to a large degree forced to run the administration out of their own pocket. Even in Rome itself, traditional republican magistrates like consuls, praetors or censors did not have their own offices or scribes tied to the magistracy, but rather clerks drawn from the pool of publicly salaried minor officers. Would there have been a shared office for the clerks of the praetors or aediles? The imperial *curae* had hired staff – in the case of the *curae*, a hierarchy of officials – but they were often led by equestrians, who could be of relatively modest means compared to senators.

Even though the numbers are hard to come by, we may decipher something about the sheer number of people involved from the indications given by legal documents, which mention how a city prefect during the time of Nero might have 400 slaves in his house in Rome, and an unspecified number of freedmen as well.[37] In fact, it has been estimated that a quarter of the entire population of Rome might have consisted of slaves, most belonging to the senatorial elite.[38]

What this meant was that in any case all mental models of a private single-family house when discussing the Roman elite should be banished. Even with the palatial scale of private houses, for the execution of certain administrative tasks, such as the handling of the *annona* or water management, there were issues of scale which made it prohibitive. Work involving public money led to security and health issues, thus a *procurator monetae* would probably not have run a minting operation or stored the coins in his private home.

The second query is trickier. Having the administration of a section of the government move from one house to another involves more than the moving of the staff assigned to that post. In cases where the personal staff of the magistrate was involved, such persons would remain behind. However, the most crucial issue is that of the archives. Would they need to be moved every time that a person was selected for a suffect post? How much material would there be?

Private houses had important archival duties, because the *commentarii*, the account of the official acts that magistrates had taken during their year in office, were kept in the *tablinum* of the house.[39] From a fairly fragmentary record, it has been estimated that the *commentarii* were derived from the records of the household itself, but later assumed a public meaning. Starting from the late Republic it has been estimated that the *commentarii* of high officials such as the consuls were deposited in public archives.[40] What these private archives would have looked like is unclear, but based on evidence from Pompeii we may assume that they could have consisted of records kept in cabinets in the *tablinum* or elsewhere in the house.

In the house of Caecilius Iucundus (V 1,26), there was found a large trove of 154 wax tablets, locked in a cabinet at the back of the peristyle. An interesting detail is that near the archival cabinet was a decorated reception room (room r). This opened to the peristyle, which has a table. In a similar manner, the Sulpicii archive was found in the *triclinium*. However, both of these archives contain documents relating only to the personal affairs of the people living there, not records of public service.[41]

The private house was also central to the workings of the communicative enterprise needed for public officeholding. The practice of *salutatio* and the preference for oral communication and personal appeals was fundamental to the way that Roman administration worked. What this meant was that even though some officials had public reception spaces, administrative activities could and would take place as part of the personal discharge of the business of the magistrates in their own homes. However, what took place in the imperial period was that some of the services grew so big and demanding that running them as side jobs became impractical and politically inexpedient. As in the famous fictitious speech of Maecenas about the Roman administration,[42] it was necessary for the public services to be run by salaried equestrian officials who would not be required to cover the costs of the office from their own means.

Scribes and secretaries were key functionaries on both sides of the public/private divide because there were public scribes working in decurions attached to each magistracy but equally people on the public career retained their private scribes. The way they both worked, taking dictation and reading texts to their principals was possibly quite similar.[43] Of course, our knowledge comes from literary individuals such as Cicero, Caesar or Pliny, who, based on the information we have, wrote constantly. They would dictate letters and texts while traveling or even before dawn,[44] and have a secretary follow them around to take notes and to bring them letters to sign, even at dinner.[45] Although there were public scribes, it appears that having a trusted scribe was a long-term relationship where a good scribe would be able to write reliably with just a general indication of the content and be knowledgeable about the principal's private and public business.[46]

What this did not mean is that the public administration was solely based on the Roman *domus*. Within those features where there was contact with the people as a multitude or something was presented publicly, the obvious choice was the Forum. This is evident from such reliefs as the *Plutei Traiani*, where the institution of *alimenta* was depicted as a meeting of the emperor and the people in the Forum. Similarly, in the depiction of the burning of the tax records, the location is the Forum.

However, it would be wrong to assume that the move from a system based on private individuals either meeting in the Forum or private homes to a system of salaried officials could be seen as purely one of bureaucratization. From the onset it is clear that the imperial government was in fact based on the blueprint of the aristocratic household. A household on steroids, but a household nonetheless. The same virtues of openness and accessibility were presented for both the house of a Roman noble like Cicero and emperors like Vespasian. What studies on republican politics show is how much the different factions relied on large houses and households as their bases: centres where their activities and communications were based.[47] By the Severan period the imperial palaces had grown to cover most of the Palatine, but it was still conceptualized as a *domus* and had the functions of a *domus* from the *salutationes* to the way that imperial officials circulated there.[48]

The locations of imperial jurisdiction are a clear indication of this. Imperial trials took place not only in public, but also in the *cubiculum* of the emperor.[49] Even during the Republic, petitioners flocked to the homes of magistrates to ask for favours, much as Cicero mentions having done to advance the case of Ligarius.[50] However, some matters were clearly thought to be in the public realm. While trials within the household were dealt with within the house, high oratory was thought to belong to the public arenas. Cicero, in his speech on Deiotarus, does imply that having a trial inside the house, as was done in this case, was something unusual for a high-profile event like that.[51] Tacitus, in his Dialogus (39.4), similarly laments the confinement of trials to small rooms and single judges, where the businesslike setting left no room for high oratory.

What these examples demonstrate is how central the model of the private house was to the administrative tradition of Rome. The *domus* was complemented by the Forum as an administrative locus where citizens would interact, but whether there would have been a secluded public administrative building or area appears unlikely as a solution to the task of administration. However, the evidence appears at times contradictory and thus our next task is to see whether there are some continuities and consistencies to be found.

IV Designated Administrative Spaces

There are a number of instances where there were designated physical spaces for the magistrates if they had a particular need for them. We will here classify these according to the purpose of that space.

During the late Republic and early Principate, the spaces of administration were in flux as the administrative processes changed. The scale of the administration was constantly growing with the concentration of new magistracies around the emperor during the Principate. It is clear that the administrative space should be approached as reflecting the changes in the administrative and political system in Rome, and while Roman authors might portray them as static, those depictions are in and of themselves part of the contested discourses on power.

The administrative apparatus that ensured the smooth operation of the city of Rome and the Roman Empire was at the same time a historically complex and an astonishingly simple system for the scale of population and area involved. By the common estimates, the city of Rome had, at its largest, a population of over a million inhabitants, while the Roman Empire enveloped the entire Mediterranean basin and much of modern Europe. The estimates are of course very vague, but a peak population of some 50–60 million inhabitants for the Empire is an educated guess.[52] For a premodern society, this was an enormous city in the centre of a vast empire, where roads had to be built and maintained; a large army raised, armed and fed; a huge operation of the transfer of grain from the provinces to the main cities had to take place with precision – all while order and security had to be upheld. Of course, the Roman state, the *Senatus populusque Romanus*, if one should even use the modern term "state" in this context, was very limited in its reach and ambition. To use another modern term, one may call it a night-watchman state.[53] Despite this, the state apparatus or at least its political class at times had a willingness to interfere with the affairs of individuals with sumptuary and marriage legislation.[54]

It may be good to define what we are talking about when we speak of administration. The traditional republican system of governance that emerged with the legendary overthrow of the kings was based on the separation of legislative and executive power. The first was held by the various assemblies, which both legislated and selected the magistrates, mostly on a yearly basis. The magistrates were tiered according to order, where the censors, chosen every five years, ranked highest. Below them were the two consuls, who had the supreme executive power, the praetors, who had both executive and jurisdictional power, and below them the aediles, who maintained public buildings, and quaestors, who oversaw the public finances. The number of magistrates and eligibility requirements varied over time. In addition to these high-ranking political offices, there were a number of other minor offices, such as the *tresviri capitales*, who oversaw public order, as well as officials with specific administrative tasks. Additionally, there were scribes and other personnel.[55] On the whole, the traditional administration of the city of Rome was comprised of just some dozens of magistrates aided by support staff.

On top of this traditional system, there emerged through the reforms of Augustus the imperial system of administration. Many of the posts were manned initially either by freedmen or equestrians. These two administrative layers, the republican and the imperial, remained extant until Late Antiquity, as may be seen in the so called *Notitia Dignitatum* that records the situation during the late fourth or early fifth century.

The founding of the imperial offices was a major step towards professionalization. However, whether this meant that there would have been public offices for the new agencies is not clear. In the organization of the imperial agencies the republican principle of yearly rotation within the *cursus honorum* was decisively forgotten. The procurators responsible for the agencies were salaried officials, who were ranked according to their pay. The very fact that they were paid a salary sets them apart from the traditional officials, who received no remuneration.[56] While republican officials may have been expected to have private means of support, it is possible that the freedmen and later equestrians who ran these agencies, especially early on, could not be assumed to have similar possibilities. It may even have been thought that it was beneficial for their loyalty and performance that they were dependent on the salaries provided by the emperor. Many of the senior posts of *curatores* were equally not handled as part of the yearly rotation nor were they part of the tendency to appoint suffect magistrates.[57]

The changes taking place in the administrative space were the result not only of the individual preferences of emperors, for example, on whether to promote freedmen, equestrians or senators to administrative posts, but equally of the tasks that the administration was expected to perform. The functions of the *curae* were labour-intensive tasks, which were crucial to the functioning of civil life in the capital. The *cura annonae*, for example, handled the import and distribution of grain to a vast number of people. Augustus had limited the number of people eligible to 200,000. The equestrian *praefectus annonae* was responsible for the workings of this machinery. Where this distribution took place is a matter of debate,[58] but in the following we shall concentrate on two other imperial agencies, the urban prefecture and the *cura aquarum* as our main examples. This arrangement of services in *curae* was replicated in the provinces.[59]

The hypothesis of the following investigation is that the spatial setting of the Roman magistrate may be determined by whether there was a particular reason why there would be an assigned space for them, a space needed for safekeeping of documents or money, or the reception of people. The main principle is the fluid field of actions between domestic and public spheres.

To a large degree, the task of the highest magistrates of the Roman Republic was to act as political, military and religious leaders. For the consuls, very little is known of whether they had something that could be described as offices or a set place of work for themselves and their staff. As the holders of *imperium*, they were accompanied by lictors and a number of scribes and messengers. They were entitled to a *sella curulis*, a folding chair that showed the person both as a Roman magistrate and a holder of *imperium*.[60] However, the fact that they were given furniture to go with the power of office does not necessarily imply that there would have been an office in which to keep that furniture.

From the Roman sources, there appear no specific locations where the consuls would have exercised their duties or that would have limited their functions, except that the *imperium* or military commanding power would only have been in force outside the *pomerium*. The consuls directed troops in the field, received embassies, performed rites, appeared in the Senate and gave speeches, but nowhere in the Roman literature does it refer to the office of the consul as a physical location. In fact, before Sulla, the consuls normally spent the vast majority of their time away from Rome on campaigns.[61] From sources extending to fairly late in the Principate, we know that consuls were expected to use their private fortune in the execution of their duties; for example, Cassius Dio mentions that he was exempted from this obligation.[62] Even the ceremonies through which the consuls took office symbolize the connection between the private house and the city, where ceremonies at home would be followed by sacrifices at the Capitol and a speech in the Senate, whereupon the procession would lead the new consul home.[63]

Meeting the People

Much of the activity of the leading magistrates was conducted publicly in the Forum or elsewhere in public. The fact that public administrative acts took place in public was most likely due to maintaining public trust and transparency. The *sella curulis* was eminently transportable, making moving around easy and allowing a consul or a praetor a seat at the assembly or in the Forum, either on the ground or on a tribunal.[64]

What this meant was the performance of duties took place in an open space, on a podium or a tribunal where the seat of the magistrate was set – for a consul proposed laws to the assemblies, held *contiones* in public, led the sessions of the Senate and met with embassies in the Comitium.[65] Beyond this we have no indication of where the consular staff was housed, the persons who dealt with his correspondence, carried his messages, stored materials from the numerous consular investigations and wrote down the speeches he made.[66] It is clear that the role of high magistrates was to be seen – to be accessible to the people of Rome. Even meetings with ambassadors most often took place in front of the Senate.[67] Visibility was central to the whole physical arrangement, prompting the use of tribunals and podia, or the peculiar Graecostasis that was set up in the Comitium to elevate visiting dignitaries.

A similar arrangement is noticeable even with provincial governance, where the governors were visible on their tribunals or podia. Cicero, in his letters, mentions some of the attributes of office, the official high tribunal on which he sits as governor,[68] but never speaks of an office.[69] There is no mention of locations where high officials would meet in private, draft their correspondence and work with their staff; as has been mentioned, even the *commentarii* of consuls and praetors were primarily stored in their own homes.

While scribes trailed their principals, including the magistrates, there is no mention of a specific location for them in public except the tribunals. Likewise, the messengers (*viatores*), heralds (*praecones*) and other staff have no mentioned places; they appear in sources only when the magistrate is holding a public session.[70] Whether there would be a set place for the *decuriones* of *apparitores* is not known. The same goes for public slaves, *servi publici*, who were attached to different offices and magistracies, from the aediles to the *aerarium* and onwards throughout the administration.[71] The question is, where did these the *apparitores* work and the slaves live and work? Slaves owned by individuals lived and worked in the house of the master, but would the public slaves have general quarters or would they stay with the slaves of the magistrate?

Of Roman magistrates, the praetors were most set to appear in public and be available for consultation.[72] From the republican sources, it is evident that as jurisdictional magistrates, the *praetor urbanus* resolved cases between citizens while the *praetor peregrinus* those between non-citizens. Both had tribunals in the Forum, whose locations varied, but during the time of Cicero, the podium of the *praetor peregrinus* was in the Forum in front of the Basilica Julia, while the podium of the *praetor urbanus* would have been beside the temple of the Dioscuri.[73] Based on illustrations, tribunals were chest-high wooden podia where the praetor and his council and staff sat. However, nothing is known about where the paperwork about cases was stored or the rolls of jurors held.[74]

The tribunal was the primary location for judicial activities even during the Principate, but the seat of praetors moved to the Forum of Augustus.[75] Tacitus mentions how Tiberius would follow the activities of courts, sitting on the edge of the tribunal in order not to disturb the praetor leading the session.[76]

The office of the urban prefect, which gained prominence during the Principate, was also located in the imperial courts, but knowledge of it is mainly from Late Antiquity. He was by and large responsible for the administration of justice as well as the whole of the urban administration, from the local administration of the *vici* to water management and grain distribution.[77] Despite the scale of the responsibilities of the urban prefect, there is very little knowledge of the location of the offices of the prefect apart from some inscriptions and a few references in literature.[78] One hypothesis is that the office would have been located at the *Templum Pacis* in the imperial *fora*. The only signs to that effect are the location of the *Forma Urbis*, the vast Severan marble map of Rome there, and a passage in Symmachus about the *Forum Vespasiani*. Whether the passage refers to the forum as the office of the urban prefect requires some reading into it and Symmachus is in any case beyond our timeframe.[79] Another theory, presented by Chastagnol, is that the offices would have been in the little-known *Secretarium Tellurense* just north of the Colosseum. Based on an inscription, he claims that the office would have been divided into two parts, the *scrinia* and the *tribunalia*, where the first would have housed the archives and the secretaries, while the latter would have housed the courts.[80]

The late antique *Notitia Dignitatum* gives a rough estimate of the staff of the city prefect, 20 managerial positions and seven different categories of clerical staff, suggesting a total staff in three figures. In the reconstructions made of the *Templum Pacis* or the Forum of Vespasian, we have a rare occasion where the space available, three large rooms adjoining the peristyle, would actually be sufficient for the staff to operate even in a modern office layout, including working archives.

In short, places for having public audiences were not necessarily combined with office space and thus in some important cases, such as that of the praetors, this appears to have been excluded. However, in the later, Augustan form of the urban prefect's duties the spaces for the clerical staff seem to be included in most reconstructions of the offices.

Handling and Storing Documents

For the archives or in general the storage and retrieval of data, there are three main alternatives of which something is known: the Aerarium for laws and public records, the Villa Publica and Atrium Libertatis for the census records and the Tabularium. For the Principate onwards, one must also factor in the existence of libraries and their use as data storage. On the whole, recent works about ancient libraries have suggested that there was little difference between an archive and a library.[81]

During the Republic, the Aerarium contained both the public records and the public funds, administered by quaestors. Both Cicero and Pliny mention the *Aerarium Saturni*, Pliny saying that public contracts, documents from debts, the *commentarii* of officials, the accounts of the state as well as the moneys of the state were kept there. Cicero says that the *aerarium* kept copies of the laws, although its scribes were reluctant to comply with requests.[82]

The census and its records, kept by censors, were at the Villa Publica and the Atrium Libertatis. Livy mentions how censors built the Villa Publica in the Campus Martius in 435 BC, arranging the first census there, later restoring it in 194 BC with the Atrium Libertatis.[83] The Villa Publica was a multifunctional building; according to Varro[84] it was used "for the cohorts to assemble when summoned by the consul for a levy, for the inspection of arms, for the censors to convoke the people for the census".[85] However, it disappears completely during the late Republic.[86] The Atrium Libertatis, located close to the Forum, provided a place for the records and for the staff of the censors, but little is known about this building as well.[87]

The most ambiguous of the archival locations is the Tabularium. The enormous substructures that now carry the name *tabularium* have only tenuously been identified with archives.[88] One of the main issues with storing documents is that knowledge of how they were preserved is mostly elusive. For instance, while we know that the fire on the Capitolium in AD 69 destroyed over 3,000 old bronze tablets that contained old documents, laws, *senatusconsulta*, treaties and others, it is not known where these documents were kept.[89] Were they inside a building, or rather posted on the outside walls to be publicly read? The evidence regarding the *tabularium*, *aerarium* and other public buildings of the area and their uses is complicated.[90] A separate entity with its own officials is the imperial *tabularium castrense*, where documents pertaining to imperial finances and legal matters were kept.[91]

Beyond the *aerarium* the evidence on archives is meagre. We have the Regia, where the annals were kept. From there onwards the evidence grows thinner. For the Augustan offices, the *curae*, there are mentions of office-places, such as the city prefect's offices at the Temple of Peace or the Secretarium Tellurense. For the large staffs of the Augustan *curae* and the other services, the relative lack of information is surprising, as they are headed by equites or freedmen, persons who were not necessarily expected to have large houses. From the written sources it is evident that administrative units and organizations ranging from *collegia* to *corpora* had their own archival units, but where they were located is again unclear.[92]

One of the main issues regarding archives is that the storage of information in Rome took considerable space, but we do not know how extensive or systematic that storage was. While we know nothing about the archival systems, we do have useful information about libraries and their methods of storing books. Rectangular or cylindrical boxes as well as different systems of shelves and cabinets were used to store rolls, while wax tablets would demand even more space for storage.

Shelves have been thought to be inbuilt and thus niches in buildings are often seen as signs of a library or archive. Because papyrus rolls were fragile, it was important to have a place for the repair of damaged manuscripts.[93]

Handling Money

The minting and storing of money was, for obvious reasons, a task that could hardly have been assigned to a magistrate to be performed at home. In addition to the censors, the quaestors are a rarity among Roman magistrates in that they have a fixed location for their activities, the *aerarium* or the treasury. Their administration of public finances began early in the Republic, and during the Empire, senatorial *praefecti aerarii* took up oversight duty of the *Aerarium Saturni*.[94] Valerius Publicola, who founded the questorship, located the *aerarium* at the Temple of Saturn because he thought it necessary to store public funds somewhere other than in a private home.[95]

The *Aerarium Saturni* employed clerks who took care of its many financial and archival duties, such as the storing of public moneys, contracts, the texts of the laws passed, the lists of taxes and debts to the state. From accounts such as Plutarch's life of Cato the younger and Pliny's letters, it is evident that the work was both technically demanding and dull.[96] The accounts mention how the *aerarium* was at the temple, but how the various duties of storage and receiving clients would have taken place is unclear. For example, Pliny uses the phrase *sedeo pro tribunali*, but would that mean that he had a tribunal inside the building or outside it? In a similar way, where were the money and the laws actually stored?[97]

It would appear that when the administration was actually tied to physical places, for example, in the case of the censors or the *aerarium*, there is a very good reason for it. In addition to the need to store much important information, the need to store money would prompt the building of a designated structure.

Public Works and Public Order

In addition to storing money, the performance of public works such as the construction and upkeep of roads, markets, water supply infrastructure and buildings as well as the preservation of public order in them including police and firefighting functions, overseeing commercial activities and traffic were tasks that required both space and a labour force. It is evident that they were beyond the use of domestic spaces. We may take a look at a few examples, from the aediles to water management.

The upkeep and maintenance of republican Rome, its roads and public places, were the duty of aediles. Before the founding of the Augustan *curae*, they were also responsible for the oversight of the grain distribution and the water supply, as well as the organization of games, the various *ludi sollemni*. We have no real sense of where their operations were based, apart from speculations relating to the plebeian origin of the office and its linkage with the temples of Ceres and Diana on the Aventine.[98] It has been suggested that they would have had a base there, but little in the way of sources is available.[99] The discrepancy between the responsibilities and the lack of dedicated space is quite significant. A similar situation is the case of the minor magistracies such as the *tresviri capitales*, who were responsible for public order and policing. They have been linked with the Mamertine Prison, but this is again conjectural.[100]

In addition to the grain supply, the task of water management was one of the main public works. The scale of the *cura aquarum*, including the engineering, building, maintenance and administrative tasks, was enormous: eleven aqueducts brought water to Rome over distances extending over 60 kilometres. In Rome, the water was distributed to different locations. Even the legal ramifications of setting out the infrastructure on private land were considerable, including establishing the rights to have pipes, aqueducts, etc. be set on private property. During the Republic, the water system was overseen by the censors, but the practical work was outsourced to contractors. Augustus set up the office of *cura aquarum*, with three senatorial *curatores aquarum* for the oversight and freedman (later equestrian) *procuratores aquarum* for the practical work. While much is known about the *cura aquarum* due to Frontinus and epigraphic sources,[101] little is known about its administrative locations. Its headquarters was called *statio aquarum*, but where it was is contested. It would need space to house the plans for the water systems, the contracts that were involved, presumably the staff that would take care of the planning work, the running of the maintenance and the payment of the subcontractors.[102] Bruun has estimated that the *cura aquarum* had some 700 persons working in the whole service. Of these, many were possibly spread out into the field, but the managers, architects and engineers, as well as the clerical staff would have been at the headquarters.[103]

Because of the lack of any references in written sources about these headquarters, let alone their location, the efforts to pinpoint them have focused on epigraphic sources. The trouble with them is that they are often at cult sites, which has led to some curious conclusions. Thus, Coarelli suggested a location for the headquarters in the temple area of Largo Argentina (between temples A and B), while others have suggested the Lacus Iuturnae at the Forum.[104] Both of these are basically cult locations of very restricted size, with little functional usability. Another suggestion is that by the end of the second century AD, the water and grain supply would have been united at the *porticus Minucia*, based on the fact that titles of curators combine both water and Minucia.[105] However, a fourth century inscription was again found at the Lacus Iuturnae, but whether that is evidence of anything is another matter.[106] In contrast, Bruun argues that the reference to a *statio* (*CIL* VI 36781: *genio stationis aquarum*) refers to a votive gift of the *genius* of the *cura*, not a sign pointing to its headquarters.[107] The result is that we do not really know anything secure about the location of the *cura aquarum*.

The conclusion is that there is no reliable information about the locations of the *curae* or other public works. This has led to either speculation or cautious avoidance of the issues in much of the history of administration.[108] A similar case is evident in the inquiries concerning local services such as the *vigiles*, where workers simply had to be physically present to maintain order and fight fires. The jurisdiction of the *praefectus vigilum* came to encompass not only fire but also thieves and escaped slaves, perhaps even a civil jurisdiction over leases,[109] indicating that the *stationes* of the *vigiles* took on, *faute de mieux*, the form of local administration. However, as Coarelli's recent attempt at locating these *stationes* illustrates, that there is a need for these services does not mean that we will be able to pinpoint their location.[110]

V Conclusions

The question of whether one may find a Roman office building or a desk must be approached through the larger investigation of administrative space and its functions. The Roman magistracies may be divided into political and administrative roles, but each magistracy contained both. What could be identified as a political side of the magistracies, taking part in the operation of assemblies and the Senate, negotiating political issues both within the citizen body and with representatives of foreign powers, all took place in public, in the Forum, Comitium, Curia and the assemblies. Within this public sphere also operated the courts of law and the praetors, who had their podia in the Forum for receiving litigants.

The only reliable information regarding dedicated administrative space comes from the censors and the quaestors, whose offices in the Atrium Libertatis and the Aerarium Saturni are attested by numerous sources. They are all situations where there was a need to store valuables or documents in large quantities: the storing of public moneys in the *aerarium*, the safekeeping of tax and census records as well as the laws and other public documents in the Atrium Libertatis and the Aerarium Saturni. The only remarks of a *statio* in the meaning of a public office are likewise from the financial administration such as tax offices.

The majority of the general administrative work was performed in hybrid spaces, in arrangements that used both public and private locations. Thus, consuls were visible and acted in public spaces, but at the same time drafted documents at home. However, where the aedile responsible for the cleaning of the streets and markets would perform his duties is not clear, but it is possible that even there the administrative work would be taken care of at home while the work crews doing the actual work would have places for their tools. While praetors could meet with litigants and give rulings in the Forum, their archives and writing would most likely be at home.

The purpose of this chapter has been to present a more nuanced hypothesis of the uses of space and the allocation of space for administrative purposes. It has sought to examine how the division of space could have been demarcated between public and private spaces and to move beyond that division. As private homes go, the dwellings of the Roman upper classes were sizable structures that housed not only the family itself, but their *familia*, consisting of a large number of slaves and, sometimes, freedmen. Business was based there, and the receiving of associates, allies and people coming for aid took place in the reception areas of the *domus*, the *tabularium* and the peristyle.

That the official business of meeting with clerks, drafting of documents and delivering them took place in the *domus* would have been a simple extension of the standard way of operation for a member of the Roman upper class. From the

Models of Administrative Space in the Roman World 67

evidence of the way Roman scribes operated, it would appear that some would work in the house of their master, others somewhere else, but always delivering the finished products to the master in his home.

The private house would have been almost the only possibility for the tasks that demanded concentration, either for the dictation of a document or sensitive negotiations between officials. The public buildings were not built to provide privacy – quite the opposite.

Notes

1. This work is part of the project "Law, Governance and Space: Questioning the Foundations of the Republican Tradition" (SpaceLaw.fi). This research has received funding from the European Research Council (ERC) under the European Union's Horizon 2020 research and innovation programme (grant agreement No 771874). The author wishes to thank the members of the SpaceLaw project for their comments and help. He also wishes to thank Dr Heta Björklund, Ms Oona Raatikainen, Ms Mirkka Koskimäki and Mr Pyry Koskinen for their editorial assistance.
2. This is evident in classical works on Roman administration such as Mommsen 1871–1888 or Hirschfeld 1905. Mommsen would only briefly refer to the built surroundings when discussing the censors, quaestors and aediles, chiefly the Villa Publica and the aerarium (Mommsen 1871–1888: 2.2:359, 545). He did put some effort into discussing the vehicles and seats of magistrates (Mommsen 1871–1888: 1:393–408). Hirschfeld has more references to minor officials and their stations (Hirschfeld 1905: 5, 41). The spatial aspect is mainly absent in more recent works such as Kolb 2006; Ausbüttel 1998; Robinson 1992.
3. Bablitz 2007; De Angelis 2010; Färber 2014.
4. Of the recent studies, one may mention Färber 2012; Mazzei 2009; Castorio 2006; Gros 2001.
5. Eich 2005; Coarelli 2019.
6. Bekker-Nielsen 2014: 132–134.
7. Tuori and Nissin 2015; Bowes 2010; Winterling 2009; Zaccaria Ruggiu 2005; Carucci 2008; Ellis 2000; Grahame 2000; Hales 2003; Riggsby 1997; Grahame 1997; Treggiari 1998; Laurence and Wallace-Hadrill 1997; Wallace-Hadrill 1994.
8. Millar 1992: 15 discusses the role of the private house for the aristocracy, but even here neglecting its role as a site of administration.
9. See, for example, Russell 2016 or Gargola 2017.
10. On the pervasiveness of the two models, see Posner 1972. On the rejection of this model, see, for example, Canevaro 2013.
11. The *praetoria* and the *principia* as centres of the Roman military camps are interesting comparisons to the municipal structures, as the Roman military camps were modelled after cities (here, one should naturally make the distinction between a *praetorium* in a camp and a provincial *praetorium*). The forum and the *praetoria* were the centres of the camps, but unlike in cities, here the *praetorium* was equally a place to live. Archaeological remains indicate that they were comprised of a structure resembling a Roman peristyle house where numerous small rooms (*cubicula*) would be arranged around a peristyle with some larger rooms. On the archaeological typologies, see Moneta and Schallmayer 2006; for the written sources, see Alessio 2006. For the arrangement of administrative functions, such a setting would work in a fashion similar to a Roman house or a villa where residential and administrative functions coincided. *Praetoria* have been identified in only roughly a quarter of the provinces. While there are great variations, they often have common characteristics with the large Roman private houses. Haensch 1997: 375–376. About the *praetoria*, see Chapter 10 in this volume by A. Álvarez Melero.

12 Purcell 1988: 150–181, at 175.
13 Bruun 1991.
14 For references, see below.
15 For example, Mols 1999 has only decorative tables, not desks.
16 See Houston 2014 for more references to images.
17 Museo Nazionale Romano, Terme di Diocleziano, inv. 475113. See Zevi 2012 for details.
18 Museo Nazionale Romano, Palazzo Massimo alle Terme, inv. 124483. On the *sella curulis*, see Schäfer 1989: 24–195.
19 On the altar, see most recently Maschek 2018. On libraries, see Houston 2014.
20 *Secretarium* comes up first in Lactant., *De mort. pers.* 15.5, Cod. Th. 1.7.1 and Cod. Just. 3.24.3, 9.3.16.
21 Vitr. 5.1–2.
22 Weiss 1929: 2210–2213.
23 *Frag. Vat.* 134 *arcarii Caesariani, qui in foro Traiani habent stationes.*
24 *CIL* VI 8446: *princeps tabulariorum in statione XX hereditatium*. Another inscription mentions Ulpius Placidus, an imperial freedman, who was a *tabularius* of *a rationibus*: *CIL* VI 8581: *Ulpius Placidus Aug. lib. tabularius a rationibus mensae Galliarum.*
25 The two main studies on *scribae* are now David 2019 and Hartmann 2020.
26 Färber 2014: 144–161; Haensch 1997: 374–377. They reflected the topography of the Roman military camp (see Moneta and Schallmayer 2006) and became shorthand for the residences of governors and emperors (Alessio 2006; Schäfer 2014). See also Upex et al. 2011.
27 Acton 2011: 107.
28 For the writing practices of the administration, we are left with three main sources: references in literature, epigraphic copies of rescripts or other documents and preserved documents either on papyri or wax tablets. A good example is imperial rescripts, which are found in epigraphy, papyri and literature. On the rescripts as documents, see Wilcken 1920; Nörr 1981; Williams 1980, 1986; Honoré 1994: 35–37; Hauken 1998: 263, 300–306; on the provincial experience, see Ando 2000: 87–90.
29 See Wallace-Hadrill 1994 using modern and ancient comparisons.
30 Carandini 2010; Coarelli 2012: 315.
31 Tr. by Schofield 2009.
32 Plin., *HN* 34.9.17; Cic., *Att.* 12.23; Dickmann 1999: 114; see also Hales 2003: 57.
33 Peachin 1996: 40.
34 König 2011.
35 Cohen 1984: 29.
36 Weiss 1929: 2212–13 underlines the relation of the *statio* to the *fiscus*.
37 The most poignant reminder of this is the case about the punishment of the slaves who had resided in the house of the city prefect, Pedanius Secundus (Tac. *Ann.* 14.42–45) in AD 61, when he was murdered by unknown assailants. Four hundred slaves, including women and children, were executed, but his freedmen were spared.
38 The total number of slaves is unknown, and estimates range from 10 to 40 per cent of the total population during the Empire. In Italy, and especially Rome as an urban centre, the percentage would have been considerably higher. See Scheidel 2007b on the challenges facing any estimates.
39 Culham 1989: 104; Posner 1972: 165.
40 Cic., *Sull.* 42; Liv. 6.1.2 *privata monumenta*. On the *commentarii*, see von Premerstein 1900: 733–756.
41 Camodeca 1999; Crook 1994. The original location of the cabinet in the house of Caecilius Iucundus is in dispute, as it was found some 4 metres from ground level, suggesting it was on an upper floor. De Vos 1991: 575–576.
42 Dio 52.23–25.

43 For example, Hartmann 2020 suggests that scribes worked independently as an *ordo* attached to a magisterial level and had a set space in public arcades to work.
44 Plut., *Vit. Caes.* 17.3–4; Plin., *Ep.* 3.5, 9.10; Cic., *Q. Fr.* 2.5.5. On the functions of secretaries in writing, see Richards 1991: 14–127.
45 Plin., *Ep.* 9.29; Plut., *Vit. Caes.* 63.4.
46 Cic., *Q. Fr.* 1.2.8, *Fam.* 16.4.3. On Cicero's views, see Treggiari 1998. The intimate nature of household staff is evident in the way Cicero reacts to the fleeing of Dionysios, his library slave.
47 Dio 66.10.54. Potter 2011 argues that the late republican nobility would already enact a similar policy of combining participation in political processes with their private households. Acton 2011 similarly sees the combination of public and private as a defining feature of the Principate. Ellis 2000: 54 maintains that Augustus would deliberately follow the architecture of a private house in his palace.
48 On the Severan court and palaces, see Schöpe 2014: 223–238.
49 The trials in *cubiculum* were often referred to as exceptions and examples of bad administration. Sen., *Clem.* 1.9; Tac., *Ann.* 11.1–2, 11.34–38. On the symbolic value, see Tuori 2016: 117, 167, 182.
50 Cic., *Fam.* 6.13–14.
51 Cic., *Deiot.* 5–7.
52 The issue of estimating population figures is highly controversial and estimates very diverse. Scheidel 2007a: 38–86; Frier 2000: 827–854. But see also Lo Cascio 1994: 23–40.
53 The phrase has a convoluted history, but currently refers to libertarian theories of a state that is limited to solely providing external and internal safety, excluding all moral or social obligations.
54 Bleicken 1982: 185–199.
55 *Dig.* 1.2.2.14–34 (Pomponius) on the history and evolution of the Roman magistracies. Mommsen (1871–1888: 2.2) compiled a full listing of the different magistrates.
56 On the origin of this system, see Dio 53.15.5. A large number of procurators are known from inscriptions.
57 On the *curatores*, see Bruun 2006.
58 Richardson 1992: 315–316; Coarelli 1997: 296–345, especially 341–342; Zevi 1993: 2, 661–708.
59 The provincial *Lex Irnitana* 75 speaks of the *cura annonae* (see Torrent 2012) while there are provincial references to *cura aquarum*; see Segenni 2005; Rémy et al. 2011.
60 On the symbolic uses of the *sella curulis*, see Tuori 2020. Imperium was conferred with a *lex curiata*. Lintott 1993: 22.
61 Pina Polo 2011: 26; Lintott 1999: 104–107; Mommsen 1871–1888: 2.1:74–140.
62 Cass. Dio 80.5.1.
63 Liv. 21.63; Ov., *Fast.* 1.81, *Pont.* 4.4.27–42; Pina Polo 2011: 21–22.
64 Mommsen 1871–1888: 1:400. Mommsen believed that the consular use of the *sella curulis* was a remnant of their jurisdiction.
65 Varro, *Ling.* 5.155. See Pina Polo 2011: 75 on the tribunals and the public reception areas used by consuls.
66 Some have suggested that there would have been a room in the Curia for consuls and their staff. Mazzei 2009: 294–298.
67 Liv. 41.8.
68 Cic., *Fam.* 3.8.2.
69 The Roman governors were often found on their tribunals, for example, Livy (31.29) relates how a Roman governor appears on a tribunal like a despot, surrounded by lictors. See also Cic., *Verr. II* 2.102, 2.94.
70 Despite this, we know that some scribes were attached to particular persons for a length of time and during various offices. Jones 1949: 155–159; Cohen 1984: 35–49.

Purcell 1983 argues that the positions for *apparitores* were an important route for social advancement, but the evidence for this is fairly limited.
71 Cohen 1984: 30–32. The issue of *servi publici* is the focus of a new project by Federico Santangelo and Franco Luciani. See Luciani 2017.
72 The most comprehensive new study of the praetors is Brennan 2000; see equally Mommsen 1871–1888: 2.1: 193–238. These studies demonstrate how much the praetors had military tasks and worked outside Rome in the provinces.
73 Cic., *Verr. II* 1.129, 5.186; Cic., *De or.* 2.24.
74 *XII Tab* I, 7; Cic. *De or.* 2.24.100; Frier 1985: 57–64; Richardson 1992: 50, 52; Purcell 1995: 325–336, 333; Coarelli 1985: 169–171, 190–191. See Carnabuci 1996: 20–29 on the locations of various courts in the Forum. See Brennan 2000: 289 on the attempts to locate the seats of the praetors in the Forum. Livy 23.32.4 writes that during the Hannibalic wars, the praetors' tribunals were located near the public baths. See, for example, Welin 1953; Richardson 1973; Coriat 2015 on the places of podia. See also the Chapter 2 by Heikonen et al. in this volume.
75 Lopez Garcia forthcoming.
76 Tac., *Ann.* 1.75.
77 Wojciech 2010; Ruciński 2009; Chastagnol 1960; Vitucci 1956.
78 Mart. 2.17, Lyd., *Mag.* 1.34. On the localization attempts, see Marchese 2007; Färber 2012: 53–60.
79 Coarelli 1999a: 67–70, at 70; Symm., *Ep.* 10.78 (the 1848 *Patrologia Latina* edition).
80 *CIL* VI 31959 *porticum cum scriniis tellurensis secretarii tribunali(bus) adherentem*. Chastagnol 1960: 247–251, pl. VI; Coarelli 1999b: 159–160; Richardson 1992: 321. Most recently, the new excavations at the *Templum Pacis* have shed light on this.
81 Martínez and Finn Senseney 2013: 412; Lopez Garcia and Bueno Guardia 2021.
82 Plin. *Ep.* 1.10.9; Millar 1964: 33–40; Corbier 1974: 671–692; Culham 1989: 103, 112–114; Cic., *Leg.* 3.20.46–48.
83 Liv. 4.22, 34.44.
84 Varro, *Rust.* 3.2.1–4.
85 Translation by Hooper and Ash 1934. *Et cum haec sit communis universi populi, illa solius tua; haec quo succedant e campo cives et reliqui homines, illa quo equae et asini; praeterea cum ad rem publicam administrandam haec sit utilis, ubi cohortes ad dilectum consuli adductae considant, ubi arma ostendunt, ubi censores censu admittant populum.*
86 Agache 1999: 202–205; Richardson 1992: 431.
87 On the Atrium Libertatis, see Liv. 43.16.13; Coarelli 1993.
88 Weiss 1932: 1963–6. Livy 43.16.13, 45.1; Serv. *Ad Verg. G.* 2.502. More recently, Purcell 2010 suggests that the substructures belong to the Atrium Libertatis, while Tucci 2013–2014 and now Coarelli 2010 claim that they are part of a temple. On the various *tabularia*, see Balty 1991: 151–161. On the Atrium Libertatis, see also Purcell 1993.
89 *CIL* I 591, 592; Tac., *Hist.* 3.71–2; Suet., *Vesp.* 8; Polyb. 3.22.4, 3.26.1; Dion. Hal. 4.58. Beard 1998: 75–101, at 76–77; Dudley 1967: 72.
90 Mazzei 2009.
91 *CIL* VI 8529, VI 8518, VI 8431: *custos tabularii a rationibus*.
92 Moatti 1998.
93 Houston 2014: 180–202.
94 Corbier 1974.
95 Plut., *Vit. Popl.* 12. On locating the *aerarium* and *tabularium*, see Mazzei 2009.
96 Plut., *Vit. Cat. Min.* 16; Plin., *Ep.* 1.10; Millar 1964: 33–40; Corbier 1974: 671–692; Culham 1989: 100–115 at 103, 112–114; Plut., *Quaest. Rom.* 42; Fest., *Gloss. Lat.* s.v. "Aerarium". Among the things preserved at the *aerarium* are the standards of the legions (Livy 3.69, 4.22, 71.23), texts of laws on brazen tablets (Suet. *Iul.* 28) and *senatusconsulta* (Joseph, *AJ* 14.10.10; Plut., *Vit. Cat. Min.* 17; Cic., *Leg.* 3.4; Tac., *Ann.* 3.50). Clerks: *CIL* VI 1930 *tabularius viatorum quaestoriurum ab aerario*.
97 Tuori 2018.

98 See Chapter 7 by A. Lopez Garcia in this volume.
99 Lintott 1999: 129–133. On the responsibilities of the aediles, such as the *vigiles* and their reorganization after Augustus, see Santalucia 2012.
100 Sall., *Cat.* 55; Fuhrmann 2012: 93–94; Richardson 1992: 150–182; Nippel 1995: 4–27; Cascione 1999.
101 The main source for the *cura aquarum* is Frontinus, who was *curator aquarum* and wrote *De aquaeductu urbis Romae* in AD 100. The *cura* was one of Augustus' new offices (Suet., *Aug.* 37 *nova officia*). Peachin 2006; Bruun 1991: 140–206; Eck 1979, 1995; Robinson 1992: 99–101.
102 Bruun 1991: 190.
103 See Bruun 1989, 1991: 140–206, 2007.
104 Coarelli 1981: 9–52; Robinson 1992: 101; Bruun 1991: 195. Most recently, see Coarelli 2019: 161–193, with discussions regarding the possible surface area for the headquarters.
105 The location is based on the inscriptions where the title contains the name of Minuciae: *CIL* V 7783 = *ILS* 1128 (*curator aquarum et Minuciae*), *CIL* VI 3902 = *ILS* 1186 (*curator aquarum et Miniciae*), *CIL* VI 1532 = *ILS* 8679 (*cur. aquar. et Miniciae*), but also *CIL* X 4752 (*consulari aquarum et Minuciae*). Robinson 1992: 101.
106 *ILS* 8943, 9050.
107 Bruun 1989: 127–147, 1991: 195–196.
108 See, for example, Kolb 1993.
109 Santalucia 2012: 401–402.
110 Coarelli 2019: 397–414.

References

Acton, K. 2011: 'Vespasian and the Social World of the Roman Court', *American Journal of Philology* 132, 103–124.
Agache, S. 1999: 'Villa Publica', in E. M. Steinby (ed.), *Lexicon Topographicum Urbis Romae II*, Roma, 202–205.
Alessio, S. 2006: '*Praetorium* e *palatium* come residenze di imperatori e governatori', *Latomus* 65, 679–689.
Ando, C. 2000: *Imperial Ideology and Provincial Loyalty in the Roman Empire*, Berkeley.
Ausbüttel, F. M. 1998: *Die Verwaltung des römischen Kaiserreichs*, Darmstadt.
Bablitz, L. 2007: *Actors and Audience in the Roman Courtroom*, London and New York.
Balty, C. 1991. Curia ordinis: *Recherches d'architecture et d'urbanisme antiques sur les curies provinciales du monde romain*, Brussels.
Beard, M. 1998: 'Documenting Roman Religion', in *La mémoire perdue. Recherches sur l'administration romaine*, Rome, 75–101.
Bekker-Nielsen, T. 2014: 'Hard and Soft Space in the Ancient World', in K. Geus and M. Thiering (eds), *Features of Common Sense Geography: Implicit Knowledge Structures in Ancient Geographical Texts*, Zürich and Berlin, 117–132.
Bleicken, J. 1982: *Zum Regierungsstil des Römischen Kaisers*, Wiesbaden.
Bowes, K. 2010: *Houses and Society in the Later Roman Empire*, London.
Brennan, C. T. 2000: *The Praetorship in the Roman Republic*, New York and Oxford.
Bruun, C. 1989: 'Statio Aquarum', in E. M. Steinby (ed.), *Lacus Iuturnae 1*, Roma, 127–147.
Bruun, C. 1991: *The Water Supply of Ancient Rome. A Study of Roman Imperial Administration*, Helsinki.
Bruun, C. 2006: 'Der Kaiser und die Stadtrömischen *curae*', in A. Kolb (ed.), *Herrschaftsstrukturen und Herrschaftspraxis. Konzepte, Prinzipien und Strategien der Administration im römischen Kaiserrecht*, Berlin, 89–114.

Bruun, C. 2007: '*Aqueductium* e *statio aquarum*. La sede della *cura aquarum* di Roma', in A. Leone, D. Palombi, and S. Walker (eds), '*Res bene gestae*'. *Ricerche di storia urbana su Roma antica in onore di Eva Margareta Steinby*, Roma, 1–14.
Camodeca, G. 1999: *Tabulae Pompeianae Sulpiciorum (TPSulp.). Edizione critica dell'archivio puteolano dei Sulpicii. 2 Vols*, Rome.
Canevaro, M. 2013: *The Documents in the Attic Orators: Laws and Decrees in the Public Speeches of the Demosthenic Corpus*, Oxford.
Carandini, A. 2010: *Le case del potere nell'antica Roma*, Roma.
Carnabuci, E. 1996: *I luoghi dell'amministrazione della giustizia ne Foro di Augusto*, Napoli.
Carucci, M. 2008: *The Romano-African Domus: Studies in Space, Decoration and Function*, Oxford.
Cascione, C. 1999: '*Tresviri capitales*'. *Storia di una magistratura minore*, Napoli.
Castorio, J.-N. 2006: 'Le'Pseudo-Marsyas' et le portrait présumé de Geta découverts à Grand (Vosges)', *Latomus* 65, 659–678.
Chastagnol, A. 1960: *La Préfecture urbaine à Rome sous le Bas-Empire*, Paris.
Coarelli, F. 1981: 'L'Area Sacra di Largo Argentina. Topografia e Storia', in *L'Area Sacra di Largo Argentina 1*, Roma, 9–52.
Coarelli, F. 1985: *Il Foro Romano II. Periodo Repubblicano e Augusteo*, Roma.
Coarelli, F. 1993: 'Atrium Libertatis', *LTUR* 1, 133–135.
Coarelli, F. 1997: *Campo Marzio I*, Roma.
Coarelli, F. 1999a: 'Pax, Templum', *LTUR* IV, 67–70.
Coarelli, F. 1999b: 'Praefectura Urbana', *LTUR* IV, 159–160.
Coarelli, F. 2010: 'Substructio et tabularium', *PBSR* 78, 107–132.
Coarelli, F. 2012: *Palatium: Il Palatino dalle origini all'impero*, Roma.
Coarelli, F. 2019: *Statio. I luoghi dell'amministrazione nell'antica Roma*, Roma.
Cohen, B. 1984: 'Some Neglected Ordines: The Apparitorial Status-Groups', in C. Nicolet (ed.), *Des ordres à Rome*, Paris, 23–60.
Corbier, M. 1974: *L'aerarium Saturni et l'aerarium militare: administration et prosopographie sénatoriale*, Rome.
Coriat, J.-P. 2015: 'I tribunali dell'impero tra I e III secolo: *status quaestionis* e prospettive', in F. Milazzo (ed.), *I tribunali dell'impero*, Milano, 3–39.
Crook, J. A. 1994: 'Review of *L'archivio puteolano dei Sulpicii*, by G. Camodeca', *Journal of Roman Studies* 84, 260–261.
Culham, P. 1989: 'Archives and Alternatives in Republican Rome', *Classical Philology* 84, 100–115.
David, J. M. 2019: *Au service de l'honneur: les appariteurs de magistrats Romains*, Paris.
De Angelis, F. (ed.) 2010: *Spaces of Justice in the Roman World*, Boston, MA.
De Vos, A. 1991: 'Casa di Cecilio Giocondo', in *Pompei: pitture e mosaici III*, Rome, 575–576.
Dickmann, J.-A. 1999: *Domus frequentata: Anspruchsvolles Wohnen im pompejanischen Stadthaus*, München.
Dudley, D. 1967: *Urbs Roma*, New York.
Eck, W. 1979: *Die Staatliche Organisation Italiens in der hohen Kaiserzeit*, München.
Eck, W. 1995: 'Organisation und Administration der Wasserversorgung Roms', in *Die Verwaltung des römischen Reiches in der Hohen Kaiserzeit*, Basel, 161–178.
Eich, P. 2005: *Zur Metamorphose des politischen Systems in der römischen Kaiserzeit. Die Entstehung einer "personalen Bürokratie" im langen dritten Jahrhundert* (Klio Beihefte N.F. 9), Berlin.
Ellis, S. 2000: *Roman Housing*, London.

Färber, R. 2012: 'Die Amtssitze der Stadtpräfekten im spätantiken Rom und Konstantinopel', in F. Arnold, A. Busch, R. Haensch, and U. Wulf-Rheidt (eds), *Orte der Herrschaft. Charakteristika von antiken Machtzentren*, Halle and Saale, 49–71.

Färber, R. 2014: *Römische Gerichtsorte: räumliche Dynamiken von Jurisdiktion im Imperium Romanum*, München.

Frier, B. W. 1985: *The Rise of the Roman Jurists. Studies in Cicero's Pro Caecina*, Princeton, NJ.

Frier, B. W. 2000: 'Demography', in A. K. Bowman, P. Garnsey, and D. Rathbone (eds), *The Cambridge Ancient History XI: The High Empire, A.D. 70–192*, Cambridge, 827–854.

Fuhrmann, C. J. 2012: *Policing the Roman Empire. Soldiers, Administration, and Public Order*, New York.

Gargola, D. J. 2017: *The Shape of the Roman Order: The Republic and Its Spaces*, Chapel Hill, NC.

Grahame, M. 1997: 'Public and Private in the Roman House: Investigating the Social Order of the *Casa del Fauno*', in R. Laurence and A. Wallace-Hadrill (eds), *Domestic Space in the Roman World: Pompeii and Beyond*, Portsmouth, RI, 137–164.

Grahame, M. 2000: *Reading Space: Social Interaction and Identity in the Houses of Roman Pompeii*, Oxford.

Gros, P. 2001: 'Les édifices de la bureaucratie impériale: administration, archives et services publics dans le centre monumental de Rome', *Pallas* 55, 107–126.

Haensch, R. 1997: *Capita provinciarum: Statthaltersitze und Provinzialverwaltung in der römischen Kaiserzeit*, Mainz am Rhein.

Hales, S. 2003: *The Roman House and Social Identity*, Cambridge.

Hartmann, B. 2020. *The Scribes of Rome. A Cultural and Social History of the Scribae*, Cambridge.

Hauken, T. 1998: *Petition and Response: An Epigraphic Study of Petitions to Roman Emperors 181–249*, Bergen.

Hirschfeld, O. 1905: *Die Kaiserlichen Verwaltungsbeamten*, Berlin.

Honoré, T. 1994: *Emperors and Lawyers: With a Palingenesia of Third-Century Imperial Rescripts 193–305 AD*, Oxford.

Hooper, W. D., and Ash, H. B. (transl.) 1934: *Cato and Varro. On Agriculture*, Cambridge, MA.

Houston, G. 2014: *Inside Roman Libraries: Book Collections and Their Management in Antiquity*, Chapel Hill, NC.

Jones, A. H. M. 1949: 'The Roman Civil Service (Clerical and Sub-Clerical Grades)', *Journal of Roman Studies* 39, 38–55.

Kolb, A. 1993: *Die kaiserliche Bauverwaltung in der Stadt Rom: Geschichte und Aufbau der cura operum publicorum unter dem Prinzipat*, Stuttgart.

Kolb, A. (ed.) 2006: *Herrschaftsstrukturen und Herrschaftspraxis. Konzepte, Prinzipien und Strategien der Administration im römischen Kaiserrecht*, Berlin.

König, A. 2011. 'Knowledge and Power in Frontinus' on Aqueducts', in T. Whitmarsh and J. König (eds), *Ordering Knowledge in the Roman Empire*, Cambridge.

Laurence, R., and Wallace-Hadrill, A. (eds) 1997: *Domestic Space in the Roman World: Pompeii and Beyond*, Portsmouth, RI.

Lintott, A. W. 1993: *Imperium Romanum: Politics and Administration*, London.

Lintott, A. W. 1999: *The Constitution of the Roman Republic*, Oxford.

Lo Cascio, E. 1994: 'The Size of the Roman Population: Beloch and the Meaning of the Augustan Census Figures', *Journal of Roman Studies* 84, 23–40.

Lopez Garcia, A., forthcoming: 'Fora Litibus Omnia Fervent: The Transfer of the Tribunals in Rome from the Forum to the Courtroom'.

Lopez Garcia, A., and Bueno Guardia, M. 2021: 'Typology and Multifunctionality of Public Libraries in Rome and the Empire', *Journal of Eastern Mediterranean Archaeology & Heritage Studies* 9(3), 247–277.

Luciani, F. 2017: 'Cittadini come domini, cittadini come patroni. Rapporti tra servi publici e città prima e dopo la manomissione', in M. Dondin-Payre and N. Tran (eds), *Esclaves et maîtres dans le monde romain. Expressions épigraphiques des liens et relations*, Rome, 1–18.

Marchese, M. E. 2007: 'La Prefettura Urbana a Roma: una tentativo di localizzazione attraverso le epigrafi', *Mélanges de l'École Française de Rome* 119, 613–634.

Martinez, V., and Finn Senseney, M. 2013: 'The Professional and His Books: Special Libraries in the Roman World', in J. König et al. (eds), *Ancient Libraries*, Cambridge, 401–417.

Maschek, D. 2018: 'Not *Census* but *Deductio*: Reconsidering the "Ara of Domitius Ahenobarbus"', *Journal of Roman Studies* 108, 27–52.

Mazzei, P. 2009: '*Tabularium – aerarium* nelle fonti letterarie ed epigrafiche', *Atti della Accademia Nazionale dei Lincei, Classe di Scienze morali, storiche e filologiche. Rendiconti* Ser. 9a 20(2), 275–378.

Millar, F. 1964: 'The Aerarium and Its Officials Under the Empire', *Journal of Roman Studies* 54, 33–40.

Millar, F. 1992: *The Emperor in the Roman World* (2nd ed.), London.

Moatti, C. (ed.) 1998: *La mémoire perdue: recherches sur l'administration romaine*, Rome.

Mols, S. 1999: *Wooden Furniture in Herculaneum*, Giesen.

Mommsen, T. 1871–1888: *Römisches Staatsrecht I-III* (3rd ed.), Leipzig.

Moneta, C., and Schallmayer, E. 2006: 'Principia, Praetorium und Augustus: Architektur als verkörperte Staatsidee', *Saalburg-Jahrbuch* 56, 115–125.

Nippel, W. 1995: *Public Order in Ancient Rome*, Cambridge.

Nörr, D. 1981: 'Zur Reskriptenpraxis in der hohen Prinzipatszeit: Wolfgang Kunkel zum Gedächtnis', *Zeitschrift der Savigny-Stiftung für Rechtsgeschichte: Romanistische Abteilung* 98, 1–46.

Peachin, M. 1996: *Iudex Vice Caesaris: Deputy Emperors and the Administration of Justice During the Principate*, Stuttgart.

Peachin, M. 2006: 'Frontinus and the Creation of a New Administrative Office', in A. Kolb (ed.), *Herrschaftsstrukturen und Herrschaftspraxis. Konzepte, Prinzipien und Strategien der Administration im römischen Kaiserrecht*, Berlin, 79–87.

Pina Polo, F. 2011: *The Consul at Rome: The Civil Functions of the Consuls in the Roman Republic*, Cambridge and New York.

Posner, E. 1972: *Archives in the Ancient World*, Cambridge.

Potter, D. S. 2011: 'Holding Court in Republican Rome (105–44)', *American Journal of Philology* 132, 59–80.

Purcell, N. 1983: 'The Apparitores: A Study in Social Mobility', *PBSR* 51, 125–173.

Purcell, N. 1988: 'The Arts of Government', in J. Boardman (ed.), *The Roman World*, Oxford, 150–181.

Purcell, N. 1993: 'Atrium Libertatis', *PBSR* 61, 125–155.

Purcell, N. 1995: 'Forum Romanum (The Republican Period)', in E. M. Steinby (ed.), *Lexicon Topographicum Urbis Romae II*, Roma, 325–336.

Purcell, N. 2010: 'Roman Urbanism', in A. Barchiesi and W. Scheidel (eds), *The Oxford Handbook of Roman Studies*, Oxford, 579–592.

Rémy, B., Brissaud, L., Mathieu, N., and Prisset, J.-L. 2011: 'Un service officiel des eaux ("cura aquarum") à Vienne?: le témoignage d'un tuyau de plomb découvert à Saint-Romain-en-Gal (Rhône)', *Zeitschrift für Papyrologie und Epigraphik* 179, 239–243.

Richards, E. R. 1991. *The Secretary in the Letters of Paul*, Tübingen.

Richardson, L. Jr. 1973: 'The Tribunals of the Praetors of Rome', *MDAIR* 80, 219–233.
Richardson, L. 1992: *A New Topographical Dictionary of Ancient Rome*, London and Baltimore, MD.
Riggsby, A. M. 1997: '"Public" and "Private" in Roman Culture: The Case of the *Cubiculum*', *Journal of Roman Archaeology* 10, 36–56.
Robinson, O. F. 1992: *Ancient Rome. City Planning and Administration*, London and New York.
Ruciński, S. 2009: *Praefectus Urbi: Le Gardien de l'ordre public à Rome sous le Haut-Empire Romain*, Poznań.
Russell, A. 2016: *The Politics of Public Space in Republican Rome*, Cambridge.
Santalucia, B. 2012: 'Incendiari, ladri, servi fuggitivi: i grattacapi del "praefectus vigilum"', *Index: quaderni camerti di studi romanistici = international survey of Roman law* 40, 387–406.
Schäfer, F. 2014: *Praetoria: Paläste zum Wohnen und Verwalten in Köln und anderen römischen Provinzhauptstädten*, Mainz.
Schäfer, T. 1989: *Imperii insignia: sella curulis und fasces: zur Repräsentation römischer Magistrate*, Mainz.
Scheidel, W. 2007a: 'Demography', in W. Scheidel, I. Morris, and R. Saller (eds), *The Cambridge Economic History of the Greco-Roman World*, Cambridge, 38–86.
Scheidel, W. 2007b: 'Slavery, in W. Scheidel, I. Morris, and R. Saller (eds), *The Cambridge Economic History of the Greco-Roman World*, Cambridge, 89–113.
Schofield, R. (transl.) 2009: *Vitruvius. On Architecture*, London.
Schöpe, B. 2014: *Der römische Kaiserhof in severischer Zeit (193–235 n. Chr.)*, Stuttgart.
Segenni, S. 2005: 'Frontino, gli archivi della "cura aquarum" e l'acquedotto tardo repubblicano di Amiternum: (*CIL*, I² 1853 = *ILLRP*, 487)', *Athenaeum* 93, 603–618.
Torrent, A. 2012: 'La *cura annonae* en lex. Irn. 75: Un intento de explicación en clave económica del control de los mercados', *Index: quaderni camerti di studi romanistici = International Survey of Roman Law* 40, 640–669.
Treggiari, S. 1998: 'Home and Forum: Cicero between "Public" and "Private"', *Transactions of the American Philological Society* 128, 1–23.
Tucci, P. L. 2013–2014: 'A New Look at the Tabularium and the Capitoline Hill', *Rendiconti della Pontificia Accademia Romana di Archeologia* 86, 43–123.
Tuori, K. 2016: *The Emperor of Law: The Emergence of Roman Imperial Adjudication*, New York and Oxford.
Tuori, K. 2018: 'Pliny and the Uses of the Aerarium Saturni as an Administrative Space', *Arctos: Acta Philologica Fennica* 52, 199–230.
Tuori, K. 2020: 'Breaking Chairs: *Sella Curulis* in Roman Law, Identity and Memory', *Arctos: Acta Philologica Fennica* 54, 257–284.
Tuori, K., and Nissin, L. (eds) 2015: *Public and Private in the Roman House and Society*, Portsmouth, RI.
Upex, S. G., Challands, A., Hall, J., Jackson, R., Peacock, D., and Wild, F. C. 2011: 'The Praetorium of Edmund Artis: A Summary of Excavations and Surveys of the Palatial Roman Structure at Castor, Cambridgeshire 1828–2010', *Britannia* 42, 23–112.
Vitucci, G. 1956: *Ricerche sulla praefectura urbi in età imperiale (sec. I-III)*, Rome.
von Premerstein, A. 1900. 'A Commentariis', in *Pauly-Wissowas Real-Encyclopädie IV 1*, Stuttgart, 743–744.
Wallace-Hadrill, A. 1994: *Houses and Society in Pompeii and Herculaneum*, Princeton, NJ.
Weiss, E. 1929: 'Statio', in *Pauly-Wissowas Real-Encyclopädie III A (2.6)*, Stuttgart, 2210–2213.

Weiss, J. 1932: 'Tabularium', in *Pauly-Wissowas Real-Encyclopädie IV A (2.8)*, Stuttgart, 1962–1964.
Welin, E. 1953: *Studien zur Topographie des Forum Romanum*, Lund.
Wilcken, U. 1920: 'Zu den Kaiserreskripten', *Hermes* 55, 1–42.
Williams, W. 1980: 'The Publication of Imperial Subscripts', *Zeitschrift für Papyrologie und Epigraphik* 40, 283–294.
Williams, W. 1986: 'Epigraphic Texts of Imperial Subscripts: A Survey', *Zeitschrift für Papyrologie und Epigraphik* 66, 181–207.
Winterling, A. A. 2009: *Politics and Society in Imperial Rome*, Malden, MA.
Wojciech, K. 2010: *Die Stadtpräfektur im Prinzipat*, Bonn.
Zaccaria Ruggiu, A. 2005: *Spazio privato e spazio pubblico nella città romana*, Rome.
Zevi, F. 1993: 'Per l'identificazione della *Porticus Minucia Frumentaria*', *Mélanges de l'École Française de Rome* 105, 661–708.
Zevi, F. 2012: 'VI, 47. Ara degli Scribi', in R. Friggeri, M. G. Granino Cecere, and G. L. Gregori (eds), *Terme di Diocleziano. La collezione epigrafica*, Milano, 355–361.

Part II
The Space of the Magistrate and Politics

4 Legislative Voting in the Forum Romanum

David Rafferty

I Introduction

One of the central themes in Amy Russell's 2016 monograph *The Politics of Public Space in Republican Rome* is the transformation of the Forum Romanum into a political space, one dominated by formal political action and accompanying expectations around how citizens should behave.[1] While in recent decades scholars have mostly been concerned with *contiones*, less formal political meetings at which an elite orator spoke and the citizen audience listened, in this chapter I focus on *comitia*, the voting assemblies of the Roman People and of the plebs. It was at these assemblies that citizens voted and so *acted* – as citizens. I argue that the politicisation of the Forum was in large part the result of the relocation of *comitia* from the smaller space of the Comitium, located between the Curia Hostilia and the Rostra, out into the wider Forum. While voting, crowds of citizens dominated the public space in their capacity as citizens and made the Forum space into political space through this action.

This move is datable to the 140s B.C.E., but it was not a one-off. Over the following generation, we see other changes to the way legislative *comitia* took place and in the physical infrastructure of public politics in the Forum. Speakers on the Rostra turned from facing an audience in the Comitium to an audience in the wider Forum; they also began to use the platform at the front of the Temple of Castor and Pollux as an alternative place from which to speak and hold legislative *comitia*. The Temple of Castor was twice remodelled, with its speaking platform made more suitable for voting. Legislation was passed to narrow the voting gangways (*pontes*). The secret written ballot was introduced for assemblies of various sorts. I argue here that, cumulatively, these changes are best interpreted as having the effect (and perhaps the intention) of making it easier for larger numbers of Roman citizens to vote with greater integrity in the process.

I also make a secondary argument in this chapter: a new attempt to understand the function and location of the voting gangways (*pontes*, literally 'bridges'). This is deliberately tentative. Our evidence is poor and untrustworthy, and more than one interpretation is possible.

II The Voting Procedure

Much about voting was formulaic, to the extent that some scholarship has seen it primarily as a consensus ritual.[2] But if it is true that the Romans were greatly concerned with the observance of correct procedure, it is equally true that they held substantive concerns about how voting on laws should take place. *Comitia* could only be held at Rome itself; Camillus's speech in Livy is proof that there was a powerful feeling, not just religious in nature, against public political activity happening anywhere other than at Rome (5.52.15–17; cf. 3.20.6–7, 7.16.7–8). *Comitia* could only be summoned by a magistrate or tribune with the right of treating with the People, and he had to operate from a *templum*. Laws had to be passed by all thirty-five tribes (at least in the tribal assembly which was almost invariably the venue for legislation), and the whole event had to take place on a single day – according to the augural law – which had to be *dies comitialis* and not a *nundinae*.[3] Together these concerns amounted to unchangeable parameters which governed how laws could legitimately be made and how voting could legitimately take place.

Most laws in the late Republic were passed in a tribal assembly summoned by a tribune of the plebs, so to keep this account simple I will only describe the process of those assemblies. In any event, the procedure when a consul or praetor presided was not much different.[4] The vote took place in the Forum, with either the Rostra or the tribunal (speaking platform) at the front of the Temple of Castor serving as the base. Beginning at dawn, the tribune held a preliminary *contio* at which he read out the text of the law and (perhaps) spoke in its favour; any such speech need not be very long. Then he told the assembled crowd to disperse (*discedite!*), i.e. separate into their tribes and clear the space required for voting. The tribune then conducted an allotment (*sortitio*) to determine which tribe would vote first; tribes voted sequentially in legislative *comitia*, as opposed to elections where they voted simultaneously. The voters gathered in an undifferentiated mass to hear this preliminary speech but had to organise themselves into tribes for the vote itself. Together with their fellow-tribesmen, voters filed up over the steps or gangways (*pontes*) and received a small wax tablet from an attendant (*custos*) standing below the *pons*. This tablet was marked with V and A (*uti rogas* for 'yes' and *antiquo* for 'no'). The voter scratched out whichever letter he did not want and dropped the tablet into a wicker basket (*cista*), from which the votes were taken away to be counted. The voter then left the *pons* on the other side. When each tribe's vote had been counted, the result was announced. Eighteen tribes were needed for a majority, but all thirty-five tribes needed to actually vote.

The evidence for all this is remarkably thin. The best image we have, and an important one for all my arguments, is a denarius produced by the moneyer P. Nerva in c. 113 (*RRC* 292/1; Figure 4.1). In it we see a voter on the *pons* being handed his ballot by a *custos* from below: from that position, the *custos* cannot see how the voter marks his ballot. To the right, another voter deposits his ballot into the *cista*. Taylor interpreted this coin differently: for her, the *custos* was the man on the *pons*

Legislative Voting in the Forum Romanum 81

Figure 4.1 Reverse of denarius of P. Nerva, c.110 B.C.E.
Source: *RRC* 292/1, American Numismatic Society, ID 1944.100.598.

handing the ballot down to the voter who was about to walk onto it. But I agree with most other scholars in thinking her wrong about this. Both figures above are togate while the figure below is smaller, and so visually less important – a point Crawford makes. The *pons* itself is also important, as this is the only image we have of one. On the coin, it is flat and level, about one metre off the ground – as it comes up to the *custos*' waist. It appears to be supported by latticework, although it is not quite clear what the cross-hatched design is. At the end of the *pons* is the basket into which the figure on the right puts his ballot; this basket is raised on a stand so that the ballot is deposited at shoulder height. Finally, there is a double line behind the standing figures, at about waist height; this may be another structure, but it is not clear enough for us to be certain. Mouritsen seems to me wrong to interpret the two voters on the coin as 'a visual compression of two stages in a sequence', since a coin is much more likely to remove figures and simplify a picture than to add them and complicate it.[5]

For now, we can draw a few implications from this simplified account. Above all, voting is a process that involves movement – it is entirely unlike standing in the audience at a *contio*. In particular, voting requires the coordinated movement of crowds of people. Obviously, this requires a considerable amount of space. But it also temporarily creates meaningful spaces: the elevated *pontes*; the inaugurated *templum* from which the tribune presides (and, perhaps, on which the act of voting takes place); the roped-off tribal pens.[6] Finally, it involves alternating periods of waiting and action for the assembled citizens: the whole process takes several hours. It helps to imagine the scene in a crowded Forum: the citizens of one tribe filing onto the gangways to give their vote, while those of the next tribe wait for their turn, and the tribes which have already voted, their duty done for the moment, enjoy the Forum and wait for the result.

III Changes to Procedure

In the second half of the second century B.C.E., we see a series of changes to the procedure of voting on laws and to the physical environment in which voting took place. These were, in order:

145: The location for voting changed from the Comitium to the broader Forum (although probably some assemblies were still held in the Comitium).
130: The Lex Papiria changed the method by which citizens gave their votes, replacing an oral declaration with a written ballot.
119: A Lex Maria made the voting gangways (*pontes*) narrower.

Considering the evidence for each will allow us to make the meaning and context clearer.

The first change was the move from the Comitium to the open space of the Forum for the purpose of voting. This is attested by two passages:[7]

> By the way, Crassus was the first man to begin the practice of facing towards the Forum in treating with the people.
> *Atque is primus instituit in forum versus agere cum populo* (Cic., Amic. 96)

> Of the same family was that Gaius Licinius [Crassus] who, when he was tribune of the plebs, 365 years after the expulsion of the kings, was the first to lead the people, for the voting of laws, from the Comitium into the seven *iugera* of the Forum.
> *Eiusdem gentis C. Licinius, tr. pl. cum esset, post reges exactos annis ccclxv primus populum ad leges accipiendas in septem iugera forensia e comitio eduxit.*
> (Varro *RR* 1.2.9)

At first glance, this looks very similar to an act which Plutarch ascribes to Gaius Gracchus in his first tribunate in 123: Gracchus turned on the Rostra so that, instead of facing the Curia as he addressed the People, he faced out into the wider Forum (Plut. *CGracch.* 5.3). Indeed, many scholars see the two events as a doublet, but that is unlikely[8]. Plutarch places Gracchus's act in the context of his enormous popularity and his early demagogic legislation; it is also connected to the Rostra rather than the Forum itself. Moreover, Plutarch is talking about *contiones*, whereas both Cicero and Varro explicitly use the legal language of *comitia* when discussing the act of Crassus.[9] Finally, there is no obvious point of connection between Gracchus and Crassus which might explain Plutarch's confusion: the two men were neither contemporaries nor closely related. It is better to regard these as two separate incidents: Crassus moved voting from the Comitium into the Forum, while Gaius Gracchus turned on the Rostra for his *contiones*. However, we need not follow Plutarch in believing Gracchus was the first to do this.[10]

Most scholars (of those who accept the two incidents were separate) interpret Crassus's action in 145 as a response to the Comitium being too small, which is indeed the simplest and most logical interpretation.[11] However, like Gracchus, Crassus is imagined to have turned on the Rostra so that he faced out into the Forum rather than towards the Curia. But this need not be the case. Cicero says nothing about the Comitium, saying only that Crassus faced the Forum. Varro says he moved the People from Comitium out into the Forum. Both of these are consistent with Crassus holding *comitia* from the tribunal, or speaking platform, of the Temple of Castor (as de Ruggiero believed). Moreover, both passages are strictly about *comitia* rather than *contiones*: Cicero's phrase is *agere cum populo* and Varro's is *ad leges accipiendas*, both terms which refer to voting on laws rather than anything to do with speech. Most recent scholarship on this question takes its lead from Lily Ross Taylor, who dismisses de Ruggiero's suggestion. However, her only reason for disagreeing with de Ruggiero was her understanding of the building phases of the Temple of Castor, based on Richter and Frank's work. She thought that it was only with the Metellan temple of c. 117 that lateral stairs were added to the tribunal, and so (in her mind) it became possible to vote at the Temple of Castor.[12] However, the Danish excavations prove that the lateral stairs were already a feature of the second century rebuilding.[13] The grounds for Taylor's disagreement with de Ruggiero thus no longer exist.

The Danish excavations of the Temple of Castor, published in the 1990s, reveal three republican phases: Temple I, built in the fifth century; a partial remodelling in the second century which the archaeologists call IA; and the temple completely rebuilt by Metellus Dalmaticus in c. 117 ('the Metellan temple').[14] The IA phase is of most interest here, as the modern excavation 'has revealed much that is new and resulted in a radically different interpretation and reconstruction of this temple phase'.[15] Nielsen and Poulsen do not date it any more firmly than 'second century' but speculate upon a connection to a Forum fire in 210 and Aemilius Paullus's censorship in 164. They base this date primarily on the use of concrete, which they think was first used in the Temple of Magna Mater in the 190s.

However, this is now in doubt. Mogetta's more recent work argues that the first datable use of concrete is in the Porticus of Caecilius Metellus, built soon after 146.[16] This is, coincidentally, around the time C. Crassus moved voting out of the Comitium. It is also, coincidentally, around the time the censor Scipio Aemilianus gave a speech *pro aede Castoris*, which very likely means from the tribunal of the new temple.[17] This collection of coincidences makes it plausible that the IA phase was built about 146, and so that it was the existence of an alternate speaking platform in the Forum that led C. Crassus to move voting *comitia* – or, indeed the opposite, that it was Crassus's action which led to the rebuilding of the Temple of Castor in this form.[18] If this is the case, we can entirely forget the idea that Crassus made any change at all to how voting in the Comitium took place. His change – or, at least, a change of about this time – was to move the seat of that voting from the Rostra to the Temple of Castor.

The next change was the written ballot for voting on laws, introduced by a Lex Papiria in 130. Before this time, the voter spoke his vote to an official called a *rogator* who kept a tally. The written ballot was nearly as simple: a voter had merely to erase one of two letters on a wax tablet. It thus required next to no literacy to exercise. However, it did require some logistical apparatus: baskets to collect the votes, people to count and tally them, and above all an adequate supply of wax tablets. This was a change from the oral system and may also have required more space, perhaps a separate area for counting. The written ballot is not likely to have slowed the voting process: the count may even have become faster (in that counting could now be done separately and more efficiently). I concentrate on these concrete aspects deliberately, as scholarship has before now aimed more at the political implications than the practicalities.[19]

The Lex Papiria in 130, which covered legislative assemblies, was the third ballot law to be introduced. A Lex Gabinia was passed for voting in elections in 139 and a Lex Cassia for popular trials in 137, and these laws are often analysed as a group. Feig Vishnia astutely notes the likely effects of the Lex Gabinia on elections: it speeded up the voting process (if, as likely, voters filled out their ballots while waiting in line) and improved the accuracy and reliability of the count.[20] With the whole process watched over by *custodes* acting as agents for the candidates, any sharp practice could easily be identified (e.g. Plut. *Cato min.* 46.2). The candidates, then, were the main beneficiaries. But Lundgreen is sceptical of our ability to know *why* the ballot laws were introduced. He believes we can only reconstruct the technical details and trace consequences from there.[21] This seems right: apart from the methodological considerations (for which Lundgreen appeals to Koselleck), the written ballot was a practice apparently without precedent in Roman experience, and so we should expect even more unintended consequences than usual. Beyond this, we should not assume that the three laws were introduced for the same reasons: they covered different spheres of popular activity, while the experience of earlier laws informed the later ones.[22] For instance, the benefits to candidates which Feig Vishnia identifies in the Lex Gabinia had no meaning in legislative assemblies: there were no obviously interested third parties (beyond the *populus Romanus* itself) watching for any misdeeds. Moreover, the risk of significant mistakes in registering the simple difference between Yes and No (compared to distinguishing between possibly dozens of candidates in elections) seems remote, to say the least.

But here we encounter the place which the written ballot enjoyed in *libertas*-ideology in the first century.[23] That it had such a place, that the secret written ballot was regarded as a bastion of popular freedom, seems clear from the numismatic evidence and from Cicero's discussion at *De legibus* 3.34–37 (cf. Asc. 78C).[24] This political value probably emerged quickly. That is, while the Lex Gabinia in 139 may have been passed for other reasons, the secrecy of the written ballot, and its importance in *libertas populi*, was soon regarded as a good in itself. So although this law may not have been passed in order to extend the *libertas* of the Roman People, it had that effect and was seen to have that effect; it thus connects to a general tendency in laws of this period.[25] This adequately explains the extension of the written ballot to voting on laws in 130. But there was also a specific need for secrecy in the legislative ballot at that time. The Lex Papiria was passed in the immediate aftermath of Tiberius Gracchus's death and, perhaps more importantly, the mass execution of his followers. In this context, protecting the People in the exercise of their vote was not an abstraction, but a matter of life and death.

The third change was the law passed in 119 by C. Marius as tribune which narrowed the voting gangways or *pontes*. We know it from Cicero's discussion of his own proposed ballot law in *De legibus* and from a reference in Plutarch.[26]

> This is the wording of my ballot law: 'let them be known to the optimates, free to the plebs'. This law has the function of voiding all those laws which were passed later, which conceal the ballot in every way – that no one should look at it, ask for it, or question the voters. The law of Marius made the voting passages narrow. Most such laws are against bribery, and I have no objection to that.
>
> *Sic enim a me recitata lex est de suffragiis: 'optimatibus nota, plebi libera sunto'. Quae lex hanc sententiam continet, ut omnes leges tollat, quae postea latae sunt, quae tegunt omni ratione suffragium, 'ne quis inspiciat tabellam', 'ne roget', 'ne appellet'; pontes etiam lex Maria fecit angustos. Quae si opposita sunt ambitiosis, ut sunt fere, non reprehendo* (Cic., *Leg.* 3.38–39).

> While serving as tribune he [Marius] introduced a law concerning the mode of voting, which, as it was thought, would lessen the power of the nobles in judicial cases.
>
> ἐν δὲ τῇ δημαρχίᾳ νόμον τινὰ περὶ ψηφοφορίας γράφοντος αὐτοῦ δοκοῦντα τῶν δυνατῶν ἀφαιρεῖσθαι τὴν περὶ τὰς κρίσεις ἰσχύν.
>
> (Plut., *Mar.* 4.2)

This, too, has been variously interpreted. Both ancient sources connect the law with removing outside influence or surveillance on voters. Feig Vishnia asserts that the law dealt with trials only, and bases this primarily on Plutarch.[27] While this is possible, especially on the model of the earlier ballot laws which dealt with different types of assembly, it seems unlikely. The context in Cicero is clearly much wider than judicial assemblies which were, in any case, long obsolete by the time *De legibus* was written. Moreover, the *pontes* were part of the physical infrastructure for assemblies, and both judicial and legislative assemblies were held in the same places, with the same tribal organisations, and using very similar voting procedures. It makes no sense why the *pontes* would be narrow for one and wide for another.

However, judicial assemblies may well have been the immediate catalyst for the law. Marius was tribune the year after L. Opimius (*cos.* 121) was acquitted in a *iudicium populi* in which he was defended by the consul C. Papirius Carbo – the same Carbo who had passed the Lex Papiria a decade earlier. I am not the first to suggest that Marius's law was a response to the failure to convict Opimius.[28] But it seems of particular interest that the defending advocate in that case was the sitting consul, a man with *coercitio* at his disposal to use against citizens whose votes displeased him. Moreover, this trial took place in a highly charged political atmosphere and in the immediate aftermath of the extra-judicial murder of many of Gaius Gracchus's followers. Carbo may have used his consular power to intimidate the voters but, even if he did not, the possibility may have been in the air.

Marshall and Mouritsen have suggested that before 119 the *custodes* stood on the *pontes* themselves and from there distributed the ballots to voters.[29] There is no positive evidence for this: it is an inference from Marius narrowing the *pontes* and from Cicero's emphasis on this measure liberating voters from surveillance. But if that is the case (as seems likely), then it is a fascinating example of a later law being used to solve the (presumably) unforeseen consequences of an earlier law. After all, intimidation by *custodes* or others could only matter in the context of a written ballot; beforehand, voters had publicly declared their vote for all to hear. Indeed, Cicero says here that there were multiple laws dealing with the technicalities of voting and that most such laws were directed against *ambitus*. This makes sense in that a secret ballot makes it uncertain whether a bribed voter carries out his end of the bargain, and those doing the bribing would exert themselves to ensure they got their money's worth. On this reading, Marius's reform (and these other laws) closed a loophole that had only opened a decade earlier. This fits both with what Lundgreen calls the casuistry of Roman legislation and with Morrell's arguments about programmes of reform in republican Rome.[30] It also matches a pattern we see in post-Sullan politics, where changes to *ambitus* laws to combat one abuse merely opened up new possibilities which required further laws to combat them in turn.

Finally, we could see a connection with the near-contemporary remodelling of the Temple of Castor (as discussed earlier). Mouritsen has suggested that the platform at the front of the Metellan temple (of c. 117) had space for four *pontes* abreast.[31] On this reading, narrower *pontes* would have the additional effect of allowing more *pontes* to fit into the same space on the *templum*, which in turn would allow more voters to vote more quickly. More generally, Marius's law is a good example of quite detailed legislation governing the process of voting, down to the level of the width of physical equipment, and Cicero tells us it was not the only such law.

IV How Many Voters?

As noted, Mouritsen suggested that the tribunal of the Temple of Castor could accommodate four *pontes* abreast after Marius's law. This is an extension of

Taylor's observation that, as *pontes* always appears in the plural when talking about legislative *comitia*, voters voted on two parallel *pontes*.[32] Generally, the principle of multiple parallel *pontes* would be familiar from electoral voting in the Campus Martius where the thirty-five tribes voted simultaneously across thirty-five *pontes*. Mouritsen's seems to me the better argument here (although later in this chapter I offer an alternate location for the *pontes*), so let us use his figures as a starting point, to see if we can work out how many citizens were, in practice, able to vote. Mouritsen follows up his argument with a guess about speed: 'it would seem that hardly more than four voters could have passed through a *pons* each minute. There was probably only one voter at a time on the *pons*'.[33] But there is no reason to think so. It is much more likely that ballots were handed out to voters as quickly as the *custos* could do so. On general grounds Staveley's estimate is preferable: He suggests fifteen voters per *pons* per minute.[34] Still, let us be conservative and use ten voters per minute, with a three-minute break between one tribe and the next. On those figures, and four *pontes* abreast, 10,000 citizens could vote on a law in about six hours and 20,000 in about ten hours. That seems eminently possible if we assume the first ballot was cast an hour after dawn – to allow for the preliminary *contio* and the division into tribal groups. The process would be even faster if the first eighteen tribes all voted in favour and the remainder sent forward a handful of voters to finish the process quickly.

What were citizens doing while this long voting process was taking place? Ovid (*Fasti* 1.53) refers to the day 'when it's lawful to pen the People in their enclosures' (*populum ius est includere saeptis*), but Fraccaro makes a good argument on practical grounds that tribal groups did not spend the whole time waiting behind their ropes.[35] He thinks an enclosure was created for the next tribe to vote, but that reasons of space prohibited making thirty-five separate tribal enclosures within the Forum. Indeed, had this been necessary, it was easier to use the Ovile in the Campus Martius which was already set up for the purpose. With this in mind, we return to Russell's picture of the Forum as a crossroads, a continually bustling hub of the city's day-to-day life.[36] Rather than spending their time waiting patiently behind a fence, we should imagine those citizens waiting to vote (or those who have already voted and who are waiting for the result) as enjoying the amenities of central Rome, just like Macrobius's dice players (3.16.15). There is also the other side of the coin: that many of those simply passing through the Forum were themselves Roman citizens and perfectly entitled to join their tribe and vote.

One of Mouritsen's overall arguments is that we should not expect high citizen participation anyway, since ordinary Romans were largely uninterested in politics and practically debarred from it by the lack of remuneration.[37] The result was 'a political process in which only a very small section of the population ever took part'.[38] To a great extent, Mouritsen rests the legislative side of this claim on Cicero's reference to *comitia* in which 'scarcely five in each tribe, and those not from their own tribe, are found to vote' (*Sest*. 109). This is supported by the parallel reference on the Tabula Hebana (ll. 32–33), and Mouritsen treats this as an accurate description of some (perhaps many) *comitia*.[39] But Cicero is not a strong support here: we are in the middle of one of the most partisan passages of one of his most partisan speeches. Cicero is attacking the legitimacy of every law Clodius ever passed as tribune and every *contio* he held, in contrast to the True People, the *verus populus*, who were bitterly opposed to the tribune (108). Robert Kaster is right to comment that 'the tendentious character of these remarks seems too often to have been ignored' and 'they are still taken at face value, imprudently' by Mouritsen.[40] If we accept Cicero's claim here as literal and truthful, presumably we must also accept as literal and truthful his claim that everyone at Clodius's *contiones* and *comitia* had been hired (106), or that the crowd for the passage of the Lex Gabinia in 67 filled the entire Forum and every available spot on a temple (*Manil.* 44). Simply, this passage of the *Pro Sestio* is no evidence at all for the attendance at *comitia*.

V The Function of the *Pontes*

So far. we have looked at changes to voting procedure and their effects. Now I will make a detailed argument about the function and location of the *pontes*; it is not obvious why the Romans used *pontes* at all, and they are central to any attempt to understand how voters moved. But we should note that the arguments I present here do not (much) affect the other arguments made in this chapter about what meaning we should attach to the changes to voting procedure in the second century. Rather, they aim to clarify what those changes might actually have been.

The most intriguing part of Roman procedure is the use of voting gangways, or *pontes*. They were temporary structures and so have left no archaeological trace, while our only visual evidence is Nerva's coin. This has left scholars to speculate. For instance, Taylor's reconstruction of the voting process after 145 was that the *pontes* were temporary wooden structures attached to the front of the Rostra (i.e. on the Forum side). Voters assembled in the Forum and were handed their ballots, walked up onto one of two *pontes* and deposited their votes into a basket (*cista*) which was on the *pons*: this is the part of the process represented on Nerva's coin. They then walked onto the Rostra (at a higher level than the *pontes*, so this must have required more steps) and down the other side into the Comitium (although we have already seen why movement from Forum into Comitium was unlikely). For voting at the Temple of Castor, the two *pontes* approached the temple from the front, with voters either walking up onto the tribunal and then leaving via the lateral stairs (in a similar process to the Rostra), or (if the *pontes* were lower) exiting directly onto those lateral stairs without climbing onto the tribunal.[41] That said, her reconstruction is not particularly clear and seems unnecessarily complex. The second option was also impossible during the IA phase, as there was a thin wall shielding the lateral steps from the front, meaning the *pontes* could not lead onto them from that direction. Mouritsen provides a much more satisfactory version, at least for the Temple of Castor: that voters came up one lateral stair, voted on *pontes* along the long east-west axis of the platform, and then left via the other lateral stair (see Figure 4.3).[42] He suggests that the platform of the Metellan temple was deep enough to fit four *pontes* abreast. The movement of voters is quite straightforward in Mouritsen's version.

However, there are difficulties with both these reconstructions. To my mind, given that we have so little evidence, any explanation for the *pontes* should start

Legislative Voting in the Forum Romanum 89

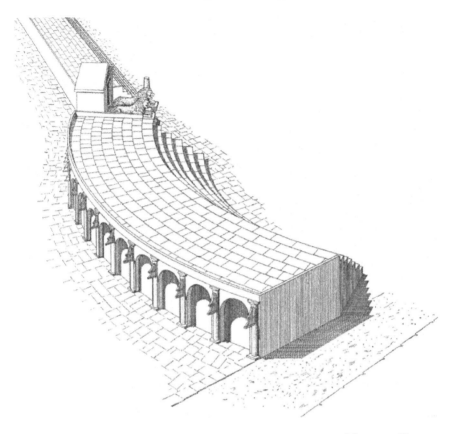

Figure 4.2 E. Gjerstad's reconstruction of the late-Republican Rostra ('Suggesto J').
Source: From Gjerstad 1941: 125.

with their function; the problem (as we shall see) is that any functional explanation that makes sense is difficult to reconcile with the evidence of Nerva's coin. That function seems clearly to be crowd control. Remember, for the Romans voting was fundamentally a process of movement, and that aspect (at least) was not altered by the changes to procedure we have discussed. Whether declaring their votes orally to a *rogator*, or depositing their written ballots into a *cista*, voters had to be organised to quickly pass a point in single file, and those waiting to vote had to be clearly separated from those who had already voted. So far, the benefits of some type of gangway are obvious. But there is more. Concentrating for the moment on the Rostra as the original location for voting, the voters of a single tribe assembled in the Comitium, filed up the steps onto the Rostra, and then moved off it on the other side and into the Forum. How this happened in practice – what the *pontes* looked like and what they did – depends on the archaeology of the Comitium and the Rostra. This is all highly uncertain (although the excavations currently underway in the Comitium will hopefully shed more light). The best representation we currently

90 *David Rafferty*

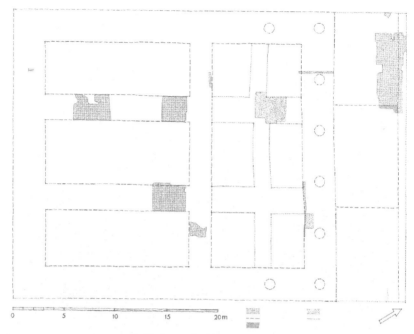

Fig. 61 – Reconstruction of the rebuilding (Temple I A).

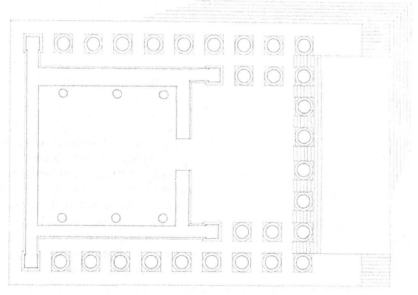

Fig. 101 – Reconstruction of the Metellan Temple. For a peripteral solution, see Fig. 100.

Figure 4.3 Plans of the Temple of Castor and Pollux: Temple Phase 1A and the Metellan temple.

Source: From Nielsen, Poulsen and Bilde 1992: 83 and 109. Reprinted with the permission of the author.

have of the Rostra is Gjerstad's (Figure 4.2), largely accepted by Coarelli and Chillet.[43] The essential features for our purpose are that the Rostra was somewhat curved and had steps on the Comitium side but a sheer drop on the Forum side, where the ships' prows were (and probably at each end as well). Therefore, steps were needed to move voters down into the Forum. However, while a gangway was clearly useful for crowd control, there was no practical need for that gangway to be raised, for it to be (giving it the Roman nickname) a *pons* rather than an *ovile* or *saepta*. If voters are moving from the Comitium onto the Rostra, there are already steps there to use. Yet Nerva's coin clearly depicts a raised *pons*.

Needless to say, this reconstruction is quite speculative: the details may well be wrong. In particular, we need to be wary about treating this coin as a realistic depiction of what voting looked like: coins are a difficult artistic medium to decipher. But what matters is understanding how *pontes* functioned in the process of voting.

VI   The Location of the *Pontes*

So far, I have accepted Taylor's assumption that the act of voting (that is, depositing the ballot) took place on the raised *templum* itself, that is the Rostra or the tribunal of the Temple of Castor. However, there is another explanation which is equally plausible: that the presiding officer watched over proceedings from that location, and probably the counting of the votes took place there too, but the *pontes* and the voters were in front of him on the Forum (or Comitium) floor. This is Cerutti's reconstruction, with which I agree in broad outline.[44] His argument is based on the height of the tribunal: too high to accommodate the voting process as it is shown on coins. 'Therefore, if voting took place at the temple it must have taken place not on the tribunal, but in front of it'.[45] He also appeals to the statement on the Tabula Hebana (l. 18) that voting baskets should be placed *ante tribunal*. The voting scene described in the Tabula Hebana is also one where the voting process is overlooked by magistrates. Finally, in all the evidence we have looked at, voters are never described as being on the tribunal itself. References to voting are always 'in the Forum' or 'in the Comitium', never 'on the Rostra', although I want to emphasise that the evidence overall is not conclusive one way or the other.

There is also Cicero's account at *Att.* 1.14.5, which only really makes sense if the *pontes* are separate from the speaking platform:[46]

> When the day came for the bill to be put to the Assembly under the terms of the senatorial decree, there was a flocking together of our goateed young bloods, the whole Catilinarian gang with little Miss Curio at their head, to plead for its rejection. Consul Piso, the proposer of the bill, spoke against it. Clodius' roughs had taken possession of the gangways. The voting papers were distributed without any 'ayes.' Suddenly up springs Cato to the platform and gives Consul Piso a spectacular dressing down, if one can apply such a term to a most impressive, powerful, in fact wholesome speech.
>
> *Nam cum dies venisset rogationi ex senatus consulto ferendae, concursabant barbatuli iuvenes, totus ille grex Catilinae duce filiola Curionis, et*

populum ut antiquaret rogabant. Piso autem consul, lator rogationis, idem erat dissuasor. operae Clodianae pontis occuparant, tabellae ministrabantur ita ut nulla daretur 'uti rogas'. hic tibi rostra Cato advolat, commulcium Pisoni consuli mirificum facit, si id est commulcium, vox plena gravitatis, plena auctoritatis, plena denique salutis.

Note that the *pontes* have already been set up and voting has already begun: Clodius' *operae* are already distributing ballots. Yet it appears that Piso is still occupying the tribunal; certainly there is room for Cato to jump up there and deliver a speech. It also seems likely that *rostra* here is generic for 'speaking platform' and so does not necessarily refer to the Rostra in the Comitium, but could be (and probably is) the tribunal of the Temple of Castor. Mouritsen's reconstruction, with up to four *pontes* abreast along the platform, does not leave room for this. And unlike other instances (e.g. Livy 25.3), on this occasion voting had already begun when the disturbance took place. Still, we cannot be too certain. Cicero may have some details wrong, or he may be talking about the original Rostra, rather than Castor's tribunal.

Vaahtera's objection to my and Cerutti's reconstruction is that the vote needed to take place inside a *templum*.[47] However, that is not certain. Vaahtera rightly points to the presiding magistrate's need to act from a *templum*, but his assertion that the People's answer also needed to be made in an inaugurated space is just that, an assertion.[48] It need not be true. As Berthelet argues, what mattered from an augural point of view was that the presiding magistrates operated *auspicato*, i.e. having taken preliminary auspices.[49] It was only he who had to act from a *templum*, not the People as well.

If voting did in fact take place in front of the Temple of Castor, rather than on the temple's tribunal, we may be able to reconcile the function of the *pontes* with their representation on Nerva's coin. The excavations on the Temple of Castor reveal that the floor of the Forum sloped down from east to west in the vicinity of the Temple, but the steepness of the slope was modified by paving work in the Forum. When the first temple was rebuilt in the second century (Temple IA), the slope from east to west was about 70cm across the width of the temple. But during the time of the Metellan temple this slope was 1.70m (although it is unclear to what extent this was affected by the repaving of the Forum in, probably, the 70s).[50] Traces have been found of steps at the front of the temple in the northwest corner, which filled the extra drop from the bottom of the tribunal to the Forum floor (see Figure 4.3). So, if the *pontes* were arranged in front of the tribunal, they would need to allow for this slope (although these frontal stairs would seem to prevent the *pontes* being attached directly to the front of the tribunal. That is, they would need to be placed a couple of metres out into the Forum). This allows us to envision how voting would take place: multiple parallel *pontes* on the sloping Forum floor in front of the Temple of Castor. The voters approach from the west, climb a ramp or a few steps onto the level gangway (which we see on Nerva's coin), proceed along it to deposit their ballot in the *cista*, and then exit the *pons* onto the Forum floor, which by now has risen to the same level.

While this reconstruction is coherent and makes good use of the evidence, it is not the only possible explanation. Our evidence, after all, is shaky: Nerva's coin is not likely to be a photographic image of what voting looked like, while it would not surprise us to learn Cicero had gotten his details wrong. To be told that we are unsure how voting happened is not a satisfying answer, but the evidence does not allow more. If anything, this chapter muddies the waters still further. But we are left with a relatively small boundary of the possible: whether on the tribunal of the Temple of Castor or in front of it, whether on the Rostra or within the Comitium, voters moved across *pontes* to deliver their vote. These *pontes* facilitated the quick movement of large crowds through the same space in order to vote, and so allowed large numbers of citizens to take part in the act of lawmaking.

VII Implications

Within a generation, much in legislative *comitia* changed. Physically, *comitia* moved from the Comitium into the Forum; the Temple of Castor was twice rebuilt and became a legislative site; the secret written ballot was introduced; the voting *pontes* were narrowed. And this was accompanied by changes in *contiones* (C. Gracchus turning on the Rostra, the use of the Temple of Castor again) and possibly also by changes in electoral procedure (although those fall outside the scope of this chapter). Even if we agree with Lundgreen (as I do) that Roman lawmaking was marked by a focus on particular changes rather than long-term programmes, this collection of discrete measures adds up to something substantial. Moreover, even individual changes to correct abuses need to have an idea in mind of what a better process should achieve – there needs to be some sort of guiding principle. Here, there was not a single act of reform, but a process over decades – we might be brave enough to call it a programme.[51] And to me the best way to interpret these changes is that they were trying to do two things: first, to allow larger numbers of citizens to vote and second, to ensure the integrity of each citizen's vote. At the very least, this speaks to a continuing concern with the mechanisms and infrastructure for making law, and with the effective rights of ordinary Roman citizens. And all within those parameters of *comitia* which were not subject to change: that voting had to take place at Rome, as a single event, presided over by a magistrate in a *templum*, and so on.

None of this happened in a vacuum, of course. These changes in legislative procedures were made at the same time as the tribunates and deaths of the Gracchi and the ideological polarisation which flowed out of them. The two decades after Marius's law were marked by a much more ideologically charged use of the *comitia*, as a vehicle for trials of individual ex-magistrates, and for legislation which tried to take over areas of public life previously under senatorial control. It is tempting to connect the *comitia*-based politics of the 100s to the change in legislative procedure I have described, but that temptation should be resisted. The two phenomena *may* be linked, but they need not be. It is interesting that we hear relatively little of any contemporary controversy over the ballot laws (as opposed to Cicero's retrospective condemnation of them), but we cannot do much with that information; given the desert of contemporary sources for the second century, it forms an argument from silence even weaker than such arguments typically are. The more interesting path forward is in comparing these changes with Morrell's other (tentatively identified) programmes of reform, to see if common features can be identified.[52] We should also ask which other mechanisms of public life were subject to change in this period. We see changes in court procedures, certainly, but not much in senatorial decision making or for magistrates.

There is also the question of public (or sacral) law, of what it meant for voting to take place in a *templum*. Following Berthelet, I have raised the possibility here that it was only the magistrate who needed to act from a *templum*, but that voters did not. That is, since a vote was formally the act of a magistrate asking a question, and the *populus* (or plebs) answering, then the question needed to be asked from a *templum*, and the answer heard from there, but the answer did not have to be given from there. If the idea is correct that early voting was by acclamation, then this was likely always true.[53] But I am reluctant to give a definite answer on this question.

Then there is the emotional content of the voting process, and the performance of Roman citizenship.[54] Since the 1990s scholarship has focused on the multiple ways in which Roman citizens performed their membership of the community within the Forum space. For instance, there is their role as the passive audience of a *contio*, and here scholars have emphasised the hierarchical relationship between speaker and audience.[55] Then there are the games, and triumphs, and elite funerals – and note here the powerful work of Favro and Johanson in trying to reconstruct the spatial experience of a spectator at an aristocratic funeral, what that person could see from different vantage points.[56] Our understanding of the experience of spectatorship in the Forum is enriched further by the reconstructions of how the piazza looked at different periods through the Digitales Forum Romanum project and through associated work on what spectators at *contiones* might be able to hear.[57] But in all these citizens were primarily spectators, notwithstanding Hölkeskamp's evocative claim (echoing Shakespeare, allegedly) that they were 'actors and spectators, too'.[58] Rather, it was only in voting that citizens became real 'actors'. And this is perhaps shown physically through another point which Hölkeskamp has emphasised (in connection with the city's monuments), that Roman visual culture 'gave high place to the highly placed'.[59] In *contiones*, the hierarchical distance between magistrate and citizen was made concrete by the magistrate's physical elevation, on a speaking platform which towered 2 or 3 metres above the crowd below.[60] But, if Mouritsen's reconstruction of the voting process is correct, then in the act of voting Roman citizens occupied those same elevated places: *they* stood in the *superior locus*. For a moment as individuals, and for hours as a collective, the *populus Romanus* saw the Forum as the magistrate saw it. One does not need much imagination to understand how this must have been highly meaningful to the ordinary citizen. A citizen felt himself to be a citizen by voting. And in doing so he was exercising that citizenship in its most powerful form, by making authoritative decisions on the affairs of his community.

Finally, there is Russell's argument about the takeover of the Forum by 'the political'. She says surprisingly little in her book about voting, but we need to put that activity back at the heart of this process of change in the Forum. While voting, Roman citizens occupied the Forum space *in their capacity as citizens*; that is, not primarily as people who just happened to be in Rome. The wearing of the toga for political action rendered this immediately visible. Domination of the space by the *populus Romanus* did what domination of space always does: it crowded out other uses of that space. The archaeological record shows how Russell's sanitised political space was created architecturally, but proper consideration of the changes to legislative practice show how this was also achieved behaviourally. After all, the coordinated movement of crowds of people is a memorable and impressive sight. It was this mass movement which went a long way to bringing 'the political' out of the axis of Curia-Comitium-Rostra and into the wider spaces of the Forum itself.

Notes

1 Russell 2016: 45.
2 Flaig 1995: 77–127.
3 Vaahtera 1993: 97.
4 My summary draws substantially on standard works on Roman legislative assemblies: Taylor 1966: xix, 175; Staveley 1972: 271; Nicolet 1980: 435.
5 Mouritsen 2001: 22. He also says (p. 21) that the coin represents voting in an election, which seems unlikely in view of the size of the ballots.
6 For the appropriateness of 'pens', see Ov., *Fasti* 1.54: *est quoque, quo populum ius est includere saeptis*.
7 Loeb translations, slightly modified.
8 Morstein-Marx 2004: 45–47; Russell 2016: 66.
9 A point made by Mouritsen 2001: 24. It is perhaps relevant that, strikingly, Plutarch refers to 'the people' here as *tōn pollōn* rather than *tou demou*, which downplays their constitutional role and emphasises the size of the crowd; I owe this observation to Christoph Lundgreen.
10 Taylor 1966: 22–23.
11 So Staveley 1972: 152; Nicolet 1980: 247; Coarelli 1985: 26; Humm 2019: §49. However, see Mouritsen 2001: 20 who argues that 'the initial incentive behind the transfer had been ideological rather than practical', wrongly in my view.
12 Taylor 1966: 41.
13 Nielsen et al. 1992: 84–86.
14 Nielsen et al. 1992.
15 Nielsen et al. 1992: 87.
16 Mogetta 2021: 66–68, 86, 88; Davies 2017: 84.
17 Festus 402L; Val. Max. 4.1.10; Cic., *Cluent*. 134. The speech attested by Festus gives the location; that attested by Cicero and Valerius Maximus gives the occasion as the *transvectio equitum* which Scipio presided over as censor. The identity of the two speeches is argued most recently by Gartrell 2021: 55.
18 So Davies 2017: 102–104, who suggests that it was Crassus's act which led to the rebuilding of the temple. In view of the uncertainty around dating, I am reluctant to commit to which direction the line of causality went.
19 E.g. Yakobson 1995: 426–442; Marshall 1997: 54–73. Lundgreen 2009 is a notable exception.
20 Feig Vishnia 2008: 337 and n. 23.
21 Lundgreen 2009: 38–39.
22 So Lundgreen 2009: 38: 'Die sukzessive Verabschiedung muss allerdings auch nicht zwangsläufig überraschen, bleibt die römische Gesetzgebung doch immer kasuistisch, auf den speziellen Anlass zugeschnitten'.

23 Arena 2012: 56–60.
24 See Marshall 1997 on the numismatic evidence.
25 Lundgreen 2009: 47–51 argues that Marius's law in 119 (on which see more later in this chapter) shows that secrecy in the ballot was a mirage. This is to miss both the ideological effect and that one's vote *could* be kept secret if desired.
26 The Cicero translation is Zetzel's; the Plutarch translation is the Loeb.
27 Feig Vishnia 2008: 338–340.
28 Marshall 1997: 61.
29 Marshall 1997: 60–61; Mouritsen 2001: 22 n. 14.
30 Lundgreen 2009: 38; Morrell forthcoming.
31 Mouritsen 2001: 21–22.
32 Taylor 1966: 41.
33 Mouritsen 2001: 22.
34 Staveley 1972: 186.
35 Fraccaro 1957: 253–254.
36 Russell 2016: 48.
37 Mouritsen 2001: 36–37.
38 Mouritsen 2001: 32.
39 Mouritsen 2001: 23–24.
40 Kaster 2006: 334.
41 Taylor 1966: 41–45.
42 Mouritsen 2001: 21–22.
43 Coarelli 1985: 370; Chillet 2019.
44 Cerutti 1998. Cerutti is primarily concerned to explain the stairs at the Temple of Castor which Clodius destroyed in 58; ironically, given how much in his article I agree with, I think he is wrong about that central point. The 'stairs' to which Cicero refers are much more likely to be those from the tribunal up to the pronaos, which according to the recent excavations continued between the columns. The bases of those columns stood around 1.5 metres higher than the stairs around them, which both created narrow passageways between the column bases and presented an appearance not unlike the ships' prows which decorated the original Rostra. It was easy to block access to the temple at this point.
45 Cerutti 1998: 299.
46 Loeb translation.
47 Vaahtera 1993: 111, 115–116. Note that this is a separate question from whether only the Rostra or the Comitium as a whole was a *templum*, on which see Coarelli 1985: 17.
48 Vaahtera 1993: 111: 'Even if the phrase *cum populo agere* is to be seen as a transaction of the magistrates, it nevertheless seems to include some sense of reciprocity; in other words it could refer both to the question placed before the people by the presiding officer, and the answer (i.e. the vote) of the people to this question. In this case the voting must also have taken place in a *templum*'. He struggles to reconcile this with the clearly non-*templum* status of the other places of assembly: 115–116.
49 Berthelet 2015: 237–240.
50 Nielsen et al. 1992: 84, 112.
51 See Morrell (forthcoming) on the possibility of reform programmes in republican Rome.
52 Morrell (forthcoming).
53 Acclamation: Staveley 1972: 157.
54 On performing citizenship (in a Greek context) see Duplouy 2018.
55 Morstein-Marx 2004: xiv, 313.
56 Favro and Johanson 2010.
57 Holter et al. 2019.
58 Hölkeskamp 2010: 58.
59 Hölkeskamp 2010: 65, quoting Kuttner 2004: 318.
60 Morstein-Marx 2004: 51; cf. Flaig 2001: 14.

References

Arena, V. 2012: *Libertas and the Practice of Politics in the Late Roman Republic*, Cambridge.
Berthelet, Y. 2015: *Gouverner avec les dieux: autorité, auspices et pouvoir, sous la République romaine et sous Auguste*, Paris.
Cerutti, S. M. 1998: 'P. Clodius and the Stairs of the Temple of Castor', *Latomus* 57, 292–305.
Chillet, C. 2019: 'Le comitium comme lieu de vote à Rome: Une relecture', in Borlenghi et al. (eds.), *Voter en Grèce, à Rome et en Gaule. Pratiques, Lieux et Finalités*, Lyon, 277–296.
Coarelli, F. 1985: *Il foro romano: Periodo repubblicano e augusteo*, Roma.
Davies, P. J. E. 2017: 'A Republican Dilemma: City or State? Or the Concrete Revolution Revisited', *Papers of the British School at Rome* 85, 71–107.
Duplouy, A. 2018: 'Citizenship as Performance', in A. Duplouy and R. Brock (eds), *Defining Citizenship in Archaic Greece*, Oxford, 249–274.
Favro, D., and Johanson, C. 2010: 'Death in Motion: Funeral Processions in the Roman Forum', *Journal of the Society of Architectural Historians* 69, 12–37.
Feig Vishnia, R. 2008: 'Written Ballot, Secret Ballot and the Iudicia Publica. A Note on the Leges Tabellariae (Cicero, De legibus 3.33 39)', *Klio* 90, 334–346.
Flaig, E. 1995: 'Entscheidung und Konsens. Zu den Feldern der politischen Kommunikation zwischen Aristokratie und Plebs', in M. Jehne (ed.), *Demokratie in Rom?: Die Rolle des Volkes in der Politik der römischen Republik*, Stuttgart, 77–127.
Flaig, E. 2001: 'L'assemblée du peuple à Rome comme rituel de consensus', *Actes de la recherche en sciences sociales* 140, 12–20.
Fraccaro, P. 1957: 'La procedura del voto nei comizi tributi romani', in P. Fraccaro (ed.), *Opuscula: Studi sull'età della rivoluzione romana, scritti di diritto pubblico, militaria*, Pavia, 235–254.
Gartrell, A. 2021: *The Cult of Castor and Pollux in Ancient Rome*, Cambridge.
Gjerstad, E. 1941: 'Il comizio romano dell'et'a repubblicana', *Opuscula archaeologica* 2, 97–158.
Hölkeskamp, K.-J. 2010: *Reconstructing the Roman Republic: An Ancient Political Culture and Modern Research*, Princeton.
Holter, E., Muth, S., and Schwesinger, S. 2019: 'Sounding Out Public Space in Late Republican Rome', in S. Butler and S. Nooter (eds), *Sound and the Ancient Senses*, London; New York, 44–60.
Humm, M. 2019: 'Les espaces comitiaux à Rome pendant la période républicaine', in A. Borlenghi, C. Chillet, V. Hollard, L. Lopez-Rabatel, and J.-C. Moretti (eds.), *Voter en Grèce, à Rome et en Gaule: pratiques, lieux en finalités*, Lyon, 261–276.
Kaster, R. A. 2006: *Cicero: Speech on Behalf of Publius Sestius*, Oxford.
Kuttner, A. L. 2004: 'Roman Art During the Republic', in H. I. Flower (ed.), *The Cambridge Companion to the Roman Republic*, Cambridge, 294–321.
Lundgreen, C. 2009: 'Geheim(nisvoll)e Abstimmung in Rom. Die leges tabellariae und ihre Konsequenzen für die Comitien und die res publica', *Historia: Zeitschrift für Alte Geschichte* 58, 36–70.
Marshall, B. A. 1997: 'Libertas Populi: the Introduction of Secret Ballot at Rome and its Depiction on Coinage', *Antichthon* 31, 54–73.
Mogetta, M. 2021: *The Origins of Concrete Construction in Roman Architecture: Technology and Society in Republican Italy*, Cambridge.
Morrell, K. forthcoming: *Reforming the Roman Republic*.

Morstein-Marx, R. 2004: *Mass Oratory and Political Power in the Late Roman Republic*, Cambridge.
Mouritsen, H. 2001: *Plebs and Politics in the Late Roman Republic*, Cambridge.
Nicolet, C. 1980: *The World of the Citizen in Republican Rome*, London.
Nielsen, I., Poulsen, B., and Bilde, P. G. 1992: *The Temple of Castor and Pollux: The Pre-Augustan Temple Phases with Related Decorative Elements*, Roma.
Russell, A. 2016: *The Politics of Public Space in Republican Rome*, Cambridge.
Staveley, E. S. 1972: *Greek and Roman Voting and Elections*, London.
Taylor, L. R. 1966: *Roman Voting Assemblies from the Hannibalic War to the Dictatorship of Caesar*, Ann Arbor, MI.
Vaahtera, J. 1993: 'On the Religious Nature of the Place of Assembly', in U. Paananen, K. Heikkilä, J. Vaahtera, K. Sandberg, and L. Savunen (eds), *Senatvs popvlvsqve Romanvs: Studies in Roman Republican Legislation*, Helsinki, 97–116.
Yakobson, A. 1995: 'Secret Ballot and Its Effects in the Late Roman Republic', *Hermes* 123, 426–442.

5 Where's Vestorius? Locating Rome's Aediles

Timothy Smith

I Introduction

A harrowing story of murder and political unrest concludes the apparently apolitical discussion of good agricultural practice in the first book of Varro's *De re rustica*. Varro sets the conversation in the temple of Tellus on the Esquiline, to which the speaker and his friends had been invited by the temple's 'sacristan' (*aedituus*) to celebrate the festival of sowing known as the *feriae Sementiuae*.[1] The fictional *aedituus*, a certain L. Fundilius, had been 'summoned by the aedile' (*accersitus ab aedile*) from the temple to an unknown location.[2] The temple fell under the unnamed aedile's *procuratio* (*cuius procuratio huius templi est*).[3] Fundilius' unsettling absence throughout the dialogue, however, informs us that the aedile exercised his *procuratio* from afar. Varro implies that the aedile summoned the *aedituus* to a certain known location. Association with or *procuratio* of a temple did not necessarily make this temple an aedile's base of operations. The dialogue ends abruptly: a tearful freedman bursts in to announce the murder of his patron Fundilius, which seems to be a case of mistaken identity.[4] This chapter explores a question left tantalisingly open by Varro. Where would the ill-fated Fundilius have found the aedile: at his home, his *tribunal* in the forum, or at another temple?

This chapter problematises the notion that Roman magistrates had defined 'headquarters'.[5] Some magistrates did have locations in the city that were closely associated with their office. Tribunes, so the ideological tradition holds, were consistently available to the *plebs* within the Basilica Porcia, the door of which was always open so that they could offer *auxilium*.[6] Physical accessibility is at the heart of the ideology of the tribunate.[7] Urban praetors, meanwhile, had a *tribunal* whence they would pass judgement on civil cases. Good recent scholarship has been devoted to both spaces.[8] But much less is written about aedilician spaces. This chapter works towards filling this gap, a gap that is quite understandable given that ancient writers seldom bother to pinpoint aediles' spaces of interaction and operation. No single space emerges clearly in the literary record. Given the lack of clear evidence, the question becomes less about where Roman aediles were based, which presupposes a static and regular presence in or around a single physical space, but about where Roman aediles tended to choose to appear publicly. This chapter considers their appearance in a broad sense: not just their physical presence *apud populum*, but the markers they left of their year of office, collegial or singular, through the *munera* they provided to the people. There were spaces in the city where aediles could choose to imprint themselves and leave a lasting memory of their year in office, but no singular space out of which they might operate. We see this most starkly in their embellishment of the city with the proceeds of fines. What this trend reveals is an attempt to affirm their 'presentness' in the city and to provide a visual reminder of their gift to the community even when not physically present.

First, a caveat. A difficulty emerges with the chronological and geographical spread of evidence for aedilician spaces. The evidence on which this chapter draws is dispersed across over 500 years of history and is not always limited to Rome itself. It therefore sets out to identify only general trends and understandings about where aediles appeared in a magisterial capacity. And I suggest that, from Plautus' day (the early second century B.C.) to Petronius' day (the mid-first century A.D.), there remained a consistent idea of where aediles interacted with the people, both at Rome and in Italian towns.[9]

II Republican Aediles in Temples

When searching for a base of operations, the temple of Ceres emerges as a strong contender. It is often identified as the plebeian aediles' 'headquarters' in (or, perhaps, from) the fifth century (onwards).[10] The temple of Ceres did have a special place in the memory of the plebeian order and of plebeian officials. Livy's account of the so-called second secession is the key evidence in favour of plebeian aediles having a base at the temple of Ceres from at least the mid-fifth century B.C. Livy relates that the consuls of 449 B.C., amidst their concessions to the *plebs*, ordered 'that *senatus consulta*, which were previously suppressed and falsified by the whim of the consuls, should be deposited in the temple of Ceres into the control of the aediles' (*ut senatus consulta in aedem Cereris ad aediles plebis deferrentur, quae antea arbitrio consulum supprimebantur uitiabanturque*).[11] Although the temple's precise location is uncertain, ancient authors universally locate it in the vicinity of the Circus Maximus near the Aventine.[12] Literary evidence attributes to this southern zone of the city (the *uallis Murcia* and below the north-eastern slopes of the Aventine) an important ideological role in the development of plebeian consciousness. It is possible, therefore, that Fundilius' last journey was undertaken between the temple of Tellus and that of Ceres, especially given the close link between these deities.[13]

Livy, however, is singular in locating plebeian aediles at this temple in particular. In fact, he does not even state that this was the only space of operation for aediles, in the fifth century B.C. or at his time of writing in the late first century B.C. Other writers consistently suggest that *aedilis* derived from the word for 'building/temple' (*aedes*) because of their association with these spaces (plural).[14] These authors saw nothing particularly important about the temple of Ceres regarding the plebeian aedileship's origins. Livy's account at face value tells us nothing about where aediles were based: the *senatus consulta* were allegedly deposited into the *aedes Cereris ad* ('into the control/possession of'?) the aediles; conclusions rest on a maximal interpolation of Livy's ambiguous preposition.[15] The ideological traditions on the creation of the aedileship – which held that aediles were created, in part, for the protection of documents (*senatus consulta* or *plebiscita*; sources vary) – imply some sort of physical presence during the fifth century B.C. But there is no hint in Livy that this space acted as a single base of operations from this time.

Still, the temple of Ceres certainly held an important ideological place in the memory of plebeian offices. Julius Caesar named a new branch of the aedileship after her.[16] In the early and middle republic, plebeian aediles are regularly attested using the proceeds of fines to embellish the temple of Ceres. The piecemeal record preserved by Livy seems to suggest a topographical trend from at least the early third century in which plebeian aediles would 'place' gold or silver items in the temple of Ceres.[17] The distributive logic is ideological and circular: aediles decorated the diverse spaces in the city most closely associated with their magistracy. Both pairs of magistrates, by the third century at least, took responsibility for the organisation of *ludi* celebrated for Jupiter (the *ludi plebeii* and *ludi Romani*) and for Ceres (the *ludi Ceriales*). Their temples and the Circus Maximus were the two most important landmarks for the celebrations. In the two sets of games for Jupiter, the *pompa circensis* traced a route through from the temple of Jupiter Optimus Maximus on the Capitoline to the Circus Maximus.[18] Livy informs us that, due to the influx of triumphs during the Samnite Wars, aediles were inspired to follow the example of conquering generals. From around the end of the fourth century, there arose a custom 'of the forum being embellished by the aediles when the processional carriages would be led through there' (*fori ornandi aedilibus cum tensae ducerentur*).[19] Aediles perceived their *ludi* as an opportunity to advertise their care for the community. These *ornatus* represented a way of displaying themselves in an appropriate context.

Aedilician benefactions tend to line or bookend this route. While, as Livy writes, *ornatus* might be placed in the forum, halfway along the processional route, to coincide with their *ludi*, lasting visual reminders of their service to the community could be placed in the temples at either end of the route. Curule aediles, for instance, tend to cluster their benefactions around the temple of Jupiter, whence departs the *pompa circensis*. The curule aedileship of the brothers Cn. and Q. Ogulnius in 296 B.C. is emblematic. From the fine money raised from usurers, they decorated the temple of Jupiter with bronze *limina*, silver bowls placed within the *cella*, and a representation of Jupiter in a *quadriga* to be placed prominently on the roof of the temple.[20] The imagery of their aedileship is here conflated into a single scene: they would organise the procession that would bear Jupiter himself (in the form of an *exuuia*) from the temple they had embellished to the circus where the people would be entertained by *quadrigae*.[21] Just as they would placate Jupiter in the circus by arranging the *ludi Romani*, so they would reinforce this association by adorning his temple.

As the *editor*, he would appear in a prominent place during his games. He would sit in the *orchestra* during the *ludi scaenici*, and would presumably feature somewhere in the *pompa circensis* before the circus games.[22] Although these appearances in the theatre and the circus were some of the aediles' most prominent activities, at least until Augustus' stripped aediles of their responsibility for games in 22 B.C., these physical appearances were ephemeral.[23] The visual reminders of one's aedileship would conflate aedilician imagery, reminding the onlooker of the initial service to the community (the trial and conviction of usurers who were lending money at extortionate rates); it would remind the people of their glorious *ludi*; and it would project this *gratia* into the future by the permanence of the display of the *quadriga*. Caesar's provocative display on the Capitol of the trophies from Marius' victories, possibly to coincide with the *ludi Romani*, signalled a clear desire to manipulate aedilician norms of display in a specific context for political ends.[24] Despite significant animosity from many influential senators, the trophies remained in place long after Caesar's death.[25] An inscription fashioned in the mosaic of the floor of the temple of Apollo Medicus confirms this memorialising intent. The curule aediles, whose names are now lost, celebrated not simply the repair of the floor of the temple, but the act of prosecution itself, boasting that they 'gifted and gave official seal of approval to this with the proceeds of fines' (*moltaticod dedere esdem probauerunt*).[26] These embellishments, however, tell us little about aedilician bases of operation. The locations described are spaces where they *chose* to display themselves. They maintained an ongoing presence at the temple, beyond even their year of office, without being present save for the obligatory *probatio* to inspect their contractors' workmanship. The intention was to maintain a presence even when absent.

Temples, then, were clearly at the heart of republican aediles' religious responsibilities, and they spent their year in office endeavouring to reinforce this connection. But there is nothing in the evidence to suggest that they found a normative base of operations in one, or any, of them. Indeed, despite the existence of an ideological tradition (concerning the fifth century B.C.) in which plebeian aediles were expected to keep a constant watchful eye over documents 'so that nothing that happened escaped their notice' (ὥστε μηδὲν σφᾶς τῶν πραττομένων λανθάνειν), their presence in temples seems to be limited to important public occasions, at least in the better-attested periods from the late fourth century B.C. onwards.[27] For instance, curule aediles performed a kind of crowning ceremony in the temple of Magna Mater during her games from (presumably) the early second century in which he takes the *corona* from the stage (*e scaena*) into the temple (*in templo*).[28] The aedile is there, we presume, simply to perform his solemn religious role for the particular occasion of the *ludi Megalenses*.

Still, aediles needed spaces to store documents and items associated with their magistracy. Items that aediles 'possessed' included torches (for weddings?) and *tensae* for *pompae circensis*; and temples were the usual storage spaces.[29] Aediles, Polybius writes, had their own *aerarium* in his day, which stored treaties between Carthage and Rome dating from a century earlier inscribed on bronze.[30] It is possible, too, that they stored their weights and measures there, or in the temple of Jupiter nearby, but the surviving evidence is imprecise.[31] The space in question seems to have been primarily for storage; it might possibly offer a space in which aedilician *scribae* could work, but not a space where aediles would typically operate.[32] But the scribes' administrative duties, it seems, were expected to be carried out in the public eye.[33] The so-called Altar of the Scribes (Figure 5.1), a funerary

Figure 5.1 The Altar of the Scribes.
Source: Author: Antonio Lopez Garcia.

monument dating from the early first century A.D. dedicated to two deceased aedilician scribes, paints a picture of scribes carrying out bureaucratic tasks for their employers not in a closed *aerarium*, but rather on a platform before a crowd. They appear to be seated on a raised *suggestus*; a crowd depicted in the panel below looks up at them admiringly as they diligently carry out their work. Although the scribes' employers are absent in the depiction, there seems to be an attempt to parallel themselves with the publicness of the aediles they worked for.[34] Still, at least in Polybius' day, the information contained in the aediles' *aerarium* was not common knowledge; in his visit to the treasury, Polybius evidently did not bump into one of the year's aediles.[35] The extent to which aediles took an active interest in the preservation and storage of decrees is questionable. After all, in 11 B.C. aediles were relieved of the duty of looking after 'decrees' (τὰ δόγματα) on the basis that they habitually deferred such duties to their *apparitores*.[36] At the very least, aediles were presumably only an occasional presence.

III Many Aedilician Spaces

None of this concretely informs us about where the Roman people might interact with their aediles on a day-to-day basis. We need to cast our net wider than republican Rome to gain a full understanding of aediles' physical spheres of activity. A conversation between two of Trimalchio's guests, Ganymedes and Echion, provides a glimpse into how a first-century A.D. author like Petronius imagined how the lower classes perceived colonial magistrates. Petronius has Ganymedes complain about the aediles of the present day in his fictional *colonia*, lamenting that they are in cahoots with the bakers in driving up food prices, starving the *populus minutus* to death. He reminisces about the good old days in the *colonia* when metaphorical *leones* had consistently taken the bakers to task, instead of colluding with them for personal profit. An aedile called Safinius is his prime example.[37]

> But Safinius comes to mind: at that time, when I was a lad, he was living by the old arch; more a hot pepper than a man. Wherever he went, he scorched the earth. Still, he was upright, trustworthy, a friend to a friend, with whom you could play *morra* confidently in the dark. How he used to dress them down in the senate: straight-up, not by using fancy language! And when he did his thing in the forum, his voice boomed like a trumpet.
>
> *sed memini Safinium: tunc habitabat ad arcem ueterem, me puero, piper, non homo. is quacumque ibat, terram adurebat. sed rectus, sed certus, amicus amico, cum quo audacter posses in tenebris micare. in curia autem quomodo singulos {uel} pilabat {tractabat}, nec schemas loquebatur sed derectum. cum ageret porro in foro, sic illius uox crescebat tamquam tuba.*

Ganymedes specifies here the three spaces in which he would expect to find his favourite, public-spirited aedile. First, he knew where he lived, in a prominent and memorable part of the city. We may presume that some of the interactions with this colonial magistrate took place within the latter's home at *salutationes*.

Second, he (unsurprisingly) would be found in the senate or local *curia*, in this case railing against evil *pistores* who hoarded supplies and distorted the market. Finally, from a position in the forum, where he would deliver public speeches with apparently similar messages. In this caricatured view of the *populus minutus*, Petronius provides a glimpse of the spaces of interaction anticipated of an imperial, colonial aedile.

The *arcus uetus* may even have been a space from which food would have been distributed. Given his repeated complaints about his hunger and poverty, Ganymedes may be making this topographical link by this passing reference. In republican Rome, *porticus* may have been important centres for aediles' *ad hoc* grain distributions of the middle and late republic; republican aediles occasionally repaired and constructed *porticus*, and other *porticus* later appear as spaces from which formal *frumentationes* were distributed (though not by aediles).[38] There seems to have been no fixed location for distributions in the earlier republic: on one occasion, the curule aediles appear to have distributed free oil in the Circus Maximus at the *ludi Romani*.[39] The temple of Ceres does not seem to have been a centre of aedilician grain distributions, despite some speculation to the contrary in modern scholarship.[40] The Circus Maximus, then, appears as one space of interaction, chiefly during aedilician *ludi*. But Ganymedes might have food in mind when he mentions Safinius' house in passing. Municipal and colonial aediles, after all, appear to have a strong link with their town's food supply.[41]

Other evidence from Rome appears to substantiate Petronius' locating of colonial aediles. Safinius' appearance *in curia* is the simplest yet most elusive. Aediles were senators at Rome. In republican Rome, election to the aedileship conferred upon its holders the right to speak in the senate, although they are seldom attested doing so: their relative influence can hardly have been as great as a loud-mouthed aedile like Safinius in a colonial *curia*. Evidence for aediles speaking in the senate is thin on the ground, though there are some examples concerning well-known first-century B.C. politicians.[42] Caesar's display of Marius' trophies on the Capitol as curule aedile was controversial enough to stir up senatorial debate. The censor Q. Lutatius Catulus spoke in vehement opposition.[43] Plutarch is vague about what Caesar said, but he was evidently persuasive enough to convince the senate (ἔπεισε τὴν σύγκλητον) that the Marian trophies should not be removed. A decade later, Cicero's introductory remarks to his senatorial speech, *de haruspicum responso*, details a bitter argument between Cicero and the then curule aedile Clodius in 56 B.C. We have only Cicero's side of the story, but he claims that he had succeeded in stopping Clodius mid-sentence in the senate.[44]

Clodius' next approach was, fittingly, to address the people from the *rostra* with a *contio*.[45] An aedile's voice was clearer in popular assemblies and *contiones* (*in foro* as Ganymedes vaguely puts it). Indeed, the space where one would most likely find an aedile is the 'forum'. For Ganymedes, Safinius' most noteworthy activity in the forum is delivering very loud speeches. A republican aedile at Rome might choose to display himself in public by convoking *contiones*, either in advance of a trial or to give political speeches. The very nature of *iudicia publica* necessitated a great deal of public speaking. Aedilician trials before the people, though far more common before the second century B.C., were drawn out affairs, requiring at least three days preceding the trial (*anquisitiones*) during which the matter would be put to the people by the magistrate and witnesses could be called.[46] One such *anquisitio* is described in vivid detail by Cicero in a letter to his brother, during which Clodius used his platform not only to attack his client, but to humiliate his prominent political enemies, especially Pompey.[47] Clodius took full advantage of his curule aedileship by giving 'countless *contiones*' in 56 B.C.[48] But such appearances were irregular and inconsistent. The extent to which an aedile might pursue popular causes or attempt to prosecute people for financial or moral crimes *apud populum* was left up to his judgement.

Aediles would have maintained a semi-regular presence in the forum in dealing with more prosaic matters. This is hardly surprising: Vitruvius defines the forum as all magistrates' central space of interaction, where 'matters of both public and private business are conducted by magistrates' (*et publicarum et priuatarum rerum rationes per magistratus gubernantur*).[49] 'In Apuleius' *Metamorphoses*, dating to the second century A.D., an 'aedile' of the Thessalian town of Hypata named Pythias 'bumps into' (*continatur*) Lucius when he was buying fish in the 'delicacy market' (*forum cuppedinis*).[50] Although Pythias is probably more to be equated with a Greek *agoranomos* (which is how Greeks translated *aedilis*), the story certainly suggests a continuous magisterial presence in the forum as aediles carry out their role as market inspectors.[51] Imperial satirists emphasise the presentness of these aediles/*agoranomoi* in the provincial forum, with their pettiness viewed with apprehension by shopkeepers.[52] And there is abundant imperial evidence for aedilician oversight of sales of slaves, animals, and goods.[53]

A passage in Plautus' *Menaechmi* suggests that an aedile might maintain a regular presence in the forum from the middle republic even when not prosecuting. The first Menaechmus grumbles about the 'stupid custom' (*mos morus*) of defending wealthy but transparently guilty clients, which obliges him to go to the forum instead of spending time with his girlfriend.[54] He speaks in defence of a client in what appears to be a civic dispute *apud aedilis*, 'in the aediles' court'.[55] Menaechmus appears to sketch a tripartite division in how such matters are adjudicated in Plautus' day: 'a case comes either before the people, to court [before a praetor], or before the aedile' (*aut ad populum aut in iure aut apud aedilem res est*).[56] Menaechmus' familiarity with the vexing *mos* and his implied habitual descent into the forum suggest that the aediles' presence here was fixed and regular. Aediles presumably had to erect their own *tribunal*, as praetors did, although surviving references to the latter are considerably more abundant.[57] There were evidently several *tribunalia* in the forum; each tribune may have had one to himself.[58] Suetonius tells the story of an aedile from Novaria in the Augustan period, C. Albucius Silus, being dragged from his *tribunal* (*e tribunali detractus est*) from which he had been 'passing judgment' (*ius diceret*).[59] The *tabula Heracleensis*, which was modelled on Roman institutional norms, states that an aedile must publish details of his letting of a contract 'around the forum before his tribunal' (*aput forum ante tribunale suom*); the singular perhaps implies that each aedile had his own distinct platform.[60] The tomb of C. Vestorius Priscus, a young Pompeian aedile who died in office (discussed further later in this chapter), depicts him above a crowd of twelve people seated on a raised *suggestus*.[61] His mother, who commissioned the artwork, clearly wanted to depict him in a setting that provided a clear visual association with his magistracy: alone, standing out from the crowd in a public setting.

Other visual depictions of aediles are even less specific about location. Two plebeian aediles from the 80s B.C., L. Critonius and M. Fannius, depicted themselves on a coin, seated side by side as paragons of collegiality, sharing their *subsellium*.[62] The aedile on the right appears to be reaching out a hand, gesturing towards an unseen audience outside the picture plane, or towards an outsized ear of corn, a product on which these aediles may have offered a discount during the notoriously difficult mid-80s B.C.[63] All that can be said is that they present themselves in a public setting as ideal magistrates. The coin lacks some of the visual signifiers of other republican coinage featuring *subsellia*. For instance, a moneyer named Palikanus (= L. Lollius Palicanus) displayed a tribunician *subsellium* on top of the *rostra* on his issues.[64] A moneyer in 13 B.C. named C. Sulpicius Platorinus celebrated Agrippa's and Augustus' collegial *tribunicia potestas* by displaying the pair seated on a *subsellium* on the *rostra*.[65] The semiotic association between the specific space in which the tribunician *subsellium* was placed seems to be much stronger than that of other magistrates, like aediles and quaestors, whose *subsellia* tend to be in nondescript public spaces.[66] The slight difference in iconography suggests a mobility and absence of a singular point of focus for the aedileship.[67]

After all, the aedile was mobile.[68] Ganymedes' chumminess with the former aedile Safinius, an *amicus amico*, appears to manifest itself in chance face-to-face interactions on the street, when an aedile would most anticipate having to *resalutare* and *nomina omnium reddere*.[69] Safinius is Ganymedes' ideal man-about-town, 'scorching the ground wherever he went' (*is quacumque ibat, terram adurebat*).[70]

Figure 5.2 The coin of Critonius and Fannius.

Source: Harvard Art Museums/Arthur M. Sackler Museum, Transfer from the Alice Corinne McDaniel Collection, Department of the Classics, Harvard University, Photo © President and Fellows of Harvard College, 2008.115.119.

A handful of anecdotes from the late republic and early empire reinforce the image of the aedile on the move. Varro complained that the aediles of his day, unlike the virtuous ones of yesteryear, now swaggered about flanked by public slaves (*stipati seruis publicis*).[71] He would have been scandalised by the story of Nero's grandfather barging the censor L. Munatius Plancus off the road as aedile.[72] Curule aediles' chairs would have to be carried along, presumably by their *uiatores* or *serui publici*. Aulus Gellius preserves a fragmentary story from the second-century B.C. historian Piso, which provides a glimpse of the magistrate's mobility. Cn. Flavius, curule aedile in 304 B.C., was visiting the home of an unwell friend. Several *adulescentes nobiles* refused to stand up in the magistrate's presence. As a riposte, Flavius 'ordered that his curule chair be brought to him; he placed it on the threshold, so that none of them could leave, and so that everyone would unwillingly see him sitting in his curule chair' (*sellam curulem iussit sibi afferri, eam in limine apposuit, ne quis illorum exire posset utique hi omnes inviti uiderent sese in sella curuli sedentem*).[73] The anecdote confirms two predictable things about aediles: that Flavius was attended by *apparitores* to whom he could deliver the orders; and that the curule chair was brought to him by his *apparitores* or *serui* when he needed to do something in his magisterial capacity. The point of this 'little scene' in which Flavius was 'dramaturge and star' was to shift the context from one in which he was acting in a private capacity to one in which he was acting in a magisterial way.[74]

IV The Aedile at Home

Ganymedes was also intimately familiar with Safinius' house: his first memory of him was the house he lived in 'when I was a boy' (*me puero*). The household, especially the *atrium*, was a space of public interaction for magistrates and wealthy private citizens alike.[75] It was important to be seen to be publicly open and available to the *populus*.[76] A *domus* needed to provide space for magisterial duties, his *officia ciuibus*: the design of these houses for men who held magistracies should, as Vitruvius puts it, be 'arranged in a manner not dissimilar to the magnificence of public building projects' (*non dissimili modo quam publicorum operum magnificentia comparatas*), because these were the spaces where *publica consilia* were relayed.[77] The aedileship is not unique in this regard. M. Livius Drusus, tribune in 91, was said to have asked his architect to design his house on the Palatine 'so that whatever I do may be seen by observed by everyone' (*ut, quidquid agam, ab omnibus perspici possit*).[78] These instructions were avowedly conveyed to his architect to develop a political persona of approachability that would be appropriate for, but not unique to, his tribunate. Opening one's doors to the people was something of a general aristocratic ideal.[79]

But it was possible to present one's private *domus* as an aedilician space. The house was an important performative space for an aspiring magistrate of any rank.[80] The author of the *Commentariolum Petitionis* advises Cicero, when canvassing for the consulship, 'to advertise your approachability by day and night, not only with the door of your home but also through your facial expression, which is the door to your mind' (*ut aditus ad te diurni nocturnique pateant, neque solum foribus aedium tuarum sed etiam uultu ac fronte, quae est animi ianua*).[81] Aediles could evidently use their homes to achieve the same effect, or illusion, of openness. There are widespread attestations of men campaigning for the aedileship at Pompeii; slogans promoting these candidates regularly feature on the exterior, and sometimes interior, walls of private houses.[82] The house was a space where the boundaries between public and private could, if one so chose, be destabilised. This was a fine balancing act for the ideal aedile. He was under social pressure from both his peers and the people at large to present himself as acting in the public good.

Cicero, for example, lambasted Clodius' brother for his last-minute decision to forego his campaign for the aedileship, despite having invested heavily in the anticipated *ornatus* inherent in a successful aedileship. As soon as he changed his mind, Cicero alleges, Ap. Claudius 'transferred his investment in the aedileship into two places: his own coffers and his private gardens' (*aedilitatem duobus in locis, partim in arca, partim in hortis suis, collocauit*).[83] Cicero is here playing on the normative expectation among the aristocracy that an essential feature of the aedileship was to display wealth in the public interest. His change of mind had 'defrauded' (*interuersa*) the people of the public display that an aedileship entailed.[84] Storing one's *aedilitas* in private property and private affairs was objectionable. Petronius' Ganymedes complains that the aediles of his *colonia* are surreptitiously in league with the bakers, working behind the scenes to cause suffering among the *populus minutus*. Unlike public-spirited Safinius, the current year's aedile 'rejoices at his house; he rakes in more money every day than someone else has for his entire fortune' (*plus in die nummorum accipit, quam alter patrimonium habet*).[85] His privateness is contrasted heavily with the spaces of interaction associated with Safinius: his doors were always open; the person on the street knew where to find him, be it at his home, in the *curia*, or in the forum. The sharp moral division between public and private (as perceived by Ganymedes) is the root of the problem, as 'people nowadays are lions at their homes, but foxes in public' (*nunc populus est domi leones, foras uulpes*). The ideal aedile might work from home. But his doors must be open.

The aedile's social responsibility seems to be at the heart of one of the prosecution's arguments in their attempted conviction of M. Aemilius Scaurus in 54 B.C. Asconius tells us that the prosecution had cited the lavishness of Scaurus' house to illustrate their argument. Cicero's verbatim (now fragmentary) response went as follows: 'not least because the proximity and busy location remove any suspicion of laziness and greed' (*praesertim cum propinquitas et celebritas loci suspicionem desidiae tollat aut cupiditatis*).[86] The prosecution, it seems, had cited Scaurus' *magnifica domus* as evidence of this greed; Cicero attempted to twist this argument by arguing that the house's very visible *locus* put paid to this allegation.[87] Although the trial concerned Scaurus' alleged indiscretions during his propraetorship of 55 B.C., the prosecution here concentrates on stories about his aedileship three years prior. His remarkably profligate aedileship was on everyone's lips, both prosecution and defence. Scaurus, too, spoke on his own behalf in the trial, citing his aedileship and the popularity that came with it as a reason to acquit; Cicero seems to have proceeded with similar, though perhaps more nuanced, arguments.[88] His removal of the largest columns used for his aedilician *ludi* to his home was, according to Cicero, an act of public-spiritedness, because his home on the Palatine was in effect a public space in which he could commemorate his aedileship beyond the *ludi Romani* of September 58 B.C.[89]

If such arguments were persuasive enough for the jury, Pliny the Elder does not seem to have been convinced. Scaurus' appropriation of the columns to decorate his *priuata domus* was taken by Pliny as emblematic of a decline in morals in the late republic.[90] Some of Scaurus' contemporaries evidently shared Pliny's belief. Questions of public and private were contestable. For Scaurus' rivals, this was a manipulation of public office for private gain, an egregious manifestation of his 'greed' (*cupiditas*). Pliny writes with thinly veiled Schadenfreude that, after some of the *deliciae* were brought to Scaurus' private villa in Tusculum (valued at thirty million sesterces), his household slaves burned the villa to the ground.[91] Likewise, his 'sloth' (*desidia*) manifested itself in his preference for showiness over hard work in his aedileship.[92] For Scaurus, on the other hand, not only did the display in his *atrium* offer an opportunity to claim that his home was now a public aedilician space; it offered a chance to prolong the *memoria* of his gift to the community, taking advantage of the contestable distinctions between public and private to create a kind of museum to his aedileship.[93]

Scaurus' *atrium* was presumably little more than a construction site for the final three months of 58 B.C.: it would have taken a long time to drag four colossal columns up to his house on the Palatine. So his household display admittedly tells us more about aedilician ideals regarding private and public space than about aediles' working-from-home arrangements. The exceptional circumstances of the magistrates' response to the Catilinarian conspiracy might offer one example. Though our sources are inexplicit, it appears that Lentulus Spinther, curule aedile in 63, imprisoned the conspirator Lentulus Sura in his house on the Palatine while the senate debated the latter's fate.[94] The crisis necessitated an activation of Spinther's aedilician *coercitio*, presumably with employment of his *uiatores* and/or *serui publici*, and his house was the safest place to guard the accused in this one exceptional case. We need not imagine other aediles regularly using their pantries to imprison notorious insurgents. It is fair to assume that aediles did conduct a significant amount of their business at home, as Vitruvius implies, but most of the evidence centres on the spectacular and exceptional.

One final piece of evidence to help us to bring together public and private spaces employed by aediles is the tomb of C. Vestorius Priscus (Figure 5.3). The various scenes depicted on the interior of the tomb of this young Pompeian aedile are designed to provide a tapestry of the last and a most notable year of his life, that of his aedileship. In the first scene the visitor sees when entering the tomb, he is depicted as an aedile at home, emerging from his *tablinum*. He looks directly at the viewer, dressed in magisterial *latus clauus*, as he enters the magistrate's *atrium*. It has been suggested that the intention of his mother who commissioned the work, Mulvia Prisca, was to depict her son as the ideal *paterfamilias* in a purely domestic and private setting.[95] But his dress and the stagedness of the scene might equally

Where's Vestorius? Locating Rome's Aediles 111

Figure 5.3 The tomb of Vestorius Priscus. After Whitehead 1993.

Source: Images reprinted with kind permission of Professor Jane Whitehead. Edited by Antonio Lopez Garcia.

suggest that the viewer is encouraged to place themselves in the position of client seeking the guidance of their magistrate. It is possible, therefore, that Vestorius is pictured receiving a *salutatio*. John R. Clarke, however, argues that the artworks within the tomb were closed off to the general public, making it unlikely that Mulvia would commission a scene of her son fulfilling his socio-political duty as aedile. The staging of half of a *salutatio*, then, would be redundant since this scene would be viewed only by the Vestorii and Mulvii.[96] By this logic, however, the political scene on the reverse side of the tomb, in which Vestorius is depicted seated on a curule chair in a public space, is also redundant. Pride in one's son's public service did not have to be displayed for public consumption, as the second scene proves. Two chairs flank the aedile, behind which are tables bearing scrolls, books, and writing implements, some of which have tumbled onto a chair.[97] A pair of shoes (*calcei*?) or slippers sits below one of the chairs; he wears light sandals and is not yet fully dressed for a journey to the forum.[98] But the artist has been asked to paint Vestorius as an aedile, with *latus clauus*, in semi-magisterial form. The intention must have been to depict Vestorius as the diligent and learned aedile both at home, where he would transact some of his administrative duties. The items in Vestorius' house are no mere generic household items, but carefully chosen to show his culture, learning, and *industria*.[99] The civic and the private are consciously blended.

On the opposite side Vestorius is depicted in an unequivocally public setting. The mural is badly damaged, but what remains has an aedile elevated above a group of twelve other standing figures. He is seated on a *sella curulis* on a large platform (*suggestus*), so that even seated he remains above others' eye-level. It is unclear how Vestorius is interacting with these people: he might be depicted demonstrating his *liberalitas* by giving out money, because the figure to his left is stretching out a hand to him, or (more plausibly) passing judgement on a matter – or simply depicted in a generic aedilician space doing generic aedilician things with little care for detail.[100] All eyes are turned to him, while he looks directly at the viewer. The presumed setting is the forum at Pompeii.[101] The emphasis on aedilician space is also emphasised by the painting of two gladiators on the west enclosure wall, entertainment that was, or would have been, so the viewer is led to believe, funded by Vestorius himself.[102] The two scenes in which he features preserve the two most important spaces of the final year of Vestorius' life, the *domus* and the forum. These were the twin aedilician spaces where Mulvia thought it most fitting to depict her son. There was nothing dissonant about painting a magistrate in his domestic setting, acting both as the ideal *paterfamilias* and ideal aedile. The scenes of Vestorius' tomb ultimately cut to the heart of the question of aedilician space. Mulvia was aware that there was no single setting appropriate for the aedile. She opted instead for two, or three including the gladiators, creating a tapestry of aedilician spaces. Even in an apparently private setting, the aedile was on the clock.

V Conclusion

Literary and material evidence tends to depict aediles in contexts where they, or their families, hoped they would be remembered. The flexibility inherent in the aedileship allowed them to associate themselves with the spaces in the city that would most effectively preserve the memory of their year in office. Administrative space is often too quotidian to warrant attention. But some positive trends emerge. What seems to unite aediles in both republic and Principate, in both Rome and Italy, is a diverse use of space. Fundilius probably knew where to find the aedile on that fateful day in January, but presumably because he told him where he was and what he was doing during the *feriae Sementiuae*. As Ganymedes' nostalgic story reveals, there were several spaces in which one might expect to encounter an aedile. He did not have a single headquarters.

Notes

1 Location: *LTUR* V, s. v. *Tellus, Aedes* (Coarelli): 24–5; Amoroso 2007. See below Chapter 7 by A. Lopez Garcia in this volume.
2 Named at Varro, *RR* 1.2.11. Cf. Green 1997: 430; Nelsestuen 2015: 109–115.
3 Varro, *RR* 1.2.9.
4 Varro, *RR*. 1.69.2. Green 1997: 431 speculates that the unnamed aedile was the intended victim.
5 Problems with defining 'office' spaces: Tuori 2018: 199–211.
6 Asc. 33C; Plut., *Cat. Min.* 5.1. Cf. Lintott 1999: 124; Arena 2012: 51. Plutarch, incidentally, did not believe that this was their fixed position: 'tribunes, then, *tended by custom* to transact their business in this space' (εἰωθότες οὖν ἐκεῖ χρηματίζειν οἱ δήμαρχοι). Other accounts of tribunician *subsellia* in slightly different locations (e.g. Suet., *Iul.* 78.2) point to their mobility. Still, their presence and normative accessibility was regular enough in the late republic for a third-century B.C. painting called the *tabula Valeria* (Plin. *NH* 35.22) to be a byword for tribunician space (Cic., *Vat.* 22; *Fam.* 14.2.2). Cf. Coarelli 1985: 53–62; Kondratieff 2009: 325–8.
7 Plut., *Quaest. Rom.* 81.
8 David 1995; Bablitz 2008; Kondratieff 2009, 2010.
9 Juvenal appears to equate aedilician responsibilities and spaces at Rome and in Italian towns in two satires. In *Sat.* 3.162, 178–9, he contrasts arrogant aediles at Rome with those of the *pars magna Italiae*, where even aediles deign to wear *tunicae albae* in the theatre. In *Sat.* 10.99–102, he presents two equally distasteful scenarios: to wear the aedile's *toga praetexta* at Rome and get bossed around by the likes of Seianus, or end up in the forum of a tinpot town like Ulubrae dealing with petty market-related offences. Both comparisons rely on a shared understanding of what *aedilitas* was (or ought to be).
10 De Sanctis 1932: 442; Spaeth 1996: 87; Wiseman 1998: 37; Davies 2017: 26; *LTUR* I, s. v. *Ceres, Liber, Liberaque, aedes; aedes Cereris* (Coarelli): 260; Latham 2016: 86.
11 Liv. 3.55.13.
12 Vitr. 3.3.5; Dion. Hal. 6.94.5; Plin., *NH* 35.154; Tac., *Ann.* 2.49; Dio 50.10.3. Numerous modern authors have attempted to locate the temple (sources listed in *LTUR* I, s. v. *Ceres, Liber, Liberaque, aedes; aedes Cereris* (Coarelli): 261). See now Pellam 2014: 86–8; Mignone 2016: 205–211.
13 Both Ceres and Tellus were propitiated during the *feriae Sementiuae* (*placentur frugum matres, Tellusque Ceresque*), since they shared an *officium commune* (Ov., *Fast.* 1.671–3). *Flamines Ceriales* carried out the *sacrum Ceriale* for both Ceres and Tellus: Numerius Fabius Pictor (*FRHist* 1.165) *apud* Serv., *Georg.* 1.21. Cf. Becker 2017: 59–61.
14 Varro, *LL* 5.81; Dion. Hal. 6.90.2–3; Fest. 12L; Pomp., *Dig.* 1.2.2.21; Zon. 7.15. Cf. Becker 2017: 47–9.
15 *OLD*, s.v. 'ad' 26.
16 Dio 43.51.3.
17 Helpfully enumerated in Piacentin 2018: 107–115.
18 Route of *pompa*: Dion. Hal 7.72.1 with Latham 2016: 72–90. The Circus Flaminius was not used for the *ludi plebeii*. This argument relies on an anachronistic citation of the Circus Flaminius in Val. Max. 1.7.4 (Wiseman 1974, 1976; *contra* Bernstein 1998: 158–163).
19 Liv. 9.40.16.
20 Liv. 10.23.11–13.
21 *Quadrigae* in the circus: Liv. 45.1.6–7.
22 Aedile in *orchestra*: App., *B Civ.* 4.41.173; cf. *Lex Colonia Genetiuae* § 127, l. 8 = *RS* 1.25 (p. 414). The jokes concerning aediles in Plautus also imply their physical presence in the theatre (e.g. *Amph.* 69–74; *Poen.* 36–9). Aediles are not mentioned in Dionysius'

description of the *pompa circensis* (7.72.1), but Val. Max. 1.1.16 implies that the aedile took an active and prominent part in the arrangement of the procession. See also Chapter 12 by J. Bartz in this volume.
23 Augustan reform: Dio 54.2.3–4.
24 Plut. *Caes*. 6.1 is unspecific about the time of year, writing only that they were surreptitiously erected overnight during 'the acme of his aedilician ambitions' (ἐν ταῖς ἀγορανομικαῖς φιλοτιμίαις ἀκμὴν).
25 Longevity: Prop. 3.11.46; Val. Max. 6.9.14; Cf. Vell. Pat. 2.43.4; Suet., *Iul*. 11.
26 *CIL* I 2675c = *ILLRP* 45. Cf. Viscogliosi 1996: 22; Coarelli 1997: 387–8; Davies 2017: 88; De Nuccio and Gallocchio 2017: 452 (with image at p. 458); Piacentin 2018: 118–119 (with p. 117 for more inscriptions explicitly citing fine money as the source).
27 Zon. 7.15.
28 Varro, *Men*. 150B. Cf. Goldberg 1998: 11; Roller 1999: 308; Latham 2016: 165; Dufallo 2021: 67–8.
29 Torches (location unspecified, but possibly in the temple of Ceres given her connection to marriage: Le Bonniec 1958: 77–88): *lex Coloniae Genetiuae* § 62 = *RS* 1.25 (pp. 401–2); Plut., *Quaest. Rom*. 2. *Tensae* (in the *sacrarium* of the temple of Jupiter): Grattius, *Cyn*. 535; Suet., *Vesp*. 5.7. Cf. Mommsen, *Röm. Staatsr*. 2^3.500 n. 1; Latham 2016: 56–7, 75–6.
30 Polyb. 3.26.1.
31 Mommsen, *Röm. Staatsr*. 2^3.500 n. 1; Berrendonner 2009: 355. Cf. Palmer 1997: 18–20.
32 *Scribae* in *aerarium*: Liv. 30.39.7. Polybius may have needed help from *scribae* to grasp the archaic Latin (Polyb. 3.22.3): Serrati 2006: 122.
33 Tuori 2018: 225.
34 Tuori 2018: 209 argues that the central figure is a 'magistrate, perhaps a curule aedile'. But see Hartmann 2020: 39–41, arguing that they are 'working in the office of the *aediles curules*'). Cf. Zevi and Friggeri 2012: 360 (the scribes are seated 'su un suggesto, quasi un *tribunal*', resulting in 'una vera e propria scena magistratuale').
35 Polyb. 3.26.3: 'those especially reputed for absorbing themselves in public affairs were unaware of them' (μάλιστα δοκοῦντες περὶ τὰ κοινὰ σπουδάζειν ἠγνόουν).
36 Dio 54.36.1.
37 Safinius is never explicitly called an aedile. Though some are cautious (Pepe 1957: 103: 'di professione avvocato'; Hall 1998: 419: 'senator'), Petronius' juxtaposition relies on the contrast between the good former aedile, Safinius, and the bad ones who are currently in office. As Rankin (1968: 254–256) has convincingly shown, Safinius was not a private 'anti-magisterial' individual (he spoke *in curia*), but an aedile who ensured that corruption was held in check. Finally, the lion metaphor recalls, perhaps consciously, Horace's description of Agrippa as aedile as an *ingenuus leo* (*Sat*. 2.3.185–6).
38 Daguet-Gagey 2015: 474. Cf. *LTUR* IV s.v. *Porticus Minucia Frumentaria* (Manacorda): 132–7; s.v. *Porticus Minucia Vetus* (Coarelli) 138–9.
39 Liv. 25.2.8.
40 See esp. Daguet-Gagey 2015: 458 with n. 16 with an important critique of the 'localisation erronée du temple'.
41 C. Iulius Polybius apparently promised good bread in his election campaign at Pompeii (*CIL* IV 429 = *ILS* 6412e); *pistores*, too, could collectively recommend their preferred candidate, who, they hoped, would espouse their commercial interests (*CIL* IV 7273).
42 Cic., *Phil*. 13.26–8 provides a glimpse of the speaking order of magistrates. But aediles on the whole were fairly quiet in the Roman senate (Ryan 1997: 261). Cf. Cic., *Verr*. 2.5.36 (with Ryan 1998: 158 n. 135) on the *ius sententiae dicendae* of aediles.
43 Plut., *Caes*. 6.6–7. Cf. Vell. Pat. 2.43.4; Suet. *Iul*. 11 (which suggests that he relied on tribunician *contiones* to support some of his political goals, in this case a command in Egypt).
44 Cic., *Har*. 1. Cf. Tatum 1999: 218; Corbeill 2018: 178.
45 Cic., *Har*. 8.

46 The first-century procedure, framed by Cicero as *a maioribus constituta*, is articulated in *Dom.* 45. But earlier evidence (*Lex Osca tabulae Bantinae*, ll. 13–18 = *RS* 1.13 (p. 277)) seems to suggest that Cicero's formulation was not 'la sola forma di processo davanti il popolo' (Lintott 2009: 17–19).
47 Cic., *QFr.* 2.3.2. Cf. Dio 39.18.2–19.1.
48 Cic., *Fam.* 5.3.1. C. Iulius Caesar Strabo Vopiscus (aed. cur. 90) was another who regularly delivered *contiones* as aedile (Cic., *Brut.* 305).
49 Vitr. 5. *praef.* 5.
50 Apul., *Met.* 1.24.
51 Migeotte 2005: 290. For a Roman audience the two offices could be described interchangeably without significant contradiction: Plaut., *Capt.* 823–4.
52 Sen., *Beat.* 7.3 notes that there were various *loca* in the city, namely places of pleasure (*uoluptas*), which 'fear the aedile' (*aedilem metuentia*).
53 Daguet-Gagey 2015: 551–619.
54 Location in 'forum': Plaut., *Men.* 597, 600.
55 Plaut., *Men.* 590. Cf. Gratwick 1993: 194.
56 Plaut., *Men.* 587.
57 Richardson 1973: 219–220. In general: David 1995; Kondratieff 2009; Lopez Garcia forthcoming.
58 Asc. 33C.
59 Suet. *Rhet.* 6.
60 *Tabula Heracleensis* l. 34 = *RS* 1.24 (p. 364). The individuality of aedilician action in the statute is introduced by the clause in which they draw lots determining *quae pars urbis* over which each should exercise *uiarum reficiendarum tuemdarum procuratio* (ll. 27–8).
61 *AE* 1911, 72 = 1913, 70 = EDR072420.
62 *RRC* 351.
63 Food shortage during *Cinnanum tempus*: Garnsey 1988: 199–200.
64 *RRC* 473. Cf. Morstein-Marx 2004: 51–3 (the amalgam evoked 'the ideological significance of the tribunician *contio*').
65 *RIC* 407. Cf. Freudenburg 2014: 105–7.
66 Cf. the issues of the quaestors Q. Servilius Caepio and L. Calpurnius Piso in 100 (*RRC* 330).
67 Still, both the quaestorian and aedilician issues nod towards the deities most closely associated with their office: Ceres for Critonius and Fannius (Fig. 5.2); Saturn for Caepio and Piso (evoking the *aerarium Saturni*, the keys of which were kept by one of the quaestors: Millar 1964: 33–4).
68 On magistrates and mobility: O'Sullivan 2011: 51–76; Östenberg 2015: 13–22; See Chapter 11 by A.M. Wilskman in this volume.
69 Petron., *Sat.* 44.10. Cf. Hall 1998 on greetings.
70 Petron., *Sat.* 44.7.
71 Varro *apud* Gell. 13.13.4.
72 Suet., *Ner.* 4.
73 Gell. 7.9.6 = Piso F29, *FRHist* 2.322–3. Cf. Liv. 9.46.9.
74 Haimson Lushkov 2015: 74.
75 Cf. Tuori 2018: 202 with bountiful references at n. 22.
76 Wallace-Hadrill 1988: 44–5; Hales 2003: 55–60; Russell 2016: 8–12, with esp. Cic., *Mur.* 76.
77 Vitr. 6.5.2.
78 Vell. Pat. 2.14.3. Cf. Cic., *Dom.* 100.
79 Cic., *Off.* 1.138–9; Plut., *Mar.* 32.1, *Cic.* 8.6. Cf. Millar 1977: 18 on the senator's house as a space 'where a significant part of his public role was played'.
80 The choice of a house on the Palatine could be used to construct a political persona in advance of winning middle-ranking offices: Cic., *Cael.* 18 (renting on Palatine by 56 B.C.; tribune in 52; curule aedile in 50).

81 Q. Cic., *Comm. Pet.* 44.
82 Viitanen and Nissin 2017: 129–135. As the authors rightly observe, however, 'a notice inside the house is not an indication of ownership of the candidate' (p. 132). Cf. Mouritsen 1988: 18–19.
83 Cic., *Dom.* 112.
84 The participle *interuersa* conjures images of deceit (Plaut., *Pseud.* 541) and embezzlement (Cic., *Verr.* 2.4.68) in addition to its plainer meaning of 'setting to one side'. Cf. Nisbet 1939: 164.
85 Petron., *Sat.* 44.13.
86 Asc. 26C.
87 According to Quint., *Inst.* 5.13.40, the prosecution complained that 'Scaurus' columns were carried through the city on wagons' (*Scauri columnas per urbem plaustris uectas esse*), potentially causing damage to other infrastructure. Cf. Alexander 2002: 107 on 'the tradition hostile to Scaurus, one that specifically related to avarice'.
88 Asc. 20C: Scaurus 'moved the jury greatly with the memory of his extravagant aedileship of with his popularity among the people' (*magnopere iudices mouit . . . aedilitatis effusae memoria ac fauore populari*). Asconius (27C) also found precise details about Scaurus' aedileship in Cicero's *Pro Scauro*: 'Scaurus had used these as aedile, as Cicero himself also states, in his adornment of the theatre' (*usus erat iis aedilis – ut ipse [sc. Cicero] quoque significant – in ornatu theatri*). Cf. Schol. Bob. 135St.
89 The columns were presumably only displayed at the *ludi Romani* and not the *Megalenses*: Plin., *NH* 36.5 writes that they were displayed publicly 'for barely one month' (*uix mense uno*).
90 Plin., *NH* 36.5–6. Cf. Wallace-Hadrill 1988: 64–6.
91 Plin., *NH* 36.115. Pliny knowingly dismisses Scaurus' aedilician endeavours as *priuatae opes* (*NH* 36.113).
92 Asc. 18C makes withering remarks about Scaurus' lack of *industria*. Cf. Lewis 2006: 217, 227.
93 Blurred boundaries between public and private: Russell 2016: 9–10; Nichols 2017: 17–18. Cf. Cic., *Att.* 4.16.6 on the lasting memory of Scaurus' aedileship.
94 Sall., *Cat.* 47.3–4, 55.2; Plut., *Cic.* 22.1. It is usually assumed that the unnamed location on the Palatine is Spinther's *domus* (Wiseman 1994: 357 n. 146; Pagán 2012: 76).
95 Mols and Moormann 1993/94: 41; Clarke 2003: 191; *contra* Spano 1943: 276.
96 Mols and Moormann 1993/94: 40; Clarke 2003: 191; Goldbeck 2010: 128 n. 4. But see Mols 1999: 12 n. 41, 51 n. 247 with a more confident identification as a *salutatio*.
97 These are not magisterial chairs: Mols and Moormann 1993/94: 40; Clarke 2003: 191; *contra* Schäfer 1990: 328–331 (*bisellium*); Campbell 2015: 137 n. 33 (*sella curulis*). The chairs in the *atrium* are clearly different from the one on which Vestorius is seated on the reverse.
98 Ambivalent: Spano 1943: 274 ('calzari verdi'); slippers: Mols and Moormann 1993/94: 40; *calcei*: Schäfer 1990: 330; Compostella 1992: 680 (perhaps '*den gesellschaftlichen Rang des Verstorbenen anzugeben*', although the shoes seem to be somewhat different from those which he wears when seated on the *suggestus*).
99 Felletti Maj 1977: 327.
100 Judgement: Spano 1943: 289, 292; Richardson 1973: 221, 1988: 97 n. 8. Money: Schäfer 1990: 331. Agnostic: Clarke 2003: 196–7.
101 A *tribunal* was also excavated within the basilica at Pompeii, a space that 'might include offices for public magistrates' (Richardson 1988: 97).
102 Clarke 2003: 201.

References

Alexander, M. C. 2002: *The Case for the Prosecution in the Ciceronian Era*, Ann Arbor, MI.
Amoroso, A. 2007. 'Il tempio di *Tellus* e il quartiere della *praefectura urbana*', *Workshop di Archeologia Classica* 4, 53–84.

Arena, V. 2012: *Libertas and the Practice of Politics in the Late Roman Republic*, Cambridge.
Bablitz, L. 2008: 'The Platform in Roman Art, 30 BC – AD 180: Forms and Functions', in C. Deroux (ed.), *Studies in Latin Literature and Roman History: Volume 14*, Brussels, 235–282.
Becker, M. 2017: 'Suntoque aediles curatores urbis . . .', *Die Entwicklung der stadtrömischen Aedilität in republikanischer Zeit*, Stuttgart.
Bernstein, F. 1998: *Ludi publici. Untersuchungen zur Entstehung und Entwicklung der öffentlichen Spiele im republikanischen Rom*, Stuttgart.
Berrendonner, C. 2009: 'La surveillance des poids et mesures par les autorités romaines: l'apport de la documentation épigraphique latine', *Cahiers du Centre Gustave Glotz* 20, 351–370.
Campbell, V. L. 2015: *The Tombs of Pompeii: Organization, Space, and Society*, London.
Clarke, J. R. 2003: *Art in the Lives of Ordinary Romans: Visual Representation and Non-Elite Viewers in Italy, 100 B.C. – A.D. 315*, Berkeley, CA.
Coarelli, F. 1985: *Il foro romano, II: Periodo repubblicano e augusteo*, Rome.
Coarelli, F. 1997: *Il Campo Marzio: dalle origini alla fine della repubblica*, Rome.
Compostella, C. 1992: 'Banchetti pubblici e banchetti privati nell'iconografia funeraria romana del I secolo d.C.', *Mélanges de l'École française de Rome* 104(2), 659–689.
Corbeill, A. 2018: 'Clodius's Contio de haruspicum responsis', in C. Gray et al. (eds.), *Reading Republican Oratory: Reconstructions, Contexts, Reception*, Oxford, 171–190.
Daguet-Gagey, A. 2015: *Splendor aedilitatum: L'édilité à Rome (Ier s. avant J.-C. – IIIe s. après J.-C.)*, Rome.
Davies, P. J. E. 2017: *Architecture and Politics in Republican Rome*, Cambridge.
De Nuccio, M., and Gallocchio, E. 2017: 'Il tempio di Apollo in Circo Flaminio a Roma: un aggiornamento sulle pavimentazioni', in C. Angelelli and D. Massara (eds), *Atti del XXII Colloquio dell'Associazione italiana per lo studio e la conservazione del mosaico*, Tivoli, 449–458.
De Sanctis, G. 1932: 'La origine dell'edilità plebea', *Rivista di Filologia* 10(4), 433–445.
Dufallo, B. 2021: *Disorienting Empire: Republican Latin Poetry's Wanderings*, Oxford.
Felletti Maj, B. M. 1977: *La tradizione italica nell'arte romana*, Rome.
Freudenburg, K. 2014: '*Recusatio* as Political Theatre: Horace's Letter to Augustus', *Journal of Roman Studies* 104, 105–132.
Garnsey, P. 1988: *Famine and Food Supply in the Graeco-Roman World: Responses to Risk and Crisis*, Cambridge.
Goldbeck, F. 2010: *Salutationes: Die Morgenbegrüßungen in Rom in der Republik und der frühen Kaiserzeit*, Berlin.
Goldberg, S. M. 1998: 'Plautus on the Palatine', *Journal of Roman Studies* 88, 1–20.
Gratwick, A. S. 1993: *Plautus: Menaechmi*, Cambridge.
Green, C. M. C. 1997: 'Free as a Bird: Varro *De Re Rustica* 3', *The American Journal of Philology* 118(3), 427–448.
Haimson Lushkov, A. 2015: *Magistracy and the Historiography of the Roman Republic. Politics in Prose*, Cambridge.
Hales, S. 2003: *The Roman House and Social Identity*, Cambridge.
Hall, J. 1998: 'The Deference-Greeting in Roman Society', *Maia* 50, 413–426.
Hartmann, B. 2020: *The Scribes of Rome: A Cultural and Social History of the Scribae*, Cambridge.
Kondratieff, E. J. 2009: 'Reading Rome's Evolving Civic Landscape in Context: Tribunes of the Plebs and the Praetor's Tribunal', *Phoenix* 63(3/4), 322–360.
Kondratieff, E. J. 2010: 'The Urban Praetor's Tribunal in the Roman Republic', in F. De Angelis (ed.), *Spaces of Justice in the Roman World*, Leiden, 89–126.

Latham, J. A. 2016: *Performance, Memory, and Processions in Ancient Rome: The Pompa Circensis from the Late Republic to Late Antiquity*, New York.
Le Bonniec, H. 1958: *Le Culte de Cérès à Rome des origines à la fin de la République*, Paris.
Lewis, R. G. 2006: *Asconius: Commentaries on Speeches by Cicero*, Oxford.
Lintott, A. 1999: *The Constitution of the Roman Republic*, Oxford.
Lintott, A. 2009: 'Provocatio e iudicium populi dopo Kunkel', in B. Santalucia (ed.), *La repressione criminale nella Roma repubblicana fra norma e persuasione*, Pavia, 15–24.
Lopez Garcia, A., forthcoming: 'Fora Litibus Omnia Fervent: The Transfer of the Tribunals in Rome from the Forum to the Courtroom'.
Migeotte, L. 2005: 'Les pouvoirs des agoranomes dans les cités grecques', in R. W. Wallace and M. Gagarin (eds), *Symposion 2001. Vorträge zur griechischen und hellenistischen Rechtsgeschichte*, Vienna, 287–301.
Mignone, L. M. 2016: *The Republican Aventine and Rome's Social Order*, Ann Arbor, MI.
Millar, F. 1964: 'The Aerarium and Its Officials Under the Empire', *Journal of Roman Studies* 54(1–2), 33–40.
Millar, F. 1977: *The Emperor in the Roman World (31 BC – AD 337)*, London.
Mols, S. T. A. M. 1999: *Wooden Furniture in Herculaneum: Form, Technique and Function*, Leiden.
Mols, S. T. A. M., and Moormann, E. A. 1993/94: '*Ex parvo crevit*. Proposta per una lettura iconografica della Tomba di Vestorius Priscus fuori Porta Vesuvio a Pompei', *Rivista di Studi Pompeiani* 6, 15–52.
Morstein-Marx, R. 2004: *Mass Oratory and Political Power in the Late Roman Republic*, Cambridge.
Mouritsen, H. 1988: *Elections, Magistrates, and Municipal Élite. Studies in Pompeian Epigraphy*, Rome.
Nelsestuen, G. A. 2015: *Varro the Agronomist: Political Philosophy, Satire, and Agriculture in the Late Republic*, Columbus.
Nichols, M. F. 2017: *Author and Audience in Vitruvius' De architectura*, Cambridge.
Nisbet, R. G. (ed.) 1939: *M. Tulli Ciceronis: De Domo Sua Ad Pontifices Oratio*, Oxford.
O'Sullivan, T. 2011: *Walking in Roman Culture*, Cambridge.
Östenberg, I. 2015: 'Power Walks: Aristocratic Escorted Movements in Republican Rome', in I. Östenberg, S. Malmberg, and J. Bjørnebye (eds), *The Moving City: Processions, Passages and Promenades in Ancient Rome*, London, 13–22.
Pagán, V. E. 2012: *Conspiracy Theory in Latin Literature*, Austin, TX.
Palmer, R. 1997: *Rome and Carthage at Peace*, Stuttgart.
Pellam, G. 2014: 'Ceres, the Plebs, and *Libertas* in the Roman Republic', *Historia* 63(1), 74–95.
Pepe, L. 1957: *Studi petroniani*, Naples.
Piacentin, S. 2018: 'The Role of Aedilician Fines in the Making of Public Rome', *Historia* 67, 103–126.
Rankin, H. D. 1968: 'Petronius 44, 3–5: Who Receives the Beating?', *Hermes* 96(2), 254–256.
Richardson, Jr., L. 1973: 'The Tribunals of the Praetors of Rome', *Mitteilungen des Deutschen Archäologischen Instituts, Römische Abteilung* 80, 219–233.
Richardson, Jr., L. 1988: *Pompeii: An Architectural History*, Baltimore, MD.
Roller, L. E. 1999: *In Search of God the Mother: The Cult of Anatolian Cybele*, Berkeley, CA.
Russell, A. 2016: *The Politics of Public Space in Republican Rome*, Cambridge.
Ryan, F. X. 1997: 'Two Missing Aediles, and Several Others', *Athenaeum* 85, 251–265.
Ryan, F. X. 1998: *Rank and Participation in the Roman Senate*, Stuttgart.

Schäfer, T. 1990: 'Der Honor biselli', *Mitteilungen des Deutschen Archäologischen Instituts, Römische Abteilung* 97, 307–346.
Serrati, J. 2006: 'Neptune's Altars: The Treaties between Rome and Carthage (509–226 B.C.)', *Classical Quarterly* 56(1), 113–134.
Spaeth, B. S. 1996: *The Roman Goddess Ceres*, Austin, TX.
Spano, G. 1943: 'La tomba dell'edile C. Vestorio Prisco in Pompei', *Memorie. Atti della Accademia nazionale dei Lincei* 7(3), 237–315.
Tatum, W. J. 1999: *The Patrician Tribune: Publius Clodius Pulcher*, Chapel Hill, NC and London.
Tuori, K. 2018: 'Pliny and the Uses of the *aerarium Saturni* as an Administrative Space', *Arctos* 52, 199–230.
Viitanen, E.-M., and Nissin, L. 2017: 'Campaigning for Votes in Ancient Pompeii: Contextualizing Electoral *Programmata*', in I. Berti, K. Bolle, F. Opdenhoff, and F. Stroth (eds), *Writing Matters: Presenting and Perceiving Monumental Inscriptions in Antiquity and the Middle Ages*, Berlin and Boston, MA, 117–144.
Viscogliosi, A. 1996: *Il tempio di Apollo in Circo e la formazione del linguaggio architettonico augusteo*, Rome.
Wallace-Hadrill, A. 1988: 'The Social Structure of the Roman House', *Papers of the British School at Rome* 56, 43–97.
Wiseman, T. P. 1974: 'The Circus Flaminius', *Papers of the British School at Rome* 42, 3–26.
Wiseman, T. P. 1976: 'Two Questions on the Circus Flaminius', *Papers of the British School at Rome* 44, 44–47.
Wiseman, T. P. 1994: *Historiography and Imagination: Eight Essays on Roman Culture*, Exeter.
Wiseman, T. P. 1998: *Roman Drama and Roman History*, Exeter.
Zevi, F., and Friggeri, R. 2012: 'Ara degli scribi', in R. Friggeri, M. G. Granino Cecere, and G. L. Gregori (eds), *Terme di Diocleziano. La collezione epigrafica*, Milan, 355–362.

6 Moving Magistrates in a Roman City Space

The Pompeian Model

Samuli Simelius

1 Introduction

The best location to find a Roman magistrate was likely the forum. However, it was not the only option. Magistrates also worked at home and moved throughout the city space as did any other person living in the city. There are literary sources that suggest that a part of the work relating to administration could have been done even when moving from one place to another. Consequently, we cannot dismiss the importance of roads and streets in Roman administrative work. This contribution aims to clarify the importance of the street for Roman administration, highlighting their character as a location to meet people, which was essential for magistrates and the people seeking an audience with an administrator. The chapter first examines the literary sources and then moves to locate the best street locations to encounter a magistrate, or for a magistrate to be visible in the Pompeii cityscape.

If one just wanted to encounter a random Roman magistrate, the easiest way was to go to the forum. However, this was not the only option. Magistrates also worked at home, and additionally they moved in the city space just as other citizens, inhabitants, or visitors. There are literary sources demonstrating that some of the work relating to administration could have been done while moving from one place to another. Consequently, dismissing the importance of roads and streets in Roman administrative work would leave the picture incomplete. This chapter investigates and models the movement of magistrates in the Roman urban environment. The focus is first on the literary sources, followed by an examination of Roman Pompeii as it was just before the eruption of Vesuvius 79 C.E. The aim is to model the best locations to meet a magistrate in Pompeii, or the best locations to be visible, which was important for persons involving administrative work – at least occasionally.

Administrative work is defined very broadly in this chapter. It includes all type of juridical and legal activity, communal decision making, and the political process involving it – including elections – as well as bureaucracy. Although the elected magistrate or people holding other offices are central to this chapter, the scope includes all of the people involved in administrative work, including those that needed the services of the persons incorporated into the administrative machinery of the Roman Empire.

DOI: 10.4324/b23090-8

This chapter has been made available under a CC BY-NC 4.0 license.

The literary sources that describe the Roman world have been under substantial scrutiny for centuries, and therefore it often seems that almost all aspects should have already been discussed – at least on some level. This is the case with movement and administrative work. In particular, legal historians keenly and diligently combed through Roman texts to find the locations and circumstances associated with Roman juridical work. Consequently, the first part of this chapter owes much to the work of scholars such as Leanne Bablitz, Francesco De Angelis, and Kaius Tuori, who have in their scholarly contributions discussed the several locations associated with Roman jurists and the legal process.

Although it might be somewhat obvious, it is essential to remember that Pompeii cannot be equated to Rome. This fact is repeated constantly by many scholars, and therefore we cannot necessarily transfer the social and administrative landscape of the capital – and consequently the world that is described in the literary sources – to a municipal city.[1] Before modelling the optimal locations to meet a magistrate, I will therefore take a look at the Pompeian sources that can be connected to magistrates and discuss what they tell us about the locations utilized by the administration. Electoral notices are one such source. They are an exceptional source group, hardly known outside Pompeii.[2] On this matter, the chapter relies largely on previous research, in particular the recent work of Eeva-Maria Viitanen and her colleagues. Their work has connected the notices to their spatial context.[3] In addition to the electoral notices, some wall paintings are discussed in this chapter. The selected paintings either depict magistrates or likely the streetscape of Pompeii, making them relevant to the subject in hand.

Timothy O'Sullivan has concluded that walking was a social and performative activity for Romans.[4] The desire to be visible is the key element of the last part of the chapter, which models the movement patterns of ancient Pompeii to map the locations that were best for reaching the maximum audience. These locations were particularly important if one anticipated being a magistrate – so before holding office – because they were good locations to meet the Pompeians who would then vote in the elections or otherwise participate in the process by supporting a candidate. These same spots can also be thought of as optimal for people who wished to meet a magistrate. Of course, the forum or other public venues where good for this purpose, but, as indicated by some literary sources, the magistrates might have been busy in those locations, making them less ideal places to consult them. The private houses of the magistrates were another location for such meetings, but as they were characteristically private, they perhaps did not offer the possibility of an audience for everyone. Consequently, this makes the streets and roads the third possible location, and they might have even been the more democratic of the three venues. They offered the magistrate the opportunity to meet many people – including those that did not or could not spend much time in the forum. For the people that were not part of the administrative apparatus, they were good locations to come across a magistrate, in particular for those who could not arrange a private audience or did not have the opportunity to spend much time in the forum.

The last part of the chapter utilizes the Space Syntax analysis developed by Bill Hillier and Julienne Hanson. It reconstructs the moving patterns of the city to help to identify the locations that were ideal for meeting a magistrate, or for a magistrate to be visible. Space Syntax analysis has been used several times before this in (classical) archaeology. For example, Fabiana Battistin has recently applied it to the movement patterns of Falerii Novii, and her article functions as an excellent introduction to Space Syntax analysis and its technical aspects.[5] The method is not a new tool for Pompeii either. For instance, Mark Grahame and Katharine Von Stackelberg have used its manually calculated application to model the movement and visibility inside Pompeian houses, and Michael Anderson has done similar work with a computer assisted method.[6] The street network of the city has also been analysed with Space Syntax by Akkelies Van Nes, Karin Fridell Anter, and Marina Weilguni. Anter Fridell and Weilguni's article "Public Space in Roman Pompeii" discusses the creation of the axial plan of Pompeii for Space Syntax analysis, which was utilized later by Weilguni in her dissertation studying wheeled traffic and the interaction between public and private in Pompeii. Van Nes' work concentrates on the shops/*tabernae*, the entrances, and public buildings, and their connection with the values produced by Space Syntax analysis.[7] Additionally, David Newsome has utilized the method to analyze the transformation of the street network on the west side of the forum.[8]

For the creation of my Space Syntax analysis, I used the DepthmapX 0.8 software. The Space syntax analysis provides only a model – no one actually walks like the patterns produced by the software. The model cannot take into account all the possible factors that a human does when selecting a route, and it is overly rational compared to human behaviour, but it can still be a helpful tool to interpret ancient life. To evaluate the Space Syntax model, I compare it to previous research done on Pompeiian movement that has been reconstructed on the basis of the archaeological evidence, such as the location of doors, electoral notices, shops, other commercial or productive activity, and by utilizing other mathematical models to calculate the moving patterns.[9]

II Private Dwellings and Streets as Locations for Administrative Work in the Literary Sources

Public spaces, such as the forum and the buildings around it, are well-known locations of administrative activity. Public venues were principally locations of meetings and decision-making. Nonetheless, the literary sources also clearly depict that administrative work was not limited to these public spaces. The private sphere likewise functioned as a location for meetings – specifically for smaller gatherings – and plenty of preparatory work seems to have occurred in private buildings. The separation between these two locations of administrative work – the forum and the house – created a third space for the magistrates: the streets and roads connecting them. These were also involved in the administrative life of the Roman world. The journey from the house to the forum turned out to be an opportunity to meet a magistrate, or even for a magistrate to perform some administrative task during his travels.

Before examining what the literary sources have to say about how streets and roads related to administrative work, I will briefly take a look at the Roman house and other private dwellings as a location of administrative work. Although legal historians have demonstrated their importance, they are not perhaps so well known for this function, and a short recap of a couple selected sources is in order.

In general, private dwellings played a significant role in the preparatory phase of administrative work but may have also been occasionally used for other stages of work, such as locations of trials.[10] Writing and dictating were a natural part of the preparatory work, and there are plenty of passages describing these activities. However, this was a quite mundane activity for the writers of the ancient texts, and therefore it is rarely stated what type of work was going on – it could be administrative or some other tasks, such as writing a study. Writing and dictating seem to have been quite flexible activities that could be done almost anywhere: Caesar is said to have signed letters while dining, and Mark Antony dictated an edict at the dinner.[11] The dining area suggests a private sphere, but more importantly, these passages make it clear that a part of administrative work did not require a grand or public setting, but could be done in the middle of everyday activities.

Vitruvius' famous passage that describes how people of different social positions needed different types of houses is often used as evidence for administrative and juridical work occurring in private houses.[12] The architect tells us that lawyers and orators need spacious and decorated spaces and rooms for meetings, and that people holding offices should have regal and high *vestibula*, large atria and peristyles, and additionally decorated gardens, walkways, libraries, *pinacothecae*, and even *basilicae* in their houses, which should all be architecturally as magnificent as public buildings.[13]

Vitruvius' focus seems to be on spaces for meetings, and he does not mention where the preparatory work related to administrative or legal processes should happen. It is possible that Vitruvius thought that the same locations could have been used for both purposes, but the text leaves this open. However, reading *De architectura* gives the picture that the *domus* was actually a key place in a magistrate's work life. For example, when Vitruvius discusses the fora and *basilicae*, he barely touches on the needs of magistrates, but rather discusses the needs of economic activity and focuses on the lines of sight (at the basilica of Fano).[14] The function of fora and *basilicae* as administrative locations might have been so obvious for Vitruvius that he did not see a need to discuss these activities in detail. Nonetheless, when he discusses houses, Vitruvius makes sure that the reader notes the needs of magistrates and lawyers, which indicates that administrative and legal activities – if relevant for the inhabitant – should be taken carefully in consideration when building a private dwelling.

In addition to Vitruvius, there are plenty of other writers who describe the house as a meeting place for administrative and legal functions. For instance, Tacitus describes a situation where the orator and politician Vipstanus Messalla enters a room and thinks that he may have interrupted the preparation of a case, because everybody in the room had such serious facial expressions.[15] Cicero mentions that people wanting to meet the eminent lawyer Q. Mucius always crowded in front of his house, and also remarks that the prominent orator Manius Manilius could be met in the forum or in his house, and consulted on legal and other matters.[16]

Tacitus' passage not only tells us about a meeting occurring in a private space, but also indicates that the preparative work for a case could be done in private dwellings, which must have been very common, as Quintilian's *Institutio Oratoria* states that the advocates prepared their work and speeches at home.[17]

Furthermore, meeting with a magistrate was also built into the Roman practice of *salutatio*, where *clientes* visited their patron's house during the morning. The exact character of the *salutatio* is not very clear, but scholars have assumed that it might have involved legal, financial, and political support, and a conversation between the host and the visitor.[18] Without a doubt, the *salutatio* was a good occasion to meet a magistrate if one's patron held such a position, or perhaps one of the other visitors in the *salutatio*. However, the *salutatio* did not guarantee that anybody could meet the house owner, but only his *clientes*. The same applies to the function of the house as a meeting place. Although a Roman house could hypothetically have been open to almost anybody,[19] it did not mean that everybody had a chance to meet the house owner or a magistrate when they entered their house. The private nature of the location restricted such encounters, but in the public, anybody could approach a person involved in administrative duties.

Consequently, a convenient location to meet a magistrate was the street between his house and the forum. In some cases, it might have been even better to meet the magistrate on the street, as the chances of getting an audience might have been higher than in other public places such as the forum. Martial tells us about the lawyer Pompeius Auctus, who could be found near the entrance of Temple of Mars Avenger, but he was so busy that he did not have time before the normal court day was over.[20] Likewise, a busy household with many visitors was not likely an optimal location to meet a magistrate in the middle of his duties.

Furthermore, the streets could create public pressure for the magistrate. Bablitz has concluded that hiring an advocate was likely often made in public, citing the story of Augustus' veteran Scutarius. He managed to secure the emperor himself as his lawyer due to the public pressure of the bad publicity that would have befallen Augustus if he had declined the veteran's petition.[21] According to Suetonius, Scutarius was Augustus' *cliens*, which might mean that not even this kind of relationship ensured a meeting during the *salutatio*, or if it did, the public location was still better for convincing Augustus to be his lawyer. Additionally, there is an anecdote about Vespasian suspecting that his muleteer was delaying their journey on purpose so that a person could approach the emperor with a petition for a lawsuit.[22] It is difficult to know how much of these stories are true, and they focus on emperors, who were obviously the most preferred persons to handle one's matters – providing that he was favourable to them. Nonetheless, they relate two important aspects: 1) a public space could produce more pressure to take on a case or address other matters, and 2) meeting a public person was not always easy, and one had to use every opportunity. These likely applied to many persons involved in administration, even if they did not hold the highest position, as the emperor did.

Although the streets offered a natural location to meet a magistrate, any movement between two locations could additionally be utilized for other tasks relating to administration. Both writing and dictating are said to have been done while traveling and moving.²³ Cicero mentions that a journey or a walk is an occasion to prepare for a case in the courts.²⁴ In addition, even manumission could be performed while moving.²⁵ The streets were not only a transitory space between the magistrate's house and the forum, but also functioned as a location for administrative activity. Compared to the forum, where administrative activities were executed on a tight schedule, as the example of Pompeius Auctus demonstrates, and private houses, which offered the opportunity to avoid possible visitors, the streets offered a good place to approach magistrates – in particular, for those who did not hold a high position in society. In this way, the streets can be considered an even more democratic location than a private house or the forum.

III Administrative Space in Pompeii

The literary sources mainly describe Rome, or perhaps can be thought of as describing the Empire in general, and therefore their accounts do not necessarily correspond to the situation in Pompeii. Literary mentions are few for the city buried by Vesuvius, and therefore the picture of the administrative and political life must be reconstructed on the basis of different material. Inscriptions have been at the core of this task. Architecture, both public and private, has also played a role in the interpretation, but it has proven a difficult source to connect to Pompeian administration and politics. Furthermore, wall paintings can also be used to reconstruct the administrative cityscape in Pompeii. All of these sources are examined in this chapter to build a reconstruction of the spatial structure of Pompeii's administrative landscape. I will begin with a brief analysis of the forum, which might be thought of as the obvious centre of administration, but the sources do not offer as clear a picture as one might think. This is followed by a short examination of the houses, focusing on the question of whether we can identify the houses involved in the administration of the city. Finally, the investigation emphasizes the role of the streets and electoral notices. The examination of the streets will then continue in the next section.

Pompeii's administrative centre is usually thought to have been located around the forum, which is in the southwest corner of the city. The buildings on the south side of the forum have often been interpreted as administrative buildings. One of them has basilica shape, three others consist of one hall with an apse (one building has a rectangular apse, two round), and there is a building with a large space with two podiums on the south side (Figure 6.1). They have been identified as the basilica, the city council chamber, the archive, the office of the duumviri, and the *comitium*, even though their specific function can be only speculated upon. For instance, the three halls have also alternatively been suggested to have been temples, and the so-called *comitium* has additionally been thought to have been a general voting place, a tribunal, or a school building. This area was excavated around the 1810s, and consequently the reports offer very little – if any at all – help to identify the functions of these buildings. Furthermore, the three hall-type buildings were apparently emptied of all material and decoration (except the floors) before the excavation.²⁶ The basilica seems to be the sole building for which scholars have arrived at a consensus on the function.

126 *Samuli Simelius*

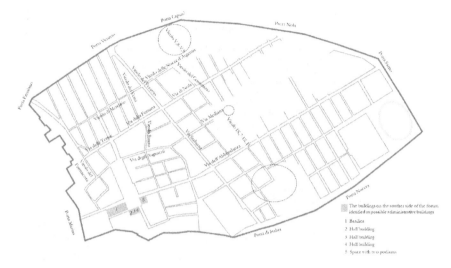

Figure 6.1 Map of Pompeii with street names. Projected streets with lighter gray.
Source: Author: Samuli Simelius.

It is possible that administrative work also occurred in the other areas of Pompeii, such as the public porticoes. These were the forum, the Triangular Forum, the Large Palaestra, and the Quadriporticus. However, some of these seem to have been devoted to other purposes, such as gladiator barracks, so they were not likely venues of administration.[27] A set of wall paintings found in the so-called *Villa di Giulia Felice* (II,4,3) has been interpreted as depicting Pompeii's forum. The paintings locate plenty of varied activity in the forum, such as selling and buying, schoolwork, and just people strolling. Additionally, there is a scene that has been interpreted as a person presenting a young girl to a sitting magistrate (Figure 6.2).[28] The painting thus seems to confirm that the magistrates met people in the forum. A porticoed space was likely a good venue for administrative activity, in particular when the activity involved writing, as they provided protection from rain but still had light. An old drawing of the painting from the *Villa di Giulia Felice* could indicate that another person was also sitting on the magistrate's seat and could have been holding an opened scroll or some type of sheet of writing.[29] However, this is difficult to confirm from the existing remains of the paintings.

If the weather conditions were really poor then a portico would not have been enough protection, and a set of rooms behind the portico was needed to offer enough light but also cover. In this case, there are not many public locations that could be used for this purpose, particularly if the Quadriporticus and Large Palaestra were used for other purposes than administration. That leaves the spaces at the south side of the forum – discussed before – and another set of buildings in its northwest corner, where the room for the official overseeing the measurement standards may have been located. John Dobbins also speculates that there were two additional offices and an *aerarium*, but these buildings may have also had a

Figure 6.2 Wall painting from the Villa di Giulia Felice (II,4,3) depicting a person presenting a young girl to a magistrate.

Source: Picture: Wikimedia Commons/Jamie Heath. Picture edited by Samuli Simelius.

commercial function. The largest building in the northwest corner has been interpreted as a granary or a market building.[30]

As the discussion earlier demonstrates, there does not seem to have been many public buildings designed for administrative work in Pompeii, and those that are interpreted as having been used for such a purpose are usually done so on speculative grounds. Furthermore, these spaces may have been used for several purposes. The paintings of the so-called *Villa di Giulia Felice* suggest that there were many other things occurring in the forum than just administration. The basilica also likely held many activities and persons related to these activities, such as bankers, businesspersons, administrators, jurists, and people involved in the legal process.[31] This leaves very little space for administrative work, particularly if we think of an office-like work environment. Additionally, we can assume that not all stages of administrative work would have necessarily been suited to a public setting but would have needed some privacy. It is therefore extremely likely that private houses had an important role as Pompeian administrative spaces, similar to the picture drawn by the literary sources for Rome.

Pompeii also hosts a collection of unique textual sources that has allowed researchers to identify house owners. Electoral notices, graffiti, and amphora texts have played a key role in this task, but other types of inscriptions have also been utilized. The electoral notices have been fundamental to this type of study, and consequently many of the identified house owners have been Pompeii's magistrates. Nonetheless, such identification has been proven to be more difficult than has been expected, and the trend in research has moved on from the old optimistic attitude introduced by Matteo Della Corte to Penelope Allison's modern and more critical approach.[32]

The identification of house owners is done on the basis of the spatial connections between the written records and the houses. However, the discovery of a scratched or painted name in the context of a house does not guarantee that it was the name of the owner, and a more refined methodology was needed. For instance, Henrik Mouritsen's method demands at least two different types of textual sources to confirm the identity of the owner, and using this system there are only a few houses where the owner can be identified.[33]

Although only a few house owners can be identified, there is still a likely connection between wealth and social position in Pompeii. Nonetheless, it cannot be stated that all of the large and decorated houses were owned by the political upper class.[34] On the other hand, a house owner did not have to be an aedile or duumvir to be a participant in the city administration, and therefore some houses that were not owned by the political ruling class might have been equally involved in the administrative work. This means that it is – at least for now – impossible to point out all of the exact houses involved in administrative work, but very likely many of the most decorated and largest houses were owned by persons involved in the administrative work of the city. These houses are spread around almost the entire excavated area of Pompeii, as Figure 6.3 shows. The exception is the southeastern part, which held the amphitheatre and the Large Palaestra, which were both

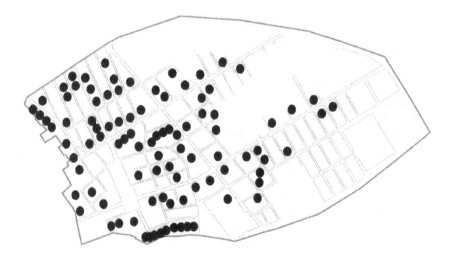

Figure 6.3 The locations of the largest and most decorated houses in Pompeii.
Source: Author: Samuli Simelius.[35]

visited – at least infrequently – by many people, some of them naturally belonging to the administrators of the city. This indicates that none of Pompeii's areas can be excluded from the investigation of the administrative life of the city, and very likely all of the areas – except perhaps the south-east corner – were at least somewhat involved in administrative work within private houses.

The electoral notices – painted on the buildings flanking the streets – provide us with a picture of the importance of these streets in the political and administrative life of Pompeii. Viitanen has recently studied the locations of these electoral notices, and she concludes that they have a strong connection with other factors that indicate a busy street life. It makes sense to locate the notices at places where many people could see them.[36] This leads to the conclusion that if the magistrates wanted to be visible, they probably would have favoured those same streets; and other way around, if one wanted to meet a magistrate, then these streets were locations where one should go. However, it is possible to identify even more precisely the best locations to make oneself visible or to meet a magistrate, and that is the task of the next section.

Other than the scenes of the forum found in the *Villa di Giulia Felice*, there are not many Pompeian wall paintings depicting the administration of the city. A painting illustrating persons and bread has been interpreted as a baker or bread seller, but because the person giving the bread is wearing a toga, he has also been interpreted as a magistrate providing the bread, and thus the paintings could illustrate a *largitio* (Figure 6.4).[37] The *Tomba di Caio Vestorio Prisco* near the *Porta Vesuvio* has a painting of a man wearing a toga sitting on a possible *sella curilis*; this person is thought to be an aedile.[38] Additionally, there is the so-called painting of the Judgement of Solomon, which has cartoon-like characters with small bodies and large heads. It (possibly) depicts three judges in the act of cutting a baby in half, similar to the story of the judgement of Solomon (Figure 6.5). However, there are parallel stories from Antiquity, and thus it is not certain that this refers to Solomon.[39] A common feature of all of these paintings is a podium situated under the seated characters. In the *largitio* painting it seems to be wooden, and thus may represent an impermanent structure. The painting in the tomb is difficult to interpret in its current condition, but previous descriptions and photographs suggest that it also featured a wooden podium. In the painting of the so-called judgement of Solomon, the podium looks distinctively different from the other two paintings. Its material is challenging to identify, but it does not look like wood, and compared to the others that have only one person on the podium there are three characters on this podium. It is possible that the painting depicts a more permanent structure. The background of the *largitio* and the painting in the tomb are ambivalent, and it cannot be certain whether the scene is occurring inside a building or outside, but the scene of the judgement takes place outside. Also, the forum scenes of the *Villa di Giulia Felice* occur outside, although their current condition makes it difficult to see whether the persons are inside or outside the portico. However, compared to other paintings of magistrates, these forum scenes do not feature a podium.

In all of the aforementioned paintings, the magistrates are not moving but sitting. The sitting posture, and the possible presence of a *sella curilis*, are a means

130 *Samuli Simelius*

Figure 6.4 Wall painting from house VII,3,30 depicting a person wearing a toga giving bread to another person.

Source: Marie-Lan Nguyen. Public domain. Wikimedia Commons.

(both for us and the Romans) to recognize a magister. Without a seat or other symbols to indicate an individual's magisterial position, it is often impossible to distinguish a magistrate from a citizen wearing a toga, as in the painting of the so-called amphitheatre riot that occurred in Pompeii. This painting depicts the fight between Pompeians and Nucerians that took place in the city's amphitheatre in 59 C.E. Most of the characters in the painting seem to be involved in the fighting, but on the lower part some persons seem to be conducting their daily life. Some of them seem to be walking near the amphitheatre, and are perhaps wearing a toga, which might suggest an elevated position in society (Figure 6.6).[40] Nonetheless, this is open to interpretation due to the condition of the painting.

Figure 6.5 The wall painting of the so-called judgement of Solomon from the Casa del Medico (VIII,5,24).

Source: Author: Samuli Simelius.

Figure 6.6 The lower part of the wall painting depicting the amphitheatre riot. The painting was found in the Casa della Rissa nell'Anfiteatro (I,3,23).

Source: Author: Samuli Simelius.

Of course, magistrates moved throughout Pompeii, even if we do not have depictions of this – Pompeian paintings actually oftentimes depict things that were not there, such as the mythological scenes.[41] However, the question of whether preparatory administrative work was done while moving in Pompeii remains open. The distances in Pompeii were quite short, so perhaps it was not a custom, as very

132 *Samuli Simelius*

little could have been achieved by doing this. However, one can easily imagine that a person helping a magistrate could make some brief notes on a clay tablet when they were moving, meaning that this activity was not entirely out of the question in Pompeii.

Visibility and performativity were a part of the magistrate's life and work, even in Pompeii. The electoral notices indicate this clearly. The streets offered a good stage to meet the inhabitants of the city, and the magistrates – or people wanting to be magistrates – benefited from this publicity. This also made them locations where Pompeii's other inhabitants could meet magistrates if they needed. What the optimal places for this may have been is examined next.

IV   Towards Mapping the Movement of Magistrates in Pompeii

Building the Street Map

Pompeii is one of the few Roman cities that is almost entirely excavated, but about one quarter of the entire area inside the city walls still remains unexcavated.[42] Additionally, even more material outside the city walls is still covered by deposition layers. The significance of Roman suburbs has recently been re-evaluated,[43] and without a doubt they also effected movement inside the city walls, but the knowledge of the area here is too scarce to be included, and so the examination is limited to the area inside the city walls.

Most of the street network of Pompeii is known, but there are few areas where we must rely on deduction. I mainly follow Eric Poehler's and his groups' understanding of Pompeii's street network.[44] Its pattern is quite similar to the several other interpretations of the street network in 79 C.E.[45] However, some parts are debated; for instance, whether there was a street in the middle of insula III,7. Here I follow Poehler's view that there was not. However, I have interpreted that the *Vicolo* IX.7 – IX.11 continues more-or-less to the *Vicolo del Centenario*, similar to Marco Giglio's interpretation, whereas Poehler sets it to meet the *Via Mediana* about 9 metres east of the intersection.[46] The street network used in this chapter is presented in Figure 6.1.

In general, the projection of unexcavated streets is based on the relative symmetry and rectangular shape of the *insulae*. Marina Weilguni has formatted this principle simply: "The assumption used is that streets always continue as straight lines if there is no evidence to contradict this".[47] On the east side of the *Via Stabiana*, the thus far excavated streets and *insulae* seem to mostly follow this pattern, making it a reasonable assumption. In addition, some projections in parts of *Regiones* III and IX have been confirmed by research done with ground penetrating radar.[48]

The projection of the street pattern is linked to the hypothesis of how the city developed. The zone including most of unexcavated areas is often considered to be one of the last unbuilt areas of Pompeii. Its planning and construction – which occurred in several phases – is usually thought to follow the grid plan, and the *insulae* are usually projected as rectangular.[49] Nonetheless, the deduction is interlinked with the shape. The shape of the *insulae* is one way to recognize the various construction periods of the city, and therefore if the unexcavated *insulae* are thought to be from the same period, they are projected to be of similar shape. Without a doubt, if future data should suggest that the street network of the unexcavated areas had anomalies in its grid plan, it would change the interpretation of the city's development.

The eastern edge of the current excavated area raises some doubts about the presence of an even grid on the east side of Pompeii. The shape of insula I,19 does not appear to be rectangular, and the *Vicolo di Lucrezio Frontone-Vicolo* IX,8-IX,9 and the *Vicolo* V,8-V,9 end in *insulae* IX,11 and V,3 and do not continue further (these locations are marked with dashed circles in Figure 6.1). The known streets around *insula* IX,11 strongly support the last assumption, but one could question the entire existence of the *Vicolo* V,8-V,9. Maija Holappa, Viitanen, and Giglio have demonstrated that topographical factors also influenced the formation of the street network, and we cannot totally exclude that this is not the case in the unexcavated areas.[50] Likewise, Poehler has proposed some changes that break the perfect symmetry of the street network in the eastern part of Pompeii during the last two centuries.[51] All of this creates uncertainty for the suggested map and its logic, but greater confidence can only be achieved after excavations, and on the basis of the current information the rectangular *insulae* are the most likely option.

Locating the Optimal Places to Meet People

The reconstructed street map creates the basis of the movement model. Pompeii provides a wealth of archaeological evidence that can suggest which streets were more active. The presence of these features, such as bars, shops, commercial facilities, and electoral notices, can reflect whether a street was likely more active than others. Scholars have noted the possibility of a circular argument in this methodology: for instance, an accumulation of shops can be interpreted as a sign of an active street, and then, as it is considered an active street, this is seen as the reason why there are so many shops.[52] Although this is certainly something to consider, there is a possibility that these both occur on the same street: a busy street attracts more commercial activity, but the commercial activity also attracts more people. This means that both can indeed be correct.

Space Syntax analysis is a tool that helps us avoid similar problems of circular arguments, as it calculates the use of space according to the most economic options, and therefore likely the most used routes in the city. On the basis of map information, Space Syntax models the areas of the city that "naturally" focus movement. This calculation does not take into account other features, such as shops, but only the shape of the street network. If the areas where Space Syntax produces high values have several shops, it is possible – although not the only option – to deduce that they are clustered there because there was plenty of people moving in that area, even before the shops arrived. Nonetheless, after the shops were established there, they also attracted more street users. This means that if we have both high Space Syntax values and archaeological evidence indicating an active street, the conclusion that many Pompeians used the street on a daily basis is convincing.

These were thus locations where a magistrate should go if he needed to be seen, or vice-versa would be a location to go to if someone wanted to meet a magistrate.

Space Syntax analysis calculates the connection of spaces in a system – which is in this case Pompeii inside the city walls – and it can be utilized to measure visibility or movement. The focus here is on the latter, meaning that calculations are made on the basis of axial lines. The examination here emphasizes the connectivity, integration, and choice values, as all of these can be interpreted as indicators of increased patterns of use. *Connectivity* is a local value that is calculated from the spaces immediately connected to the location under investigation, the so-called space of origin. *Integration* is a global value used to calculate the distance between the space of origin and all other locations in the map. *Choice* instead calculates how likely an axial line is to be passed through on all of the shortest routes from all spaces to all other spaces in the street map of Pompeii. These values can also be depicted on maps using different colours that represent different levels of integration/connectivity/choice: red for the highest level, orange the second highest, followed by yellow, green, and blue as the lowest. I use this colour-coding as the basis for the analysis, rather than the root numerical values also produced by DepthmapX.

Space Syntax, as with any model, is not without its problems. When studying Pompeian houses one issue is that the upper levels are scarcely known, and some connections inside the houses remain unidentified, creating a problem for the model.[53] With regard to the ancient streets, this is not a significant issue. Another problem commonly noted relates to definition of the room/space borders.[54] It might be easy to define a square room, but what about an open public space, such as a piazza or a forum? The borders of these spaces might be very different depending on who is defining them. The computer software (mostly) eliminates the definition problem, as it utilizes a grid (for visual analysis) or axial lines (for movement), making it unnecessary to divide the map into smaller units. Nevertheless, there is still a significant human decision involved in the process: drawing the map from which the analysis is made.

A vital question is the number of details included in the map used in the Space Syntax analysis. All maps are somewhat distorted views of space, but to a certain degree we can influence this by selecting the level of details included in the map. Streets and walls are usually drawn straight – including in Pompeii – although in actuality they are not.[55] In a visual analysis, a slightly curving wall drawn as straight might affect the results, creating a distorted visibility model. However, when studying movement, a schematic plan – not too detailed – might actually be better.

The DepthmapX 0.8 software measures the possible movement patterns by creating lines that cover all of the spaces of the map. In sum, this can mean that the more corners are drawn on the map, the more axial lines it produces, and thus models more movement in that area. Nevertheless, if we consider how people think about their movement – particularly in a city – the small corners of the street do not affect that. For instance, there is a corner on the north side of the *Vicolo di Mercurio* between the *Vicolo di Modesto* and *Via Consolare*. Although this corner has influence on the physical space, hardly anyone would consider it important for

Moving Magistrates in a Roman City Space 135

the decision of whether to walk along the street or not. Yet, if the corner is drawn on the map, it will increase the number of axial lines, indicating more movement there (Figure 6.7). The Fewest Line Map function in the software eliminates much of this problem, as it aims to cover the spatial system with as few lines as possible. However, if the number of details in the depicted system is high, they will also eventually affect the fewest line map. For instance, in Pompeii, if the details

Figure 6.7 The effect of adding a corner on a Space Syntax analysis. Vicolo del Farmacista is first drawn as a rectangular unit that is enclosed by imaginary lines to the north and south. Second, a corner is added to the same street, which adds three lines to the analysis.

Source: Author: Samuli Simelius.

of the locations of the statue bases in the forum are added to the map level they significantly change the results of the analysis, and indicate that there was much more movement in the forum when compared to a map were they are not included. Yet, it is difficult to think that a statue base had a very important role when people navigated the street network of Pompeii – after all, it is an obstacle that is easy to avoid. Of course, this is a very simplistic interpretation, and it is possible that a single element, such as a statue base or a particular corner in the middle of the street, might have had an important role in the city, but to correctly take this into account would require some ancient sources that actually indicate that.

Consequently, I have decided to use a very schematic map, wherein the streets are rendered as perhaps overly straight (Figure 6.8). One can imagine that a person planning his route inside a city would mainly consider a street or block/*insula* as a unit, and then the decision of route is made at the intersections. Therefore, the minor irregularities do not affect to the choice of streets. The principle is somewhat reminiscent of the ancient itinerary lists.[56]

Weilguni's axial grid is quite similar to the axial maps produced in this study (Online Appendix Figures 1, 2, 3, https://zenodo.org/record/7763121),[57] so the principles of creating them must have been alike, although they are not exactly equal. For example, in my plan the *Via Stabiana* is a single straight line, whereas Weilguni has two lines, which indicates that her map has a slight curving of the street.[58] Nonetheless, it is hard to imagine that anyone would consider that curving so remarkable that it would have been highly influential on the decision to use the *Via Stabiana* as a route, so the single line may model movement better.

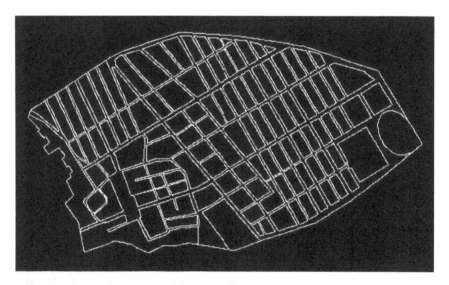

Figure 6.8 The map used for the Space Syntax analysis.

Source: Author: Samuli Simelius.

The correlation of high Space Syntax values and business activity has already been examined by Van Nes, who located the shops on a map of Pompeii and paralleled them with the Space Syntax integration values. Although her identification of shops – based on Hans Eschebach and Liselotte Eschebach's work – is likely too positive, it demonstrates that on a general level there is a correlation between the streets of high integration values and the locations of the shops.[59] In addition to shops, there is the possibility of examining Pompeii's bars, other types of retail and industrial buildings, public fountains, crossroad shrines, masonry benches, and electoral notices as indicators of high street activity. They were already mapped by earlier scholarship.[60] Furthermore, other indicators such as the frequency of doors, the depth values of the streets, and the number of intersections have been used to calculate street activity, and the street use of cart traffic has also been studied extensively.[61]

All of the available sources almost unanimously highlight the importance of the same three streets: the *Via della Fortuna-Via di Nola-Via della Terme*, *Via dell'Abbondanza*, and *Via Stabiana-Via del Vesuvio*. The first mentioned is clearly an important artery, highlighted by the red colour in all of the Space Syntax maps. The *Via Stabiana-Via del Vesuvio* also has its integration marked in red, and on the choice map it is yellowish orange, making it the second most active route of the map. The connectivity colour of the street is light green. The *Via dell'Abbondanza* does not stand out so much as the other two, but in all of the maps its eastern part is on the higher end of the spectrum (connectivity and choice: yellowish green; integration: orange), making it one of the more important streets of Pompeii (Online Appendix Figures 1, 2, 3).[62] All of these streets can thus be interpreted as having been highly active, as confirmed by both the archaeological sources and the Space Syntax analysis.

The *Via degli Augustali-Via Mediana* is not often considered as one of the most important routes in Pompeii.[63] However, the combination of the Space Syntax values and the archaeological data suggests the contrary.[64] Although it does not stand out as clearly as the three streets mentioned earlier when looking at the choice and integration maps, it still has higher values than many of the other Pompeian streets (Online Appendix Figures 2 and 3), and its connectivity is among the four highest streets of the city (Online Appendix Figure 1). It can be considered as the third major east-west link in Pompeii, which makes sense as it runs through the middle of the city, flanked by the vital *Via dell'Abbondanza* and *Via della Fortuna-Via di Nola*, and the movement on these streets must have spilled over onto the *Via degli Augustali-Via Mediana*. The importance of the *Via degli Augustali-Via Mediana* also explains the concentration of commercial activity on the *Vicolo Storto*.[65] It connected the two main east-west arteries and was a route to the *Porta Vesuvio*, through the *Vicolo dei Vettii*, which might have been a politically important space, as the concentrations of electoral notices along it suggest.[66] However, the Space Syntax values of the *Vicolo dei Vettii* are low (Online Appendix Figures 1, 2, 3). The Space Syntax analysis ignores the importance of the gates, which might explain this. The electoral notices on the *Vicolo dei Vettii* indicate that the *Porta Vesuvio* might have been quite important for the citizens of Pompeii, because it makes sense to advertise one's candidacy were the people who could vote moved. The importance of the gate might have been because of the agricultural significance of Vesuvius,[67] and many Pompeians may have used this gate frequently.

The *Vicolo di Mercurio-Vicolo delle Nozze d'Argento* in the northern part of the map has quite high Space Syntax values (Online Appendix Figures 1, 2, 3). However, the archaeological evidence does not locate much activity on the *Vicolo di Mercurio*, but at least there is a concentration of electoral notices on the *Vicolo delle Nozze d'Argento*, suggesting that this street had political significance on the east side of the *Via Stabiana*.[68]

To sum up, the best locations to meet people or a magistrate, if excluding the forum and private houses, are then the three crossroads of the *Via Stabiana* (Figure 6.9 numbers 1, 2, and 3). All of these crossroads had a public fountain, which would have added to the number of people visiting these places. Although one might assume that people coming to these fountains were not important to the magistrate, this seems not to be the case. First, the persons visiting these fountains were not necessarily enslaved people or servants, as not all households would have had them, and second, the political process of Pompeii involved many other people than only the *paterfamilias*.[69] The northmost crossroad (Figure 6.9 number 1) also had a public altar, which would have attracted even more people. The two others (Figure 6.9 numbers 2 and 3) were instead architecturally monumentalized with arches, and the political significance of the southernmost was highlighted by a statue of M. Holconius Rufus, a significant Augustan era political figure in Pompeii. John D'Arms considers the location undignified for his statue, and thinks that it must have originally been in the forum.[70] However, as demonstrated, it is actually in a very visible location, and therefore was a prominent and suitable place for a political statue.

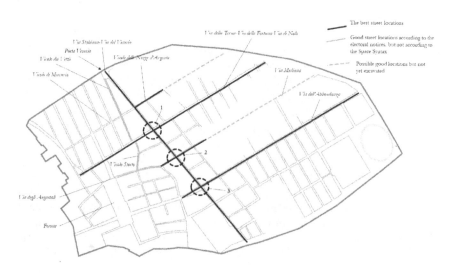

Figure 6.9 The best places to be visible or meet people in Pompeii.

Source: Author: Samuli Simelius.

V Conclusions

The streets were an integral part of the Roman administrative landscape, even though they were not *per se* planned for that purpose. One could even argue that they were a more democratic space than fora – or other public places were administrative functions traditionally occurred – or magistrate's private houses, which were also an essential location for administrative work. The streets were particularly good places for meeting a magistrate, or the other way around, a good location for a magistrate to meet people. In the street, a magistrate could not hide behind the workload of the forum or the privacy of their house. For a person involved in administrative work, the street may have even occasionally offered the possibility to do some small tasks related to administration.

Pompeian depictions of city life are rare, but there are a few paintings that illustrate magistrates. These, however, do not inform us much about the role of the streets in the city's administrative work. Nonetheless, the electoral notices indicate that the streets were important political locations in Pompeii, and therefore connected to the administration of the city. When estimating the best locations to meet a magistrate, or for a magistrate to meet people, in Pompeii, three locations rise above others: the crossroads of the *Via Stabiana* and the *Via dell'Abbondanza* and the *Via della Fortuna-Via di Nola*, but the crossroad of the *Via degli Augustali-Via Mediana* and *Via Stabiana* should also be included. This suggests that, in addition to the forum, the geographical centre of the city was an important administrative and political space. Some of the entrances leading to the forum were closed before the final period of ancient Pompeii, which likely caused greater predictability to locate magistrates moving in Pompeii's streets.[71] A Space Syntax analysis of the different phases of Pompeii's street network would shed more light on the issue and open possibilities to further investigate the change of the administrative cityscape of Pompeii.

Notes

1 Ciarallo and Mariotti Lippi 1993: 110–116; Pesando 1997: 6, 9; Allison 2001: 53; 2004, xv; Hackworth Petersen 2006: 128; Viitanen and Ynnilä 2014: 142; Speksnijder 2015: 88; Simelius 2022: 3.
2 Viitanen 2021: 281.
3 Viitanen et al. 2013; Viitanen and Ynnilä 2014; Viitanen 2020, 2021.
4 O'Sullivan 2011: 6–7.
5 Battistin 2021: 1–3, for other applications and discussions of Space Syntax analysis in classical archaeology, see e.g. Assassi and Mebarki 2021; Crawford 2019; Hilder 2015; Laurence 2011: 397–399; Stöger 2011.
6 Anderson 2011; Grahame 2000; Von Stackelberg 2009.
7 Fridell Anter and Weilguni 2002; Van Nes 2011; Van Nes and Yamu 2021: 121–122; Weilguni 2011.
8 Newsome 2009.
9 For shops: Viitanen et al. 2013: 63 Fig. 2.; van Nes 2011: 105–106. For bars: Ellis 2004: 375; 2018: 66–69. For bars, industry and retail: Monteix 2010: pl. IV; 2017: 218–219 Fig. 7.2. For bars, public fountains, crossroad shrines, masonry benches, and electoral notices: Viitanen et al. 2013: 62 Fig. 1, 70 Fig. 5; Viitanen and Ynnilä 2014: 147 Fig. 4,

148 Fig. 5. For electoral notices: Viitanen 2020: 279 Fig. 1. For other indicators, such as the frequency of doors, the depth values of the streets, the number of intersections, and the use of cart traffic: Laurence 1994: 88–103; Poehler 2006: 54, 2017a, 2017b: 173–188; Kaiser 2011a: 77–105; 2011b: 178.
10 Bablitz 2007: 33, 2015: 64–66, 72; De Angelis 2010: 16.
11 Plut., *Vit. Caes.* 63.4; Sen. *Clem.* 1.9.3–4.
12 Bablitz 2007: 33, 213 n. 118; 2015: 64–65, 72; De Angelis 2010: 14–16. See also Tuori's Chaper 3 in this volume.
13 Vitr. 6.5.1–2.
14 Vitr. 5.1.
15 Tac., *Dial.* 14.1. See Bablitz 2007: 171.
16 Cic., *De orat.* 1.199–200, 3.133. See also De Angelis 2010: 16; Tuori 2010: 22.
17 Quin., *Inst.* 4.1.54.
18 Goldbeck 2010: 231–235; Speksnijder 2015: 87, 90.
19 For a short summary of the discussion on the level of openness of the Roman house, see Simelius 2022: 58.
20 Mart. 7.51.1–6, 11–12. See Bablitz 2007: 156.
21 Bablitz 2007: 81. See Suet., *Aug.* 56.4; Dio 55.4.2; Macrob., Sat. 2.4.27.
22 Suet., Vesp. 23.2. See also, Tuori 2016: 231.
23 Plut., *Vit. Caes.* 17.3–4; Plin., *Ep.* 3.5, 9.10, 9.36; Cic., *Att.* 2.23.1; Q. *Fr.* 2.5.4, 3.3.1; Sen., *Ep.* 15.6. O'Sullivan 2011: 82–83.
24 Cic., *Off.* 1.144. O'Sullivan 2011: 6, 88.
25 Gai., *Inst.* 1.7.20. Tuori 2018: 202.
26 Romanelli 1817: 169; Bonucci 1827: 163; Dobbins 2007: 56–159, 177–178 nn. 23, 26. The excavators of the time did not seem to have much interest in recording the small finds in order to interpret the building functions. They were mainly interested in finding statues and reporting inscriptions. As these were rarely found, the notion of 15 January 1815 "*Nella Basilica non è occorsa cosa alcuna, che meriti essere ricordata*" (Nothing worth remembering has been found in the basilica) describes well the many entries of the excavation reports of this area. See, Fiorelli 1860: 102–221; for the floors of the hall-like buildings, see Fiorelli 1862: 160.
27 For the Large Palaestra as a gladiator barracks, see Zanker 1998: 129. For the Quadriporticus as a gladiator barracks, see Pesando 2001: 191–194.
28 MANN inv. 9057, 9059, 9061–9070. Sampaolo 1991: 251–257.
29 *Raccolta* 1843, Tav. 75. The drawing was likely made by Giuseppe Abbate.
30 Dobbins 2007: 159–160.
31 E.g., Vitruvius 5.*praef.*5, 5.1.5–8. About the persons and functions associated with the *basilicae*. See also Heikonen 2017: 56. The same purposes and users are often connected to the Basilica of Pompeii, e.g. Dobbins 2007: 159; Keegan 2016: 249.
32 Della Corte 1954: 13; Allison 2001: 69; Simelius 2022: 174.
33 Mouritsen 1988: 14–19, 182 n. 60; Simelius 2022: 174–175, 193–195.
34 Simelius 2022: 195.
35 Simelius 2022b: 4 Fig. 3.
36 Viitanen 2021: 285, 287–296, 313.
37 MANN inv. 9071. Mols and Moormann 1994: 43; Sampaolo 1996: 948–949.
38 Mols and Moormann 1994: 29–30, 43–44; Dunbabin 2003: 85; Hackworth Petersen 2006: 69.
39 MANN inv. 113197. Bragantini 1998: 605–606; Barrett 2019: 196–201.
40 MANN inv. 112222. Sampaolo 1990: 80–81; Castrén 2008: 16.
41 E.g. Simelius 2022: 146–148.
42 Simelius 2022: 23–24.
43 Emmerson 2020; Zanella 2021.
44 Pompeii Bibliography and Mapping Project's map is published online: Poehler and Stepanov 2017.

45 Poehler 2017a: 49–52, 2017b: 181 Fig. 6.7. Cf. Giglio 2017: 22; Weilguni 2011: 62–63.
46 Giglio 2017: 22 Fig. 6.
47 Weilguni 2011: 62.
48 E.g. Anniboletti et al. 2009.
49 For the development of Pompeii, see Geertman 2007: 86–90; Giglio 2016, 2017: 21–34; Poehler 2017a: 22–52. See also Newsome 2009: 122–123.
50 Holappa and Viitanen 2011: 182; Giglio 2017: 21–26.
51 Poehler 2017a: 44–52.
52 For the circular argument of estimating movement, see Poehler 2017b: 180; Stöger 2011: 242.
53 Grahame 2000: 41–42; Von Stackelberg 2009: 59. For the upper floors, see Spinazzola 1953: 282–283.
54 On the problems, and discussions of the problems, see Ratti 2004; Hillier and Penn 2004; Fredrick and Vennarucci 2020; Simelius 2022: 40, 67–68 n.13.
55 Giglio 2017: 21–23; Weilguni 2011: 61.
56 For the lists, see Laurence 1999: 86.
57 The colourful Space Syntax maps are published online: https://doi.org/10.5281/zenodo.7763121.
58 For the creation of the plan, see Fridell Anter and Weilguni 2002: 88–91.
59 Van Nes 2011: 105–106; Eschebach and Eschebach 1993; cf. Viitanen et al. 2013: 63 Fig. 2; for the problems with identifying shops, see Ellis 2018: 9, 76–83.
60 Bars: Ellis 2004: 375, 2018: 66–69, bars, industry and retail: Monteix 2017: 218–219 Fig. 7.2, 2010: pl. IV, bars, public fountains, crossroad shrines, masonry benches, and electoral notices: Viitanen et al. 2013: 62 Fig. 1, 70 Fig. 5; Viitanen and Ynnilä 2014: 147 Fig. 4, 148 Fig. 5, electoral notices: Viitanen 2020: 279 Fig. 1.
61 Kaiser 2011a: 77–105, 2011b: 178; Laurence 1994: 88–103; Poehler 2006: 54, 2017a: 173–188, 2017b.
62 https://doi.org/10.5281/zenodo.7763121.
63 E.g. Anniboletti et al. 2009: 5; Kaiser 2011a: 100; Poehler 2017a: 36.
64 For archaeological indicators, see Monteix 2017: 218–219 Fig. 7.2; Poehler 2017b: 172 Fig. 6.3; Viitanen 2020: 297 Fig. 1; Viitanen et al. 2013: 63 Fig. 2.
65 Monteix 2017: 218–219 Fig 7.2; Viitanen et al. 2013: 63 Fig. 2.
66 Viitanen 2020: 297 Fig. 1.
67 For agriculture of the Vesuvian area, see De Simone 2017.
68 For electoral notices, see Viitanen 2020: 297 Fig. 1.
69 See e.g. Savunen 1995.
70 D'Arms 2003: 433–436. Cfr. Haug 2021: 57.
71 For the blocking of the entrances of the forum and their influence of Space Syntax analysis of the streets west side of the forum, see Newsome 2009: 122–126.

References

Allison, P. 2001: 'Placing Individuals: Pompeian Epigraphy in Context', *Journal of Mediterranean Archaeology* 14(1), 53–74.

Allison, P. 2004: *Pompeian Households: An Analysis of the Material Culture*. Los Angeles, CA.

Anderson, M. 2011: 'Disruption or Continuity? The Spatio-Visual Evidence of Post Earthquake Pompeii', in E. Poehler, M. Flohr, and K. Cole (eds), *Pompeii: Art, Industry and Infrastructure*, 74–87. Oxford

Anniboletti, L., Befani, V., and Boila, P. 2009: 'Progetto Rileggere Pompei: Per Una Nuova Forma Urbis Della Città. Le Indagini Geofisiche Nell'area Non Scavata e l'urbanizzazione Del Settore Orientale', *The Journal of Fasti Online*. http://eprints.bice.rm.cnr.it/867/

Assassi, A., and Mebarki, A. 2021: 'Spatial Configuration Analysis via Digital Tools of the Archeological Roman Town Timgad, Algeria', *Mediterranean Archaeology and Archaeometry* 21(1), 71–84.
Bablitz, L. 2007: *Actors and Audience in the Roman Courtroom*, London.
Bablitz, L. 2015: 'Bringing the Law Home: The Roman House as Courtroom', in K. Tuori and L. Nissin (eds), *Public and Private in the Roman House and Society* (Journal of Roman Archaeology Supplementary Series 102). Portsmouth, 63–76.
Barrett, C. 2019: *Domesticating Empire: Egyptian Landscapes in Pompeian Gardens*. Oxford.
Battistin, F. 2021: 'Space Syntax and Buried Cities: The Case of the Roman Town of Falerii Novi (Italy)', *Journal of Archaeological Science: Reports* 35, 1–18.
Bonucci, C. 1827: *Pompei descritta* (3rd ed.). Napoli.
Bragantini, I. 1998: 'VIII 5, 24 Casa del Medico', *Pompei: pitture e mosaici* 8, 604–610.
Castrén, P. 2008: 'Storia di Pompei', in P. Castrén (ed.), *Domus Pompeiana: una casa a Pompei. Mostra nel Museo d'arte Amos Anderson, Helsinki, Finlandia 1 Marzo – 25 Maggio 2008*. Helsinki, 11–17.
Ciarallo, A, and Mariotti Lippi. M. 1993: 'The Garden of the'Casa Dei Casti Amanti' (Pompeii, Italy)', *Garden History* 21(1), 110–116.
Crawford, K. 2019: 'Visualising Ostia's Processional Landscape Through a Multi-Layered Computational Approach: Case Study of the Cult of the Magna Mater', *Open Archaeology* 444–467.
D'Arms, J. 2003: 'Pompeii and Rome in the Augustan Age and beyond: The Eminence of the Gens Holconia', in F. Zevi (ed.), *Romans on the Bay of Naples and Other Essays on Roman Campania* (Pragmateiai: Collana Di Studi per La Storia Economica, Sociale e Amministrativa Del Mondo Antico). Bari, 415–439.
De Angelis, F. 2010: 'Ius and Space: An Introduction', in F. De Angelis (ed.), *Spaces of Justice in the Roman World, Columbia Studies in the Classical Tradition, 35*. Leiden, 1–26.
Della Corte, M. 1954: *Case ed abitanti di Pompei* (2nd ed.). Roma.
De Simone, G. 2017: 'The Agricultural Economy of Pompeii: Surplus and Dependence', in M. Flohr and A. Wilson (eds), *The Economy of Pompeii* (Oxford Studies on the Roman Economy), Oxford, 23–51.
Dobbins, J. 2007: 'The Forum and Its Dependencies', in J. Dobbins and P. Foss (eds), *The World of Pompeii* (The Routledge Worlds). New York, 150–183.
Dunbabin, K. 2003: *The Roman Banquet: Images of Conviviality*, Cambridge.
Ellis, S. 2004: 'The Distribution of Bars at Pompeii', *Journal of Roman Archaeology* 17, 371–384.
Ellis, S. 2018: *The Roman Retail Revolution: The Socio-Economic World of the Taberna*, Oxford.
Emmerson, A. 2020: *Life and Death in the Roman Suburb*, Oxford.
Eschebach, H., and Eschebach, L. 1993: *Gebäudeverzeichnis Und Stadtplan Der Antiken Stadt Pompeji*, Köln.
Fiorelli, G. 1860: *Pompeianarum antiquitatum historia*. Vol. 1, Naepoli.
Fiorelli, G. 1862: *Pompeianarum antiquitatum historia*. Vol. 2, Naepoli. https://archive.org/details/gri_33125012606733/page/160/mode/2up.
Fredrick, D., and Vennarucci, R. 2020: 'Putting Space Syntax to the Test: Digital Embodiment and Phenomenology in the Roman House', *Studies in Digital Heritage* 4, Special Issue 3D Methodologies in Mediterranean Archaeology, 185–224.
Fridell Anter, K., and Weilguni, M. 2002: 'Public Space in Roman Pompeii', *Nordisk Arkitekturforskning*, 87–97.

Geertman, H. 2007: 'The Urban Development of the Pre-Roman City', in J. Dobbins and P. Foss (eds), *The World of Pompeii* (The Routledge Worlds), New York, 82–97.

Giglio, M. 2016: 'Considerazioni Sull'impianto Urbanistico Di Pompei', *Vesuviana: An International Journal of Archaeological and Historical Studies on Pompeii and Herculaneum* 8, 11–48.

Giglio, M. 2017: 'L'insula IX 7 nel contesto urbanistico di Pompei', in F. Pesando and M. Giglio (eds), *Rileggere Pompei V: L'insula 7 della Regio IX* (Studi e ricerche del Parco Archeologico di Pompei 36). Roma, 21–28.

Goldbeck, F. 2010: *Salutationes: Die Morgenbegrüßungen in Rom in der Republik und der frühen Kaiserzeit*, Berlin.

Grahame, M. 2000: *Reading Space: Social Interaction and Identity in the Houses of Roman Pompeii. A Syntactical Approach to the Analysis and Interpretation of Built Space* (BAR International Series 886), Oxford.

Hackworth Petersen, L. 2006: *The Freedman in Roman Art and Art History*, Cambridge.

Haug, A. 2021: 'Emotion and the City: The Example of Pompeii', in M. Flohr (ed.), *Urban Space and Urban History in the Roman World* (Studies in Roman Space and Urbanism 3). London, 39–65.

Heikonen, J. 2017: *San Clemente in Rome: A New Reconstruction of the Early 5th Century Basilica and Its Origins*. Doctoral Dissertation, Espoo, Aalto.

Hilder, J. 2015: 'Inner Space: The Integration of Domestic Space at Volubis in the 3rd c. A.D.', in K. Tuori and L. Nissin (eds), *Public and Private in the Roman House and Society* (Journal of Roman Archaeology Supplementary Series 102), Portsmouth, 161–176.

Hillier, B., and Penn. A. 2004: 'Rejoinder to Carlo Ratti', *Environment and Planning B: Planning and Design* 31(4), 487–499.

Holappa, M., and Viitanen, E. 2011: 'Topographic Conditions in the Urban Plan of Pompeii: The Urban Landscape in 3D', in S. Ellis (ed.), *The Making of Pompeii: Studies in the History and Urban Development of an Ancient Town* (Journal of Roman Archaeology Supplementary Series 85). Portsmouth, 169–189.

Kaiser, A. 2011a: 'Cart Traffic Flow in Pompeii and Rome', in R. Laurence and D. Newsome (eds), *Rome, Ostia, Pompeii: Movement and Space*. Oxford, 174–193.

Kaiser, A. 2011b: *Roman Urban Street Networks: Streets and the Organization of Space in Four Cities* (Routledge Studies in Archaeology 2), New York.

Keegan, P. 2016: 'Graffiti as Monumenta End Verba: Marking Territories, Creating Discourses in Roman Pompeii', in R. Benefiel and P. Keegan (eds), *Inscriptions in the Private Sphere in the Greco-Roman World* (Brill Studies in Greek and Roman Epigraphy), 7. Leiden, 248–264.

Laurence, R. 1994: *Roman Pompeii: Space and Society*, London.

Laurence, R. 1999: *The Roads of Roman Italy: Mobility and Cultural Change*, London.

Laurence, R. 2011: 'Endpiece. From Movement to Mobility: Future Directions', in R. Laurence and D. Newsome (eds), *Rome, Ostia, Pompeii: Movement and Space*, Oxford, 386–401.

Mols, S., and Moormann, E. 1994: 'Ex parvo crevit: Proposta per una lettura iconografica della Tomba di Vestorius Priscus fuori Porta Vesuvio a Pompei', *Rivista di Studi Pompeiani* 6, 15–52.

Monteix, N. 2010: *Les lieux de métier: boutiques et ateliers d'Herculanum* (Bibliothèque des Écoles françaises d'Athènes et de Rome 344). Rome.

Monteix, N. 2017: 'Urban Production and the Pompeian Economy', in M. Flohr and A. Wilson (eds), *The Economy of Pompeii* (Oxford Studies on the Roman Economy), Oxford, 209–243.

Mouritsen, H. 1988: *Elections, Magistrates and Municipal Élite: Studies in Pompeian Epigraphy* (Analecta Romana Instituti Danici, Suppl. 15), Roma.

Newsome, D. 2009: 'Traffic, Space and Legal Change around the Casa del Marinaio (VII 15.1–2)', *Babesch: Bulletin Antieke Beschaving* 84, 121–142.
O'Sullivan, T. 2011: *Walking in Roman Culture*, Cambridge.
Pesando, F. 1997: *Domus: Edilizia private e societá pompeiana fra III e I secolo a.C* (Ministero per i beni culturali ed ambientali soprintendenza archeologica di Pompeii, Monografie 12). Roma.
Pesando, F. 2001: 'Gladiatori a Pompei', in A. La Regina (ed.), *Sangue e arena*, Milano, 175–197.
Poehler, E. 2006: 'The Circulation of Traffic in Pompeii's Regio VI', *Journal of Roman Archaeology* 19, 53–74.
Poehler, E. 2017a: 'Measuring the Movement Economy: A Network Analysis of Pompeii', in M. Flohr and A. Wilson (eds), *The Economy of Pompeii* (Oxford Studies on the Roman Economy), Oxford, 163–207.
Poehler, E. 2017b: *The Traffic Systems of Pompeii*, New York.
Poehler, E., and Stepanov, A. 2017: Pompeii: Navigation Map 2. Pompeii Bibliography and Mapping Project. https://digitalhumanities.umass.edu/pbmp/?page_id=1258.
Real Museo Borbonico. 1843: *Raccolta delle più interessanti dipinture e de più belli musaici rinvenuti negli scavi di Ercolano, di Pompei, e di Stabia: che ammiransi nel Museo Reale Borbonico*, Naples.
Ratti, C. 2004: 'Space Syntax: Some Inconsistencies', *Environment and Planning B: Planning and Design* 31(4), 501–511.
Romanelli, D. 1817: *Viaggio a Pompei, a Pesto e di ritorno ad Ercolano ed a Pozzuoli*, Napoli.
Sampaolo, V. 1990: 'I 3, 23 Casa dell'Rissa nell'Anfiteatro', *Pompei: pitture e mosaici* 1, 77–81.
Sampaolo, V. 1991: 'II 4, 3 Villa di Giulia Felice', *Pompei: pitture e mosaici* 3, 184–310.
Sampaolo, V. 1996: 'VII 3, 30', *Pompei: pitture e mosaici* 6, 943–973.
Savunen, L. 1995: 'Women and Elections in Pompeii', in R. Hawley and L. Levick (eds), *Women in Antiquity: New Assessments*, London, 194–207.
Simelius, S. 2022: *Pompeian Peristyle Gardens* (Studies in Roman Space and Urbanism 8), London.
Simelius, S. 2022b: 'Unequal Housing in Pompeii: Using House Size to Measure Inequality', *World Archaeology* 54, 602–624.
Speksnijder, S. 2015: 'Beyond 'Public and 'Private': Accessibility and Visibility during Salutationes', in *Public and Private in the Roman House and Society* (Journal of Roman Archaeology Supplementary Series 102). Portsmouth, 87–99.
Spinazzola, V. 1953: *Pompei: Alla Luce Degli Scavi Nuovi Di Via Dell'Abbondanza (Anni 1910–1923)*. Vol. 1.2, Roma.
Stöger, H. 2011: 'The Spatial Organization of the Movement Economy: The Analysis of Ostia's Scholae', in R. Laurence and D. Newsome (eds), *Rome, Ostia, Pompeii: Movement and Space*, Oxford, 215–242.
Tuori, K. 2010: 'A Place for Jurists in the Spaces of Justice?', in F. De Angelis (ed.), *Spaces of Justice in the Roman World*, Leiden, 43–65.
Tuori, K. 2016: *The Emperor of Law: The Emergence of Roman Imperial Adjudication* (Oxford Studies in Roman Society and Law), Oxford.
Tuori, K. 2018: 'Pliny and the Uses of the Aerarium Saturni as an Administrative Space', *Arctos – Acta Philologica Fennica* 52, 199–230.
Van Nes, A. 2011: 'Measuring Spatial Visibility, Adjacency, Permeability and Degrees of Street Life in Pompeii', in R. Laurence and D. Newsome (eds), *Rome, Ostia, Pompeii: Movement and Space*, Oxford, 100–117.

Van Nes, A., and Yamu, C. 2021: *Introduction to Space Syntax in Urban Studies*, Cham.

Viitanen, E. 2020: 'Painting Signs in Ancient Pompeii: Contextualizing Scriptores and Their Work', *Arctos – Acta Philologica Fennica* 54, 285–331.

Viitanen, E. 2021: 'Pompeian Electoral Notices on Houses and in Neighborhoods? Re-Appraisal of the Spatial Relationships of Candidates and Supporters', *Arctos – Acta Philologica Fennica* 55, 281–317.

Viitanen, E. Nissinen, L., and Korhonen, K. 2013: 'Street Activity, Dwellings and Wall Inscriptions in A. Bokern, M. Bolder-Boos, S. Krmnicek, D. Maschek and S. Page (eds), Ancient Pompeii: A Holistic Study of Neighbourhood Relations', in *TRAC 2012: Proceedings of the Twenty-Second Annual Theoretical Roman Archaeology Conference Which Took Place at Goethe University in Frankfurt*, Oxford, March 29–April 1, 2012, 61–80.

Viitanen, E., and Ynnilä, H. 2014: 'Patrons and Clients in Roman Pompeii – Social Control in the Cityscape and City Blocks?', in J. Ikäheimo, A. Salmi, and T. Äikäs (eds), *Sounds Like Theory. XII Nordic Theoretical Archaeology Group Meeting in Oulu 25. – 28.4.2012* (Monographs of the Archaeological Society of Finland 2), Helsinki, 141–155.

Von Stackelberg, K. 2009: *The Roman Garden: Space, Sense, and Society* (Routledge Monographs in Classical Studies), London.

Weilguni, M. 2011: *Streets, Spaces and Places: Three Pompeiian Movement Axes Analysed*. Doctoral Dissertation, Uppsala University.

Zanella, S. 2021: 'The Tabernae Outside Porta Ercolano in Pompeii and Their Context', in M. Flohr (ed.), *Urban Space and Urban History in the Roman World* (Studies in Roman Space and Urbanism 3). London, 286–306.

Zanker, P. 1998: *Pompeii: Public and Private Life* (L. Schneider Deborah (transl.), Revealing Antiquity 11), London.

Part III
The Space of the Institutions

7 The Rise and Consolidation of a Bureaucratic System

New Data on the *Praefectura Urbana* and Its Spaces in Rome[1]

Antonio Lopez Garcia

I Introduction

The *Praefectura Urbana* was an essential body of the Roman administrative system that incorporated thousands of officials, slaves, and military staff spreading to every corner of Rome in different directions from the early Empire to Late Antiquity. The purpose of this chapter is to review the sources related to the magistracy of the prefect of the city in order to understand the impact of this magistrate on the development of the city administration. We will examine the sources that mention the functioning of this body of government, the spatial implementation of the *Praefectura Urbana* and its subaltern offices, the changes in the management of urban policies and the bodies in charge of these tasks, the acquisition of legal responsibilities by the *Praefectus Urbi*, the functioning of the judicial system, and the evolution of the spaces under the authority of the prefects. In recent decades, several scholars have attempted to locate the headquarters and dependencies of this institution inside the urban fabric of Rome.

This contribution aims to further the dissection of the topography of the city by discussing the different problems involved in the location of the physical spaces related to the *Praefectura Urbana* through the examination of several kinds of sources including ancient literature, epigraphy, historical cartography and, of course, the archaeological record. The examination of these sources will focus on some of the questions about the deployment of the administration within the city. To examine the expansion of the *Praefectura Urbana* it is necessary to examine how the roles of the prefects evolved through time and how the complexity of their tasks required the use of several types of spaces to undertake the vast number of assignments they had. How large was the *Praefectura Urbana* and how did its structures influence the urban fabric of Rome? The progressive acquisition of duties and responsibilities by the urban prefects throughout the Empire makes it difficult to figure out how large this institution was and how many workers it had under its command. The measurement of the size of this institution is necessary in order to understand the expansion of its various components within the city.

Much has been written about the urban prefects and the development of their magistracies, but, by contrast, the spaces occupied by the prefects and their subalterns is a topic that has offered less information to scholars.

The most representative works about the spaces of the *Praefectura Urbana* have their origin in a contribution by one of the fathers of Roman topography, R. Lanciani, in 1892. He approached the topic and attempted to locate a complex containing the headquarters of the prefect in the *Carinae* and the *Vicus in Tellude* in the foothills of the Esquiline in the *III regio*.[2] Not much later P. E. Vigneaux published a monograph on the institutional history of the *Praefectura Urbis* in 1896.[3] Later on, several authors treated the development of the institution and the jurisdiction of the magistrate. The great attempts at making a definitive work on the organization and the duties of the urban prefect came with G. Vitucci and A. Chastagnol, who independently compiled and analyzed most of the sources discovered up to 1956/62.[4]

Perhaps the definitive contribution on the development of the magistracy and its hierarchy arrived in 2009 with the monograph of S. Ruciński on the *Praefectus Urbi* during the High Empire.[5] Some other remarkable works on the subaltern bodies of the *Praefectura Urbana* had an important impact on the understanding of the hierarchy and the spaces used by some of its main units such as the urban cohorts, the *vigiles*, and the *curae*.[6]

Some archaeological and epigraphic discoveries in recent years have supplemented the knowledge provided by the previous contributions and shed some light on the spaces used by the different bodies of the prefecture,[7] but so far nobody has completed a compilation that unifies all the new data and hypotheses on the spaces of the urban prefecture in one place.[8] To understand the difficulty of that task it is necessary to examine the complex structure of the *Praefectura Urbana* from its origins to Late Antiquity.

II The Rise of the Magistracy

One of the key elements of the Roman constitution was the prefect of the city. The creation of this administrative position has its origin in the *custos urbis*, a title conferred by the king on the *princeps senatus*.[9] This official originally exercised the function of the guardian of the city and representative of the royal power during the absence of the king from Rome.[10] During the early republican period, the office of *custos urbis* became a magistracy. Access to the post was limited to persons of consular rank since in the absence of the consuls, the prefects exercised consular powers. Among those powers was to convene the Senate and the *comitia* as well as being the commander of the civil legions in times of war. With the institution of the urban praetorship in 367 B.C., the office of the prefect of the city lost most of its power.[11] It became a minor magistracy that was only summoned once a year, its power being limited to the replacement of the consuls during the period of the Latin Festival.[12]

In 47 B.C., the magistracy reappeared when the master of the cavalry Marcus Antonius appointed L. Iulius Caesar as urban prefect.[13] During the time of Augustus, the position of *Praefectus Urbi* was reformed. Tacitus tells us in his Annals that during the Civil Wars, Cilnius Maecenas received the *Praefectura Urbana* from Augustus to maintain order in the capital and this was the germ of the consolidation of this magistracy.[14] The final consolidation of this magistracy happened during the early principate when the urban prefect became a perennial institution that served to protect the city against any subversive force.[15] At that time, the magistrate acquired authority over the police units and the power to exercise *potestas* and jurisdiction over criminal matters. The urban prefect performed several tasks to prevent social disturbances. He prosecuted any type of criminal charge and led the authorized unit for the capture, prosecution, and execution of sentences against criminals.

One clear example of the consolidation of this magistracy happened in A.D. 13, when L. Calpiurnius Piso was appointed by Augustus to hold the urban prefecture, serving for almost twenty years until the time of Tiberius.[16] To understand the process of concentrating the authority over the city it is necessary to examine the reforms made by Augustus to manage Rome in a more efficient and effective way.

III The Spreading of the Institution Over the Cityscape

In 7 B.C., Augustus reorganized the city of Rome into fourteen *regiones*. These districts were in turn divided into a smaller unit, the *vicus*. The creation of these urban subdivisions seems to be a key to the expansion of the authority of the prefect of the city, as his subalterns were deployed all across the cityscape. In A.D. 5, Augustus established the urban cohorts, an elite body commanded by a tribune under the control of the urban prefect. The cohorts were a key element in maintaining the social peace, acting as a sort of police force for the city. One of the main tasks of the *urbaniciani* was to assist the prefect of the city in the exercise of his criminal and civil jurisdiction, protecting the rights and safety of citizens.

The number of members of this large body varied depending on the period because when the body was created at the time of Augustus it amounted to three cohorts of about 480 to 500 men each.[17] During Julio-Claudian times, the body was enlarged by another cohort, reaching ca. 2,000 men. At the time of Vitellius, the number of members of each cohort was doubled and the urban cohorts reached a maximum of ca. 4,000 members in total. By the time of Nero, there were seven cohorts, although it is not clear whether this number included the members of the praetorian guard. Nevertheless, by the time of Septimius Severus, the number of cohorts was reduced to four that included 1,500 men each.[18]

Scholars seem to differ on the location of the urban cohorts. Some maintain that, from A.D. 23, the urban cohorts shared the *Castra Praetoria*[19] on the Viminal with the praetorian cohorts, based on several facts: The *urbaniciani* did not oppose Sejanus in A.D. 31, the discovery of votive dedications of the urban corps at the headquarters of the praetorian cohorts, and the soldiers of the praetorian guard and the urban cohorts shared burial sites.[20]

Under Aurelian,[21] a new camp was built to host the urban cohorts. The erection of this garrison at the *Campus Agrippae* in A.D. 270 led to the transfer of the urban cohorts to a place in central Rome close to the Forum Suarium, where the soldiers could take control over the meat distribution of the city.[22] Other scholars like Coarelli and Ricci suggest that the new garrison for the *cohors urbana* was built earlier in the Antonine period.[23]

The *cohortes vigilum* was a body of watchmen for the regions that had its origins in the republican period but under Augustus was reorganized to better suit the necessities of the city. Each cohort of watchmen was responsible for the surveillance of two regions.[24] All these units depended directly on the authority of the urban prefect, who deployed his influence all over the city in different directions. The seven cohorts were commanded by a prefect of the watchmen (*praefectus vigilum*) who directly served the urban prefect.[25] The main aim of this prominent component of the prefecture was to watch for and fight fires, patrol the streets at night, and monitor the maintenance of social peace.[26]

It is difficult to estimate the real numbers, but most of the studies agree that the body of the watchmen was composed of 3,000 to 6,000 men within the seven barracks deployed all over the fourteen regions. Given that both the cohorts of the watchmen and the urban cohorts were police, firemen, and paramilitary bodies, it is obvious that the number of members was very high. Some scholars have proposed that the prefect of the watchmen probably had his office at the headquarters of the I cohort in the *VII regio*, in a barracks discovered in 1642 in Piazza SS. Apostoli containing several inscriptions mentioning the prefects.[27] Nevertheless, other authors suggest that the office of the *praefectus vigilum* had to be elsewhere – possibly in

Figure 7.1 Possible locations of the barracks of the *vigiles* and the *urbaniciani*.

Source: Author: Antonio Lopez Garcia.

the Campus Martius – in a more prominent location considering that a high magistrate would have needed an autonomous office independent of the barracks.[28]

Most scholars seem to agree that each of the seven cohorts of *vigiles* had a headquarters – *castra* or *stationes* – in a *regio* and served its contiguous neighbourhood with a guard post – *excubitorium*.[29] These barracks were mostly positioned in the margins of the city, very close to the gates of the walls, allowing a quick response when necessary, both inside the enclosure of the walls and outside (Figure 7.1). We know the locations of three barracks of the watchmen including the aforementioned headquarters of the I cohort: The barracks of the V cohort discovered in the nineteenth century on the Caelian Hill, in the *II regio*,[30] as well as the famous guard post of the VII cohort found in Trastevere (*XIV regio*) in the nineteenth century.[31] Other barracks have only been attested epigraphically, as the headquarters of the II cohort at the *V regio* in the area of via Conte Verde and via Principe Eugenio,[32] as well as the barracks of the IV cohort in the *XII regio* on the Aventine near the ancient Porta Naevia.[33] More dubious are the cases of the barracks of the III cohort in the *VI regio* identified by Lanciani in the surroundings of Porta Viminale,[34] or the case of the VI cohort in the *VIII regio* which the Regionary Catalogues place near the Basilica Argentaria and the Forum of Trajan.[35] Hence, the cohorts of *urbaniciani* and *vigiles* made up the bulk of the surveillance apparatus of the urban prefect for the city, which permitted him to quickly impose his authority and implement protection over the citizens in any part of the city when necessary.

Another important body that deployed the authority of the urban prefecture around the city was the *vicomagistri*. This institution, originated in republican times, was formed by freedmen that originally kept watch over the *vici* – the smaller portions of the districts – but in the time of Augustus they also became a religious organization dedicated to the cult of the Lares Compitales[36] and the *Genius Augusti* that constituted the religious centre of each *vicus*. For each of the known 265 *vici* there were four *vicomagistri* that were supported by up to four slave auxiliaries – *ministri*.[37] Thus, the size of this body could reach more than 4,000 people in total. The cult sites where the *vicomagistri* and the *ministri* worshipped the local spirits of each *vicus* – known as *compita* – were usually positioned at major crossroads in the neighbourhoods.[38]

No less important for the city was the body of commissioners in charge of the execution of public works and the collection of taxes and tolls – *vectigalium*.[39] These commissioners (*curatores*) were under the control of the urban prefect. At the time of Severus Alexander, there were fourteen commissioners that commanded an unknown but surely vast number of lower-ranking officials that directly oversaw the public works.[40] The number of commissioners doubled at the time of Constantine according to the *Curiosum*.[41] It is impossible to calculate the size of this body, but their influence over the cityscape must have been remarkable as they had a direct impact on the development of the urban fabric (Figure 7.2). Among the *curatores* there were different types of commissioners that surveyed the day-to-day tasks of building and maintaining the city facilities. To assist the *curatores* in their duties, they had *adjutores* or *subcuratores* and a junior staff assigned to administrative, technical, and accounting tasks.[42] In many cases, we do not know when most of the *curatores*, as well as their subalterns, were incorporated under the authority of the urban prefect, but they all ended up being part of the apparatus of the *Praefectura Urbana* at least from the early fourth century if we consider all the available sources.

The *cura sacrarum et operum publicorum* was one of the main offices that was held by a pair of senatorials who carried out the tasks of maintenance in the public works.[43] One of the most important offices was responsible for watching over the water supply of the city.

Other important commissioners were the *curatores aquarum*. This office was established by Augustus to provide control over the water infrastructure through a *procurator aquarum*, three *curatores*, and further staff[44] that consisted of architects, public slaves, clerks, copyists, orderlies, and criers, reaching a number of ca. 700 men.[45] Some authors interpret the fact that Agrippa was chosen as water commissioner in 33 B.C. as a sign of the creation of an autonomous office for water management.[46] There is a controversy among scholars about the spaces occupied during the imperial era by the water commissioners within the layout of Rome. An inscription with the expression *Aquaeductium* found in one fragment of the Severian *Forma Urbis* corresponding to the Neronian aqueduct of the Caelian Hill led Bruun to propose that location as the headquarters of the *statio aquarum* and its archives during the imperial era.[47] Nonetheless, Coarelli dismissed this possibility considering that the expression *Aquaeductium* refers to the water distributor (*castellum aquarum*) located in that area.[48] For Coarelli, the Temple of Juturna at the *Campus Martius* would be the location of the headquarters of the water commissioners.[49] The location of the Temple of Juturna at the Field of Mars is not clear. Several locations have been proposed for that temple, but it seems that one of the most plausible options is one of the temples in the sacred area of Largo Argentina or the temple at via delle Botteghe Oscure.[50] Some archaeological remains of *cocciopesto* basins and two buildings made in *opus reticulatum* and *opus latericium* respectively found near the temples of Largo Argentina dated to the beginning of the Augustan period led Coarelli to identify therein a complex dedicated to water management.[51]

It seems that at the beginning of the fourth century A.D. the headquarters of the water commissioners might have been transferred to the Spring of Juturna at the Roman Forum, coinciding with the transfer of the authority over water management to the hands of the urban prefect.[52] Some inscriptions mentioning the *statio aquarum* and a *curator aquarum et Miniciae* discovered in the surroundings of the Spring of Juturna link the place directly with the water administration.[53] Steinby argued in favour of the identification of the *statio* in the area of the spring, but nuanced his solution to account for the suspicions created by such a space that only with difficultly can be adapted to the requirements of a proper office with a place to host the officials, clerks, and archives necessary for the functioning of the institution. Steinby interprets the spaces of the Oratorio dei Quaranta Martiri, St. Maria Antiqua, and the so-called Temple of Augustus as possible locations for the office of the water commissioners.[54]

The *cura riparum et alvei Tiberis* was another important element of the local administration that likely ended up under the command of the urban prefect, as precautions against the floods of the Tiber and the control of navigation was key to the city of Rome.[55] It is not clear when this office was established. Suetonius[56] relates the creation of the position with the other commissioners created by Augustus, but Cassius Dio[57] and Tacitus[58] contradict this and ascribe the creation of the office to Tiberius, after the great flood of A.D. 15.[59]

The body was composed of a board of five members and from the time of Trajan they incorporated other functions such as watching over the sewers of the city. The only footprint of the existence of the *Statio Alvei Tiberis* is an epigraph preserved in the Church of St. Maria in Trastevere that mentions the commissioner Aurelius Artemidorus from the mid-third century A.D.[60] The *Statio alvei Tiberis* was located in an ancient building corresponding to the current area of via San Bartolomeo dei Vaccinari and the river – by the end of the vicolo Cenci – whose traces were identified by Rodríguez Almeida in the famous marble Plan of via Anicia.[61]

Other important positions involved in the management of the city that likely remained under the authority of the urban prefects were the *curatores viarum* that took care of the streets and roads[62] and the two *curatores regionum* that superintended each of the fourteen *regions* of the city.[63] Other minor offices were, for instance, the commissioner of the theatre of Pompey (*curator operis theatri*)[64] and the commissioner of the statues (*curator statuarum*) among many others that appear in the epigraphic record but unfortunately are not traceable in the topography of Rome.[65]

As of Diocletian's mandate, Rome was no longer the capital of the Empire, nor was it the residence of the emperors. However, it was still the largest city and the cradle of Roman civilization, so it was necessary to provide it with a figure capable of handling any type of situation and act as a vicar of the emperor. The urban prefect was the only consular magistrate left in the city when the senatorial elite transferred to Constantinople.[66] For that reason, he became the most important authority in the city after the emperor himself. During this time, the urban prefect became the honorary president of the Senate and acted as an intermediary between the emperor and the people of Rome.

After the victory of Constantine in the Battle of the Milvian Bridge (A.D. 312), the praetorian cohorts were dissolved and then the urban cohorts under the command of the urban prefect became the most significant military force in Rome.[67] Over the next decades, the *Praefectura Urbana* acquired total control over all the key administrative elements of Rome. These included control over the census, the aqueducts, the public works, the imperial granaries, and the harbour of Ostia, where the main suppliers of goods for the *Annona* were located. Some scholars affirm that, already in the second century, the prefect of the Annona became dependent on the *Praefectura Urbana*.[68] Others think that the prefect of the *Annona* became a dependent of the urban prefect at the time of Septimius Severus.[69] According to Chastagnol, the only authority of the urban prefect over the care for the grain supply was essentially the administration of the list of persons entitled to free distribution of grain (*frumentationes*) or management of the access to certain entertainment shows.[70]

The relationship between the Annona and the urban prefecture is not very clear, but it seems that among the attributes of the urban prefects was surveillance over the

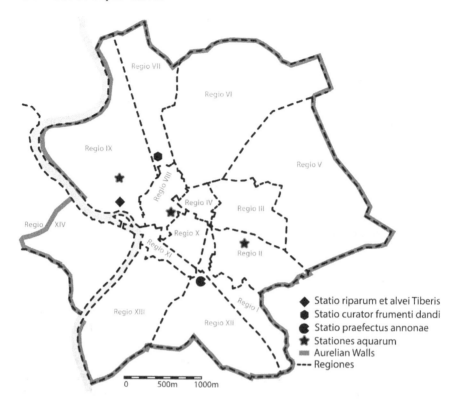

Figure 7.2 Possible locations of the main *stationes* linked to the urban prefect.
Source: Author: Antonio Lopez Garcia.

city markets as well as over the prices and supply of meat at the Forum Suarium.[71] Since the early Empire, the commissioners (*curatores* or *praefecti frumenti dandi*) were in charge of the food distribution, the distribution of food in the city, control over the measurement and weight system, and the preservation of the supply at the public warehouses. The *praefectus annonae*, who was the ultimate authority over the food supply in the city, had an office which likely was located close to the Temple of Ceres.[72] The office of the prefect of the *Annona* was composed of an *adiutor* and a *subpraefectus* that assisted him in the tasks of controlling the supply. The prefects of the Annona exercised direct authority over judicial cases concerning the food supply, but at the time of Septimius Severus the jurisdiction over these cases passed to the authority of the prefect of the city. But how did the urban prefects reach this level of authority over all these fundamental elements of the city?

IV The Consolidation of the Urban Prefect in the Legal System

It is difficult to understand the extension of the powers of the urban prefect without examining the incremental growth of his influence over the legal system. The expansion of the control of the urban prefect over the city happened during the early and high Empire when the legal authority of the magistrate took over the powers that had traditionally been in the hands of the praetors. Throughout the first two centuries, there was a development of the legal aspect of the magistracy. Previously, during the republican period, the most important judicial tasks were assumed by the urban praetor and the peregrine praetor. During the first century, the prefect of the city was still subordinate to these praetors and had to compete with the courts of republican origin that were under the control of the *aediles* and the *tresviri capitales*.[73] Nonetheless, from the mid-first century A.D., the urban prefect began to monopolize some of the tasks that had customarily been performed by the praetors, thus becoming the chief judge of criminal proceedings in Rome. At this time, the *quaestiones perpetuae* – which then were the most common type of judicial procedure – passed directly to the authority of the prefect.[74] Nevertheless, civil proceedings – which were still a fundamental type of procedure – remained in the hands of the praetors during this period.[75] But even in the civil causes, the *Praefectus Urbi* became the highest appeal magistracy above the praetors. Thus, the praetors lost their prominent place in the hierarchy in favour of the prefect. This increase in influence brought other responsibilities into the hands of the prefects.

Between the principate of Tiberius and the time of Trajan, the urban prefect achieved control over the local administration and the police forces to maintain the social peace. To reinforce the *status quo* of the city, the prefect had secret agents called *curiosi* who were dedicated to controlling the society. The *curiosi* kept some kind of archive with information about suspects that served to maintain control over the unorthodoxy that might expose the Roman institutions to undesired risks.[76] But it was from time of Hadrian on that his legal powers expanded widely. The urban prefect took over the *causae pecuniariae*.[77]

The true consolidation of the judicial authority of the magistrate occurred mainly between the mandates of Caracalla and Diocletian. During this period, the magistrate became the judge of initial jurisdiction and on appeal. In the transition between the second and the third century, a type of judicial process called *cognitiones extra ordinem*, which originated in the Augustan era, became the most common procedure, meaning the decline of the *quaestiones perpetuae*.[78] The emperors also became a fundamental part of the Roman judiciary system[79] and a council (*consilium*) of senators and knights – including the urban prefect among them – became a permanent body for the administration of justice.[80] The urban prefect was the highest authority in the judiciary processes but had the guidance of the council that supported his decisions in court verdicts. We have some knowledge of this institution thanks to Pliny the Younger, who personally was part of a council during Trajan's era.[81] Originally, the council was formed by young men of senatorial rank[82] but from the end of the second century, some of the members of the council had consular rank, so the importance and influence of this auxiliary body should have increased. Regarding the number of members of this fundamental structure of the judicial system, we know that during the Severian period it was composed of fourteen members.[83] The practical tasks of the courts of justice were carried out by auxiliaries of the *officium* of the urban prefecture,[84] but we do not know the number of officials in charge of these matters.

From the late third century, senatorial magistrates lost most of their roles. A letter from the time of Septimius Severus compiled by Ulpian in the Digest[85] defines the powers of the urban prefect Fabius Cilo and, presumably, it is possible to infer that his predecessors had similar responsibilities. From this time, the praetors remained only as judges of minor civil proceedings. The territorial competence of this magistrate was limited to the city and 100 miles beyond Rome.[86] To balance the authority of the urban prefect when the magistracy reached its maximum peak of control over the city, a new figure was created at the time of Constantius II: The *vicarius*.[87] This position served to preserve the equilibrium in the late antique Roman institutions through the subordination to the prefect of the praetorium of Italy.

V The Headquarters of the *Praefectura Urbana*

The *officium* was the administrative unit of the *Praefectura Urbana*. All the bureaucratic tasks of the institution were centralized in this body. These offices had to have a very large staff of officials, capable of managing and coordinating all the prefectural tasks. As regards the personnel that should be part of the institution, some scholars have tried to reconstruct the hierarchy through a comparative study with the provincial offices of the *praetoria*.

At the head of the institution would be the *cornicularius*, an official who was devoted to controlling and organizing criminal proceedings. According to some historians, it is possible that there were up to three *corniculari* in the *officium*. At a lower rank were the *commentarienses*, in charge of the supervision of the archives and the criminal jurisdiction. According to the Acts of the Martyrs, these officials would have been in charge of interrogating the suspects and executing the capital sentences. Third, there were the *beneficiarii*, a body of considerable size since each *centuria* of the urban cohorts had two *beneficiarii*. There should be about 48 *beneficiarii* in the *officium*. The *beneficiarii* acted as police chiefs in the territory of Rome and performed important duties as supervisors of prisons and messengers. On the last step of the *officium* hierarchy were freedmen and official slaves who were engaged in bureaucratic tasks. It has not been possible to determine the dimensions of this bureaucratic body through sources, but it was likely made up of several hundred people.

The location of the *Praefectura Urbana* is a controversial matter within the community of Roman topographers. One of the main problems we face in Rome is the multi-stratification of the city. Most of the old buildings that have survived to this day belong to the ancient period, so it is difficult to know the exact location of some buildings, although some sources tell us about the approximate position. At the time of the re-foundation of the magistracy, during the reign of Augustus, the office of the prefect of the city was situated in a basilica, as mentioned in a work by Johannes Lydus.[88] The unclear location of that basilica has offered several options for scholars to elucidate. The passage of Lydus refers to a lost work by Suetonius. Traditionally this basilica – founded by Augustus – has been identified with the *Basilica Iulia*,[89] although some authors have placed it at the *Basilica Antoniarum*

Duarum[90] or the *Basilica Paulli*.[91] However, it is a complicated problem since we do not know for sure how many basilicas existed in Augustan Rome and perhaps there are no archaeological remains of the one we are looking for.

A series of scholars, such as Jordan and Gatti, later supported by Coarelli, floated a hypothesis about one of the Temple of Peace rooms in which the marble plan of Rome was exhibited in the Severian period. Coarelli's hypothesis about the *Basilica Paulli* links the building with the later Temple of Peace (inaugurated in A.D. 75) and the discovery of several fragments of marble plans[92] – some of them dated to the Augustan period – which would have belonged to an office of the city cadastre, one of the functions of the *officium* of the urban prefect.[93] According to this hypothesis, the urban prefecture would have had its main headquarters in this building since the Flavian era. This controversial hypothesis has been contested several times because we do not have any other information about the use of the Temple of Peace as a cadastre or an office.[94]

Through a passage from Martial[95] that mentions a place used for torture, some scholars have proposed that the headquarters of the urban prefect should be located near the *Subura*, close to the *Argiletum* – in the surroundings of the *Templum Pacis*. Nevertheless, this vague reference cannot be considered as evidence of such an assertion.[96]

The Domus of Cilo on the Piccolo Aventino, owned by the famous *Praefectus Urbi* Fabius Cilo (A.D. 203) and mentioned by Ulpian in the letter about the powers of the prefect included in the *Digestae*, is the only private building that appears explicitly represented in the Severian *Forma Urbis*.[97] This is one of the few elements that may link the map situated at the Temple of Peace – at least its later iteration after the fire of A.D. 192 – with the figure of the urban prefect, but it is more a matter of speculation than clear evidence of the relation of the building with the *Praefectura Urbana*.

Another element that may link the Temple of Peace – also known as the *Forum Vespasiani* – is the mention of a getaway of the urban prefect Symmachus and his vicar after a revolt of two factions of people in the area. But again, the reference to the place does not necessarily concern the office of the urban prefecture.[98]

A building excavated between 1990 and 1997 on the Oppian Hill underneath the Baths of Trajan has constantly been related to the *Praefectura Urbana*. This building was identified by some archaeologists as the *officium* of the prefecture during the time of Vespasian.[99] The building might have had a monumental entrance and quite flamboyant decoration. However, until now no hypothesis has been brought forth about the practical use of spaces within this complex. The only relationship of the building with the tasks developed by the prefecture of the city could be a wall mosaic with agricultural scenes, which some scholars interpret as an allegorical representation of the function of supplying Rome with wine – one of the tasks undertaken by the urban prefects.[100] During the excavation a fresco was located with an urban representation – famously known as *La Città Dipinta* – that aroused considerable interest among historians due to its monumentality. The fresco has quite large dimensions, almost 10 square metres. It represents a bird's-eye view of a walled city that has not yet been identified, but some scholars have suggested that it could be a representation of Antioch, London, Arles, or even Rome, although there has been no consensus among them.[101] In Trajan's time, the building was buried by the construction of the baths but could continue to function as an underground space. Although the Flavian building seems to be a public complex due to its grandiosity, it is not possible to confirm that its purpose was to serve the *Praefectura Urbana*.[102] The disappearance of most of the building with the construction of the Baths of Trajan seems to suggest looking for the headquarters of the *officium* elsewhere.

It is quite difficult to determine what the location of the *officium* was between the second and the fourth centuries. The archaeological evidence does not offer a clear candidate to identify as the headquarters of the *officium* and the Temple of Peace is the only building that seems to offer a tenuous link with the urban prefecture. However, from the fourth century on, it seems that there was an area of influence of the urban prefect in the surroundings of St. Pietro in Vincoli, perceptible in the frequent emergence of inscriptions mentioning the magistrate.[103] But no traces of a specific building have been discovered in the area yet. Nonetheless, some of the epigraphs discovered have offered invaluable information about the magistracy during Late Antiquity.

Especially important are two epigraphs of the fifth century found in two different localities. One of the epigraphs was found at via degli Annibaldi (on the Velia)[104] and the other one appeared in via Marco Aurelio (on the Caelian Hill)[105] – two objectively distant locations.[106] In both cases the restoration of a series of buildings belonging to the prefecture by the urban prefect Valerius Bellicius[107] is mentioned in a similar manner. The spaces referred in the inscriptions include a *porticus*, which should serve to publish the laws emanating from the prefecture; the *scrinia*, which should function as archives and offices; the *Secretarium Tellurense*, which some interpret as a space used for interrogations and others as a secret enclosed tribunal containing the archive of the high magistrate; the *tribunalia*, which were an essential part of the urban prefect's spaces as the head of the justice administration in Rome at the time; and finally, an *Urbanae sedis*, which might be the headquarters of the *officium*.

According to E. Carnabuci, the south-western hemicycle of the Baths of Trajan would have hosted the *scrinia* of the *Praefectura Urbana* during the Trajan era, incorporating this space into the aforementioned building of *La Città Dipinta*, which is situated underneath.[108] That hemicycle presents a series of great niches that have often been interpreted as a library. According to this new hypothesis, the archive of the urban prefecture would have been established in that location from the second century. Nevertheless, this interpretation, based on the visual similarity of the hemicycle with libraries – especially the Library of Timgad – does not consider the difficulty of accessing the niches that supposedly hosted the documents, which likely were more appropriate for holding statues.[109] This building, in turn, was interpreted as the *[po]rticu[m] cum scriniis Tellurensis secretarii tribunalib(us) adherentem* mentioned in the inscriptions of Junius Valerius Bellicius.[110] This hypothesis has been modified by A. Amoroso,[111] who, although

The Rise and Consolidation of a Bureaucratic System 161

supporting the possibility that the hemicycle building functioned as the *scrinia*, denies a direct relationship with the *Secretarium Tellurensis* because of the differing chronology of the building and the first references to the *secretarium* that appear much later.[112] The name *Tellurensis* likely alludes to a part of *Regio IV* close to the Temple of Tellus.[113] The location of the Temple of Tellus is a much-debated topic since its location would allow us to determine the position of some of the buildings of the headquarters of the *Praefectura Urbana* in the late antique period. Several studies have tried to locate a specific building within the area with little success.[114] There are several locations proposed so far (Figure 7.3): The most recent investigations pose a location near the current via dei Fori Imperiali and Largo G. Agnesi.[115] Other scholars place it in via del Cardello; still others in the area next to the church of S. Pietro in Vincoli and via Eudossiana[116]; others in the vicinity of via della Polveriera[117]; and yet others place it in the via Venere Felice area.[118] The most accepted theory among scholars locates the *Secretarium Tellurense* in a complex to the north of the Temple of Venus and Rome and to the east of the Basilica of Maxentius,[119] which is visible in two Renaissance drawings attributed to Pirro Ligorio and Francesco da Sangallo.[120] The drawings, although not completely coincident, show a massive building composed of large porticoed halls of which

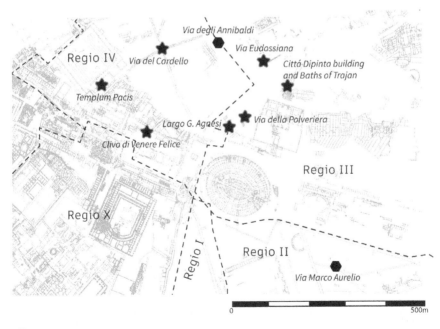

⬢ Place of discovery of the epigraphs of Valerius Bellicius
★ Hypothetical locations of the *officium* of the *Praefectura Urbana*

Figure 7.3 Possible locations of the headquarters of the urban prefect.
Source: Author: Antonio Lopez Garcia.

one included an apse and a courtyard with a monumental staircase. It seems plausible that this complex could contain some of the spaces mentioned in the epigraphs of Valerius Bellicius, as it seems to be a monumental construction adequate for hosting several activities, but this remains in the realm of speculation. This area suffered radical changes in recent centuries that make it impossible to recover the information eradicated by the urban works of the sixteenth century and the construction of via dell'Impero in the early twentieth century. In any case, the *officium* of the *Praefectura Urbana* should have been an impressive space that contained the operations centre of the most fundamental official of the bureaucratic machinery of Rome.

VI The Judicial Apparatus of the Urban Prefect

The management of the court and other apparatus for the exercise of justice and punition was an essential component of this magistracy. As we have seen in the previous pages, the accumulation of judicial authority by the urban prefect was a slow process that occurred across four centuries. Simultaneously, a process of spatial evolution materialized in the trials that little by little was transferred from the open spaces of the Roman Forum and the Imperial Fora to the enclosed spaces of the courtrooms.[121]

The overcrowded and sometimes intense public courts of the early Empire, pictured by Martial[122] and reflected by many other ancient authors when referring to the trials, evolved into a much safer situation. At the beginning of the Empire, the centumviral court settled at the Basilica Iulia was the only special court that met in an enclosed space.[123] However, most of the praetorian tribunals maintained a location in open spaces such as the Roman Forum or moved into precincts such as the porticoes of the Forum of Augustus[124] that somewhat allowed them to restrain the access of large crowds and to avoid the effects of the weather.[125]

No information regarding the court of the urban prefect during the early years of the Empire has survived to our days, but we could presume that it had to take place in similar settings within the fora. A passage of Aulus Gellius mentions the court of a consul functioning at the Forum of Trajan,[126] but the exact place within the forum and the arrangements are completely unknown. Much has been speculated about the arrangement of tribunals at the Forum of Trajan, especially about the hemicycles[127] and the Basilica Ulpia.[128]

During the early second century A.D., the urban praetor was replaced by the urban prefect as the central figure of the judiciary system when the prefect became the main authority over civil and criminal cases. From the transformations of the judiciary system at this time – for example, the substitution of the *quaestiones perpetuae* for the *cognitiones extra ordinem*[129] or the inclusion of a permanent council presided over by the urban prefect in the judicial system from the time of Hadrian[130] – we could conjecture that the arrival at the top of the hierarchy of the urban prefect particularly influenced the development of the courts.[131] The establishment of the council led to the creation of new spaces to host the secret discussions *intra cubiculum* and to the consolidation of the *cognitiones* as the most common type of judicial procedure.

This context is where we interpret a building of the Hadrian era discovered in Piazza della Madonna di Loreto as the main court of Rome at the time. The complex consists of three attached halls that include lateral steps on the long sides of each hall following a style similar to the hall of the Curia Iulia.[132] This building – known as the *Auditoria* of Hadrian – could host up to 400 people meeting in each hall. Each hall could work independently of the others, allowing different kinds of gatherings. The construction of this complex may be a response to the changes in the legal process as well as to the overcrowded courts of the fora in the second century A.D., but the relation of the building to the urban prefecture only comes from sources of the fifth century: The discovery of two statue bases dedicated by the urban prefect Fabius Felix Passifilus Paulinus with his own resources[133] could be a key to the identification of the building as one of the *tribunalia* that worked under the authority of the prefects of the city. How many tribunals were under the supervision of the urban prefect is a question that we cannot infer the answer to from the written sources.

Additional changes in the judiciary procedures from the end of the second century A.D. to the fifth century may have led to the creation of more spaces to suit the judiciary necessities of Rome. During this long period, a new practice of secret judiciary meetings appears and with it, a new type of arrangement for the courts is born. This new arrangement is known as *secretarium*.[134] Some of the *cognitiones extra ordinem* became a secret event,[135] although during the fourth century civil and criminal trials were still open to the public.[136]

These *secretaria* mentioned in the sources seem to be a fundamental part of the late antique judicial system led by the urban prefect. Some authors have attempted to locate the *secretaria* mentioned in the sources (Figure 7.4). Coarelli interprets the northern apse of the Basilica of Maxentius as a secret tribunal – the *Secretarium Commune* mentioned by Symmachus[137] – in which the magistrate and the *iudices* could use a podium to isolate them from the other attendants of the trials and be more visible.[138] The space could be blocked off using a gate (*cancellum*) or a curtain (*velum*) to prevent the entrance of undesired people into the hall and to subdivide the space. The interpretation of Coarelli remains controversial, as most of the authors attribute other functions to this space and its podium.[139]

The relation between the *Secretarium Commune* and the *Secretarium Tellurensis* mentioned in the epigraphs of Valerius Bellicius[140] is unclear.[141] The other known *secretarium* is the *Secretarium Circi*, which Coarelli locates in a building in front of the *carceres* of the Circus Maximus whose basement housed a Mithraic temple.[142] In contrast, Chastagnol identified this complex as being somewhere near the imperial box on the east side of the Circus Maximus facing the Palatine.[143] Fraschetti proposed a different hypothesis for the *Secretarium Circi*, positioning it at the Circus Flaminius, which was a common location for acts of martyrdom and popular assemblies.[144] This tribunal was used for the trial of Fulgentius, a senator who had interfered in a legal case.[145]

Another *secretarium* mentioned by the sources is the *Secretarium Senatus*. This space is only mentioned in an inscription discovered in the surroundings of the Curia Iulia.[146] The space mentioned in the inscription probably alludes to a room created near the Senate House in response to the judicial innovations of the late fourth

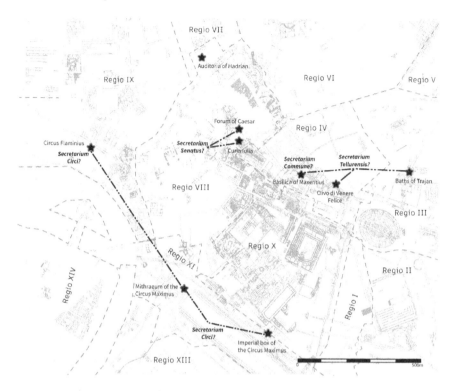

Figure 7.4 Possible locations of *secretaria* and *tribunalia*.
Source: Author: Antonio Lopez Garcia.

century when the senators received the right to sit in judgement of each other.[147] This new practice likely required a new space to host the secret trials among the senators, and most probably the prefect of the city was the person leading these trials as the president of the Senate. To complete the list of places of justice depending directly on the *Praefectura Urbana* we should consider the penitentiary spaces. The urban cohorts and the watchmen might have had a very important role in enforcing the judiciary sentences imposed by the courts. Some specific officials that were *beneficiarii* of the cohorts such as the *quaestionarius* supervised interrogations.[148] It is not clear how many *carceres* there were in Rome. It seems possible that in addition to the famous *Carcer Tullianum* on the slopes of the Capitoline hill, other prisons or guardhouses existed at the barracks of the cohorts.[149] The *optio carceris* and the *optio custodiarum* oversaw the prisons with the support of a *clavicularius*.[150]

VII Conclusions

To conclude, it is important to consider the extent to which the complexity of the hierarchical structure of the *Praefectura Urbana* complicates the distinction of certain spaces within the urban fabric of the city. When adding to that mixture the element of change and the evolution of the tasks of the magistracy, the transfer of tasks from one space to another and an infinite number of practical reasons, the task of obtaining an overview of the spaces related to the prefecture becomes extremely complex. The figure of the urban prefect rose from being just one more of the high magistrates that ruled within the city in the early Empire to become the vicar of the emperor in Late Antiquity. The magistracy evolved so much that it appears almost impossible to figure out how the minor magistrate that acted as the replacement for the consuls during the Latin Festival became in practice the ruler of the city in a few centuries. The effectiveness of this magistrate leading the police forces in times of destabilization, especially in the last years of the Republic, led to an increase in his authority.

The reforms of Augustus with the establishment of cohorts of watchmen again increased his power over the urban structure and likely, the success of some prefects against attempts to subvert the public order may have gained the favour of the emperors and thereby led to the incorporation of new duties in the administration of justice – in contraposition to the praetors that proportionately lost their traditional authority over justice. Under the umbrella of the urban prefect there was space for other officials that little by little were incorporated into the hierarchy of the *Praefectura Urbana* such as the commissioners that oversaw the public works and maintenance of the public infrastructure of the city, as well as the *vicomagistri* and those who oversaw the *Annona* that supplied food to the city.

The location of the spaces used by all the bodies amalgamated into the *Praefectura Urbana* is a debatable topic, as most of the spaces proposed so far remain speculative (Table 7.1). In Roman topography, the written sources are not very specific about the locations, but very often allow scholars to make approximate estimations that help recreate the cityscape and position the institutions that ruled Rome within it. In this respect, the location of the *officium* of the urban prefect is the most controversial topic within the studies about the magistracy. There are so many open possibilities that clearly identify a building as the seat of the urban prefect is constantly impeded. The only agreement among scholars seems to be that the *Urbana Sedis* mentioned in the epigraphic record might be in a large area that covers from the current church of St. Pietro in Vincoli, to the Temple of Venus and Rome, and the Temple of Peace.

Being more specific in this debate about the location of the *Praefectura Urbana* seems more a question of faith than of tangible fact. New data about the spaces have shed light on activities that can be linked to the urban prefect. For example, in recent years, thanks to the archaeological campaigns in connection with the construction of the Metro C line, some interesting spaces have come to light, like the complex of *auditoria* found in Piazza della Madonna di Loreto or – perhaps – the *excubitorium* of an unknown cohort found in the excavations of Viale Ipponio. Clearer seems to be the reconstruction of the hierarchy of the prefecture. The studies of Chastagnol, and more recently Ruciński, have shed some light on the duties of the urban prefects and their subalterns, but also about the process of the consolidation of the magistracy.

Table 7.1 Main hypotheses to date about the location of the spaces of the *Praefectura Urbana* within the topography of Rome[151]

Institution	Organ or Space	Location	Bibliography and Sources
Carceres	Carcer Tullianum	Slopes of the Capitoline Hill. Building behind St. Giuseppe dei Falegnami	Robinson 1992: 168; *LTUR* I, s.v. *Carcer* (Coarelli): 236–238.
Cohortes Urbanae	Castra Praetoria (Early Empire)	Viminal Hill	Freis 1967: 6. Tac., *Ann.* 4.2.1L; Dio 42.19.6; Suet., *Tib.* 37.2; Aur. Vict., *Caes.* 2.4.
Cohortes Vigilum	Castra Urbana (Late Empire)	Campus Agrippae	Busch 2007. *Dig.* 1.12.1.11 (Ulp.).
	Headquarters of the prefect of the *vigiles*	In the surroundings of the *Crypta Balbi*	Coarelli 2019: 397–398.
	idem	Piazza SS. Apostoli, *VII regio*. At the barracks of the I Cohort	De Rossi 1858: 269–278; *CIL* VI 233.
	I Cohort	Piazza SS. Apostoli, *VII regio*	*LTUR* I, s.v. *Cohortium Vigilum Stationes* (Ramieri): 292–294. *CIL* VI 233; *CIL* VI 1092; *CIL* VI 1226.
	II Cohort	Area of via Conte Verde and via Principe Eugenio, *V regio*	Sablayrolles 1996: 269. *CIL* VI 1059; *CIL* VI 414a-b.
	III Cohort	Porta Viminale, *VI regio*	Lanciani *FUR*: tab. 17; Sablayrolles 1996: 270.
	IV Cohort	Porta Naevia, Aventine, *XII regio*	Sablayrolles 1996: 267–268. *CIL* VI 643.
	V Cohort	Caelian Hill, *II regio*	De Rossi 1858: 289–294. Sablayrolles 1996: 257–262.
	VI Cohort	Near the Basilica Argentaria and the Forum of Trajan, *regio VIII*	Sablayrolles 1996: 250. See Regionary Catalogues.
	VII Cohort	Trastevere, *XIV regio*	De Magistris 1898; Sablayrolles 1996: 251–257.
Curatores Aquarum	Statio (Early Empire)	Neronian aqueduct of the Caelian Hill	Bruun 2007: 5. Cod. Vat. Lat. 3439; *FUR Stanford* 4a.
	idem	Near the *Aedes Iuturnae*, Field of Mars. Largo Argentina	Coarelli 2019: 177–180. Ovid, *Fast.* 1.463.
	Statio (Late Empire)	Near the *Lacus Iuturnae*, Oratorio dei Quaranta Martiri, St. Maria Antiqua, and the so-called Temple of Augustus	Kajava 1989, n. 6; Steinby 2012: 98. *CIL* VI 36951.
Curatores Frumenti Dandi	Statio	*Forum Suarium*	*Dig.* 1.12.1.11 (Ulp.); Ruciński 2009, 99–100.
Curatores Riparum et Alvei Tiberis	Statio	Area of via San Bartolomeo dei Vaccinari and the river by the end of the Vicolo Cenci	Rodriguez-Almeida 1988: 124; *CIL* VI 1224.

Praefectura Annonae Tribunalia	*Statio* of the prefect of the Annona	Robinson 1992: 136; *LTUR* IV, s.v. *Statio Annonae* (Coarelli): 345–346. *CIL* VI 8470 = *ILS* 1705.
	Auditoria of Hadrian	Forum of Trajan	Egidi 2010; Orlandi 2010; Orlandi 2013; Lopez Garcia 2015, 2021. *LSA* 1819; *LSA* 2664.
	Secretarium Circi	Mithraeum at the *Circus Maximus*	Coarelli 2007: 321. Symm., *Rel.* 23.9.
	idem	Near the imperial box at the *Circus Maximus*	Chastagnol 1960: 252–253. Symm., *Rel.* 23.9.
	idem	*Circus Flaminius*	Fraschetti 1999: 228–230. Symm., *Rel.* 23.9.
	Secretarium Senatus	Southern portico of the Forum of Caesar, behind the *Curia Iulia*	Fraschetti 1999; Coarelli 2019: 381; Salvagni 2021; *CIL* VI 1718 = *EDR* 111471.
	idem	*Taberna* at the Forum of Caesar	Nash 1976: 191–205; Richardson 1992: 347; Kalas 2015: 157–159; *CIL* VI 1718 = *EDR* 111471.
	Secretarium Tellurensis/Commune	Basilica of Maxentius	Coarelli 2019: 380–383. Symm., *Rel.* 23: 4–6.
	Secretarium Tellurensis	Via Venere Felice	Amoroso 2007: 70. Symm., *Rel.* 23: 4-6.
Urbanae Sedis	*Officium* (Early Empire)	*Basilica Iulia*	Vigneaux 1896: 124; Palombi 1997: 150, n. 45. Lyd., *De Mag.* 1.34.
	idem	*Basilica Antoniarum Duarum*	La Rocca 2001: 193–195; Carnabuci 2006: 182. Lyd., *De Mag.* 1.34.
	idem	*Basilica Paulli*	*LTUR* IV, s.v. *Praefectura Urbis* (Coarelli): 159–160. Lyd. *De Mag.* 1.34.
	Officium (Flavian era)	*Città Dipinta* building, Oppian Hill, under the Baths of Trajan	Volpe 2000: 511–512; Caruso and Volpe 2000: 55.
	Officium (Late Empire)	St. Pietro in Vincoli area	Marchese 2007. *CIL* VI 37114 = *EDR* 071667; *CIL* VI 31959 = *EDR* 093152.
	idem	Via dei Fori Imperiali and Largo G. Agnesi	Colini 1933; *LTUR* IV, s.v. *Praefectura Urbis* (Coarelli): 159–160. Terrenato 1992; Häuber 2005.
	idem	Via del Cardello and via Eudossiana	Jordan and Hülsen 1907; Platner and Ashby 1929.
	idem	Via della Polveriera	Lanciani 1892; Chastagnol 1960; Palombi 1997; Carnabuci 2006.
	Scrinia	South-western hemicycle of the Baths of Trajan	Carnabuci 2006: 182; Marchese 2007: 628; Amoroso 2007: 73.
	Cadastre office	Temple of Peace	Coarelli 2019: 317–318. Symm. *Ep.* 10.78; *Cod. Vat. Lat.* 3439 – Fo. 18r.

Notes

1 This work is part of the project "Law, Governance and Space: Questioning the Foundations of the Republican Tradition". This research has received funding from the European Research Council (ERC) under the European Union's Horizon 2020 research and innovation programme (grant agreement No 771874). Also, this research has received funding from the Next Generation framework of the European Commission through the programme "María Zambrano" for the attraction of international talents that I have at the University of Granada. I want to acknowledge Robert Whiting for the language revision.
2 Lanciani 1892.
3 Vigneaux 1896.
4 Vitucci 1956; Chastagnol 1960, 1962.
5 Ruciński 2009.
6 Freis 1967; Bruun 1991; Robinson 1992; Sablayrolles 1996; Daguet-Gagey 1997; Steinby 2012.
7 Caruso and Volpe 2000; Carnabuci 2006; Amoroso 2007; Marchese 2007; Färber 2012; Lopez Garcia 2021.
8 Besides the magnificent *Lexicon Topographicum Urbis Romae* edited by E. M. Steinby (1993–1999), only F. Coarelli's book *Statio* (2019) has partially compiled the information about the locations of the dependencies of the *Praefectura Urbana* in Rome.
9 Lyd., *Mag.* 1.34.38. The dignity of *Custos Urbis* as well as the title of *princeps senatus* was conferred on one of the *decem primi*. Liv. 1.59.50; Dionys. 2.12.
10 Tac., *Ann.* 6.11; Liv. 1.59; Dionys. 2.12; Lyd., *Mens.* 1.19; Lyd., *Mag.* 2.6.
11 Ruciński 2009: 21.
12 Tac., *Ann.* 6.11; Suet., *Ner.* 7; Suet., *Claud.* 4; Dio 54.17; J. Capitol., *Antonin. Phil.* 4.
13 Dio 43.48.1.
14 Tac., *Ann.* 6.12.
15 Suet., *Aug.* 37.
16 Tac., *Ann.* 6.11.3.
17 Robinson 1992: 161.
18 Dio 55.24.6.
19 Freis 1967: 6; Tac., *Ann.* 4.2.1L; Dio 42.19.6; Suet., *Tib.* 37.2; Aur. Vict., *Caes.* 2.4.
20 Ricci 2011: 5, n.18.
21 *Chron. ad 354*, 48: *hic muro urbem cinxit, templum solis et castra in campo Agrippae dedicavit, genium populi Romani aureum in rostra posuit.*
22 *Dig.* 1.12.1.11. (Ulp.); Busch 2007.
23 *LTUR* I, s.v. *Castra urbana* (Coarelli): 255; Ricci 2011: 5, 2014: 471–3; *CIL* VI 217 = *ILS* 2106.
24 Suet., *Aug.* 49; *Tib.* 37.
25 *Dig.* 1.15.4 (Ulp.). The fire-fighting responsibilities were originally under the command of the *tresviri capitales*, but at the time of Augustus this task was controlled by the prefect of the watchmen. *Dig.* 1.15.1 (Paul.).
26 *Dig.* 1.15.3.3 (Paul.). Cf. *CIL* VI 32327, vv. 21–2; Petron., *Sat.* 78.
27 *CIL* VI 233; *CIL* VI 1092; *CIL* VI 1226. See *LTUR* I, s.v. *Cohortium Vigilum Stationes* (Ramieri): 292–4.
28 Coarelli seems to identify the office of the prefect of the *vigiles* in the surroundings of the Crypta Balbi because of the discovery of an inscription dedicated to Vulcan mentioning the prefect of the watchmen Cn. Octavius Titinius Capito who might be the patron of the corps. Coarelli 2019: 397–8.
29 Some authors claim that the difference between the *castra* and the *excubitoria* is nonexistent or unclear. See Coarelli 2019: 402–4.
30 Sablayrolles 1996: 257–262.
31 De Magistris 1898; Sablayrolles 1996: 251–7.

32 *CIL* VI 1059; *CIL* VI 414a-b; Sablayrolles 1996: 269.
33 Sablayrolles 1996: 267–8.
34 Lanciani *FUR*: tab. 17; Sablayrolles 1996: 270.
35 Sablayrolles 1996: 250.
36 Known as Lares Augusti from the time of Augustus after his reorganization of the cult in 7 B.C. See Lott 2004: 181–209; Russell 2020: 28.
37 *ILS* 3219 (= *CIL* VI 35); 3610–12 (= V 3257; X 1582; VI 446–7).
38 Russell 2020: 27–28.
39 Ruciński 2009: 193–4.
40 *SHA, Alex. Sev.* 33.1.
41 *Not. Urb. Rom. et Cur. Urb. Rom.*, 105.13–16.
42 Daguet-Gagey 1997: 36–37.
43 Suet., *Aug.* 37.
44 Frontin., *Aq.* 100: *placere huic ordini, eos qui aquis publicis praeessent, cum eius rei causa extra urbem essent, lictores binos et servos publicos ternos, architectos singulos et scribas, librarios, accensos praeconesque totidem habere, quot habent ei per quos frumentum plebei datur.* See also Frontin., *Aq.* 116.3.4; Robinson 1992: 86–88. This office was originally controlled by the peregrine praetor, but it passed to the control of the *Praefectus Urbi* when the authority of the praetors declined.
45 This number was reached at the time of Claudius when the *Familia Aquaria Publica* formed by some 240 slaves and the *Familia Aquaria Caesaris* formed by 460 workers were reunited to create a larger technical office for the construction, maintenance, and repair of the water supply infrastructure. Frontin., *Aq.* 2.105; Aicher 1995: 23.
46 Frontin., *Aq.* 98.1; Coarelli 2019: 176.
47 Bruun 2007: 5.
48 Coarelli 2019: 166–7.
49 Coarelli 2019: 164, 168.
50 Coarelli 2019: 172, n. 95.
51 Steinby 1981: 302; Coarelli 2019: 177–180.
52 Chastagnol (1960: 214–218) placed the foundation of this *statio* at the time of Constantine. Nevertheless, Coarelli (2019: 192) supports a pre-Constantinian creation, possibly at the time of Maxentius.
53 *CIL* VI 36951; Kajava 1989: n. 6. It seems that the *curator aquarum et Miniciae* also oversaw the distribution of free grain at the Porticus Minucia Frumentaria at this time. C. Bruun argued for the existence of an office at the *Lacus Iuturnae*. Bruun 1991; *contra* Steinby 2012: 98.
54 Steinby 2012: 98.
55 *Dig.* 43.15.
56 Suet., *Aug.* 37.
57 Dio 57.14.7–8
58 Tac., *Ann.* 1.76.
59 Aldrete 2007: 199.
60 *CIL* VI 1224: Statio·Al[vei·Tib·et-Ripar·et]/Cloacaru[m·Sacrae·Vrbis·] Cvr[a·Agen]te/ Avrelio·A[rte]midoro·C·V/Devoto·Nv[min]i·Maiestatiq/[ei]vs·
61 Rodríguez-Almeida 1988: 124.
62 Dio 54.8; Suet., *Aug.* 37.
63 Suet., *Aug.* 30; *SHA, Alex. Sev.* 33; *SHA, M. Ant.* 12
64 *ILS* 1347 (= *CIL* VIII 822). See also a *procurator operis theatri Pompeiani*: *ILS* 1430 = *CIL* VIII 14.39.
65 *ILS* 1222 (= *CIL* VI 1708); Cf. *Not. Dig. Occ.* 4.12–15.
66 Ruciński 2009: 68.
67 Chastagnol 1960: 64–66; Ruciński 2009: 190.
68 Vigneaux 1896: 109–112
69 Ruciński 2009: 191.

70 Chastagnol 1960: 54–56.
71 *Dig.* 1.12.1.11 (Ulp.): *Cura carnis omnis ut iusto pretio praebeatur ad curam praefecturae pertinet, et ideo et forum suarium sub ipsius cura est: sed et ceterorum pecorum sive armentorum quae ad huiusmodi praebitionem spectant ad ipsius curam pertinent.* See Ruciński 2009: 99–100.
72 *CIL* VI 8470 = *ILS* 1705. Cf. Robinson 1992: 136.
73 See above chapter 4 by T. Smith.
74 The *quaestiones perpetuae* were standing courts for investigation and trial of cases that involved *delicta publica* that replaced the primitive custom of judging the cases through the assembly of the people or the use of an appointed commission. See Lopez Garcia forthcoming: 11–3.
75 This changed in the time of Septimius Severus when the urban prefects took over the civil cases. Chastagnol 1960: 85.
76 Tert., *Persec.* 13.3.
77 Ruciński 2009: 216.
78 Santalucia 1992: 125–216; Coarelli 2019: 316.
79 Bablitz 2007: 44. The first epigraphic testimony of the urban prefect acting as a vicar of the emperor is from the time of Gordian III (*iudex sacrarum cognitionum/ vice sacra iudicans*). *CIL* XIV 3902 = *ILS* 1186. See Chastagnol 1960: 131; Ruciński 2009: 155.
80 Santalucia 1992: 219–220.
81 Plin., *Ep.* 7.11.1.
82 Ruciński 2009: 189.
83 *SHA, Alex. Sev.* 33.1.
84 See below about the *officium*.
85 *Dig.* 1.12.
86 *Dig.* 1.12.4 (Ulp.): *Initio eiusdem epistulae ita scriptum est: "cum urbem nostram fidei tuae commiserimus": quidquid igitur intra urbem admittitur, ad praefectum urbi videtur pertinere. sed et si quid intra centensimum miliarium admissum sit, ad praefectum urbi pertinet: si ultra ipsum lapidem, egressum est praefecti urbi notionem.* See Vitucci 1956: 59.
87 Chastagnol 1960: 26–7.
88 Lyd., *Mag.* 1.34.
89 Vigneaux 1896: 124; Palombi 1997: 150, n. 45.
90 La Rocca 2001: 193–5; Carnabuci 2006: 182.
91 *LTUR* IV, s.v. *Praefectura Urbis* (Coarelli): 159–160.
92 Meneghini and Santangeli Valenzani 2006; D'Ambrosio et al. 2011.
93 Coarelli 2019: 317–8. The urban prefecture was the main tax office, and thus it required effective control of the city and its territory. To support this hypothesis on the *Templum Pacis*, Coarelli compares the shape of the building with the plan of the Library of Hadrian in Athens which some authors have linked with the office of the proconsul of Achaia – but this hypothesis about the Greek building is not completely satisfactory among the research community either.
94 Palombi 2016: 20; Tucci 2017: 140–3.
95 Mart. 2.17: *Tonstrix Suburae faucibus sedet primis,/Cruenta pendent qua flagella/ tortorum Argique letum multus obsidet sutor./Sed ista tonstrix, Ammiane, non tondet,/ Non tondet, inquam. Quid igitur facit? Radit.*
96 Marchese (2007: 613, n. 5) pointed out that a place to inflict torture in the *Argiletum* should not be surprising because of the existence of the court of the urban praetor and the peregrine praetor at the Forum of Augustus, but in any case, it is not possible to link this with the urban prefect.
97 This piece of the *Forma Urbis* was discovered in 1562 in the surroundings of St. Cosmas and Damian and was reproduced in Renaissance drawing Cod. Vat. Lat. 3439, fol. 18r.

98 Symm., *Ep.* 10.78: *Et cum ad forum Vespasiani tam ego quam vir spectabilis vicarius perurgente populo fuissemus ingressi, ut quietem utriusque partis multitudini suaderemus, subito armati servi telis et saxis, aliquanti etiam ferro, populos partis Eulalii aggressi sunt, qui inermes convenerant, ut quod praeceptum de episcopo Spoletino esset agnoscerent: quosque ita sauciaverunt, qui parati adversus imparatos venerant, ut me quoque et virum spectabilem vicarium crederent appetendos, dum seditioso furore nullam admittunt penitus rationem, nisi ad liberandum nos divinitas adfuisset, egressique per secretiorem partem ictum saxorum et impetum conspirantis multitudinis vitassemus, minime potuissemus evadere.*
99 Caruso and Volpe 2000: 55.
100 Vitucci 1956: 56; Chastagnol 1960: 322; *contra* Coarelli 2019: 386–7.
101 Volpe 2000: 511–2.
102 Coarelli 2019: 387.
103 Marchese 2007.
104 *CIL* VI 37114 = *EDR* 071667: Salvis d]d. nn. inclytis semper Augg., [po]rticu[m] cum scriniis Tellurensis secretarii tribunalib(us) adherentem, Iunius Valerius Bellicius, v(ir) c(larissimus), praef(ectus) urb(i), vice sacra iudicans, restituto specialiter urbanae sedis honore perfecit.
105 *CIL* VI 31959 = *EDR* 093152: Florentib(us) dd. [nn. H]onorio [et] Theodosio incc[lyti]s semper Augg., Iunius Valerius [Bellici]us, v(ir) c(larissimus), p[r]aef(ectus) u[rb(i)] vice sac(ra) iud(icans), port[icum cum sc]r[i]ni[is] tellurensis secr[etarii tribunalibus] adherentem red[integravit et] urbanae sedi vetustatis h[o]nor[em resti]tuit.
106 The distant positions of the two discoveries – ca. 1 km – could suggest that the spaces mentioned in the epigraphs could be scattered in different areas of the city. Nonetheless, it is difficult to determine if the epigraphs were found in primary or secondary locations.
107 *PLRE* II, s.v. Iunius Valerius Bellicius: 223.
108 Several epigraphs mentioning urban prefects have been discovered in the area between via della Polveriera and via delle Sette Sale (*CIL* VI 40783b = *CIL* VI 41335a; *CIL* VI 1657; *CIL* VI 1714 = *CIL* VI 31909; *CIL* VI 1120b = *CIL* VI 1656c = *CIL* VI 31882; *CIL* VI 1656a = *CIL* VI 31882; *CIL* VI 41391b; *CIL* VI 1670 = 31889). Carnabuci 2006: 182; Marchese 2007: 628.
109 This traditional interpretation of a library at the hemicycle of the Baths of Trajan has been contested on several occasions. On this controversy see Lopez Garcia and Bueno Guardia 2021: 11.
110 *CIL* VI 37114 = *EDR*071667; *CIL* VI 31959 = *EDR*093152. See above.
111 Amoroso 2007: 73.
112 An epigraph from Thracia dated A.D. 238 mentions a *porticus Thermarum Traianorum* that would be a place to exhibit public documents. *CIL* III 12336. Other authors interpret the hemicycle as a place for the training of athletes known as the *curia Athletarum*. See Palombi 1997: 158; Rausa 2004.
113 The temple was originally founded sometime after 268 B.C. at the Carinae. It was restored on several occasions in the republican period. Flor. 1.14.2; Frontin., *Strat.* 1.12.3; Iordan., *Rom.* 160; Varro, *Rust.* 1.2.1; Cic., *QFr.* 3.1.14; *Har. resp.* 31; Suet., *Gramm.* 15; Serv., *Aen.* 8.361; Ps. Acro., *Hor. Epist.* 1.7.48; Dion. Hal. 8.79.3; Fast., *Praen.* 13 dic. It is likely that the temple was restored after the fire of A.D. 192 during the time of Commodus. Dio 72.24.1–2.
114 *LTUR* V, s.v. *Tellurenses* (Lega); *LTUR* V, s.v. *Tellus, Aedes* (Coarelli); *LTUR* V, s.v. *Tellus, Templum* (De Spirito), and more recently, Amoroso 2007: 53–84; Marchese 2007: 613–634.
115 Colini 1933; *LTUR* V, s.v. *Tellus, Aedes* (Coarelli); Terrenato 1992; Häuber 2005.
116 Jordan and Hülsen 1907; Platner and Ashby 1929.
117 Lanciani 1892; Chastagnol 1960; Palombi 1997; Carnabuci 2006.
118 Amoroso 2007: 70.

119 The Basilica of Maxentius itself is interpreted by Coarelli as the "judicial basilica of the prefecture" during the fourth century. Specifically, the northern apse of the basilica has been identified as a *secretarium* – an enclosed courtroom.
120 Lanciani 1891; *contra* Palombi 1997: n. 49.
121 Lopez Garcia forthcoming.
122 Mart. 2.64.
123 This type of trial was reserved only for some cases of *querela inofficiosi testament* or *hereditatis petitiones* that sometimes required a massive panel of 105 to 180 judges under the authority of a *praetor hastarius* to examine the evidence and impose sentence. See Gagliardi 2002: 352–358.
124 The *Tabulae Herculanenses* and *Tabulae Sulpiciorum* show that the location of the tribunal of the urban praetors, and perhaps the peregrine praetors as well, in the period between A.D. 40 and 75 was within the Forum of Augustus. See Camodeca 1999, 2017.
125 Gagliardi 2005: 438.
126 Gell., *NA* 13.25.1–2.
127 Anderson 1984: 166.
128 Giuliani and Verducchi 1993: 178; Packer 1997.
129 Santalucia 1992: 215–216.
130 Santalucia 1992: 219–220.
131 Also, at that time the emperor became a fundamental figure of the judiciary system, conducting legal activities in several locations within the city. See Bablitz 2007: 44.
132 Lopez Garcia 2021: 164–5.
133 Orlandi 2013: 49. The statues dedicated by the urban prefect were likely part of the programme of restorations carried out on public buildings after the sack by Ricimer. See also Ambrogi 2011: 522.
134 *Cod. Theod.* 13.9.6, 2.1.8.3; Cf. Nash 1976: 194.
135 The *cognitiones* were accessible only to the *exceptores,* the *honorati,* and the *iudices.* Cf. De Giovanni 2007: 294.
136 *Cod. Theod.* 1.12.1; Amm. Marc. 26.3.2. Between A.D. 384 and 395 the custom of meeting secretly was extended to all cases. See Chastagnol 1960: 381.
137 Symm., *Rel.* 23.4–6: *Nam cum ad examinandos actus v. c. Bassi ex praefecto urbi potestas uicaria ad secretarium commune prodiisset, nescio quis, ut aiunt libello dato, de officii mei conludio uel iniquitate conquestus est.* Färber (2012: 53) interprets the *Secretarium Commune* as the official building that the urban prefect – Symmachus himself – shared with the *vicarius Urbis Romae*. This location also served to store the official diaries of the prefects, but the relation of the term *secretarium* with the tribunal of the urban prefect is not entirely clear.
138 Coarelli 2019: 380–3.
139 Caré 2005: 38; Liverani 2020.
140 See above about the epigraphs of Valerius Bellicius.
141 Chastagnol 1960: 247; Färber 2012: 53–4. Some acts of martyrdom led by the urban prefects happened in the *Secretarium Tellurensis*, so it seems to be an equivalent place to the *Secretarium Commune*. Cf. Vigneaux 1896: 124; Ruciński 2009: 213.
142 Coarelli 2007: 321.
143 Chastagnol 1960: 252–3.
144 Fraschetti 1999: 228–230.
145 Symm., *Relat.* 23.9: *Quod cum sibi Fulgentius v. c. auctor contumeliae meae invidiosum putaret, ad circi secretarium convocavit.*
146 *CIL* VI 1718 = *EDR* 111471. The exact location of this space is controversial. Some scholars identified the location of the *secretarium* at the *tabernae* of the Forum of Caesar. See Nash 1976: 191–205; Richardson 1992: 347; Kalas 2015: 157–159. Others locate the space in a late fourth- or early fifth-century building that occupied the southern portico of the Forum of Caesar behind the Curia Iulia. Fraschetti 1999; Coarelli 2019: 381; Salvagni 2021.

147 Lopez Garcia forthcoming: 41.
148 Robinson 1992: 167.
149 Juvenal lamented about the happy days when one prison sufficed the city. Cf. Juv. 3.312–314. See Robinson 1992: 168.
150 *ILS* 2117; *ILS* 2126; *CIL* III 15190–1.
151 The bibliography includes the most important contributions about the spaces related to the institutions discussed in this chapter.

References

Aicher, P. 1995: *Guide to the Aqueducts of Ancient Rome*, Wauconda, IL.
Aldrete, G. S. 2007: *Floods of the Tiber in Ancient Rome*, Baltimore, MD.
Ambrogi, A. 2011: 'Sugli occultamenti antichi di statue. Le testimonianze archeologiche a Roma', *Römische Mitteilungen* 117, 511–566.
Amoroso, A. 2007: 'Il tempio di Tellus e il quartiere della praefectura Urbana', *Workshop di archeologia classica: paesaggi, costruzioni, reperti* 4, 53–84.
Anderson, J. C. 1984: *The Historical Topography of the Imperial Fora*, Brussels.
Bablitz, L. 2007: *Actors and Audience in the Roman Courtroom*, New York.
Bruun, C. 1991: *The Water Supply of Ancient Rome. A Study of Roman Imperial Administration, Commentationes Humanarum Litterarum-93*, Helsinki.
Bruun, C. 2007: 'Aqueductium e statio aquarum. La sede della cura aquarum di Roma', in A. Leone, D. Palombi, and S. Walker (eds), *Res bene gestae. Ricerche di storia urbana su Roma antica in onore di E.M. Steinby*, Roma, 1–14.
Busch, A. W. 2007: ' "Militia in urbe". The Military Presence in Rome', in L. De Blois, O. Hekster, G. Kleijn and E. Lo Cascio (eds), *Proceedings of the Sixth Workshop of the International Network Impact of Empire (Roman Empire, 200 B.C. – A.D. 476)*, Capri, March 29–April 2, 2005, 315–341.
Camodeca, G. 1999: *Tabulae Pompeianae Sulpiciorum: edizione critica dell'archivio puteolano dei Sulpicii*, Roma.
Camodeca, G. 2017: *Tabulae Herculanenses: edizione e commento*, Roma.
Caré, A. 2005: *L'ornato architettonico della Basilica di Massenzio*, Roma.
Carnabuci, E. 2006: 'La nuova forma del Foro di Augusto: Considerazioni sulle destinazioni d'uso degli emicicli', in R. Meneghini and R. Santangeli Valenzani (eds), *Formae Urbis Romae. Nuovi frammenti di piante marmoree dallo scavo dei Fori Imperiali*, Rome, 173–195.
Caruso, G., and Volpe, R. 2000: ' "Preesistenze e persistenze delle Terme di Traiano", in E. Fentress (ed.), *"Romanization and the City": Creation, Transformations, and Failures. Proceedings of a Conference Held at the American Academy in Rome to Celebrate the 50th Anniversary of the Excavations at Cosa, 14–16 May, 1998*', Journal of Roman Archaeology 38, 42–56.
Chastagnol, A. 1960: *La préfecture urbaine à Rome sous le Bas-Empire*, Paris.
Chastagnol, A. 1962: *Les Fastes de la Préfecture de Rome au Bas-Empire*, Paris.
Coarelli, F. 2007: *Rome and Environs. An Archaeological Guide*, Berkeley, CA.
Coarelli, F. 2019: *Statio. I luoghi dell'amministrazione nell'antica Roma*, Roma.
Colini, A. M. 1933: 'Scoperte tra il Foro della Pace e l'anfiteatro', *Bullettino della Commissione di Archeologia Comunale* 61, 79–87.
Daguet-Gagey, A. 1997: *Les opera publica à Rome: 180–305 ap. J.-C*, Paris.
D'Ambrosio, E., Meneghini, R., and Rea, R. 2011: 'Nuovi frammenti di piante marmoree dagli scavi dell'area di culto del Templum Pacis', *Bullettino Della Commissione Archeologica Comunale Di Roma* 112, 67–76.

De Giovanni, L. 2007: *Istituzioni, scienza giuridica, codici nel mondo tardoantico. Alle radici di una nuova storia*, Rome.
De Magistris, E. 1898: *La militia vigilum della Roma imperiale*, Rome.
De Rossi, G. B. 1858: 'Le stazioni delle coorti dei vigili nella città di Roma', *Annali dell'Instituto di Correspondenza Archeologica* 30, 265–297.
Egidi, R. 2010: '"L'area di Piazza Venezia. Nuovi dati topografici", Archeologia e infrastrutture. Il tracciato fondamentale della linea C della metropolitana di Roma: prime indagini archeologiche', *Bollettino d'Arte*, Serie VII, 93–124.
Färber, R. 2012: '"Die Amtssitze der Stadtpräfekten im spätantiken Rom und Konstantinopel", in F. Arnold, A. W. Busch, R. Haensch, and U. Wulf-Rheidt (eds), *Orte der Herrschaft. Charakteristika von antiken Machtzentren, Menschen – Kulturen – Traditionen.* Studien aus den Forschungsclustern des Deutschen Archäologischen Instituts, Forschungscluster 3: Politische Räume', *Band* 3, 49–71.
Fraschetti, A. 1999: *La conversione. Da Roma pagana a Roma cristiana*, Rome.
Freis, H. 1967: *Die cohortes urbanae, Epigraphische Studien 2* (Bonner Jahrbücher, Beihefte, 21), Köln.
Gagliardi, L. 2002: *Decemviri e Centumviri: Origini e competenze*, Milano.
Gagliardi, L. 2005: 'La divisione in Consilia del Collegio Centumvirale e la Basilica Iulia', *Bullettino dell'Istituto di Diritto Romano Vittorio Scialoja* XL–XLI, 385–445.
Giuliani, C. F., and Verducchi, P. 1993: 'Basilica Iulia', in E. M. Steinby (ed.), *Lexicon Topographicum Urbis Romae*, 1, Roma, 95–102.
Häuber, C. 2005: 'Das Archäologische Informationssystem "AIS ROMA": Esquilin, Caelius, Capitolium, Velabrum, Porta Triumphalis', *Bullettino della commissione archeologica comunale di Roma* 106, 9–59.
Jordan, H., and Hülsen, C. 1907: *Topographie der Stadt Rom im Alterthum*, Berlin.
Kajava, M. 1989: 'Le iscrizioni ritrovate nell'area del Lacus Iuturnae', in M. Steinby (ed.), *Lacus Iuturnae I, Lavori e studi di archeologia 12*, Rome, 34–56.
Kalas, G. 2015: *The Restoration of the Roman Forum in Late Antiquity: Transforming Public Space*, Austin, TX.
Lanciani, R. 1891: 'Quatre dessins inédits de la Collection Destailleur', *Mélanges d'archéologie et d'histoire* 11, 159–168.
Lanciani, R. 1892: 'Gli edifici della prefettura urbana fra la Tellure e le Terme di Tito e di Traiano', *Bullettino della Commissione Archeologica Comunale di Roma* 20, 19–37.
La Rocca, E. 2001: 'La nuova immagine dei Fori Imperiali. Appunti in margine agli scavi', *Mitteilungen Des Deutschen Archaelogischen Instituts. Roemische Abteilung* 108, 171–213.
Liverani, P. 2020: Recension of *Statio. I luoghi dell'amministrazioni nell'antica Roma. Topografia antica, Archeologia, Storia Antica Romana*, Rome 2019, Histara. Les Comptes Rendus. http://histara.sorbonne.fr/cr.php?cr=3624.
Lopez Garcia, A. 2015: *Los Auditoria de Adriano y el Athenaeum de Roma*, Florence.
Lopez Garcia, A. 2021: 'Una corte di giustizia presso il Foro di Traiano? Analisi sulla funzionalità degli auditoria adrianei', *Mélanges de l'École Française de Rome* 133(1), 149–171.
Lopez Garcia, A. forthcoming: 'Fora Litibus Omnia Fervent: The Transfer of the Tribunals in Rome from the Forum to the Courtroom'.
Lopez Garcia, A., and Bueno Guardia, M. 2021: 'Typology and Multifunctionality of Public Libraries in Rome and the Empire', *Journal of Eastern Mediterranean Archaeology & Heritage Studies* 9(3), 247–277.
Lott, J. B. 2004: *The Neighborhoods of Augustan Rome*. Cambridge.
Marchese, M. E. 2007: 'La prefettura urbana a Roma: Un tentativo di localizzazione attraverso le epigrafi, Mélanges de l'École Française de Rome', *Antiquité* 119, 613–634.

Meneghini, R., and Santangeli Valenzani, R. 2006: *Formae Urbis Romae. Nuovi frammenti di piante marmoree dallo scavo dei Fori Imperiali*, Roma.
Nash, E. 1976: 'Secretarium Senatus', in L. Bonfante and H. von Heintze (eds), *In memoriam Otto J. Brendel. Essays in Archaeology and the Humanities*, Mainz, 191–204.
Orlandi, S. 2010: "L'iscrizione del praefectus Urbi F. Felix Passifilus Paulinus", in *Archeologia e infrastrutture. Il tracciato fondamentale della linea C della metropolitana di Roma: prime indagine archeologiche, Bollettino d'Arte*, Volume Speciale 2010 – Serie VII, Florence, 124–127.
Orlandi, S. 2013: 'Le testimonianze epigrafiche', *Bollettino di Archeologia On Line, Direzione Generale per le Antichità* IV(2–4), 45–59.
Packer, J. E. 1997: *The Forum of Trajan in Rome*, Berkeley-Los Angeles, CA, Oxford.
Palombi, D. 2016: *I Fori prima dei Fori. Storia urbana dei quartieri di Roma antica cancellati per la realizzazione dei Fori Imperiali*, Rome.
Palombi, D. *Tra Palatino ed Esquilino: Velia, Carinae, Fagutal. Storia urbana di tre quartieri di Roma antica*, Roma, 1997.
Platner, S. B., and Ashby, T. 1929: *A Topographical Dictionary of Ancient Rome*, London.
Rausa, F. 2004: I luoghi dell'agonismo nella Roma imperiale. L'edificio della Curia Athletarum, *Römische Abteilung* 111, 537–554.
Ricci, C. 2011: 'In custodiam urbis: Notes on the cohortes urbanae (1968–2010)', *Historia* 60(4), 484–508.
Ricci, C. 2014: 'The Urban Troops Between the Antonines and Severus', in W. Ec and P. Funke (eds.), *Öffentlichkeit – Monument – Text: XIV Congressus Internationalis Epigraphiae Graecae et Latinae. 27.-31. Augusti MMXII. Akten*, Vol 4, Berlin, Boston, 471–473.
Richardson, L. Jr. 1992: *A New Dictionary of Ancient Rome*, Baltimore, MA and London.
Robinson, O. F. 1992: *Ancient Rome. City Planning and Administration*, London.
Rodríguez-Almeida, E. 1988: 'Un frammento di una nuova pianta marmorea di Roma', *Journal of Roman Archaeology* 1, 120–131.
Ruciński, S. 2009: *Praefectus Urbi. Le gardien de l'ordre public à Rome sous le Haut-Empire Romain*, Poznań.
Russell, A. 2020: 'The Altars of the Lares Augusti. A View from the Streets of Augustan Iconography', in A. Russell and M. Hellström (eds.), *The Social Dynamics of Roman Imperial Imagery*, 25–51.
Sablayrolles, R. 1996: *Libertinus Miles: Les Cohortes De Vigiles*, Rome.
Salvagni, I. 2021: 'Il Secretarium Senatus e la chiesa di Santa Martina al Foro Romano: Frammenti dalla storia', *Bollettino di Archeologia Online* XII(1), 99–137.
Santalucia, B. 1992: 'La giustizia penale', *Storia di Roma* 2(3), 211–236.
Steinby, E. M. 1981: 'I bolli laterizi dell'area sacra di Largo Argentina', in I. Kajanto (ed.), *L'Area Sacra di Largo Argentina*, I, Rome, 299–332.
Steinby, E. M. (ed.) 2012: '*Lacus Iuturnae, II. Saggi degli anni 1982–1985*. Relazione di scavo e conclusioni', *Acta Institutum Romani Finlandiae* 38.
Terrenato, N. 1992: 'Velia and Carinae: Some Observations on an Area of Archaic Rome', *Papers of the Fourth Conference on Italian Archaeology* IV(2), 31–46.
Tucci, P. L. 2017: *The Temple of Peace in Rome*, Cambridge.
Vigneaux, P. E. 1896: *Essai sur l'histoire de la praefectura urbis à Rome*, Paris.
Vitucci, G. 1956: *Ricerche sulla praefectura urbi in età imperiale (sec. I – III)*, Rome.
Volpe, R. 2000: 'Paesaggi urbani tra Oppio e Fagutal', *Mélanges de l'école française de Rome* 112, 511–556.

8 *Scholae* and *Collegia*

Spaces for 'Semi-Administrative' Associations in the Imperial Age[1]

Marco Brunetti

I Introduction

This chapter is focused on the *collegia*, the (private) professional and religious associations that, at least officially, did not have any administrative functions. Through the analysis of the impact that their activities and tasks had on some public services, we aim to assess whether and which *collegia* can be considered 'semi-official' associations. Their *publica utilitas* is here investigated through the analysis of the logistic and material support that some collegia gave to specific public services (e.g., the *annona*, public building, and the supply of goods and services: be they material – e.g., wood, military clothing – or immaterial, e.g., athletic education, firemen). At last, considering the numerous benefits granted to *collegia*, this chapter investigates how the social relevance was also expressed by these associations through architectural and topographical features of their seats, as if they claimed a sort of 'non-official' administrative function. As such, the final goal is to foster a reconsideration of our idea of 'Roman administration' including these private intermediate *corpora* that acted between the central power and the society.

In recent decades our knowledge of Imperial administration has changed considerably, especially from an archaeological perspective. From the second half of the 19th century onwards, an increasing number of studies have been provided on the logistic processes of the Imperial administration and how its tasks were performed through different institutions and public figures.[2] Recently, more attention has also been focused on the archaeological spaces and buildings of those in charge of such administrative processes and tasks, i.e. the *stationes* – often characterized by the presence of archives.[3] However, as these very studies have pointed out, the lack of material evidence (e.g., inscriptions, mosaics, literary sources) strains our attempts to recognize administrative seats in specific buildings and architectural structures. Unfortunately, we have to admit that, even the presence of such material evidence does not necessarily mark a building as a seat of an 'administrative office'. Nevertheless, through a collection of cross-referenced data, in some cases, scholars have supposed that some buildings could house specific administrative tasks. The co-presence of these clues is however so rare that, in many instances, the real existence of administrative offices as we understand it in modern terms has been questioned.[4]

DOI: 10.4324/b23090-11

This chapter has been made available under a CC BY-NC 4.0 license.

Undoubtedly, the existence of concrete spaces devoted to administrative functions cannot be questioned, as some inscriptions reveal (e.g., the s*tatio aquarum* of the *Lacus Iuturnae* at the Roman Forum[5]) or the administrative spaces devoted to the water supply mentioned by Julius Sextus Frontinus's text (*On aqueducts*, end of the 1st century A.D.).[6] Coarelli's recent publication has cast fresh light on this field of research, mostly in relation to the case of the city of Rome. Nevertheless, this topic is still open to further investigation because of some unresolved issues and the necessity of including other spatial contexts outside Rome, such as municipal spaces that accommodated Imperial demands at the local level.[7] On the other hand, there is one underlying problem for the very concept of administration: which competences/activities can be ascribed to the Imperial administration and which not? Can we provide a precise and stable definition of 'Imperial Administration' so that we can also specify which tasks and offices constituted its range of action? And, moreover, can we include within the 'imperial administrative tasks' those 'public services' that the Empire guaranteed for its citizens but were ensured by private associations such as the *collegia* (e.g., the *annona*)?

Starting with these questions, this chapter aims to focus on the *collegia*, the private professional or religious associations that, at least officially, did not have any administrative functions. Specifically, we are going to investigate whether and which *collegia* could instead be considered 'semi-official' associations because of their 'public utility' and how their tasks indirectly impacted the services that the Imperial administration guaranteed. As such, in the next section of this chapter, despite the wide chronological and geographical boundaries that characterize the long life of these associations, we are going to mention some of the numerous social benefits granted to *collegia* in order to stress their social relevance in the eyes of the Imperial/municipal power.[8] In the final part of this contribution, we are going to investigate how the social relevance of these associations was also expressed from an architectural and topographical point of view as if they claimed a sort of 'non-official administrative function'. Of course, we are going to collect all the architectural typologies that concern the seats of these associations, a task both ambitious and partially reached by Beate Bollmann.[9] But we are going to stress the public utility that these associations had for the Empire (especially in relation to some logistic and essential public services). Not by chance, as will be discussed further shortly, some tax or legal benefits suggest a sort of special legal status and indirectly a public role that, therefore, could also be expressed through architectural/topographical aspects of their seats.

II *Scholae* or *Collegia*: A Terminological Distinction and Evidence for the 'Public Service'

As clearly pointed out by Pierre Gros, the words *schola* and *collegium* are sometimes used as synonymous in the academic literature, but their meaning is different. While *collegium* refers to the 'association' as a legal entity made up of a group of members,[10] the word *schola* is usually used by inscriptions for indicating the structure that hosted the *collegium*.[11] The terminological issue concerning the different words used by inscriptions and texts for *schola* and *collegium* has been explored by Beate Bollmann in the third chapter of her publication on Roman *scholae*.[12] Although the scholar excludes Greek materials almost completely, the existence of *collegia* is already testified to in the Hellenistic world. A famous example is the *schola* of the *negotiatores* (traders) from Beirut who had a representative building in Delos characterized by different uses (i.e., employed as a sort of sanctuary, guesthouse, and stock exchange for prices).[13]

On the other hand, in the West, we have scanty evidence of *scholae* during the republican age (at that time, the associations likely used to meet in porticos, *cauponae*, and private houses).[14] During the 1st century B.C. the creation of *collegia* was fostered by politicians for their own political consensus, but despite that, the phenomenon of building seats for the *collegia* mostly concerns the Imperial age.[15]

Even though several definitions for the *collegium* can be provided, *collegia* can generally be meant to be private corporations/associations of members with different social status but united by a similar working profession, commercial interest, or religious cult (e.g., artisans [*collegia opificum*], doctors, traders, members of Genius Augusti's worship [*Augustales*]).[16] In the *Digest*, the jurist Gaius clearly states that an association has three characteristics: it has *res communes*, a common treasury, and an *actor* as its legal business.[17] Practically, the main goals of a *collegium* were essentially those of creating social connections through rituals and banquets, to defend some professional rights (when it came to a professional association),[18] and to ensure the mutual assistance of the internal members in case of economic/business troubles – including financial support for the funerals and burials of the internal members.[19] Although each *collegium* was characterized by a specific cult or religious practices, not all *collegia* had a space (*schola*) exclusively reserved for the meeting of internal members and their activities. For instance, in some cases, as for the *collegia tenuiorum*, meetings could be held in private houses.[20]

Although *collegia* in Roman society were not in charge of administrative services and were essentially regulated by private laws and inner rules, the activities and decisions taken within a *collegium* had an indirect impact on public and social life.[21] This is particularly evident in the case of some *collegia* (e.g., *fabri, navicularii, centonarii*) that were involved in important aspects of daily life. The clearest case is the *collegium* of *navicularii*, i.e., the shipowners who were in charge of the transport of the goods for the *annona* and other goods deemed essential to the State. Once shipowners gathered their estates for founding their own *societas* (or, *corpus naviculariorum*), they benefited from several advantages provided by the Empire because of their public utility (e.g., no permissions were needed for founding their own *collegium* and several tax exemptions).[22] They had such strong bargaining power with the Empire that the inscription about the famous strike of the *navicularii* in Arles (A.D. 201) clearly speaks about the relevance of this *collegium* and the difficulties that the Empire was forced to face because of the complaints.[23]

In addition to *navicularii*, the so-called *tria collegia* (*dendrophori, fabri*, and *centonarii*) represent other cases of associations that had a social relevance for public services and, in fact, some inscriptions mention their *utilitas publica*.[24] Wrongly (and simply) considered as firemen by the 19th-century academic literature, over recent decades scholars have had long debates on the surprisingly widespread distribution of these *tria collegia*.[25] Their recurrent mention in inscriptions in Rome and in Roman *municipia* clearly speaks about the social relevance and public utility that these associations had.[26] For instance, in Pesaro (*Pisaurum*), one inscription mentions the fact that two important figures were *patroni* of the most prestigious and relevant local *collegia*, namely the *collegia* of *navicularii, dendrophori, fabri*, and *centonarii*.[27] As we will soon see, scholars have provided various opinions about the activities and tasks that characterized each *collegium* of the so-called *tria collegia* and, therefore, there are still no common and definitive positions on this matter.

According to recent studies, we can sum up the main tasks of these *collegia* in the following way. The *fabri* were essentially builders and artisans in different materials (e.g., *fabri tignarii*: carpenters; *fabri navales*: ship builders; *fabri aurarii*: goldsmiths, etc.). If we consider the case of *fabri tignarii* and *fabri navales*, it is sufficiently clear how much their presence and competence were considered essential for public and private assignments. Literary sources and inscriptions speak about their *utilitas publica* and, specifically, about their employment in the construction of public buildings.[28] Owing to a letter to Trajan by Pliny, at that time governor of Bithynia, scholars have supposed the employment of *fabri* as firemen.[29] The category of *fabri* included several types of specialization (including the *figuli* – i.e., ceramists – for instance).[30] As such, if *fabri* were effectively used as firemen in some cases,[31] we should expect that this would have been the *tignarii* and *fabri navales*, experts in wooden structures, rather than other types of *fabri* (e.g., *figuli* or *fabri aurarii*) who were less familiar with phenomena of combustion.

We have less information on the function and activities of *centonarii* who took their name from the *cento/centones* meant as 'patch', 'patchwork', and also heavy cloaks, blankets, and protective clothing, often used for agricultural workers and the military. As recently shown by Liu, the *centonarii* were instead artisans/tradesmen in low-to-medium quality woollens.[32] In this sense, *centonarii* could facilitate military purchases or requisitioning and, hence, had no role as firemen as Jean Pierre Waltzing thought.[33] Not by chance, the law of the Theodosian Codex that stresses the strict connection with the *collegium* of *dendrophorum* (*De centonariis et dendrophoris*) does not mention any role of the *centonarii* as firemen.[34]

More challenging is the attempt to identify the 'public service' and social relevance of the *dendrophori* (i.e., the 'tree-bearers'). This is the most recent *collegium* founded in Rome, created at the hands of Emperor Claudius.[35] Because of the few data available, scholars do not agree on its function and activities: while some think that it had a purely religious purpose (i.e., the cult of Attis and Cybele),[36] others suppose that, in addition to that, the *collegium* was in charge of the procurement of wood as raw material, its transportation, and likely of its conversion into charcoal – necessary for the heating of public buildings (consequently, the *fabri tignari* would have been in charge of the final processing of the wood for its selling or building for private/public assignments).[37] Indeed, its mere religious character would not motivate the widespread distribution of this *collegium* in many Roman *municipia*.[38] Therefore, as Francesca Diosono suggests, we cannot dismiss the hypothesis that

Claudius gave a religious value to this *collegium* although it already had a professional character and performed public service (i.e., wood-cutters and tree transporters through the exploitation of Imperial-owned forests).[39] Some clues suggest this possibility, for instance, the fact that the *collegia* were *sub cura quindecemvirorum*, namely under the control of the Imperial administration[40] and, moreover, one of Constantine's dispositions that commands the praetorian prefect to increase the number of *dendrophori*, *fabri*, and *centonarii* because of their 'public utility'.[41]

Membership in a *collegium* could bring so many economic/social advantages and duties (e.g., the payment of membership fees)[42] that public lists of the members (*alba* or *fasti*) were inscribed in monumental inscriptions and displayed in the *scholae* of the *collegium*.[43] Regarding these advantages, the members of the *tria collegia* and other *collegia* of artisans/traders received several benefits because of their contribution to these important services. For instance, the *negotiatores frumenti* received some *immunitates* from Augustus onwards,[44] the *mercatores olearii* were exempted from some *munera publica*,[45] the *pistores* received the Roman citizenship,[46] the *centonarii* of Solva had the benefit of not having their riches tied up,[47] and the *fabri* were exempted from the payment of the *chrysargyrum* tax.[48] So long is the list of benefits granted by the Empire – especially, in the case of the *tria collegia* mentioned earelier – that, during the 3rd and 4th centuries A.D., many workers or political individuals (e.g., municipal decurions and curials) aimed to be included in the *collegia* of *fabri* and *centonarii* to profit from these advantages.[49] Moreover, from the 3rd century, the Empire became increasingly 'dependent' on these *collegia* that it made their commitments compulsory and no longer indentured by a contract.[50]

The *collegia* mentioned earlier were not the only ones that had significant advantages granted by the Empire because of their contribution to crucial public services (e.g., the *annona*, the (re)construction of public buildings, and the supply of raw materials or essential goods). Across the decades, many other *collegia*, *corpora*, or *societates* (e.g., *societates publicanorum*, *conductores*, *susceptores*) took over the management of activities deemed of 'public utility'.[51] We can mention a few of them, such as the collection of taxes in the provinces, the exploitation of salt mines and mines, and the supplying of the army. These *societates* are rightly not considered by scholars as part of the Imperial administrative apparatus, although we should not forget their role in the smooth functioning of such essential 'services' that the Empire guaranteed and controlled. They did not have the same bargaining power with the Empire that we have mentioned for some *collegia* (e.g., *navicularii*), and this was essentially due to the limited duration of their task (e.g., *conductores* and *susceptores*). Therefore, they did not even try to have their own seat with a stable and permanent structure (be it a building or halls within other building complexes). The fact that several *collegia* did have their own *scholae* – sometimes with monumental architecture – clearly speaks about the difference between their legal/social status and that of other *societates*.

Considering the data and examples mentioned here, it is clear how the geographical distribution and existence of some *collegia* can be explained through the crucial contribution that they made to the successful fulfilment of public services.

However, in scholarly publications on Roman administration, the *collegia* have not had the proper attention that they deserve, both in architectural and historical terms. Although they consist of associations ruled by internal laws and not by the public administration, their activities had a significant interaction with those public services that the Empire assured and controlled but did not directly manage.

III Public Architectural Models and Topographical Markers for Private Associative Spaces

Every scholar who wants to investigate the topographical and architectural aspects related to Roman *scholae* has to start with Bollmann's study. This significant work is focused on the professional *collegia* in Italy and, as the title clearly states, the religious ones are also included. A specific focus is addressed to the *collegium* of the *Augustales*, i.e., the religious association devoted to Imperial worship and not characterized by or having any professional purpose. The attention devoted to this *collegium* in Bollmann's book is justified by the fact that the *collegia* (be they religious or professional) reached their peak of prosperity in the 2nd century A.D. (both in architectural and geographical terms), and this was also due to the prosperity that the freedmen class had in this timeframe. In fact, although a substantial part of the *Augustales* come from this upwardly mobile class, it also played a central role for other *collegia*. Indeed, several inscriptions record the acts of evergetism addressed to *scholae* by this freedmen class (e.g., donations, restoration, etc.).[52]

Unfortunately, Bollmann's study is limited to the context of Italy and, even within these boundaries, the scholar does not include a number of cases: e.g., Greek *collegia* in Italy (e.g., Dionysiac artists in Rome and Naples), soldiers' associations, *collegia iuvenum*, *scholae* within grave structures,[53] and baths (e.g., *Curia Athletarum*). As such, the conclusions of Bollmann's book have to be considered in relation to the geographical and typological boundaries set by the scholar and, obviously, not in general terms. Moreover, in recent decades, many other studies have enriched our knowledge on some specific *collegia*[54] and further studies have also been provided on other *scholae* in Rome and outside Italy.[55]

Unfortunately, shadows hover around some typologies of *scholae*: this is the case for *scholae* of *centonarii* that had a widespread geographical distribution, at least according to epigraphic sources. In fact, although this *collegium* is frequently mentioned by inscriptions, the unique building discovered so far – that can be assumed to be a *schola* – is at Aquincum in Pannonia (dated to the 2nd century A.D. or earlier).[56] However, even in this case, the evidence gives us no significant insights about the architectural aspects of this building which seems to be a private building. Together with the inscriptions found in this building complex, the only findings are storage and preparation vessels as well as mortars, jugs, and cups.[57] Therefore, regarding the *collegium* of *centonarii*, we can recognize an unusual discrepancy between the rich epigraphic documentation, on one side, and the scant archaeological evidence, on the other. This fact could be explained by the possibility that the meeting spaces of this *collegium* – as with the *collegia tenuiorum* – were in private houses or public temples/shrines/porticos through building additions or conversions of the space.[58]

A similar example can be found in the *schola* of the athletes (*curia athletarum*) on the Esquiline Hill. As Caldelli's study has shown, even in this case, we have no evidence of the *schola* from the archaeological point of view, but the epigraphic evidence allows us to recognize the seat of this *collegium* in a space next to Trajan's Baths and not far from the current church of San Pietro in Vincoli.[59] Greek epigraphic documents tell us that in A.D. 143 one famous Roman athlete (Marcus Ulpius Domesticus) from Ephesus obtained a permanent seat for his *collegium* (or better *synodos*) of athletes near Trajan's Baths from the Emperor.[60] According to Caldelli, the *synodos* received permission to have its own seat because of the Emperor's determination to compete with the Greek athletic tradition.[61] Such an ambition had already started after the foundation of the *agon Capitolinus* in A.D. 86 and, therefore, the Imperial administration required a permanent organizational structure in charge of the recruitment of athletes and their training. Since Rome did not preserve the Greek tradition of *gymnasia* as other cities did, Trajan's Baths became an inevitable surrogate.[62] As such, the *curia athletarum* represents an important case for illustrating how a *collegium* was in charge of the recruitment and training of athletes for public games and ceremonies. Even in this case, we are dealing with a non-public association that, however, had an active and relevant role in the fulfilment of a public service guaranteed by the Empire (i.e., 'public games').[63] Moreover, the *curia athletarum* provides a chance to show how other types of *scholae* can be found in addition to the three main categories highlighted by Bollmann (*insula/domus*-type, temple-structures, and halls/*tabernae*).[64]

Bollmann's general macro-categories must be treated with caution, as some affinities within one category might be not so immediate and granted. For instance, the so-called Bauten mit Portikushöfen (i.e., '*insula/domus*-type') include substantially different buildings like the 'Caseggiato dei Triclini' in Ostia and other porched buildings, such as the so-called Building of Eumachia in Pompeii and the so-called 'Basilica' in Herculaneum (Figure 8.1).[65] Of course, these three cases are united by the presence of a central court/*peristylium* but, at the same time, other relevant architectural differences are evident as well (cf. several affinities with Bollmann's second category, i.e. 'temple-structures'). For instance, from the architectural point of view, these two buildings from Pompeii and Herculaneum reveal similarities with another significant example of *scholae* in Rome, i.e., the case of the so-called Basilica Hilariana, the *schola* of the *dendrophori* on the Caelian Hill, recently re-examined by Pavolini.

From the Claudian to the Antonine Age, archaeological evidence has shown different phases for the Basilica Hilariana. In fact, in this timeframe, the building passed through radical changes, even in the orientation of the building itself (Figure 8.2). In the Claudian Age, the building was oriented N–S with a structure essentially made up of one central porticoed court and two naves per each of two sides. At the centre of the court, a base for an altar and a small religious space with two rooms can be seen. At the side opposite the entrance, three exedras were located and, in the central one, a base for a statue was likely located. In A.D. 140–145, the

Scholae *and* Collegia 183

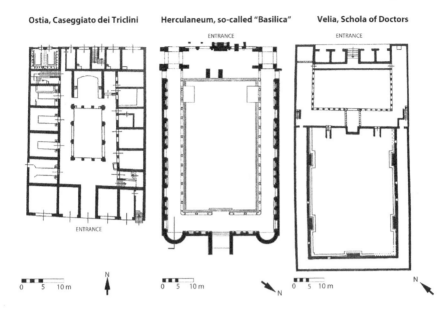

Figure 8.1 From left to right: Ostia, 'Caseggiato dei Triclini'; Herculaneum, so-called Basilica; Velia, *schola* of doctors. Plans based on Zevi 2008; Laird 2015; Galli 2014.

Source: Edited by Marco Brunetti and Antonio Lopez Garcia.

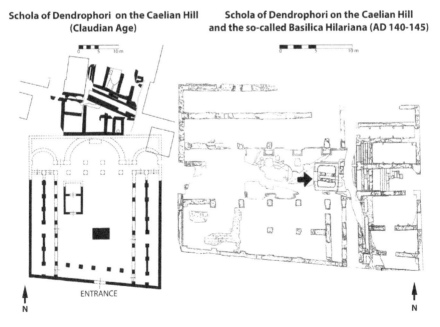

Figure 8.2 *Schola* of *dendrophori* on the Caelian Hill. After Pavolini 2020.

Source: Edited by Marco Brunetti and Antonio Lopez Garcia.

building reached its peak of fame, taking its name from Manius Poblicius Hilarus, *margaritarius* (pearl merchant) and *quinquennalis perpetuus* of the *collegium*.[66] In this brief timeframe, the building completely changed its orientation from N–S to E–W. The new building maintained its function as a *schola*, but the building changed its orientation and also reduced its dimensions. Such a phenomenon was likely due to the need for leaving space for the street that was built at that time next to the building.[67] On the other hand, scholars have not yet figured out the reason why this area of the Caelian Hill, a very densely populated area of Rome, was chosen for the *schola* of the *dendrophori*. Generally, the *collegia* assembled near their place of work or in proximity to the city centre or, sometimes, used pre-existing temples (e.g., Minerva's temple on the Aventine or the *sacellum* of the Augustales at Misenum).[68] Taking into account these three macro-trends, the Claudian seat of the *dendrophori* on Caelian Hill might have been located in this area because of a pre-existing space devoted to the worship of Attis and Cybele.[69] Although the Basilica was not next to the city centre, its location within the urban fabric reveals the role that the *collegium* had because of its worship and, possibly, profession.

Different circumstances inform the *collegium* that, according to one inscription at the Vatican Museums, was devoted to the worship of the god Silvanus and that had its *schola* in the countryside between the second and third miles of the Via Appia.[70] The inscription specifies that the *collegium* was created to provide a funeral and a guarded tomb for its members (Figure 8.3). The land devoted to the *collegium* was donated by a private donor (Iulia Monime) for the symbolic sum of a sestertius and, according to the inscription, the property would have returned to

CIL VI 10231: est schola sub por[ticu] / consacrata Silvano et collegio eius sodalici / mancipio"

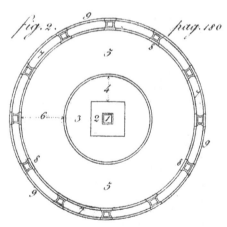

Structures of the temple of the "collegium Silvani" discovered by Carlo Fea in Vigna Cassini (via Appia)

Figure 8.3 Inscription and plan of *collegium Silvani* on the Via Appia. After Della Giovampaola 2008.

Source: Edited by Marco Brunetti.

the donor in the event that the association ceased to exist or performed activities other than those permitted (i.e., sacrifices and banquets). The circular shrine of the *collegium* was discovered by Carlo Fea already in 1820 next to the vigna Cassini on the via Appia and, hence, the location of the *schola* has to be assumed to be in its proximity.[71] Compared to the Basilica Hilariana, the *schola* of Silvanus shows how, excluding religious considerations (the devotion to a deity connected to forests and nature), the peripheral area occupied by this *collegium* reflected the minor social relevance of the *collegium* itself. While it is not always easy to identify the reasons for the peripheral position of a *schola*, we can be more confident that its position in proximity to the city centre was due to the greater social and political role of the *collegium*. The position of the so-called Ucetis' Monument in *Alesia* (Alise-Sainte-Reine) next to the forum clearly speaks of the role that this *collegium* of *fabrum aerariorum* (or *ferrariorum*) had from a local perspective.[72]

Regardless of which categories of *collegia* the *scholae* belonged to, all of them were designed for both social and religious activities. Surely, as in all of the *scholae*, no commercial activity took place inside.[73] The Ucetis' Monument takes this name from one of the deities that were worshipped in the underground *crypta*. The functions of the rooms that flanked the east and south sides (Figure 8.4) are still unknown, but according to some recurrent architectural features (very few *scholae* have clear traces of *triclinia*, kitchens, or latrines) these spaces can be interpreted as multi-purpose rooms, including subsidiary porticos also functioning in this sense.

The reputation of this *collegium* was so widespread that even Pliny mentioned this city because of its metal craftsmen.[74] Such fame can be explained by the fact that the valuable metal production in Alesia not only met the local needs but also the Imperial ones and those of international customers. Therefore, through the central location of its *schola* and its significant dimensions, the members of the *collegium* aimed to '*manifester leur présence par une fondation qui institutionnalise en quelque sorte leur* "leadership" *économique*'.[75]

In addition to that of having a monumental and sumptuous architecture (e.g., the *scholae* of *Augustales*), the proximity of a *schola* to the city centre is undoubtedly one of the main markers for stressing the social relevance of the *collegium*. In a similar manner to the Ucetis' Monument, we can mention several cases, such as the aforementioned 'Caseggiato dei Triclini' in Ostia, the so-called Basilica of Herculaneum, and the *schola* of doctors in Velia (Figure 8.1). These buildings reveal some similarities not only in the sense of the architecture (e.g., a peristyle next to the entrance, central open space, multipurpose rooms, niches/exedras for religious purposes, etc.). They are also characterized by common aspects concerning the topography within the urban plan: namely, their proximity to the city centre and, specifically, to the main streets of the city. For instance, the 'Basilica' of Herculaneum that housed the *collegium* of *Augustales* had its entrance doorway (the short south side) of the building on the *decumanus maximus*.[76] Similarly, the 'Caseggiato dei Triclini' in Ostia, the seat of the *fabri tignuarii*, was flanked by the *decumanus maximus* and was located next to the square of the *forum*.[77] Lastly, the *schola* of doctors in Velia was also flanked by 'via delle Terme', one of the main streets of the city.

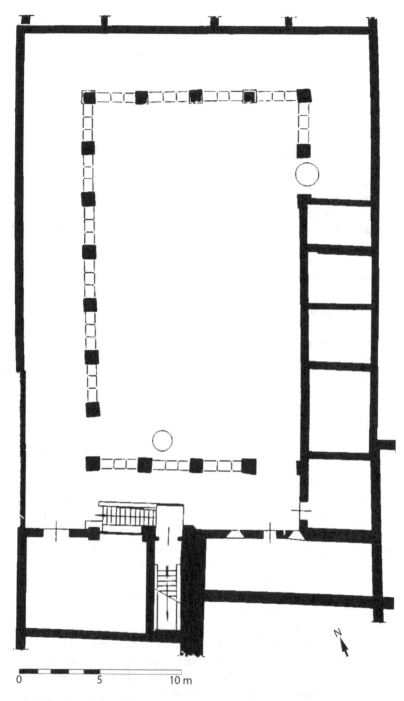

Figure 8.4 Alesia, *schola* of *fabri aerariorum*. After Martin and Varène 1973.
Source: Edited by Marco Brunetti and Antonio Lopez Garcia.

Considering the case of Velia, the building was made up of two main spaces. The smaller one consisted of a covered space with a porticoed court, and one could access the rest of the building through it. On the opposite side from the entrance, one niche probably had a function connected to some cult and here statues of famous doctors have been found. The remainder of the building consisted of a wider space, probably a garden, which was surrounded by galleries and not porches. In this area, statues of gods and figures of the mythical repertoire and members of the Imperial family were found.

As pointed out by Marco Galli, the *schola* of the doctors in Velia represents an interesting example of a *schola*, a case in between a seat of a professional association and a religious space reserved for different cults, including the Imperial one.[78] There is a substantial difference between this building and other *scholae* specifically devoted to the worship of the Imperial cult, such as the 'Basilica' of Herculaneum. In fact, the *schola* of Velia included aspects of Imperial worship in addition to its own pre-existing cults connected to Asclepius. Therefore, in a certain way, the *collegium* aimed to reach a public and Imperial reputation that other *collegia*, such as the *collegium* of *Augustales*, had had since their foundation. Even the internal furnishings of the *schola* of doctors in Velia was so rich that it seems to emulate the sumptuous furnishings of the public spaces. In a similar manner, in the 'Caseggiato dei Triclini' in Ostia, several elements of statuesque furnishings have been found with the same emulative spirit (e.g., a statue of the nymph Leukothea; a huge head of Minerva; a dedication to Mars as the protective deity of the builders). In the *schola* of the *collegium fabrum* at Tarraco, dated to the Hadrianic period, similar rich furnishings of statues have also been found.[79] These and further examples let us hypothesize that we are faced with a recurrent architectural practice within professional *scholae*.

The social relevance that some *collegia* had in general (be they professional or religious) is particularly clear in the case of the *Augustales*, but also for the *navicularii* and *fabri navales* in Ostia. In addition to the already mentioned case of the 'Caseggiato dei Triclini' (*fabri tignuarii*), the *navicularii* and *fabri navales* were important associations for some services that directly (*navicularii*) or less directly (*fabri navales*) were connected to the *annona*. We do not repeat here the architectural descriptions of these *scholae* that Bollmann and Fausto Zeri have skillfully provided so far, although new archaeological evidence and recent studies have shown that, in some cases (e.g., the *stationes* in Piazzale delle Corporazioni and even more the '*schola* del Traiano'), we cannot properly speak of *scholae*.[80] Simply, we include these cases among those already mentioned in order to note that the monumental dimensions of the *scholae* and their central positions reflected their social and economic relevance. These associations in fact guaranteed an essential public service, the *annona*, that officially was in the charge of the Imperial administration. Therefore, through these cases, it can be seen how the emulation of monumental/sumptuous architecture and of the internal furnishings – both typical of some civic spaces – clearly speak to the influence that the *scholae* of the *Augustales* had on the rest of the *collegia*.[81]

We have discussed earlier the 'public utility' of some *collegia* and we have now seen how the social relevance of these *collegia* to the Imperial administration was also claimed through the quasi civic structures of the *scholae*, as shown by the cases of Ostia (e.g., 'Caseggiato dei Triclini'). Nevertheless, one point has to be stressed even though it might seem obvious. Some features that we have mentioned earlier (i.e., monumental architectural dimensions, topographical proximity to the city centre, and the luxury furnishings of the interiors) did not necessarily correspond to an effective 'public utility' of the *schola*. The case of Velia is quite clear in this sense. Although the *collegium* of doctors surely had a social and political influence locally (so that its *schola* reflected its local prestige in architectural and artistic terms), the *collegium* in itself cannot be listed among those *collegia* that we could proffer as a 'non-public association' because of their 'public utility'. Therefore, as we will see soon, a clarification of the *publica utilitas* concept has to be made in order to understand under what conditions we could speak of 'non-public' or 'non-administrative' *collegia*.

IV Some Final Conclusions: *Publica Utilitas* for 'Semi-Administrative' Associations

The *publica utilitas* of Roman associations was implicit in the very concept of *collegia* since the time of the *lex Iulia de collegiis* (c. 49–44 B.C.), promulgated by Julius Caesar. Owing to this law, no new association was to be permitted unless it performed useful functions and services for the community.[82] On the other hand, the *senatus consultum de collegiis tenuiorum* (dated to the Tiberian – Claudian Age) fostered the creation of *collegia tenuiorum* as they guaranteed their members a proper funeral, acting as a social safety net for the lower social classes.[83] As Marcian explains in the *Digest*,[84] this *senatus consultum* included among the *collegia illicita* those that "did not perform any useful function for the Roman State" (i.e., *collegia sodalicia*).[85] As such, the principle of *publica utilitas* is not new in recent scholarship, although different definitions – and not always in agreement – have been provided for it.[86] Numerous types of *collegia* were founded during the 2nd and 3rd centuries A.D. (especially if we consider the religious ones, e.g., the *collegium* of *Dianae et Antinoi*).[87] In view of that, it could be said that almost all *collegia* were considered of *publica utilitas* in the end, as in the case of *collegia tenuiorum* that had a role in guaranteeing funeral services for its members. As such, the increasing number of *collegia* during the 2nd and 3rd centuries A.D. was probably due to the very concept of *publica utilitas*: be it effective or not, the 'public utility' was understood in a very flexible way, becoming a sufficient reason for founding new *collegia*.

Moreover, besides this idea of *publica utilitas*, some *collegia* have also been defined by scholars as 'semi-public associations' because their members could be nominated by the local town council and assembly (e.g., those of *Augustales, neoi, iuvenes*, and *gherontes*).[88] Therefore, the concept of 'semi-public' has been tied to the fact that the selection of internal members reflected public decisions. However, scholars did not link the 'semi-public' character of these associations to an effective contribution of the *collegium* to the public sphere.

On the other hand, what we have tried to point out here is that, although during the 2nd and 3rd centuries A.D. authorizations for the creation of new *collegia* were given in a quite generous way, some *collegia* effectively had different levels of *publica utilitas*. This 'utility' can be observed in their contribution to specific public services that, at least officially, were guaranteed and supervised by the central state.[89] As shown earlier, the different level of *publica utilitas* is testified to by inscriptions and literary sources that mention numerous benefits granted to these associations, mostly the *navicularii* and *tria collegia*. Also, the widespread geographical distribution of these *collegia* reveals the relevance that these associations had for local and peripheral urban contexts, like the *municipia*. We have also stressed how, at least for some of these *collegia*, the 'semi-civic architecture' and topographical centrality of their *scholae* proclaimed this economic and social relevance.

Of course, as pointed out at the beginning of this chapter, the *collegia* cannot be considered part of the Imperial administration or 'public-*corpora*' in general terms – even if in some cases the internal members were selected by public assemblies or councils. Nevertheless, it is clear that we can speak of a 'semi-public' character of the *collegia*, even beyond the members' nomination in certain *collegia*. This can be said in view of the economic and logistic support that they provided for some public services, such as the *annona*, public building, and the supply of goods and services – be they material (e.g., wood, military clothing) or immaterial (e.g., athletic education, firemen). These associations collaborated with public structures and offices to manage such important services, acting as if they were 'quasi-administrative' *corpora*. As just pointed out, even from an architectural and topographical point of view, some *scholae* reveal affinities with the seats of administrative offices, i.e., *stationes* (e.g., *Schola Xanthi* in Rome).[90] At last, we should not forget that archives were even preserved within the *scholae* of *collegia* and not only in the *stationes* of 'administrative offices'.[91]

As pointed out so far, several points of connections ran between the *scholae* of *collegia* and the 'official' *stationes* of administrative 'offices' and we hope that this evidence will make this topic deserving of more attention by scholarship. Surely, before doing so, we should be ready to reconsider and expand our idea of 'Roman administration', including those intermediate *corpora* that, like the *collegia*, acted between the central power and the society.

Notes

1. I would like to express my deepest gratitude for the support and feedback of Simone Ciambelli, Gian Luca Gregori, Paolo Liverani, and Eric M. Moormann. Of course, any faults or errors that remain are all my own.
2. Here are just a few examples: Kelly 1957; Rougé 1966; Nicolet 1988; Robinson 1994; Moatti 2001; Bérenger 2014; Coarelli 2019.
3. E.g., Gros 2001; Coarelli 2019; for the presence of archives in a few *collegia*: Rüpke 1998.
4. Coarelli 2019: 7–20.
5. *CIL* VI 36951.
6. On the *statio aquarum*, see Brunn 1989, 1991; Burgers 1999; Rodgers 2004; Coarelli 2019: 161–193.
7. For issues and insights coming from Coarelli's book, see Liverani 2020 and Smith 2020.

8 Tran 2006: 1–20.
9 Bollmann 1998.
10 For the *collegia* in Imperial age, see the recent work of Ciambelli 2022.
11 Gros 1996: 377; Goffaux 2011, 2016: 149–165.
12 Bollmann 1998: 22–56.
13 Bruneau 1978.
14 See the Murecine *triclinia*: Bollmann 1998: 161–3 and Camodeca 2003.
15 De Ligt 2000; Jiy 2005; Verboven 2007. The *lex Iulia de collegiis* and the *senatus consultum de collegiis tenuiorum* were the two main laws that regulated the *ius coeundi* of *collegia* (De Robertis 1971, 1: 209, 341–5). Because of the political instability that *collegia* fostered, in 49–44 B.C., Julius Caesar promulgated the *lex Iulia de collegiis* for abolishing nearly all associations (*cuncta collegia praeter antiquitus constituta distraxit*: Suet., *Iul*. 42; De Robertis 1971, 1: 198–208).
16 For a general overview, see Cracco Ruggini 1972; Bollmann 1998: 22–7; Diosono 2007; Sangriso 2009: 91–113; Tran 2006.
17 *Dig*. 3.4.1.1 (Gai.)
18 For a different position that sees the *collegia* as a group of members tied by common rituals, traditions, and ceremonies, rather than a mere group of workers/professionists: Ciambelli 2022: 34–48.
19 'Collective activities such as burials, religious ceremonies, and banquets were certainly of pivotal importance for sociability, as well as for maintaining and displaying their connections with patrons and benefactors. Conceivably, however, these activities were much more than mere occasions for socializing or pleasure but would have provided important occasions for information diffusion and discussions with respect to work, apprenticeship, marriage, price, and so on. It is to be regretted that it is particularly in this area that our sources are relentlessly parsimonious'. (Liu 2009: 300); for the *vexata quaestio* among scholars of whether *collegia* did or did not have economic concerns and regulatory functions like the medieval guilds, see Liu 2009: 14–5.
20 Randazzo 1998.
21 Jonathan Scott Perry has investigated the reason why, since the 19th century, modern scholars have been interested in these types of associations as if they anticipated medieval guilds and fascist corporatism: Perry 2006 (cf. De Robertis 1995) and Ciambelli and Morard 2023 (cf. also Tran 2012, 2013).
22 From the time of Augustus, all *collegia* had to request public permission to be recognized as a licit institution: only the *collegia* of *navicularii* were excluded from this requirement (Broekaert 2013: 216–223); moreover, from the time of Hadrian, they were excluded from municipal and Imperial taxes (*Dig*. 60.6.6.5.5; *Dig*. 50.6.6.5.10). For the *ius coeundi* by *senatus consultum* or permission of the Emperor: De Robertis 1971, 1: 252–4 (in Italy, twelve professional *collegia* obtained the *ius coeundi* from the Senate).
23 *CIL* III 14165.
24 For a brief introduction to the *tria collegia* with an updated bibliography, see Liu 2009: 50–55 and Cordovana 2016; for the occurrence of the expressions in inscriptions: *tria collegia licita* (*CIL* V 7881), *tria collegia principalia* (*CIL* XI 5749), *tria collegia* (*CIL* V 7905, *AE* 1965, 194; *CIL* XI 5416; *AE* 1997, 405).
25 For the firemen in Roman society, see Wallat 2004.
26 Maué 1886: 8–18; Waltzing 1895–1900, 2: 194–205.
27 *CIL* IX 6362, 6378.
28 E.g., Cic., *In Verr*. 5.19,48; Aur. Vict., *Ep*. 14,5; Symm., *Relat*. 14.3.
29 Plin., *Ep*. 10.33, 1–3; Pliny also refers to a debate held by the senate *de instituendo collegio fabrorum*: Plin., *Paneg*. 54.4 (cf. *Dig*. 3.4.1.*pr*.).
30 E.g., the inscription from *Lugdunum* (*CIL* XIII 1978) states that a ceramist was part of the local *fabri* (i.e., *fabrii* included different type of artisans).
31 Liu 2009: 160.
32 Liu 2009.

33 Liu 2009: 123; *contra* Waltzing 1895–1900, 2: 195 and Diosono 2007: 65: Diosono understands the name *centonarii* in the sense of 'patch/patchwork' (i.e., the idea of a great variety [of goods]) and, hence, the scholar conjectures that the *centonarii* were a sort of retail traders.
34 *Cod. Theod.* 14.8.2; Liu 2009: 280–291.
35 The most ancient inscription that speaks about the *collegium* of *dendrophori* is dated to A.D. 79 (*CIL* X 7); for the link of the *collegium* with Emperor Claudius, see Lyd., *De Mens*. 4.59.
36 Waltzing 1895–1900, 1: 240–253; 2: 122–4, 148.
37 For an updated bibliography on those two different positions, see Brunetti et al. 2022: 55, n. 44.
38 For the geographical distribution of the *collegium*, see Van Haeperen 2012.
39 Diosono 2007: 67, 2008: 80–84.
40 Boscolo Chio 2006: 505; Diosono 2007: 67; for the *dendrophori* of *Berua* and *Feltria* and their activity in wood transportation by river, see Zamboni 1974–1975.
41 *Cod. Theod.* 14.8.1; furthermore, commenting *Pro Cornelio de maiestate* 75, Asconius Pedianus wrote: *propter quod postea collegia et s.c. et pluribus legibus sunt sublata praeter pauca et certa quae utilitas civitatis desiderasset, sicut fabrorum fictorumque* (Lewis 2006: 150).
42 For the membership fees, consider the significant example of the religious association of Athenian Iobachhoi in Egypt that, in the late 2nd century A.D., collected an amount of money that corresponded to a fifth of the annual gross earnings of artisans employed by the Empire: Monson 2006: 228–238.
43 Van Nijf 2002: 332–4.
44 Suet., *Aug*. 42.
45 *Dig*. 50.4.5 (cf. *Dig*. 50.6.6.5.3 (Callistr.).
46 *Dig*. 1.34 (Gai.); Trajan already fostered the foundation of the *collegium* of *pistores* and we may assume that this was due to their role in relation to the *annona*: Aur. Vict. 13.5; for the *pistores* in Ostia, see Bakker 1994: 165–8 and Zevi 2008.
47 For this and other benefits (e.g., the public financial support for the restoration of the productive seats of the collegium in *CIL* VI 1682 and 1696), see Diosono 2007: 84.
48 *Cod. Theod.* 13.1.10.
49 See *Cod. Theod*. 12.1.62 and 63 for limiting this phenomenon; for this reason, it became necessary to be a member of the *collegium* to profit from these benefits (and not simply cooperate with the *collegium* or be a relative of one member): *Dig*. 50.4.5; 50.6.6.5.6 and 8–9 and 12.
50 Cracco Ruggini 1971: 135–143.
51 For the trade meant as an activity of 'public utility' between the late republican age and imperial age (and relating to the case of *Hispania*): Stannard et al. 2019.
52 Bollmann 1998: 12–5.
53 E.g., Flambard 1987.
54 E.g., Liu 2009; Broekaert 2013; Laird 2015
55 E.g., Dondin-Payre and Tran 2012; Palazzo and Pavolini 2013; Rodríguez, Tran, and Soler 2016; Coarelli 2019.
56 Zsidi 1997.
57 Zsidi 1997 (cf. Nagy 1941).
58 E.g., in *Sentinum*, the *collegium* of *centonarii* – called *domus* – had a *triclinium* for collegial events (*CIL* XI 5749); in *Brigetio* (Pannonia) the *centonarii* had their convivial meetings in a *porticum* (*AE* 1944, 110): Liu 2009: 249–277.
59 Caldelli 1992.
60 *IG* XVI 1055.
61 'È per questa branca che viene creata la *Curia Athletarum*, laddove per Curia s'intende ovviamente la *schola*, il luogo di riunione, naturalmente in questo caso dell'associazione degli atleti': Caldelli 1992: 79.

62 Cf. the Augustan 'Palestra Grande' in Pompeii and the *schola* of *iuvenes* in Mactar (near Tunis). According to Zanker, in the 'Palestra Grande' the Greek architectural tradition of *gymnasia* meets the Roman tradition of the *castrum*. It was the Pompeian seat of the *collegium iuvenum*, and, therefore, young Romans went there for practicing sports and military training, emulating the model of Gaius and Lucius Caesar, *principes iuventutis* (Zanker 1998: 114–8). The building complex had only one latrine and one room for religious purposes on the south side. Thus, its structure excludes the possibility that it was a meeting space in the sense that we assume for *collegia*.
63 On this topic see Chapter 12 by J. Bartz in this volume.
64 Bollmann 1998: 57–128.
65 Within the group 'Bauten mit Portikushöfen', Bollmann includes the cases of 'Portikusanlagen' buildings and, for this last group, she means the so-called Building of Eumachia in Pompeii and Herculaneum's Basilica: Bollmann 1998: 72–8.
66 Regarding the archaeological findings and excavations, see Palazzo and Pavolini 2013, and Pavolini 2020; for the figure of Manius Poblicius Hilarus, see also Van Haeperen 2018: 35–8.
67 '*Ciò, tuttavia, avviene in un quadro nel quale – per superiori esigenze urbanistiche – i seguaci della Magna Mater devono accettare una notevole decurtazione dello spazio a loro disposizione*': Pavolini 2020, no. 54.
68 For the Temple of Minerva used as a meeting-place by the *collegium* of *scribae et histriones* and that of *tibicines*, see Bollmann 1998: 258–9; regarding the *sacellum* of *Augustales Mercuriales* or *Herculei* in Misenum: De Franciscis 1991 (cf. Bollmann 1998: 356–363); Camodeca 2000; Rosso 2016: 101–3.
69 Pavolini 2020, n. 40.
70 *CIL* VI 10231 (Città del Vaticano, Vatican Museums, Inv. 6856, wall 45, position 45).
71 Della Giovampaola 2008: 493–5.
72 Martin and Varène 1973.
73 Bollmann 1998: 54–6.
74 Plin., *NH* 34.162.
75 Gros 1996: 383.
76 Laird 2015: 100–138.
77 Zevi 2008: 480–2.
78 Galli 2014.
79 E.g., a statue of Herakliskos, a statue of a possible figure of Victory, a portrait of Minerva, a statue with *paludamentum*, a sleeping nymph, and a portrait of Claudius: Koppel 1988.
80 Zevi 2008; as Taco Terpstra has shown in a convincing way, rather than being a proper seat of the *collegia* of *navicularii*, the 'Piazzale delle Corporazioni' – that hosted 61 rooms (*stationes*) faced on the porched square – was mainly a sort of showroom spaces for African *navicularii* that chose to have here their 'stores': Terpstra 2013: 124–5 (cf. Ciambelli 2022: 62, n. 15); for the recurrent mistake of considering the '*Schola del Traiano*' as an effective *schola*: Morard 2018; Bocherens 2018; Ciambelli and Morard 2023.
81 Bollmann 1998: 39–46, 200; Laird 2015: 73–99.
82 Suet., *Iul.* 42 (cf. Suet., *Aug.* 32).
83 *Dig.* 11.7.43 (Pap.): *Nam propter publicam utilitatem, ne insepulta cadaveraiacerent, strictam rationem insuper habemus* (cf. Patterson 1992); regarding the dating and legal implications related to the *senatus consultum de collegiis tenuiorum*: De Ligt 2000 (*contra* De Robertis 1971, 1: 275–293).
84 *Dig.* 47.22.1.*pr.* (Marc.)
85 De Ligt 2001: 356 (De Ligt takes this definition of *collegia sodalicia* from that of De Robertis: '*i collegi a scopi esclusivamente privati*': De Robertis 1971, 2: 41); according to the *senatus consultum de collegiis tenuiorum*, even the *collegia tenuiorum* became *collegia illicita* if they had the habit of holding two or three non-religious meetings a month (De Ligt 2001: 349–350).

86 De Robertis 1971, 1: 232–4, 296; Van Nijf 1997: 9–11; De Ligt 2001; Liu 2009: 97–103.
87 *CIL* XIV 2112, col. 2, lines 10–11.
88 Van Nijf 1997: 74; De Ligt 2001: 357.
89 For a synthesis of the urban and social impact of *collegia* on societies, see Bollmann 1998: 204–212.
90 Coarelli 2019: 42–6.
91 Rüpke 1998.

References

Bakker J. T. 1994: *Living and Working with Gods. Studies of Evidence for Private Religion and its Material Environment in the City of Ostia*, Amsterdam.
Bérenger, A. 2014: *Le métier de gouverneur dans l'empire romain: de César à Dioclétien*, Paris.
Bocherens, C. 2018: 'iLa Schola du Trajan: un bâtiment de l'annone?', in C. De Ruyt, T. Morard, and F. Van Haeperen (eds), *Ostia Antica. Nouvelles études et recherches sur les quartiers occidentaux de la cité* (Actes du Colloque International, Rome-Ostia Antica, 22–24 septembre 2014), Bruxelles-Roma, 289–294.
Bollmann, B. 1998: *Römische Vereinshäuser: Untersuchungen zu den Scholae der römischen Berufs-, Kult- und Augustalen-Kollegien in Italien*, Mainz.
Boscolo Chio, F. 2006: 'I dendrophori nella *Venetia et Histria*', in M. G. Angeli Bertinelli and A. Donati (eds), *Misurare il tempo. Misurare lo spazio*, Faenza, 487–514.
Broekaert, W. 2013: 'Navicularii et Negotiantes', in *A Prosopographical Study of Roman Merchants and Shippers*, Rahden.
Bruneau, P. 1978: 'Les cultes de l'établissement des Poseidoniastes de Bérytos à Délos', in M. B. de Boer (ed.), *Hommages à Maarten J. Vermaseren. Recueil d'études offert à l'occasion de son soixantième anniversaire le 7 avril 1978*, Leiden, 160–190.
Brunetti, M., Ciambelli, S., and Gregori, G. L. 2022: 'Un'inedita statua della *VIRTVS CORP. COLL. DENDROPHORVM* da Careiae (Santa Maria di Galeria)', *Papers of the British School at Rome* 90, 35–61.
Brunn, C. 1989: 'Statio aquarum', in E. M. Steinby (ed.), *Lacus Iuturnae I*, Rome, 127–147.
Brunn, C. 1991: *The Water Supply of Ancient Rome: A Study of Roman Imperial Administration*, Helsinki.
Burgers, P. 1999: '*Statio aquarum*', in E. M. Steinby (ed.), *Lexicon Topographicum Urbis Romae*, 4, Rome, 346–349.
Caldelli, M. L. 1992: '*Curia athletarum, iera xystike synodos* e organizzazione delle terme a Roma', *Zeitschrift für Papyrologie und Epigraphik* 93, 75–87.
Camodeca, G. 2000: 'Domiziano e il collegio degli Augustali di Miseno', in G. Paci (ed.), *Epigraphai. Miscellanea epigrafica in onore di Lidio Gasperini*, Tivoli, vol. 1, 171–187.
Camodeca, G. 2003: 'Altre considerazioni sull'archivio del Sulpicii e sull'edificio pompeiano di Moregine', *Ostraka. Rivista di antichità* 12, 249–258.
Ciambelli, S. 2022: *I Collegia e le relazioni clientelari. Studio sui legami di patronato delle associazioni professionali nell'Occidente romano tra I e III sec. d.C.*, Bologna.
Ciambelli, S., and Morard, T. 2023: 'Dalla corporazione fascista alla corporazione romana: teoria e propaganda', in F. Oppedisano, P. Salvatori, and F. Santangelo (eds), *Costruire la nuova Italia: miti di Roma e fascismo*, Rome.
Coarelli, F. 2019: *Statio. I luoghi dell'amministrazione nell'antica Roma*, Rome.
Cordovana, O. D. 2016: 'Le organizzazioni dei lavoratori', in A. Marcone (ed.), *Storia del lavoro in Italia: l'età romana. Liberi, semiliberi e schiavi in una società premoderna*, Rome, 175–203.

Cracco Ruggini, L. 1971: 'Le associazioni professionali nel mondo romano bizantino', in R. Sabatino Lopez et al. (eds), *Artigianato e tecnica nella società dell'alto medioevo occidentale*, 1, 1971, 59–193.

Cracco Ruggini, L. 1972: 'Stato e associazioni professionali nell'età imperiale romana', in *Akten des VI Internationalen Kongresses für Griechische und Lateinische Epigraphik*, München, 271–311.

De Franciscis, A. 1991: *Il Sacello degli Augustali a Miseno*, Naples.

De Ligt, L. 2000: 'Governmental Attitudes Towards Markets and *Collegia*', in E. Lo Cascio (ed.), *Mercati permanenti e mercati periodici nel mondo romano*, Bari, 237–252.

De Ligt, L. 2001: 'D. 47 22 1 pr-1, and the Transformation of Semi-Public Collegia', *Latomus* 60, 345–358.

De Robertis, F. 1995: 'Dai *collegia cultorum* pagani alle medievali *congregationes fratrum* attraverso il superamento della discriminazione Giustinianea *in pro dei tenuiores*', *Studia et Documenta Historiae et Iuris* 61, 433–445.

De Robertis, F. M. 1971: *Storia delle corporazioni e del regime associativo nel mondo romano*, 2 vols., Bari.

Della Giovampaola, I. 2008: 'La vigna Cassini tra il II e il III miglio della via Appia: gli scavi settecenteschi', *Mélanges de l'École Française de Rome* 120–122, 475–505.

Diosono, F. 2007: *Collegia. Le associazioni professionali nel mondo romano*, Rome.

Diosono, F. 2008: *Il legno. Produzione e commercio*, Rome.

Dondin-Payre, M., and Tran, N. (eds) 2012: *Collegia. Le phénomène associatif dans l'Occident romain*, Bordeaux.

Flambard, J. M. 1987: 'Eléments pour une approche financière de la mort dans les classes populaires du Haut-Empire', in F. Hinard (ed.), *La mort, les morts et l'au-delà dans le monde romain (Actes du colloque de Caen 20–22 novembre 1985)*, Caen, 209–244.

Galli, M. 2014: 'Ritratto romano e memoria greca: il caso della c.d. scuola dei medici di Elea – Velia', in J. Griesbach (ed.), *Polis und Porträt. Standbilder als Medien der öffentlichen Repräsentation im hellenistischen Osten*, Wiesbaden, 155–187.

Goffaux, B. 2011: 'Schola: vocabulaire et architecture collégiale sous le Haut-Empire en Occident', *REA* 113-1, 47–67.

Goffaux, B. 2016: *La vie publique des cités dans l'Occident romain*, Rennes.

Gros, P. 1996: *L' architecture romaine du début du IIIe siècle av. J.-C. à la fin du Haut-Empire*, vol.1, Paris.ss

Gros, P. 2001: 'Les édifices de la bureaucratie impériale. Administration, archives et services publics dans le centre monumental de Rome', *Pallas* 55, 107–126.

Jiy, J. 2005: 'Local Government and Collegia: A New Appraisal of Evidence', in J. J. Aubert and Z. Varhélyi (eds), *A Tall Order. Writing the Social History of the Ancient World*, München-Leipzig, 285–315.

Kelly, J. M. 1957: *Princeps Iudex. Eine Untersuchung zur Entwicklung und zu den Grundlagen der kaiserlichen Gerichtsbarkeit*, Weimar.

Koppel, E. M. 1988: *La Schola del Collegium Fabrum de Tarraco y su Decoración Escultórica*, Bellaterra.

Laird, L. M. 2015: *Civic Monuments and the Augustales in Roman Italy*, New York.

Lewis, R. G. 2006: *Asconius. Commentaries on Speeches of Cicero. Translated with Commentary by R.G. Lewis*, Oxford.

Liu, J. 2009: *Collegia Centonariorum. The Guilds of Textile Dealers in the Roman West*, Leiden and Boston, MA.

Liverani, P. 2020: 'Recensione: *Statio. I luoghi dell'amministrazione nell'antica Roma*, Filippo Coarelli, 2019', *Histara*. http://histara.sorbonne.fr/cr.php?cr=3624&lang=es&quest=gia

Martin, R., and Varène, P. 1973: *Le Monument d'Ucetis à Alesia*, Paris.
Maué, H. C. 1886: *Die Vereine der fabri, centonarii und dendrophori im römischen Reich. mit einem Anhang, enthaltend die Inschriften 1, Die Natur ihres Handwerks und ihre sacralen Beziehungen*, Frankfurt am Main.
Moatti, C. 2001: 'La mémoire perdue. Recherches sur l'administration romaine: les documents du census', *Mélanges de l'École Française de Rome* 113(2), 559–563.
Monson, A. 2006: 'The Ethics and Economics of Ptolemaic Religious Associations', *Ancient Society* 36, 221–234.
Morard, T. 2018: 'Éléments de réflexions à propos de l'occupation de la parcelle de la Schola del Traiano (IV, V, 15–15) à Ostia Antica', in C. De Ruyt, T. Morard, and F. Van Haeperen (eds), *Ostia Antica. Nouvelles études et recherches sur les quartiers occidentaux de la cité* (Actes du Colloque International, Rome-Ostia Antica, 22–24 septembre 2014), Bruxelles-Rome, 167–190.
Nagy, L. 1941: 'La maison du collège des pompiers de la ville civile d'Aquincum (Schola collegii centonariorum)', in *Laureae Aquicenses. Memoriae Valentini Kuzsinsky dicate*, 1, Budapest, 182–231.
Nicolet, C. 1988: *L'inventaire du monde. Géographie et politique aux origines de l'Empire romain*, Paris.
Palazzo, P., and Pavolini, C. (eds) 2013: *Gli dèi propizi. La Basilica Hilariana nel contesto dello scavo dell'Ospedale Militare Celio (1987–2000)*, Rome.
Patterson, J. R. 1992: 'Patronage, *Collegia*, and Burial in Imperial Rome', in S. Bassett (ed.), *Death in Towns. Urban Responses to the Dying and the Death, 100–1600*, Leicester, 15–27.
Pavolini, C. 2020: 'Una prima schola dei dendrofori di Roma sul Celio?', *Mélanges de l'École Française de Rome* 132-1. https://doi.org/10.4000/mefra.9347.
Perry, J. S. 2006: *The Roman Collegia. The Modern Evolution of an Ancient Concept*, Leiden and Boston, MA.
Randazzo, S. 1998: 'I *collegia tenuiorum*, fra libertà di associazione e controllo senatorio', *Studia et Documenta Historiae et Iuris* 64, 229–244.
Robinson, O. F. 1994: *Ancient Rome. City Planning and Administration*, London and New York.
Rodgers, R. 2004: *Sextus Iulius Frontinus. De aquaeductu urbis Romae*, Cambridge.
Rodríguez, O., Tran, N., and Soler, B. (eds) 2016: *Los espacios de reunión de las asociaciones romanas, diálogos desde la arqueología y la historia, en homenaje a Bertrand Goffaux*, Sevilla.
Rosso, E. 2016: 'Le genius des collèges: un marqueur de leurs espaces de réunion et de représentation', in O. Rodríguez, N. Tran, and B. Soler (ed.), *Los espacios de reunión de las asociaciones romanas, diálogos desde la arqueología y la historia, en homenaje a Bertrand Goffaux*, Sevilla, 93–114.
Rougé, J. 1966: *Recherches sur l'organisation du commerce maritime en Méditerranée sous l'Empire romain*, Paris.
Rüpke, J. 1998: 'Les archives des petits collèges. Le cas des vicomagistri', in École Française de Rome (ed.), *La mémoire perdue: recherches sur l'administration romaine*, Rome, 27–44.
Sangriso, P. 2009: 'I collegi professionali e la loro valenza economica: il caso dei figuli', in *Studi Classici e Orientali* 55, 91–136.
Smith, C. J. 2020: 'Review: *Statio. I luoghi dell'amministrazione nell'antica Roma*, Filippo Coarelli, 2019', *Ocnus* 28, 215–217.
Stannard, C., Sinner, A. G., and Ferrante, M. 2019: 'Trade between Minturnae and 'Hispania' in the Late Republic', *The Numismatic Chronicle* 179, 123–171.

Terpstra, T. T. 2013: *Trading Communities in the Roman World: A Micro-Economic and Institutional Perspective*, Leiden-Boston, MA.
Tran, N. 2006: *Les membres des associations romaines. Le rang social des* collegiati *en Italie et en Gaule sous le Haut-Empire*, Rome.
Tran, N. 2012: 'Associations privées et espace public', in M. Dondin-Payre and N. Tran (eds), *Collegia: le phénomène associatif dans l'Occident romain*, Bordeaux, 63–80.
Tran, N. 2013: 'Les collèges dans les espaces civiques de l'Occident romain: diverses formes de dialogue entre sphère publique et sphère privée', in A. Dardenay and E. Rosso (eds), *Dialogues entre sphère publique et sphère privée dans l'espace de la cité romaine. Vecteurs, acteurs, significations*, Paris, 144–159.
Van Haeperen, F. 2012: 'Collèges de dendrophores et autorités locales et romaines', in M. Dondin-Payre and N. Tran (eds), *Collegia. Le phénomène associatif dans l'Occident romain*, Paris and Bordeaux, 47–62.
Van Haeperen, F. 2018: 'Su alcuni fedeli della Mater Magna', in C. Bonnet and E. Sanzi (eds), *Roma. La città degli dèi*, Rome, 29–38.
Van Nijf, O. 1997: *The Civic World of Professional Associations in the Roman East*, Amsterdam.
Van Nijf, O. 2002: '*Collegia* and Civic Guards. Two Chapters in the History of Sociability', in W. Jongman and M. Kleijwegt (eds), *After the Past. Essays in Ancient History in Honour of H.W. Pleket*, Leiden, 305–339.
Verboven, K. 2007: 'The Associative Order. Status and Ethos among Roman Businessmen in the Late Republic and Early Empire', *Athenaeum* 95, 861–893.
Wallat, K. 2004: *Sequitur clades. Die Vigiles im antiken Rom: eine zweisprachige Textsammlung*, Frankfurt am Main.
Waltzing, J. P. 1895–1900: *Étude historique sur les corporations professionnelles chez les romains depuis les origines jusqu'à la chute de l'Empire d'Occident*, Louvain.
Zamboni, A. 1974–1975: 'Berua', *Aquileia Nostra* 45–46, 83–98.
Zanker, P. 1998: *Pompei. Public and Private Life*, Cambridge, MA (or. ed. 1995).
Zevi, F. 2008: 'I collegi di Ostia e le loro sedi associative tra Antonini e Severi', in C. Berrendonner and M. Cébeillac-Gervasoni (eds), *Le quotidien municipal dans l'Occident romain*, Clermont-Ferrand, 477–505.
Zsidi, P. 1997: 'An Unusual Archaeological Excavation at the Schola Collegii Centonariorum', *International Symposium 'Organ of Classical Antiquity: The Aquincum Organ AD 228*, 45–57.

9 Civic Archives and Roman Rule

Spatial Aspects of Roman Hegemony in Asia Minor from Republic to Empire[1]

Bradley Jordan

I Introduction

The concepts of space and administration are crucial to understanding the functional and practical elements of imperial rule and its local experience. With the 'spatial turn', historians have productively focused on topographical questions and the organisation of urban spaces to reveal new insights into how ancient states and empires functioned.[2] A critical element of governance in literate societies is the collection, storage, and use of written documents pertaining to local, regional, and imperial administration. The existence (or non-existence) of specific spaces for administrative documents (i.e., archives), their organisation, and their development over time, can reveal significant aspects regarding the organisation and priorities of the community at large and any external hegemon. There has been an increasing focus on the administrative spaces of Rome itself under the Republic and, especially, the Principate, fuelled by the copious archaeological material.[3] However, to date, little attention has been paid to how pre-existing administrative spaces in provincial contexts were affected by the establishment of Roman hegemony. This chapter offers a preliminary investigation of this issue, focusing on how Roman power affected the administrative topography of the Greek-speaking communities in Asia Minor during the late Republic and early Principate. The arrival of Roman magistrates and the gradual coalescence of provincial administration had a major impact on power dynamics, introducing new levels of governance and new practices. The analysis here concentrates on a single aspect of this issue, asking how Roman hegemony affected civic archival spaces. After defining the term 'archive' for the purposes of the chapter, it will proceed to explore the distinct concepts of archival space in Hellenistic and Roman contexts. It will then analyse two specific themes: (i) what impact these differences had during the establishment of Roman hegemony in Asia Minor; and (ii) the significance of the deliberate display and monumentalisation of archival documents in civic spaces. Overall, this chapter will argue that across this period, despite the fundamental differences between Roman and local approaches to archival spaces and the occasional assertion of Roman power over provincial archives, local communities retained significant agency over their own civic spaces.

II Definitions

First, a problem of definition: what are archives in this context? Most clearly, the term 'archive' should be restricted to collections of documents deliberately gathered and stored together for some purpose in Antiquity.[4] For Moatti, the use of the term 'archive' to describe state run administrative spaces presumes both the existence of a central repository of documents, which it is then possible to consult (subject to state-imposed rules), and the concept of documents which belong to the state rather than individuals.[5] This narrow definition, while functional, excludes the relatively common situation where the state collects and preserves documents of importance to individuals.[6] Accordingly, following DePauw, this chapter takes archives as "physical collections of documents pertaining to the business of a given community, which act as a repository for future consultation".[7] The documents included within them could contain those produced by the institutions of a *polis* itself (e.g., decrees of the *demos*, *boule*, or other civic body), communications from royal, Roman, or other peer actors (e.g., letters or *senatus consulta*), as well as personal documents of citizens (e.g., wills, property deeds, contracts, etc.). Under this definition, archives were functional spaces which collected and kept documents which acted as 'vectors of power' within and between communities.[8] Crucially, archives could serve as repositories of 'civic memory', by preserving a record not only of the political acts of a community and its relations with neighbours, but also of the myriad socio-legal interactions between its inhabitants. Where archives were relatively open spaces, that is, allowing (certain) interested parties to consult deposited documents, this allowed motivated individuals to construct their own views of their community. More frequently, access to these repositories was restricted: however, significantly, archives allowed contemporary or later iterations of civic institutions to selectively display or monumentalise documents in other public spaces and to thereby fashion a curated history of civic interaction for its own citizens and visitors.[9] Although archaeologically attested specialised archives from the Hellenistic world are rare, the epigraphic evidence does allow some conclusions to be reached.[10] Similarly, while Boffo rightly stresses the important distinction between the use of archives and display of documents, the publicisation of administrative material is a crucial consequence of archival practice, with flow-on effects for the spatial organisation of communities.[11] Accordingly, this chapter will focus on both the implications of both sides of local practices.

III Hellenistic Archives

Although archival practices varied substantially across the Hellenistic world, some comments can be made regarding pre-Roman practice. Generally, until the Hellenistic period, archives were not necessarily an identifiable space: rather, they were the documents received by a named magistrate tasked with monitoring private contracts or legal cases, then deposited in the public building associated with that office. Though Aristotle implies that these magistrates would have received material pertaining to the business of citizens, including contracts, land registers, or documents pertaining to personal status, he also acknowledges that these responsibilities varied from state-to-state.[12] One early example, an inscribed decree from Ephesos dated to 299 B.C., provides evidence for the creation of two copies of judicial decisions in debt cases, with one copy to be stored by the *neopoiai* in the Artemision and the second by an *antigrapheus*, whose role was to facilitate public access to said decisions (κοινὴμ μὲν διαίρεσιν | ταύτην εἶναι, ll. 23–4).[13] This points to the existence of at least two distinct spaces in early third century Ephesos for archiving this single set of documents: one sacred and one, in a practical sense, civic and political, with distinctive aims and intentions.

Three late Hellenistic inscriptions provide evidence for the expansion of such approaches to securing documents in specific civic-regulated spaces. First, a fragmentary first century B.C. inscription from Kos refers explicitly to the retention of public decrees in a physical archive. This decree sought to regulate the "best administration of the business of the *polis*" (τὰ τε τᾶς πόλιος πράγματα [κατὰ βέλτιστ] ον διοικῆται . . .) and refers to an earlier decree which Harter-Uibopuu convincingly argues provided for a permanent repository of public documents, perhaps in the late second century B.C.[14] A second Koan inscription, dating to either the first century B.C. or A.D., seems, by contrast, to refer to the collection and storage of private legal documents under state auspices in a public building (τὸ ἀρχεῖον, l. 17).[15] The text refers to the involvement of multiple officials, including the *prostatai*, a *chereophylax* (lit. guardian of debts), and public slaves, and insists on the use of the civic seal (σφραγίς, ll.15, 19). This seems to be a voluntary process, but emphasises the extent to which, throughout the second and first centuries B.C., Koan civic bodies were designating spaces for archival purposes and establishing rules to ensure the authenticity of important documents, both public and private.

More comprehensively, a well-known decree from Paros, dating to the second quarter of the second century B.C., establishes new archival practices in response to tampering with private legal documents deposited with the *mnemones* at the temple of Apollo, Artemis, and Leto, known as the Pythion.[16] In response, moving forward, the decree required that all documents referred to these officials were to be copied, with the original deposited in the Pythion and the copy – after being received, checked, and confirmed as accurate by the civic *archontes* – handed to the *apodektes* in charge of civic affairs (ἀποδέκτης ὁ ἐπιμελόμενος τῶν κατὰ πόλιν), who sealed and placed them in the temple of Hestia.[17] The involvement of the *archontes* and the *apodektes*, an official usually given charge of civic financial records, implies that these copies were to be stored along with the records of the *polis* community in a public archive.

While the Pythion remained a working archive, the inclusion of copies of its private legal contents with civic documents in the temple of Hestia highlights the importance accorded by the Parians to ensuring their authenticity. As Lambrinudakis and Wörrle highlight, these new regulations offered "staatlicher Vertrauensschutz für Urkunden über private Rechtsgeschäfte" (Eng. "state protection of confidence in documents related to private legal matters").[18] That said, the decree also asserted centralised control more firmly over these ostensibly private texts. It restricts access to the copies in the temple of Hestia in all cases except: "[that] it will be possible for anyone wishing to check the documents in the temple of Hestia against copies held in the Pythion". Even so, the constraints placed on such checks were onerous. Should a citizen suspect flaws in the copying process, a request should be made of the *archontes* in the civic assembly. The *archontes* would then examine the two copies in the temple of Hestia on a fixed date.[19] The Hestia archive, then, was explicitly a closed space, under the close control of the *archontes* and the *apodektes*, without further oversight. The text established that in early second century Paros, there existed at least two parallel spaces, both sacred, which served as practical archives, albeit with different functions.

Taken together, these texts suggest that in Late Hellenistic Asia, although local practices varied, archives were increasingly consolidated into identifiable spaces, preserving political and private documents in a fashion which intended to establish their authenticity. There seems to have been a trend towards producing multiple copies to ensure an authoritative, state-guaranteed, version.[20] These defined civic archives, while distributed across multiple locations, were largely associated with temples or other public structures, designated ἀρχεῖα, which word later came to indicate 'archive' in a general sense. These developments may have been prompted by organic demands by citizens for certainty around contracts and other sensitive documents. However, the key point is that the act of deposition and existence of copies are what created the guarantee, through generating a practical means of checking a presented text against an authoritative, state-approved copy.

IV Roman Archives

Roman traditions surrounding the storage, reuse, and archiving of documents evolved along a different trajectory to those of Greek-speaking communities. Written documents in the form of *tabulae* (originally, boards with a layer of inscribed wax) were crucial to Roman social life. The term *tabula* (*publica*) was used to describe both publicly issued documents, including *leges*, *senatus consulta*, census documents, and magistrates' accounts or *acta*. However, *tabulae* (*privatae*) were also an important medium for private business, used for wills, contracts, and property deeds *inter alios*. Ancient authors often fail to explicitly qualify their use of the term.[21] Their use in the legal sphere is firmly attested for the second century B.C., and rhetorical handbooks from the late Republic establish their authority as evidence.[22] As Meyer has shown, *tabulae* were generally treated as factual documents, perhaps due to the comparative difficulties in tampering with them as compared to other media such as papyri. This greatly constrained the opposing advocate's freedom of action, and the failure of one side to produce *tabulae* in support of their claim could be exploited as suspicious.[23]

However, private *tabulae* were not necessarily deposited publicly to ensure their authenticity. Instead, seals and the presence of witnesses were key elements in establishing and maintaining accuracy.[24] Even public documents, pertaining to administration by magistrates, appear to have been held by the responsible individual, and continued to be so after their term of office. Cicero notes that *more maiorum*, public documents (*tabulae publicae*) were kept in private hands – that is, distributed across numerous private archives, which were, in practice, closed, except though social connection. As he notes in *pro Sulla*, referring to documents from his own consulship:

> Since I knew that the information had been reported in the public record, but that said record, in accordance with ancestral practice would be in private safe-keeping, I did not conceal it, did not retain it at home, but at once I commanded that it be copied by all the scribes, be distributed everywhere, be published and announced to the Roman People.[25]

Senatus consulta and *leges*, that is, operative documents, were held in the *aerarium* – and after 78 B.C., in an associated *tabularium* – under the purview of the annual quaestors, along with documents relating to state finances.[26] However, as Culham notes, the space was not designed as an accessible archive. Indeed, the inscription of these documents on bronze and their storage in this space seems to be ritualised rather than functional.[27] Livy states that the Atrium Libertatis served as the workspace for the censors, which may have housed some records on an ongoing basis; we also hear of censorial records in the Nymphaeum on the Campus Martius.[28] However, Cicero, while arguing for reform in *de Legibus*, laments how even these documents were, in practice, not above reproach: *legunt custodiam nullam habemus – itaque eae leges sunt, quas apparitores nostri volunt* ("we have no guardianship for the laws – therefore, these laws are whatever our clerks wish") ... *publicis litteris consignatam memoriam publicam nullam habemus* ("for public documents, we have no certified public copies").[29] Indeed, Cicero employs this attitude in opposing the tribune Rullus' proposed *lex agraria* in 63 B.C., arguing that *senatus consulta* referenced in the text could be forged by Rullus and the *decemviri* to be appointed under the law. Since many of the magistrates, during whose office such documents were passed, had died, Cicero argued that authenticity could not be guaranteed:

> However, perhaps it is due to shame that these things are omitted from the law. But it is more credible and more concerning that the audacity of *decemviri* is given great licence to falsify public documents and to fashion *senatus consulta*, which have never been passed, since most who were consuls in those years have [already] died.[30]

Such an attitude clearly suited Cicero's argument. However, his words were constrained by the expectations of his audience. This points again to the crucial role of, in this case aristocratic, witnesses in ensuring the validity of documents over and above that of state copies in the late Roman Republic.

This is not to say that *tabulae publicae* had limited value or were beyond practical use. Indeed, there was a movement towards reform and utility during the first century B.C., though this was still taking shape.[31] The crucial distinction for the purposes of this chapter is that where, in the Hellenistic world, deposition of documents in formal archives enhanced their value and validity, in republican Rome, it was the act of sealing and the reputation of the witnesses which were the key factors. Deposition in a public archive was unnecessary and a secondary factor in determining the authenticity and value of documents.

V Public Documents and Archives in *Pro Flacco*

Consequently, the arrival of Roman hegemony inevitably affected how *poleis* in Asia Minor used archival spaces. While little explicit evidence exists for how practices evolved within individual communities, there are hints of important conflicts between Roman and local attitudes. One significant source is Cicero's speech *pro Flacco*, delivered in 59, in defence of L. Valerius Flaccus, governor of Asia in 62, who had been accused of extortion.[32] The prosecution had assembled witnesses from numerous communities, who in turn appear to have brought a plethora of documents as supporting evidence. Cicero refers extensively to 'public documents' (*tabulae* or *litterae publicae*) and civic decrees (*decretae*) throughout the speech: mostly to cast doubt on their accuracy. Most significantly, he notes that one Asclepiades claimed that an earlier decree of Akmoneia praising Flaccus was deceptive (*falsa*), despite bearing the civic seal (*signum publicum*). Specifically, Cicero summarises Asclepiades' charge as that: *solere suos civis ceterosque Graecos ex tempore quod opus sit obsignare* ('his own fellow-citizens and the other Greeks were accustomed to seal what(ever) was necessary at the time').[33] Cicero notes that Asclepiades does not deny that an honorific decree was passed, rather that he claimed his fellow-citizens would pass expedient decrees. We might see this as a pragmatic response to gubernatorial power and misbehaviour; however, Cicero was delighted to concede this point, as it shed doubt on all of the prosecution's hard-won documentary evidence.[34] In any case, Cicero goes on to argue that documents provided by Asclepiades were forged, since they were sealed with wax (*cera*) rather than a material which he terms *creta Asiatica* (lit. Asian chalk; likely, clay), as with his own evidence. Drawing on the personal experience of his jurors, Cicero emphasises the ubiquity of this sealing material in public documents from Asia and, especially, private letters from expatriate Romans.[35] However, Cicero deliberately conflates norms across the breadth of Asia, refusing to account for potential differences in the use of material between major cities of the coastal region, such as Ephesos, a hub for Roman *publicani* and *negotiatores*, and small communities in the rural hinterland, like Akmoneia. Through broad familiarity with Asian practices for guaranteeing the integrity of documents and clever use of Asclepiades' ill-guarded statement, Cicero was able to exploit Roman attitudes towards documentary evidence to his advantage.

His critique of the witnesses from Dorylaion follows a similar rationale. The *tabulae publicae* of Dorylaion had been lost (or perhaps stolen) en route. Cicero claims this was staged by the witnesses themselves, worried about presenting forged documents at trial, after considering the likelihood of punishment on their return home.[36] This raises the interesting question of whether the sealed *tabulae* sent with the ambassadors were approved copies of documents retained in civic archives or the originals. The former would seem the most reasonable assumption, though it is worth noting that the wording of a first century A.D. letter of a Roman

Civic Archives and Roman Rule 203

governor implies that he received a sealed original (or original copy) of a *senatus consultum* issued in 81 from a Chian embassy.[37] Though Cicero's pointed suggestion seems highly questionable, the capacity to check documents used at trial in Rome against copies in Asia makes concerns over the falsification or subtle emendation of documents reasonable. Crucially, here, Cicero evinces confidently both the belief that laws against forgery were stricter at Dorylaion than in other cities and that these documents could (and perhaps would) be checked on the witnesses' return, again emphasising his familiarity with processes in Asia.

Most significantly, he reveals intimate knowledge of the chequered legal history of Lysanias of Temnos – and his companions, Heraclides and Nicomedes – including the fact that the former was present at the drafting of the decree from Temnos supporting their claim.[38] Finally, he notes that one C. Appuleius Decianus sought unsuccessfully to register property he had forcibly acquired with the archives at Pergamon. Moreover, he cites two honorific decrees; one passed for L. Castricius at Smyrna and another for Decianus at Pergamon, which he claims mocks the latter through its grandiose language.[39] While this may simply reflect the diligence of Cicero's agents in the province – aided by his brother, the current governor – it seems reasonable to posit that these agents had or secured access to the original documents. If so, then these civic archival spaces were either open, or opened through the influence of Roman actors. Cicero's attempts to discredit the prosecution witnesses show a Roman awareness of how civic archival spaces worked, how to use them to gain information, and how to critique them for a Roman audience. The time spent by Cicero arguing against the validity of these documents emphasises the extent to which these practices were familiar to a Roman elite audience.

VI Roman Official Documents and Greek Archival Spaces

Another perspective is offered by the surviving inscriptions of Roman official documents in Asia Minor. Civic communities had a long history of monumentalising their own civic decrees or communications from Hellenistic monarchs.[40] This trend continued with the advent of Roman hegemony. As Cooley has demonstrated, it is unlikely that the Romans routinely required the publication or more precisely monumentalisation of official documents – local interests often explain the inscriptions which do survive.[41] Indeed, we have examples of local attempts to acquire documents from Rome which pertained to privileges. During the Triumviral period, an ambassador from Aphrodisias requested from the public records (ἐκ τῶν δημοσίων δέλτων) copies of an *edictum*, *senatus consultum*, treaty, and *lex* pertaining to the city.[42] The *senatus consultum de Aphrodisiensibus* contains a preamble referring to the Rome-based files from which that document was copied including the tablet (Gr. δέλτος, Lat. *tabula*) and wax-leaf 'page' (Gr. κήρωμα, Lat. *cera*).[43] Given the find-context of both these inscriptions in the misleadingly named 'archive wall', which dates to the third century A.D., there is no evidence to suggest that these documents were monumentalised at the time of their receipt.[44] However, this evidence does underline the twin facts that the city did not have copies of these recently issued documents and that the civic authorities actively sought to acquire these as soon as practicable. The benefits of a written record of a community's status vis-à-vis Rome are clear, but this does indicate that the provision of such records by Rome should not be taken for granted.

One particularly revealing example emerges from the modern village of Arızlı, around 35km southeast of Synnada.[45] It is well known as the source for the so-called *senatus consultum Licinnianum*, which declared the decisions of Mithridates V of Pontus, who had been granted control of Phrygia from c. 126–116 B.C., valid, thereby giving them standing within Roman jurisdiction.[46] The text reflects the similar *senatus consultum Popillianum* of 132 B.C., which similarly transposed the decisions of Attalus III into a Roman legal context.[47] Extracts from both texts recur in another fragment from Arızlı, most likely a magistrate's letter.[48] This document seems to distil important elements from both Roman documents into a single format, raising questions over the purpose and impact of these inscriptions, which likely date to the first or second century A.D.[49] Though the absence of context for the finds makes it impossible to reconstruct the way in which these two documents interacted with one another, the shared orthography would imply that they consciously did so, that is, they were inscribed at the same time for a similar purpose. Though it is possible that the unknown *polis* was attempting to secure specific grants from either or both of Attalus III and Mithridates V, perhaps pertaining to its lands, or even its status as a community, the chances that a Roman magistrate or their representative would routinely visit a minor community in the vicinity of Synnada must be small. One possibility is that the display of a document dating from the earliest days of the *provincia* allowed the community to define itself. By publicly erecting monuments emphasising the early establishment of a relationship, even a generic and subordinate one, with Rome, the *polis* and its neighbours drew on and created a civic history which set them apart from other settlements within their new *provincia* of Galatia.[50] Critically, for the purposes of this chapter, these Roman documents in monumental form would seem to have dominated the public space of a small community. Beyond still unpublished fragments of letters from Eumenes II, reported by Drew-Bear, no other public documents are known to survive from Arızlı and its environs, which, while inconclusive, suggests that few such documents were inscribed.[51]

Beyond the community's choice to display a text, the location, size, and material of a monument had a bearing on its reception. Even where Roman documents did insist on their reproduction, for the most part they restricted their instructions to display in the ἐπιφανέστατοι τόποι ('the most prominent locations'). The careful ambiguity of this phrase, often employed in local honorific decrees of the second and first centuries, disguises the intense contestability and mutability of public space.[52] No single place fulfilled this criterion, as shown by the ubiquitous plural. Instead, it offered the locals a further opportunity to frame the audience and interpretation of the document. Unfortunately, problems such as reuse, lack of provenance, or lack of co-ordinated excavation prevent a complete study of the space and positioning of Roman documents within Asian communities. However, some examples suggest how location could be used to reinforce or shape the messaging of a Roman text.

A decree of Pergamum responding to the conclusion of a treaty with Rome in 129 B.C., provides an intriguing example. The text states: καθήκει καὶ | [πα]ρ' ἡμ[ῖν] ἀναγραφῆν[αι αὐτὰ ε]ἰς πίνακας | [χ]αλκοῦς δύο καὶ τε[θῆναι ἔ]ν τε τῶι ἱερῶι | [τ]ῆς Δήμητρος καὶ ἐ[ν τῶι β]ουλευτηρίωι | [παρ]ὰ τὸ ἄγαλμα τῆς [Δημοκ]ρατίας ("and it is right that these [documents] are inscribed by us on two bronze tablets and erected both in the temple of Demeter and in the *bouleuterion* next to the statue of *Demokratia*").[53] The matter of publication is framed positively as a local choice: the words of the community obscure any suggestion of Roman commands or requests.[54] The text's display in two named locations underscores the symbolic importance of place. Neither the interior of the temple of Demeter, nor the *bouleuterion* were likely to have been highly trafficked locations by most of the citizen body. The precise importance of the temple of Demeter is unclear, though Ma has suggested that it was one of the limited number of locations at which honorific statues were regularly placed.[55] The implications of the *bouleuterion*, the political centre of the newly independent community, are much easier to grasp. The strong link between δημοκρατία and ideas of 'freedom' in this period are similarly well attested. The Pergamenes, in their decision to inscribe and display the treaty with Rome in these locations, were utilising a Roman document to make a clear ideological statement of their own crafting.

Consequently, instances where the Roman administration explicitly required the public display of official documents by civic actors and sought to impose themselves upon local civic archival practices are significant. The *lex de provinciis praetoriis*, promulgated in early 100 B.C., most likely by a tribune working independently of the senatorial consensus, includes a clause ordering the dissemination and publication of letters related to its contents.[56] Specifically, the text orders the current praetor in Asia to write to "the cities and states (to whom) it is appropriate under this statute". Despite the wide geographic scope of the law – laying out tasks for magistrates in Macedonia and Cilicia – the discretion granted to the praetor must have been limited to his own area of command, i.e., *provincia Asia*. The text goes on to require that the letters which he sent: πρὸς οὕς ἂν κατὰ τοῦτον τὸν νόμον γράμ[ματα ἀπ]εσταλμένα ᾖ, εἰς δ(έλ)τον χαλ|κῆν γράμματα ἐνκεχαραγμέ[να, εἰ δὲ μὴ ἢ ἐν λίθῳ μαρμαρίνῳ ἢ κ]αὶ ἐν λευκώματι, ὅπως ἐν ταῖς πόλεσι ἐκκέ[ηται ἐν ἱερῷ] ἢ ἀγορᾶι φανερῶς, ὅθεν δυνή|σονται ἑστακότες ἀναγινώσ[κειν ὀρθῶς ("[according to the customs of those] to whom . . . they are sent engraved on a bronze tablet, [or . . . on a marble slab or even] on a whitened board, be openly [published] in the cities [in a sanctuary] or *agora*, in such a way that people shall be able to read (them) [properly] from ground level").[57] Crucially, the text of the letters was to be displayed, rather than the statute itself, and the promulgator does not explicitly require that the text be permanently recorded – the provision is made for it to be displayed on whitened boards for example – leaving that choice in the hands of local actors. Finally, the proposer required the praetor to encroach upon the capacity for local communities to regulate their own public space and access to public documents. As the statute goes on to explain: [καὶ οὗτος μὴ ἄλλ]ως ἢ οὕτως γραψάτω | ἵνα ταῦτα πα[ντα]χοῦ [γένηται] ("he is to write in this way [and in no other way] in order that this [may happen] everywhere").[58] While the impact of this law within Asia should not be overstated, and its unique political context noted, the text as preserved emphasises: (i) the limited nature of the Roman command (at least, per the instructions of the statute); (ii) the lack of differentiation between cities of different statuses; and (iii) the emphasis on universal dissemination of information and display of the associated letters. For our purposes, it is important to note that the law provides for the sending of documents by Roman official, and their local display, leaving the details of publication and preservation to local actors.

Another example, a letter from Octavian to the *koinon* and *conventus* centres of Asia in 30/29 B.C., found at Priene and Miletus, reinforces the extent to which Roman administration affected civic spaces. The text concerns the shamelessness of unnamed individuals and the author's intent to rectify this situation.[59] It has an unusually prescriptive publication clause: the soon-to-be Princeps requires that each *polis* despatch copies of his letter to the other communities in their διοικήσις or *conventus* district and display the letter: ἔν τε τῶι ἐπ[ι]φανεστάτωι τόπωι ἐν στυλοπαραστάδι ἐπὶ λίθου λευκοῦ ἐνχαραχθῆναι ("engraved in the most conspicuous places, on a stele of white stone").[60] Again, the motivation clause stresses the broad context considered by Octavian: ἵνα κοινῶς πάσηι τῆι ἐπαρχεία[ι τὸ] δίκαιον ἐσταμένον ἦι εἰς τὸν ἀεὶ χρόνον, αἵ τε ἄλλαι πᾶσαι πόλεις καὶ δῆμοι τὸ αὐτὸν παρ' αὑτοῖς ποιήσωσιν ("so that in common for all the province justice might be established for all time, and that all the other cities and peoples might do the same things among themselves").[61] Here, particularly with his prominent use of the adverbial κοινῶς, the author widens a sense of community to include the whole province, i.e., the group of communities subject to the commander in Asia, establishing a single Roman standard. This interfaces neatly with the use of the *koinon* as a conduit to facilitate communication between the imperial centre and local *poleis*. Such sentiments are unparalleled in earlier examples and suggest the author's conscious intent to frame the inhabitants of the whole *provincia* as a single unit, the antithesis of a series of autarchic *polis*-communities.

The evidence for Roman republican impact on the administrative space of Asian communities during this period concerns the display, rather than archiving of Roman official documents. Though we can surmise that official copies did find their way into archives, this was based on their utility to local communities rather than the requirements of Roman administrators. What these examples do show is an encroachment on local public spaces and their organisation by elements of the Roman state. Increasingly, Roman documents were included in civic archives, displayed prominently in public spaces, and occasionally monumentalised alongside the most important pronouncements of local authorities. As Roman governors became more familiar with – and more concerned with and more critical of – civic archival practices, local inhabitants were increasingly exposed to Roman normative documents in their public spaces. Monumentalised archival material, the public presentation of civic identity, and memory now included Roman texts, if organised and chosen by local actors. Individuals who consciously engaged with the documents, as texts or otherwise, were exposed to the interplay between Roman and local systems of authority: these texts carried significant force and, by

Civic Archives and Roman Rule 207

interacting with local frameworks of power, created a sense of legitimacy around Roman ideology and state action.[62]

VII Q. Veranius at Myra and After

One final example is a well-known ἐπικρίμα of Q. Veranius, first Roman *legatus* of Lycia in the 40s A.D., which sheds a crucial light on the Roman assertion of control over civic administrative spaces.[63] The Greek text was found in the coastal city of Myra but begins with a detailed account of Veranius' punishment of a public slave at Tlos, some 100km northwest, in mountainous central Lycia.[64]

Τ[ρύ]φῳ[να δημ]όσιον τῆς Τλωέων | πόλεω[ς οὔτε] διατάγμασιν ἐμοῖς οὔ|τε ἀπειλαῖς, ἀλλ᾽ οὐδὲ κολάσει τῶν | περὶ τὰ ὅμοια ἡμαρτηκότων δούλων | διδαχθέντα, ὅτι οὐ χρὴ παρενγραφὰς | κ[αὶ ἀ]παλοιφὰς ἔχοντα πιττάκια τῶν οἰ|κ[ον]ομουμένων προσδέχεσθαι.

Tryphon, public slave of the city of the Tlosians, has not been taught either by my edicts or threats or even the punishment inflicted upon slaves who have committed similar crimes, that he must not accept [into the civic archive] **documents of an official nature** with interpolations or erasures.[65]

Veranius chose to reinforce his point by having Tryphon publicly flogged – as well as warned that any repeat offence would result in his execution – and reiterating that official documents (οἰκονόμημα) with interpolations or erasures or written on palimpsests were not to be accepted by the public slaves into civic keeping. He then proceeds to list these documents, which include various types of contracts (*symbolia, cheirographia, syngraphia*), as well as sets of specific instructions, accounts rendered, legal challenges, and disclosures about a legal situation or decisions of arbitrators or judges.[66] These categories span the administration of civic decisions and those of private individuals. Such documents, already crucial to everyday life within a Greek city and collected accordingly, were here subject to the heavy-handed oversight of a Roman commander.[67]

Veranius' words also reveal a certain exasperation with the depositors (whether local citizens or residents). He issues his decision: "in order that those conducting business . . . should stop working against their own security" (οἱ χρηματίζοντες . . . παύσωνται τῆι ἑαυτῶν ἀντιπρασσόντες ἀσφαλείαι). Accordingly, Wörrle has argued that the aim of Veranius' intervention was to not to impose Roman ideas around order or Roman practices on a civic system, but rather to make the local practices functional again.[68] We certainly should see this as representing continuity in local practices and standards: the ἐπικρίμα makes clear that private documents could still be voluntarily registered in public archives. Though Meyer judiciously highlights that Veranius' decision reflects earlier concerns regarding counterfeit documents in both Greek and Roman contexts, his intervention simultaneously represents the imposition of Roman standards over local praxis.[69] Veranius own expectations concerning the validity of documents resulted in the imposition of new standards at a level above that of the city. The arrival of Roman hegemony in Lycia led directly to changes in archival practice, with greater control over the documents admitted and a new level of organisation of civic documents, backed by the threat of Roman-imposed punishment.

Veranius' edict and subsequent actions parallel the near contemporary introduction of a new, centralised archival system in Egypt, which seems to have been aimed at streamlining the Roman administration.[70] Crucially, however, unlike in Egypt, the Lycian decision asserted, in a robust fashion, Roman hegemony over a purely civic administrative space. Jördens, working from Egyptian evidence, plausibly argues that the role of the governor in guaranteeing order encouraged them to intervene beyond the degree that state interests required.[71]

As with most of the examples mentioned earlier, how that space was organised in Tlos remains unclear – however, it is likely that this was a building or series of buildings run at civic expense, staffed by public slaves and ultimately under the oversight of a minor magistrate, which protected and guaranteed the accuracy of documents contained within. Veranius' choice to impose new standards limited which documents could be stored in the public archives, with potentially significant social implications for the citizens and denizens of Tlos. Finally, the appearance of this decision at Myra emphasises the wide purview of Veranius' jurisdiction and the fact that his new standards, though issued in response to a specific incident were to be widely applied.

A logical progression from Veranius' actions can be seen in a second century A.D. inscription, likely a gubernational edict, from Sibidounda in Pisidia.

[κ]αὶ ἐν ἄλ[λοις] πολλοῖς | [ἔ]θνεσιν [διατ]εταγμένο[ν] | [ἐσ]τὶν πάντα τὰ συμβό|[λ]αια διὰ τῶν δημοσίων | [γ]ραμματοφυλακείων | [ἀ]ναγράφεσθαι. ὑμᾶς δὲ | [π]υνθάνομαι καὶ ἄλλων | [μ]ᾶλλον τοιούτου τρό|[π]ου δεῖσθαι συναλλα|[γ]μάτων διὰ τὸ ἐπιπολάζειν | πολλὰς παραποιήσεις ἐν τῷ | ἔθνει, καὶ διατετάχθαι δὲ ἤ[δη] | [π]ολλάκις ὑφ' ἡγεμόνων τὸ | πρᾶγμα, καὶ μηδὲν ὄφελος | [τ]ῆς ἐκείνων γνώμης γενέσ|[θ]αι διὰ τοὺς οὐ πειθομένου[ς]· | [ν]ῦν δὲ ἐγὼ κελεύω . . .

In many other provinces also it is prescribed that **all contracts** be registered in the public records-office. But in your case, I learn that you desire rather to have more transactions of this kind, owing to the prevalence of forgeries in the province, and that the matter has, on many previous occasions, been the subject of pronouncements by the governors, and that their decisions were of no aid due to non-compliance. So now I command . . .[72]

Bean, cautiously, notes that it cannot be assumed that the compulsory registration of contracts (συμβόλαια) was already mandated, but the key point is that provincials, whether at Sibidounda specifically or across Pisidia more broadly, felt that this decision did not go far enough and requested further measures.[73] This is a fundamentally different dynamic to the previous examples: civic actors are no longer acting on their own initiative, or in response to Roman demands, but actively requesting that Roman issued instructions go further. Indeed, this is a logical development from the assertion of Roman power over civic archival spaces and fits well with the broader, well-recognised phenomenon of provincials seeking to bolster their wishes with Roman authority.[74]

VIII Conclusions

This chapter set out to investigate the spatial implications of changes to archival practice in Asia Minor as the region became subject to Roman hegemony. In a strict sense, archives are repositories of documents consciously collected and stored for future use. They are, consequently, functional spaces. Prior to permanent Roman governance archival spaces in Asia Minor, tended to be run by civic magistrates and contain documents of community-wide relevance, such as civic decrees, alongside those of relating to private individuals, such as contracts and wills: that is, they played a vital role in maintaining civic order. Though caution is warranted, given the diversity of practices in late Hellenistic Asia Minor, some trends are apparent. First, important documents, pertaining to both political and private business, tended to be preserved in several copies to guard against forgery or tampering. This resulted in multiple archives containing copies of the same document, such as at Ephesus and Kos, which could then be used for separate purposes. Second, the available evidence points to the use of temples and, increasingly, public buildings as archives, emphasising the critical role of state authority in generating trust in documents. Finally, across the second and first centuries, civic authorities came to assume responsibility for maintaining private legal contracts, perhaps in response to organic demand. Crucially, the authenticity of archival documents was secured through the processes surrounding their deposit into archival spaces.

By contrast, in late republican Rome, archival spaces had a more limited purview. Though some public documents were similarly stored in temples, most material generated by magistrates was stored *more maiorum* under private authority. Furthermore, while written documents in the form of *tabulae* had substantial authority by virtue of their form, practices of authentication were grounded in the reputation of the (preferably aristocratic) witnesses present at the drafting or copying of a document and in the practice of sealing, rather than in its deposition with state authorities. Consequently, the extension of Roman power over Asia Minor led to critiques of civic practices, especially when the interests of powerful Romans ran counter to them, as in the case of Cicero's defence of Flaccus.

The evidence offered by Roman documents inscribed in Asia offers a different perspective. Often, the decision to monumentalise these documents seems to have rested on local agents, motivated by various concerns. Critically, however, beyond the significant expense this involved, such decisions normalised the appearance of Roman instructions, normative documents, and rulings in civic spaces. The display and, especially, permanent inscription of documents played a major role in shaping civic memory, especially when framed in alongside important civic documents in symbolically meaningful locations. At Arızlı, the monumental inscription of venerable *senatus consulta* and governor's letters points both to the effectiveness of local archival practices and the ways in which such permanent display could dominate public space within a small community. Likewise,

Pergamon was able to make a conscious and clear ideological statement through the placement of their Roman treaty in the temple of Demeter and next to the statue of *Demokratia*.

While Roman documents explicitly requiring publication in local contexts are limited, they are a clear example of imperial sensibilities imposing upon local agency and practice. Even here, however, the evidence is not clear-cut. The *lex de provinciis praetoriis* did not require the praetor to demand permanent inscription of his letters; though the letter of Octavian to the *koinon* of Asia explicitly does, seeming to aim at placing imperial instructions and benefaction permanently in the public eye across the whole *provincia Asia*. The well-known intervention of Veranius at Tlos presents another stage of this process – interfering directly in the practice of deposition of material in archival contexts in Lycia. The new governor imposes higher standards on documents to be accepted, the practical consequence of which – even if this instruction aligned with existing local regulations – to use Roman authority to restrict on the space as a repository and guarantor of civic interaction. This flows through into the Sibidounda edict which sees local demands for Roman regulation of local archival spaces.

In sum, the evidence from Asia Minor shows that archival spaces retained their importance to and within Greek-speaking communities across the period of study – both from a community-wide and individual perspective. However, as Roman hegemony took hold, the state and its representatives exercised a growing control over local communal archives.

Notes

1 This work was carried out primarily during a research stay at the British Institute at Ankara, whose support I am very appreciative of. I am also grateful to the SpaceLaw team, particularly Kaius Tuori and Antonio Lopez Garcia, for organising the initial conference, inviting my contribution, and for their helpful editorial comments. Likewise, I would like to thank the other participants, especially Lina Girdvainyte, as well as Kimberley Webb and Margrethe Havgar for their insightful criticisms. All remaining errors and infelicities are my own, as are all translations.
2 E.g., Ma 2013; Russell 2016; Gargola 2017.
3 Note especially the volumes arising out of Claude Nicolet's research group investigating the archival practices of the late Republic and early Principate (Demougin 1994; Moatti 1998). More recently, e.g., Tuori 2010 and Heikonen et al. (this volume).
4 Faraguna 2015.
5 Moatti 2011: 124–5.
6 Tlili 2000: 153, n. 8.
7 Depauw 2013: 259–265.
8 Boffo 2013: 201–9.
9 Boffo (2013: 230–3) emphasises the inclusion of revisions and transitions.
10 Coqueugniot 2013: 32–3; Faraguna 2015. For examples, see the catalogue of Coqueugniot 2013: 67–150.
11 Boffo 1995.
12 Arist. *Pol.* 1321b. Lambrinudakis and Wörrle 1983: 328–341. Cf., evidence for Classical Athens prior to the use of the Metröon as a centralised archive: Boegehold 1972: 28–30; Sickinger 1999: 62–83.

13 *IvEph*. 4.14–24. Walser 2008: 238–249. See also *IvEph*. 14, a late first century text recording the charges for registering life events at the ἀντιγραφῖον.
14 *IG* 12.4.1.84.7–8: δεδόχθαι κυρωθέ[ντος τοῦδε το]ῦ ψημίσματος [περὶ τῶν χρημα]|τιζομένων **ἐπὶ τῶν ἀρχείω[ν** - - νενο]μοθετημένα . . . "sobald das Dekret über die öffentliche Beurkundung von Rechtsakten bei den Behörden in Kraft gesetzt wurde" (Harter-Uibopuu); "it is decreed that, when the decree concerning public registration in the archives (lit. public office) is ratified . . . what is laid down by law" (my translation). Harter-Uibopuu 2013: 275–7.
15 *IG* 12.4.1.85. Harter-Uibopuu 2013: 277–280. Though Harter-Uibopuu translates τὸ ἀρχεῖον as 'Archiv' (Eng. 'archive'), as the earliest firm evidence for this usage dates to 144 B.C. (*SIG*³ 684.6–7, 21–2) I have chosen the conversative translation.
16 Lambrinudakis and Wörrle 1983 = *SEG* 33.679.
17 Lambrinudakis and Wörrle 1983: ll. 32–65.
18 Lambrinudakis and Wörrle 1983: 363; Coqueugniot 2013: 31.
19 Lambrinudakis and Wörrle 1983: ll. 65–83.
20 Though note *SIG*³ 684.6–7, 14 (with Kallet-Marx 1995a: 134–7), noting that chaos at Dyme in Achaia upon the destruction of τὰ αρχεῖα καὶ τὰ δημοσία γράμματα ("the archives and the public documents"), implying the absence of a second archive.
21 Meyer 2004: 36–43; Tuori 2018: 205.
22 Macrob. *Sat*. 3.16.14–6, (quoting C. Titius in *c*. 160); *Rhet. Her*. 1.16; Cic. *Top*. 24.; *de Orat*. 2.173; *Inv*. 2.134. Note especially Cicero's definitive statement in *de Oratore* 2.173: *hoc sequi necesse est; recito enim tabulas* ('this must follow: for I recite *tabulae*'). Meyer 2004: 218–227, with references.
23 E.g., Cic. *Font*. 11–2; *Flacc*. 35; *Scaur*. 18–9.
24 Meyer 2004: 158–163.
25 Cic. *Sull*. 42: *Cum scirem ita esse indicium relatum* **in tabulas publicas***, ut illae tabulae* **priuata** *tamen* **custodia** *more maiorum continerentur, non occultaui, non continui domi, sed statim describi ab omnibus librariis, dividi passim et peruolgari atque edi populo Romano imperaui*. See Culham 1989: 104–5. Cf. Dion. Hal. *Ant. Rom*. 1.74.4, 4.22.2; Varr. *LL*. 6.86–7; Festus, 356M; Plut. *Tib. Gracch*. 6.2. Rawson 1985: 238–9.
26 Millar 1964: 33 (though note Purcell 1993: 135–141 on *tabularium*); Tuori 2018: 213.
27 Williamson 1987: 164–170, 175–8; Culham 1989: 110–113; Purcell 1993: 141, *pace* Williamson 1995: 241.
28 Liv. 43.16.13; Cic. *Mil*. 73. Nicolet 1980: 63–4. On the oft-cited 'plebeian archive' in the Temple of Ceres, Liber, and Libera, see: Pellam 2014: 82–4.
29 Cic. *Leg*. 3.46.
30 Cic. *de leg. agr*. 2.36–37: *Verum haec fortasse propter pudorem in lege reticentur. Sed illud magis est credendum et pertimescendum, quod audaciae decemvirali corrumpendarum tabularum publicarum fingendorumque senatus consultorum, quae facta numquam sint, cum ex eo numero, qui per eos annos consules fuerunt, multi mortui sint, magna potestas permittitur*. Cf. Plut. *Cat. min*. 17; Schol. Bob. Sest. p. 140 Stangl. Millar 1964: 34; Williamson 1995: 248.
31 Culham 1989: 113–4. See, e.g., the requirements of the *lex Iulia de pecuniis repetundis* of 59 that gubernatorial accounts be deposited at two cities within a governor's *provincia* and at the *aerarium* (Cic. *Fam*. 5.20.2; *Att*. 6.7.2; *Pis*. 61). Morrell 2017: 133.
32 On this speech: Classen 1985: 180–217; Vasaly 1993: 198–205; Steel 2001: 53–73.
33 Cic. *Flac*. 36.
34 On pragmatism dictating honours: e.g., Ferrary 1997: 199–207; A.B. Kuhn 2017a.
35 Cic. *Flac*. 37–8. On this passage: Macdonald 1979.
36 Cic. *Flac*. 39.
37 Bitner 2014, ll. 11–2: εὗρον τοῖς μὲν χρόνοις ἀρχαιοτάτου δόγμα[τος]‖ συνκλήτου ἀντισφράγισμα γεγονότος Λουκίῳ Σύλλᾳ τὸ δε[ύτε]‖ρον ὑπάτωι . . . "I found the oldest record [to be] a sealed document of a *senatus consultum* passed in the second consulship

of L. Sulla . . .". The form ἀντισφράγισμα does not imply copy (*pace* Bitner 2014: 644–5, compare Johnson et al. 1961: 129; Sherk 1984: 138–9) and the reference to the sealing is superfluous unless intended to draw attention to the document's authenticity and originality.
38 Cic. *Flac*. 43, 54. See also, *Flac*. 34 on Asclepiades.
39 Cic. *Flac*. 71–6. Eberle 2016: 54–6; C.T. Kuhn 2017b: 6–13.
40 E.g., Ma 2000.
41 Cooley 2012.
42 *IAph2007* 8.25.27–39.
43 *IAph2007* 8.27.1–4. Compare the *senatus consultum* included in the consular letter to Oropos (*RDGE* 23.57–9); and the *lex portorii Asiae*, Cottier et al. 2008: ll. 1–6.
44 Though they may have been displayed in some other form, e.g., on painted boards. Misleading name: Jones 1985: 263; Chaniotis 2003: 251–252. On the 'archive wall' generally, see Kokkinia 2015–6.
45 Drew-Bear (1972: 79, n.2) rejects the identification of the site with the territory of Lysias (stated without argument by Ramsey 1895: 761–2; followed by Robert 1962: 135) but does not offer an alternative. See: Reger et al. 2014.
46 *RDGE* 13 = Drew-Bear 1978, no. 2.
47 *RDGE* 11 with Wörrle 2000: 567.
48 *SEG* 28.1208 = Drew-Bear 1978, no. 1.
49 Drew-Bear 1978: 3–5.
50 See Jordan 2023: 199–203.
51 See Drew-Bear 1976: 247 n. 2; Drew-Bear 1978: 8.
52 Ma 2012: 246–8, 2013: 67–9; Chaniotis 2014: 135–6.
53 *IGR* 4.1692.27–31.
54 Cooley 2012: 163.
55 Ma 2013: 102–3.
56 Contra Crawford, who sees this as referring to the statute itself (1996: 19, 263). On the *lex de provinciis praetoriis*: Ferrary 1977; Crawford 1996: 234–7, 258–270.
57 *RS* 12.Delphi.B.21–5.
58 *RS* 12.Delphi.B.26.
59 *I.Priene*² 13.41–2. On the date: Bowersock 1970: 226–7 *contra* Sherk 1969: 275–6.
60 *I.Priene*² 13.47–9.
61 *I.Priene*² 13.50–3.
62 Ando 2000: 78–9, 101–6.
63 On the circumstances of Lycia's provincialisation, see the *stadiasmus Patarensis* (*SEG* 51.1832) with commentary from Jones 2001; Thornton 2001.
64 *SEG* 33.1177 = Wörrle 1975.
65 *SEG* 33.1177.5–11.
66 *SEG* 33.1177.30–4: ἐάν τε συμβόλαιον, ἐάν τε χειρόγρ[α]φον, ἐάν τ[ε] | [σ]υνγρ[α]φή{ν}, ἐάν τε δῆλ[ω]σις, ἐάν τε σημείωσ[ις], | [ἐ]άν τε ἀπόλογος, ἐάν τε πρόκλησις, ἐάν τε πε|ρὶ δίκης ἐμφανισμός, ἐάν τε φερνιμαία, ἐάν τε δι|αιτητῶν ἢ δ[ικασ]τῶν ἀπόφασις ὑπάρχῃ.
67 Meyer 2004: 185–6.
68 Wörrle 1975: 284; Jördens 2010: 175.
69 Greek: Lambrinudakis and Wörrle 1983: 285, ll. 8, 15–6; Roman: Plut. *Cat. Min.* 16–7; Dio 54.36.1; 57.16.10.
70 Meyer 2004: 185–6.
71 Jördens 2010: 176.
72 *SEG* 19.854.3–19.
73 Bean 1960: 72.
74 E.g., Millar 1977; Kallet-Marx 1995a, esp. 125–181; Ando 2000.

References

Ando, C. 2000: *Imperial Ideology and Provincial Loyalty in the Roman Empire*, Berkeley, CA.
Bean, G. E. 1960: 'Notes and Inscriptions from Pisidia. Part II', *Anatolian Studies* 10, 43–82.
Bitner, B. J. 2014: 'Augustan Procedure and Legal Documents in *RDGE* 70', *Greek, Roman, and Byzantine Studies* 54, 639–664.
Boegehold, A. L. 1972: 'The Establishment of a Central Archive at Athens', *Americal Journal of Archaeology* 76, 23–30.
Boffo, L. 1995: 'Ancora una volta sugli 'archivi' nel mondo greco: conservazione e 'publicazione' epigrafica', *Athenaeum* 83, 97–130.
Boffo, L. 2013: 'La "presenza" dei re negli archivi delle poleis ellenistiche', *Faraguna* 201–244.
Bowersock, G. 1970: 'Review of Sherk, Roman Documents from the Greek East', *American Journal of Philology* 91(2), 223–228.
Chaniotis, A. 2003: 'The Perception of Imperial Power at Aphrodisias: The Epigraphic Evidence', in L. de Blois, O. Hekster, G. de Kleijn, and S. Mols (eds), *The Representation and Perception of Imperial Power. Proceedings of the Third Workshop of the International Network Impact of Empire (Roman Empire, 200 B.C. – A.D. 476), Rome, March 20–23, 2002*, Amsterdam, 250–260.
Chaniotis, A. 2014: 'Mnemopoetik: die epigraphische Konstruktion von Erinnerung in den griechischen Poleis', in O. Dahly, T. Hölscher, S. Muth, and R. Schneider (eds), *Medien der Geschichte. Antike Griechenland und Rom*, Berlin, 132–169.
Classen, C. J. 1985: *Recht, Rhetorik, Politik. Untersuchungen zu Ciceros rhetorischer Strategie*, Darmstadt.
Cooley, A. 2012: 'From Document to Monument: Inscribing Roman Official Documents in the Greek East', in J. K. Davies and J. J. Wilkes (eds), *Epigraphy and the Historical Sciences*, Oxford, 159–182.
Coqueugniot, G. 2013: *Archives et bibliothèques dans la monde grec: édifices et organisation, Ve siècle avant notre ère – IIe siècle de notre ère*, Oxford.
Cottier, M., Crawford, M. H., Crowther, C. V., Ferrary, J.-L., Levick, B. M., Salomies, O., and Wörrle, M. (eds) 2008: *The Customs Law of Asia*, Oxford.
Crawford, M. H. (ed.) 1996: *Roman Statutes*, London.
Culham, P. 1989: 'Archives and Alternatives in Republican Rome', *Classical Philology* 84(2), 100–115.
Demougin, S. (ed.) 1994: *La mémoire perdue: À la recherche des archives oubliées, publiques et privées, de la Rome antique*, Paris.
Depauw, M. 2013: 'Reflections on Reconstructing Private and Official Archives', in M. Faraguna (ed.), *Archives and Archival Documents in Ancient Societies*, Trieste, 259–267.
Drew-Bear, T. 1972: 'Three *Senatus Consulta* Concerning the Province of Asia', *Historia* 21(1), 75–87.
Drew-Bear, T. 1976: 'Local Cults in Graeco-Roman Phrygia', *Greek, Roman, and Byzantine Studies* 17(3), 247–268.
Drew-Bear, T. 1978: *Nouvelles inscriptions de Phrygie*, Amsterdam.
Eberle, L. P. 2016: 'Law, Empire, and the Making of Roman Estates in the Provinces During the Late Republic', *Critical Analysis of Law* 3(1), 50–69.
Faraguna, M. 2015: 'Archives, Documents, and Legal Practices in the Greek Polis', in E.-M. Harris and M. Canevaro (eds), *The Oxford Handbook of Ancient Greek Law*, Oxford.

Ferrary, J.-L. 1977: 'Recherches sur la législation de Saturninus et de Glaucia', *Les Mélanges de l'École française de Rome. Antiquité* 89(2), 619–660.

Ferrary, J.-L. 1997: 'De l'évergétisme hellénistique à l'évergétisme romain', in M. Christol and O. Masson (eds), *Actes du Xe congrès international d'épigraphie grecque et latine. Nîmes, 4–9 Octobre 1992*, Paris, 199–225.

Gargola, D. J. 2017: *The Shape of the Roman Order: The Republic and Its Spaces*, Chapel Hill, NC.

Harter-Uibopuu K. 2013: 'Epigraphische Quellen zum Archivwesen in den griechischen Poleis des ausgehenden Hellenismus und der Kaiserzeit', *Faraguna* 273–306.

Johnson, A. C., Coleman-Norton, P. R., and Bourne, F. C. 1961: *Ancient Roman Statutes*, Austin.

Jones, C. P. 1985: 'Review of Reynolds, J. 1982, *Aphrodisias and Rome*', *American Journal of Philology* 106, 262–264.

Jones, C. P. 2001: 'The Claudian Monument at Patara', *Zeitschrift für Papyrologie und Epigraphik* 137, 161–168.

Jordan, B., 2023: *Imperial Power, Provincial Government, and the Emergence of Roman Asia, 133 BCE – 14 CE*, Oxford.

Jördens, A. 2010: 'Öffentliche Archive und römische Rechtspolitik', in K. Lembke, M. Minas-Nerpel, and S. Pfeiffer (eds), *Tradition and Transformation: Egypt under Roman Rule. Proceedings of the International Conference, Hildesheim, Römer- and Pelizaeus-Museum, 3–6 July 2008*, Leiden, 159–179.

Kallet-Marx, R. 1995a: *Hegemony to Empire: The Development of the Roman Imperium in the East from 148 to 62 B.C.*, Berkeley, CA.

Kallet-Marx, R. 1995b: 'Quintus Fabius Maximus and the Dyme Affair (*Syll.* 684)', *Classical Quarterly* 45(1), 129–153.

Kokkinia, C. 2015–2016: 'The Design of the "Archive Wall" at Aphrodisias', *Tekmeria* 13, 9–55.

Kuhn, A. B. 2017a: 'Honouring Senators and Equestrians in the Graeco-Roman East', in A. Heller and O. van Nijf (eds), *The Politics of Honour in the Greek Cities of the Roman Empire*, Leiden, 317–338.

Kuhn, C. T. 2017b: 'The Castricii in Cicero: Some Observations on *pro Flac.* 75', *Museum Helveticum* 74(1), 6–18.

Lambrinudakis, W., and Wörrle, M. 1983: 'Ein hellenistisches Reformgesetz über das öffentliche Urkundenwesen von Paros', *Chiron* 13, 283–368.

Ma, J. 2000: *Antiochos III and the Cities of Western Asia Minor*, Oxford.

Ma, J. 2012: 'Honorific Statues and Hellenistic History', in C. Smith and L. M. Yarrow (eds), *Imperialism, Cultural Politics, & Polybius*, Oxford, 230–251.

Ma, J. 2013: *Statues and Cities: Honorific Portraits and Civic Identity in the Hellenistic World*, Oxford.

Macdonald, C. 1979: 'Cicero, *Pro Flacco*, 37', *Classical Quarterly* 29(1), 217–218.

Meyer E. 2004: *Legitimacy and Law in the Roman World: Tabulae in Roman Belief and Practice*, Oxford.

Millar, F. G. B. 1977: *The Emperor in the Roman World, 31 BC – 337 AD*, London.

Millar, F. G. B. 1964: 'The *Aerarium* and Its Officials Under the Empire', *Journal of Roman Studies* 54, 33–40.

Moatti, C. (ed.) 1998: *La mémoire perdue: recherches sur l'administration romaine*, Rome.

Moatti, C. 2011: 'La mémoire perdue: À la recherche des archives oubliées de l'administration romaine', *Cahiers du centre Gustav Glotz* 22, 123–130.

Morrell, K. 2017: *Pompey, Cato, and the Governance of the Roman Empire*, Oxford.

Nicolet, C. 1980: *The World of the Citizen in Republican Rome*, London.
Pellam, G. 2014: 'Ceres, the Plebs, and *Libertas* in the Roman Republic', *Historia* 63(1), 74–95.
Purcell, N. 1993: 'Atrium Libertatis', *Papers of the British School at Rome* 61, 125–155.
Ramsey, W. M. 1895: *The Cities and Bishoprics of Phrygia*, vol. 1, Oxford.
Rawson, E. 1985: *Intellectual Life in the Late Roman Republic*, London.
Reger, G., McKesson Camp II, J., Talbert, R., Gillies, S., and Elliot, T. 2014: 'Lysias: A Pleiades Place Resource', *Pleiades: A Gazetteer of Past Places*.
Robert, L., 1962: *Villes d'Asie Mineure: études de géographie ancienne* (2nd ed.), Paris.
Russell, A. 2016: *The Politics of Public Space in Republican Rome*, Cambridge.
Sherk R. 1984: *Rome and the Greek East to the Death of Augustus*, Cambridge.
Sherk, R. K. 1969: *Roman Documents from the Greek East*, Baltimore, MD.
Sickinger, J. 1999: *Public Records and Archives in Classical Athens*, Chapel Hill.
Steel, C. E. W. 2001: *Cicero, Rhetoric, and Empire*, Oxford.
Thornton, J. 2001: 'Gli aristoi, l'akriton plethos e la provincializzazione della Licia nel monumento di Patara', *Mediterraneo Antico* 4, 427–446.
Tlili, N. 2000: 'Les bibliothèques en Afrique romaine', *Dialogues d'histoire ancienne* 26(1), 151–174.
Tuori, K. 2010: 'A Place for Jurists in the Spaces of Justice?', in F. De Angelis (ed.), *Spaces of Justice in the Roman World*, Leiden, 43–65.
Tuori, K. 2018: 'Pliny and the Uses of the *Aerarium Saturni* as an Administrative Space', *Arctos* 52, 199–230.
Vasaly, A. 1993: *Representations: Images of the World in Ciceronian Oratory*, Berkeley, CA.
Walser, A. V. 2008: *Bauern und Zinsnehmer. Politik, Recht und Wirtschaft im frühhellenistischen Ephesos*, Munich.
Williamson, C. 1987: 'Monuments of Bronze: Roman Legal Documents on Bronze Tablets', *Classical Antiquity* 6, 160–183.
Williamson, C. 1995: 'The Display of Law and Archival Practice in Rome', in H. Solin, O. Salomies, and U.-M. Liertz (eds), *Acta colloquii epigraphici Latini Helsingae 3–6 sept. 1991 habiti*, Helsinki, 239–251.
Wörrle, M. 1975: 'Zwei neue griechische Inschriften aus Myra zur Verwaltung Lykien in der Kaiserzeit', in J. Borchhardt (ed.), *Myra. Ein lykische Metropole*, Berlin, 254–300.
Wörrle, M. 2000: 'Pergamon um 133 Chr.', *Chiron. Mitteilungen der Kommission für Alte Geschichte und Epigraphik des Deutschen Archäologischen Instituts* 30, 543–576.

10 Between Private and Public

Women's Presence in Procuratorial *Praetoria*

Anthony Álvarez Melero[1]

I Introduction

As is widely known, during Roman imperial times women were barred from holding public *officia*. However, they could freely move within the private sphere. Nevertheless, when their male relatives, as members of the equestrian order, had to travel due to a procuratorial appointment in cities far away from their birthplaces or hometowns, were women allowed to follow them? If so, where did they stay? This chapter focuses on the women related to Roman procurators, examining on the one hand legal texts specifying the moments at which they could accompany their fathers or husbands. Then, on the other hand, I also scrutinise the literary texts and epigraphic sources alluding to the female kin of procurators to better depict their public and private activities in their temporary homes.

A few hours prior to his execution, Jesus was brought before Pontius Pilate,[2] who was to decide his fate. The meeting apparently took place at Herod's Palace, where the prefect of Judea resided when he was in Jerusalem,[3] since he otherwise lived in the provincial capital of *Caesarea Maritima*.[4] In this instance, he had travelled to Jerusalem on the occasion of the Jewish Passover. Among those who attended the trial, or at least were informed of its sequence of events, was the governor's wife. According to the Gospel of Matthew, while Pilate was sitting on the judgement seat (ἐπὶ τοῦ βήματος), she warned him not to condemn Jesus, as such an outcome had disturbed her sleep.[5]

The rest of the story is well known. However, some information is regrettably still lacking. Indeed, if this excerpt confirms the presence of Pilate, it also informs us that his wife, whose name remains unknown to us,[6] had followed him in Jerusalem as well. The couple may also have been accompanied by their retinue, of which no trace has been preserved.

This example is not unlike that of Seneca's aunt, who was married to a prefect of Egypt.[7] According to the Spanish philosopher, she remained by his side for 16 years, without ever having interfered in matters relating to the administration of the province, nor having accepted a petition from anyone to intercede with her husband.[8] In other words, she led a secluded life while in Alexandria.[9]

Therefore, on the basis of these two almost contemporary testimonies, which refer to events that took place during the reign of Tiberius, it is clear that the wives of high officials accompanied them when they travelled far from Rome and that they resided in an edifice set up for this purpose. But were these isolated cases? Did they engage in public activities? What did the law say about this?

II Legal Sources

If we look first at the legal references, it quickly becomes apparent that the available data almost exclusively concern the senatorial order, as is confirmed by the large number of works devoted to it in recent decades.[10] Indeed, the famous excerpt reproduced in the year 21 by Tacitus,[11] which relates the fierce debate on the appropriateness of allowing spouses and families of senators to accompany them when they held office outside Italy, makes no reference to procurators or equestrian officers. We know, however, that Augustus did not allow the wives of *legati* to join them at any time other than the winter truce,[12] while Ulpian was critical of their presence, as the male relatives would be held responsible for any misdeeds by the women,[13] thus confirming another text from Tacitus dated to the year 24.[14] It is therefore quite possible that the authorisation allowing a magistrate to take his wife, and *a fortiori* his children, with him, an authorisation vehemently opposed by A. Caecina Severus, must be attributed to Tiberius.[15] It should be noted that the princesses of the imperial family were not subject to this prohibition: think, for example, of Livia.[16]

Can the same be said of Roman knights?[17] In fact, the edict of Sex. Sotidius Strabo Libuscidianus,[18] dated between 14 and 19 or from 20 onwards,[19] concerning the transport of officials or (sub-)officers passing through *Sagalassos*, then situated in *Galatia*,[20] seems to indicate that the sons of procurators could be found at their side, as is apparent from lines 13–15 (in Latin) and 35–38 (in Greek).[21] A careful reading of the text reveals that no mention is made of the procurator's wife, whose presence is perhaps overlooked. This text thus appears to provide proof, at the beginning of Tiberius' reign, that procurators could travel with their sons, who then enjoyed the same privilege as their father in their jurisdiction, unlike the other categories of persons mentioned in the edict (senators, Roman knights, centurions). Indeed, the procurator resided in the province, sometimes for many years, and consequently also took his family with him. However, his son was only allowed to use the transport service within the boundaries of his constituency, if, as an adult, he was part of the senior official's staff, as frequently happened with the descendants of senators.[22] Furthermore, it can be assumed that the other members of his family had to provide themselves with a means of transport, unless they were not allowed to leave the capital, the seat of the administration.

However, it is quite likely that at least one daughter of a Roman knight followed her spouse during the reign of Augustus: namely (Ovidia),[23] Ovid's[24] daughter, but the case remains problematic for several reasons. Indeed, the poet tells us that at the time of his forced departure for *Tomis*, his daughter was in Africa.[25] The idea that she was travelling alone must be dismissed out of hand in defence of the far greater likelihood that she remained with her husband in an official capacity. Yet, the problem is far from resolved, since according to Ovid we know that he was twice a grandfather thanks to the children she gave birth to from two different beds.[26] We know of one of Ovid's sons-in-law in the person of the senator Cornelius Fidus,[27] but we cannot determine whether he was the first or second husband of the poet's daughter. In any case, neither her senatorial union nor her second marriage should surprise us. On the other hand, the fact that her spouse belonged to the *ordo senatorius* is an additional argument in favour of our hypothesis accounting for her presence in Africa. Unfortunately, a careful examination of Seneca's text does not make it clear whether or not Fidus was Ovid's son-in-law at the time that the latter was sentenced to exile. In any case, the chronology of Ovid's journey to the shores of the Black Sea tells us that his departure took place in the autumn, since he crossed the Adriatic in December.[28] It may well be that (Ovidia)'s removal fell within the conditions set by Augustus, if one accepts that the measure concerned all officials of senatorial or equestrian rank and not just *legati*.[29] However, (Ovidia), as the wife of a senator, may have been subject, by virtue of her marriage,[30] to legislation specific to members of the first order, since we do not know whether relatives of knights were subject to such restrictions during Augustus' lifetime.

Thus, the testimonies in our possession seem to confirm that these women began to travel with their relatives on missions as early as the time of Tiberius. Subsequently, despite the recommendations of the legislator, they began to travel quite often, if not systematically, according to their free choice.[31] Contrary to what one might think, though, the relocation did not always proceed peacefully and may even have led to their death. Indeed, they may have paid with their lives for the misdeeds imputed to or the decisions taken by their husbands, as Suetonius reminds us of when writing of the exactions committed by Galba shortly after his accession to power.[32] Moreover, at the same time the wife[33] of Lucceius Albinus, procurator of the two *Mauretaniae*,[34] was murdered at his side by henchmen of Vitellius as soon as they set foot in *Mauretania Caesariensis*.[35]

III Places of Residence

Hence, since the relatives of Roman knights, and of procurators or prefects in particular, travelled with them, this begs the question of just where they stayed. What term(s) were used to describe their place of residence? In fact, the statements relating to Pontius Pilate in the Christian sources (in the Gospels as well as the writings of late antique authors) refer to the edifice that served as the seat of his power as, e.g. a πραιτώριον/*praetorium*.[36] It should therefore come as no surprise that literary sources refer to it time and again. However, limitations of space prevent me from dealing with the question of terminology in detail. For this reason, I refer the reader to the most recent works, not without underlining the polysemous character of the term, whose meaning has varied over time, as it has been used to designate facilities with a diverse array of purposes, but whose common feature is the official nature of the public building, which was intended to provide temporary accommodation for representatives of the state, their staff and their relatives.[37]

However, questions still remain unanswered at present, as in most cases we do not know the location of the *praetorium* in which they lived. Even when we do possess this information, it is difficult to identify their living quarters, as we shall see next.

Ephesus

To appreciate the difficulties, let us first go to *Ephesus* to examine the only case to date of a non-Ephesian procurator's wife attested epigraphically in the city. Her name was Desidiena Cincia[38] and she was married to Appius Alexander, by then ducenarian procurator – as he was later promoted to the senatorial order.[39] They were honoured separately during the reign of the emperors Philip the Arab and his son (244–249)[40] on two bluish marble bases, respectively by Iulia Atticilla, high priestess of the imperial cult and priestess of Artemis,[41] and by the asiarch M. Aurelius Daphnus.[42]

The presence of the couple in the province of Asia is hardly in doubt. On the other hand, it is more difficult to establish whether they had stayed in the edifice, where other prominent personalities must obviously have also resided.[43] Indeed, it is an imposing-looking building with a history spanning several centuries (mid-second century BC through seventh century AD) and located above the theatre on the western slope of Mount Peion (Panayır Dağ). Its location, overlooking the harbour and the Hellenistic and Roman quarters, was by no means left to chance, since the Ephesians would easily have recognised it as a place of power.[44] After a partial exploration in 1929–1930, it was excavated in 2009–2014, but due to the lack of epigraphic evidence and in view of similar constructions attested from the Hellenistic period, archaeologists proposed that it had potentially served as a *praetorium*. Unfortunately, it is not possible to say whether the proconsul, the procurator, or any other representative of Roman power and their family, whose duties required them to reside in *Ephesus*, lived there.[45] In other words, is it the place where Desidiena Cincia may have remained, as she does not seem to have accompanied her husband while he travelled to *Smyrna*, where he received a homage from a prominent dignitary?[46] It is hardly possible to know.

Sarmizegetusa

In fact, this example from *Ephesus* reminds us that we know of only a few *praetoria* that were occupied by procurators and their families. This is the case with the one in *Sarmizegetusa*, seat of the financial procurator of *Dacia Apulensis*,[47] where approximately 30 inscriptions have been discovered, mostly votive and in the sacred area of the building.[48] I. Piso, editor of these stones,[49] provides the plan and a description of the building, but excavations of it, carried out between 1979 and 1989, have unfortunately not been resumed.[50] The edifice, to the best of our knowledge (since only a third of it is known in detail), is located in the north-eastern part of the city, inside the walls and in the immediate vicinity of the northern gate. Moreover, it was delimited by the *cardo maximus* to the west, by a *decumanus* to the south and by *horrea*, built at the time of Trajan, to the north and east. The sacred area mentioned earlier was bordered by the northern *horreum*, while to the south there was a *serapeum*. Finally, the *praetorium* had two thermal complexes: the smaller one, east of the sacred area, was meant for officials of a lesser category, whereas the larger one, west of the eastern *horreum*, belonged to the procurator.

Although not much is known about the living quarters of the procurator and his family, since they are located in the unexplored areas, we can be certain of their passage to *Dacia* based on several inscriptions found in the sacred area of the complex. We thus learn of Aelia Romana,[51] wife of Q. Axius Q. f. Pal. Aelianus[52] and mother of Q. Axius Aelianus,[53] between 235 and 238[54]; Aelia Saturnina[55] alongside her husband Herennius Gemellinus[56] and their three sons during the joint reign of Septimius Severus and his sons[57]; Apronilla[58] and Caesidius Respectus[59] during the reign of Caracalla[60]; Hostilia Faustina[61] and M. Lucceius Felix[62] during the reign of Severus Alexander[63]; and Maxima[64] and Aelius Apollinaris[65] between 212 and 235.[66]

Asturica Augusta

This phenomenon of erecting votive dedications at the initiative of couples or even families is attested at the same time in *Asturica Augusta*, where, for example, the procurator *ducenarius* was in charge of administering the mines and maintaining the *legio VII Gemina*, perhaps as early as the time of Augustus, but certainly from the reign of Nerva and until that of Diocletian.[67] The Hispanic testimonies are in fact the result of exceptional circumstances, such as the discovery, at the end of the 1960s, of a set of inscriptions in the eastern section of the wall. The stones must have come from the sacred area of the *praetorium*, which we knew existed, but which has still not been identified.[68] This is the case with (Otacilia),[69] daughter of C. Otacilius Octavius Saturninus[70] during the later years of the Severan dynasty,[71] and of the anonymous wife[72] of Pul(lius?) Maximus not long after 211.[73] To this group can be added two inscriptions known for a long time and referring to Iustina,[74] wife of Calpurnius Quadratus,[75] and Marrinia M. f. Procula,[76] married to Sex. Truttedius Clemens,[77] both of whom died while their husbands were in office in *Asturica Augusta*, during the first half and mid-second century, respectively.[78]

Misenum

Although the location of the *praetorium* in *Asturica Augusta* is still unknown, we can be more certain in the case of (Plinia),[79] as she appears in the writings of her son, Pliny the Younger,[80] who mentions her presence together with Pliny the Elder, *praefectus classis*,[81] in *Misenum* in two of his letters.[82] The location of the building from which Pliny the Younger and his mother witnessed the volcanic eruption has not yet been excavated, but the edifice must have been somewhere on Cape Miseno, in an entirely residential space, separated from the military quarters, not excluding the fact that it was a private maritime villa owned by the prefect. In fact, Pliny's description rather evokes such a place, without making it possible to determine whether it was a private residence or simply served the function of being reserved for the commander.[83]

IV The Sardinian Example

Another example that illustrates the challenges and, at the same time, the potential of the subject takes us to *Forum Traiani* in *Sardinia*, about 30 km inland, in the central-western part of the island. Indeed, this *uicus*, founded most likely in the time of Augustus with the name *Aquae Hypsitanae* (Ὕδατα Ὑψιστανά) and originally pertaining to the *pertica* of *colonia Iulia Augusta Uselis*, was a spa town, a crossroads of the routes leading to *Turris Libisonis* and *Karales*, the provincial capital,[84] as well as a place of settlement for the *cohors I Corsorum*.[85] It was also a meeting point with the Roman authorities for the populations from the *ciuitates Barbariae* – the site marked the limits of their territory, a point to which I will return later.[86] In 111, in close vicinity to the *Aquae Hypsitanae* complex, the proconsul L. Cossonius L. f. Stell. Gallus Vecilius Crispinus Mansuanius Marcellinus Numisius Sabinus,[87] proceeded, at a time when *Sardinia* returned temporarily to the control of the Senate,[88] to establish *Forum Traiani*, which was then assigned the category of *ciuitas* during the Severan dynasty, and then that of the *municipium* during the third century.[89]

The thermal complex constitutes the nucleus of the site and is of pre-Roman origins, with the city having later been built around the bath facilities.[90] It has preserved numerous traces of a cult devoted to male and female divinities linked to water, including dedications that not only reveal the names of the governors of the island but also sometimes those of close relatives who accompanied them.[91] Among such persons, we should mention a dedication from the first half of the third century by Flavia T. f. Tertulla[92] and her children, (Flavius) Honoratianus[93] and (Flavia) Marcellina,[94] who made a vow to the Nymphs, although it is not known whether their husband and father, the *procurator et praefectus* L. Flavius Honoratus, came with them or even if such an eventuality would have been probable.[95] Another woman is also attested in the thermal complex, as the author of a dedication to the Nymphs: it is Valeria Modesta, freedwoman of the *procurator Augusti praefectus prouinciae Sardiniae* M. Valerius Optatus, until then unknown, who was in charge of the province under the Severans.[96]

However, the presence in *Forum Traiani* of other procurators, from the Julio-Claudian period until the third century, perhaps invites us to consider that the city, or even the entity that preceded it, may have had an administrative function, possibly as a conventual seat, for the populations of the island's interior.[97] This fact would explain the presence of these women at the site, following their relative or patron, who moved around *Sardinia* during their term of office. A. Ibba has attempted to reconstruct more precisely whether this led them to stay for some time in *Forum Traiani* during the exercise of their judicial functions.[98] It goes without saying that we do not know the exact location of their place of residence at a particular site.

Furthermore, the discovery of a white marble plaque at Muru de Bangius during the excavation of a building that can be called a *praetorium*, as the text of the inscription indicates, and which included a *balneum*, among other facilities, is enlightening in many ways.[99] The complex, excavated between the late 1980s and the first decade of the twenty-first century, was built on the edge of a secondary road that served as a *compendium itineris*. This road, running through the western slopes of Monte Arci, linked *Forum Traiani* directly to the pathway that connected *Karales* and *Turris Libisonis* through the Campidano plain and the western coast of the island, without having to make a diversion via *Othoca*.[100] The building was erected in the second century and later restored during the reign of Caracalla alone (212–217), as confirmed by the title *Dominus noster M. Aurelius Antoninus*. It was made possible thanks to the good care of the *ciuitas* of *Forum Traiani* before being inaugurated in the presence of a procurator, of whom only the name *Aurelius* has been preserved – D. Faoro identified him together with M. Aurelius Sebastenus.[101] In any case, the structure was abandoned during the second half of the sixth century.[102] It was intended for *commeantes* (travellers), who should be equated with the travelling authorities and their relatives as well as the holders of *diplomata* or *euectiones* rather than with simple commuters along the road.[103] Therefore, due to the location of this *praetorium*, it is probably appropriate to see it as a stopover point for the procurator and his family on their way to *Forum Traiani* or *Karales*, including, therefore, Flavia T. f. Tertulla and her children as well as the freedwoman Valeria Modesta, which the chronology does not contradict.

V Homages in Public

As we have just seen, sometimes it is possible to find records of the presence of relatives of procurators in cities that were clearly not the chief town of the province being governed by their father or husband.

A good example comes from *Singilia Barba*. In this small Flavian *municipium* in *Baetica*, Acilia Plecusa,[104] widow and freedwoman of the *praefectus fabrum* M'. Acilius Quir. Fronto,[105] had a statue base erected in the *forum* for her *amica* Carvilia P. f. Censonilla,[106] who was the wife of P. Magnius Q. f. Quir. Rufus Magonianus, who for his part held three different procuratorships in *Baetica*.[107] Acilia Plecusa also dedicated two other statue bases, one of which came from the theatre of *Singilia Barba*,[108] while the provenance of the other is not known,[109] although their original location in a public space where all could see them is not in question. In any case, both stones were moved to Antequera in the sixteenth and seventeenth centuries, where they are still preserved, and they refer to Magonianus, whom Plecusa called *amicus* as well. Since the procurator's office was most likely located in *Hispalis*,[110] this not only tells us about the couple's possible move to *Baetica*, as an African origin cannot be excluded in their case, but also about the moment at which they met Plecusa. Did the latter know them in *Hispalis*, where Magonianus was supposed to reside, or in *Corduba*, the assumed provincial capital,[111] where he may have gone for reasons related to his office? Or did the couple visit *Singilia Barba* while on an official inspection tour, during which time Plecusa hosted them? These are questions that we would like to have answered.

VI Women of the Lower Social Strata

However, sometimes it is possible to mention women of more humble social origins, who most certainly frequented the homes of procurators and governors of equestrian rank. I mention here two examples. The first is Philtate, buried in *Lucus Augusti*, where she served as the hairdresser or chambermaid (*ornatrix*) for a *clarissima femina* originally from *Augusta Taurinorum*, whose name was actually voluntarily hammered out, making it possible to only read part of it: Cattunilla.[112] One might think that I am straying from my point, but this is not the case, as the dating of this limestone altar between the reign of Caracalla and the year 238, at latest, as well as the context in which the stone was erected, suggest that the *clarissima femina* may have been the wife of a high-ranking equestrian official serving as governor of the province of *Hispania Superior*, though the province only existed for a very short time.[113] Indeed, *Lucus Augusti* had previously been the seat of the *conuentus*, and the *legatus Augusti pro praetore*, the *iuridicus* or the *procurator* had passed through it.[114] The city must then have had the infrastructure to accommodate the provincial authorities.[115] We do not know the exact location of such an edifice, but it is more than likely that Philtate, who may have accompanied Cattunilla from Italy, must have worked and been housed there.

The second example concerns the procurator of *Mauretania Caesariensis*, Sex. Baius Pudens.[116] As evidence confirms, there is proof that during his stay in *Caesarea*, where the *praetorium* has not yet been identified,[117] he was accompanied by freedmen, while the presence of his wife, Septi[mia? – –] M. f.,[118] and daughter, Baia P[udentilla?],[119] attested in *Cures Sabini*,[120] is not certain in the absence of conclusive documentation. Indeed, a marble plaque discovered in the provincial capital reads that his freedman Verecundus buried his wife, Ygia (*sic*), described as *liberta Bai Pudentis, procuratoris Augusti*, which leaves little doubt about her close relationship with the high official.[121] The freed couple may have accompanied the procurator from Italy, and even from *Cures Sabini*, where he was originally from and where he was buried. However, we do not know (and the same is true for the procurator's wife and daughter) whether Verecundus and Ygia had followed him on his previous appointments, such as to *Noricum* or *Rhaetia*.

VII Conclusion

This study has demonstrated that the presence of procurators' relatives in the *praetoria* is not in doubt, as they travelled with them from at least the time of Tiberius. If some of them were voluntarily discreet, as was Seneca's aunt, whose name still remains unknown to us, this was not the case for all of them. Some of them were the subject of public tributes, such as Carvilia P. f. Censonilla in *Singilia Barba*, while others erected dedications themselves, as did Flavia T. f. Tertulla and her children in *Forum Traiani*. The law obviously did not prevent them from doing so.

Moreover, the movements of officials did not only involve women of the elite, but also members of their *familia* of servile or freed extraction, as was the case with the *ornatrix* Philtate or Ygia, who passed away respectively in *Lucus Augusti* and

Caesarea, where they travelled with their masters or *patroni*. Another good example is that of Valeria Modesta in *Forum Traiani*, which was not even the provincial capital, meaning that she followed her *patronus* during his tour of the island in the exercise of his judicial function.

Finally, and rather unfortunately, the archaeological sources, which are quite useful for our knowledge of local urbanism, do not always allow us to identify the location of the *praetoria*, and when they do, it is never possible to know the layout of the spaces inside.

Hence, while the literary, epigraphic and archaeological sources certainly shed some light on a sometimes unknown reality, unanswered questions will always remain. Indeed, it is hardly possible to overcome the obstacles posed by both the poor state of existing documentation and the systematic absence of excavations, thereby making it difficult to learn more about women's presence in procuratorial *praetoria* given the generally marginalised position of women and the fact that they could not always express themselves as desired.

Notes

1 This publication is part of the R&D&I project PID2022-138873NB-I00, funded by MCIN/AEI/10.13039/501100011033/ and 'ERDF. A way of making Europe'. Unless otherwise stated, all dates are AD.
2 *PIR*² P 815 (L. Vidman); *CJC* 284.
3 Cf. Philo, *Leg.* 299 and 306: ἐν τοῖς κατὰ τὴν ἱερόπολιν Ἡρῴδου βασιλείοις and ἐν οἰκίᾳ τῶν ἐπιτρόπων. See Haensch 1997: 234–6. The palace may have been located on the future site of the camp of the *legio X Fretensis*: 235, n. 24. See also 548–9.
4 See Haensch 1997: 227–234. On the *praetorium* of *Caesarea Maritima*, see Patrich 2011: 205–223; Schäfer 2014: 288–307.
5 NT, *Mt.* 27.19: Καθημένου δὲ αὐτοῦ ἐπὶ τοῦ βήματος ἀπέστειλεν πρὸς αὐτὸν ἡ γυνὴ αὐτοῦ (sc. τοῦ Πειλάτου) λέγουσα· "Μηδὲν σοὶ καὶ τῷ δικαίῳ ἐκείνῳ, πολλὰ γὰρ ἔπαθον σήμερον κατ' ὄναρ δι' αὐτόν".
6 Kany 1995.
7 See *PIR*² H 79 (L. Petersen); K. Abel, in *RE Suppl.* XII, 1970, col. 429–433; Navarro Caballero 2017: 523–5, nr. 232; *PFCR* 351.
8 Sen., *Dial.* 12.19: *ad Heluiam matrem*.
9 For more on the identification of the provincial administration buildings in Alexandria, see Haensch 1997: 209–212. The discretion of Seneca's aunt appears in clear contrast to the case of Funisulana Vettula, wife of the prefect of Egypt C. Tettius C. f. Ouf. Africanus Cassianus Priscus (*PIR*² T 136 (M. Horster)), who visited Thebes for a third time in the hope of hearing the famed 'singing' noise emanating from the northern Colossus of Memnon on 12 February 82, although it is not certain that her husband accompanied her: *CIL* III, 35 (= *ILS* 8759c) = *I.Colosse Memnon* 8: *Funisulana Vettulla/C(ai) Tetti Africani, praef(ecti) Aeg(ypti),/uxor, audi Memnonem pr(idie) Id(us) Febr(uarias), hora I s(emissem),/anno I Imp(eratoris) Domitiani Aug(usti),/cum iam tertio uenissem.* See *PIR*² F 571 (A. Stein); *FOS* 395; Navarro Caballero 2017: 694, nr. 497; *PFCR* 327.
10 For more on this issue in broad terms, see Albana 2017, where a bibliography on the subject can be found.
11 Tac., *Ann.* 3.33–4.
12 Suet., *Aug.* 24.2.
13 *Dig.* 1.16.4.2. (Ulp.).
14 Tac., *Ann.* 4.20.4.

15 Marshall 1975: 119.
16 See Barrett 2002: 34–5.
17 On this subject, see more specifically Álvarez Melero 2018: 187–8 and Fertl 2019 (who also deals with *clarissimae*).
18 See *PIR*² S 790 (M. Heil).
19 For more on this last dating, which could be extended to the rest of the reign of Tiberius, see Coşkun 2009.
20 See Mitchell 1976: 113, 1986: 27.
21 Mitchell 1976 (= *AE* 1976, 653 = *SEG* XXVI, 1392) = *I.Mus. Burdur* 335.
22 Kolb 2000: 74–5.
23 *PFCR* 512.
24 *PIR*² O 180 (K. Wachtel); *CJC* 218.
25 Ov., *Tr.* 1.3.19–20.
26 Ov., *Tr.* 4.10.75–6.
27 Sen., *Dial.* 2.17.1. See *PIR*² C 1360 (E. Groag).
28 Ov., *Tr.* 1.11.3–4.
29 Suet., *Aug.* 24.2.
30 By stating this, I am opting for the hypothesis that, at the time of Ovid's exile, Cornelius Fidus was a senator and not a Roman knight later adlected to the Senate.
31 In any case, this is the conclusion that should be drawn for the *clarissimae* according to Raepsaet-Charlier 1982, 2016: 57–71.
32 Suet., *Galb.* 12.1.
33 *PFCR* 749.
34 *PIR*² L 354 (L. Petersen); *CP* 33; *CJC* 665; Faoro 2011: 324–5, nr. 2.
35 Tac., *Hist.* 2.59.1.
36 Haensch 1997: 548–9.
37 On the concept of *praetorium*, see Mommsen 1900; Cagnat 1907; Egger 1966; Zucca 1992; Haensch 1997: 45–6; Alessio 2006; Schäfer 2014: 11–33, 337–342 and 345–8; Leveau 2016; Le Guennec 2019: 24–5. For other buildings that could accommodate travellers, see also Corsi 2000; Le Guennec 2019.
38 *PIR*² D 51 (A. Stein). She may have come from *Dalmatia*, and more specifically from *Salona*, if one thinks of Desidienus Aemilianus, *praefectus cohortis* in 258 and to whom the same origin is attributed according to Alföldy 1969: 81; Wilkes 1970: 542, 549, nr. 23, and *PME* D 6. On the other hand, according to Christol et al. 2005: 283 and Christol and Pont 2017: 70–1 she may have had an African origin. On her family connections and her senatorial offspring, see Raepsaet-Charlier 1999: 227–8, 231 = Raepsaet-Charlier 2016: 206–7, 210; Christol et al. 2005: 280–4; Christol and Pont 2017.
39 On Alexander, see *PIR*² A 945 (A. Stein); *CP* p. 1101; *SCP* p. 150. See also Christol et al. 2005; Christol and Pont 2017.
40 The dating of his time in office to the reigns of Philip the Arab and his son is credited to Herrmann and Malay 2003: 5. See also Christol et al. 2005: 271, 279–280; Christol and Pont 2017: 55.
41 Engelmann and Knibbe 1978–1980: 26, nr. 17 (= *AE* 1982, 870) = *I.Ephesos* III, 617: Δησιδιήνην Κινκίαν,/τὴν κοσμιωτάτην/γυναῖκα/Ἀππίου Ἀλεξάνδρου,/τοῦ κρατίστου/ ἐπιτρόπου τῶν Σεββ(αστῶν),/Ἰουλ(ία) Ἀττίκιλλα, ἱέρεια/τῆς ἁγιωτάτης Ἀρτέμιδος/ καὶ ἀρχιέρεια Ἀσίας ναῶν/τῶν ἐν Ἐφέσῳ,/τὴν ἑαυτῆς εὐεργέτιν. On Iulia Atticilla, see Keil 1951: 289–290, nr. 43 = Merkelbach 1977: 185 = *I.Ephesos* VII/2, 4343 and Campanile 1994: 124, nr. 134a; van Bremen 1996: 319, nr. 20 and Kirbihler 2019: 28, nr. 47.
42 Engelmann and Knibbe 1978–1980: 26, nr. 16 (= *AE* 1982, 869) = *I.Ephesos* III, 616: Ἄππιον Ἀλέξανδρον,/τὸν κράτιστον ἐπίτροπον/τῶ[ν] κυρίω[ν ἡ]μῶν/[[Μ(άρκων) Ἰουλίων Φιλίππων Σεββ(αστῶν)]],/τὸν πολλάκις δουκηνάριον,/τὸν φιλόσοφον,/ τὸν ἁγνὸν καὶ δίκαιον/καὶ πάσῃ ἀρετῇ κεκοσμημένον,/Μ(ᾶρκος) Αὐρ(ήλιος) Δάφνος, φιλοσέβ(αστος)/ἀσιάρχης ὑμνῳδός,/πολλάκις ἀγωνοθέτης,/τὸν ἐν πᾶσιν τῆς πατρίδος/ καὶ ἑαυτοῦ εὐεργέτην. On Daphnus, see Miltner 1960: col. 54–5, nr. 2 = *I.Ephesos* III, 624;

Keil 1923: 152–3, nr. 70 = *I.Ephesos* VII/1, 3070 and Keil 1951: 289–290, nr. 43 = Merkelbach 1977: 184 = *I.Ephesos* VII/2, 4343 and Campanile 1994: 124, nr. 134; Kirbihler 2008: 114, 132, nr. 79, 143–4.
43 Baier 2013, 2021.
44 For the memorial symbolism of the place, see Baier 2017. For the function of the building, see Baier 2013: 53–61. See also Baier 2021.
45 Haensch 1997: 299–300, n. 7. See W. Alzinger, in *RE Suppl.* XII, 1970, s.v. Ephesos B. Archäologischer Teil, coll. 1639–40 and, more specifically, Baier 2013 and 2021. On *Ephesus* as seat for the senatorial as well as procuratorial administration, see Haensch 1997: 298–321.
46 See Herrmann and Malay 2003: 4–6, nr. 3; Christol et al. 2005.
47 Haensch 1997: 345–6.
48 For a specific example, see Scheid 1998: 267–271. For a summary of honoured deities, see 271, n. 34. For the dating of this area at the time of Marcus Aurelius' reign and his reorganisation of the Dacian provinces, see Piso 2013: 4.
49 Piso 1983, 1998; see also Haensch 1997: 731–2.
50 Piso 1998: 253–4; Piso 2001: 21, 31 and 35 (maps) = Piso 2005: 442–3, 450 and 454.
51 *PIR*² A 309 (A. Stein); *PFCR* 34.
52 *PIR*² A 1688 (A. Stein); *CP* 328; Piso 2013: 227–235, nr. 102.
53 *PIR*² A 1689 (A. Stein).
54 *CIL* III, 1423 = *IDR* III/2, 244: *I(oui) O(ptimo) M(aximo), Iuno/ni Reginae, M[i]/neruae, omni/bus dis immor/⁵talibus,/Q(uintus) Axius Aelia/nus, u(ir) e(gregius), proc(urator)/ Aug[[g]](ustorum), et Aelia/Romana, eius,/Ioni.*
55 *PIR*² A 311 (A. Stein); *PFCR* 35.
56 *PIR*² H 109 (L. Petersen); *CP* 254; *PME* H 14; Piso 2013: 201–4, nr. 97.
57 *CIL* III, 7901 = *IDR* III/2, 188: *Deo Aeterno,/Herennius Gemellinu[s],/u(ir) e(gregius), pro(curator) Auggg(ustorum) nnn(ostrorum), pro [– –]/Saturnina co<n>iuge et [He]/⁵renniis Vrso et Gemel[lino]/et Sup<e>ro Saturnino u[ot(um) lib(ens) sol(uit)]*; *CIL* III, 1625 (p. 1018 and 1424) = *IDR* II, 640 = *IDR* III/2, 342: *[– – Ael(ia) Saturna]/pro Heren(nio)/Gemellino,/u(iro) e(gregio), proc(uratore)/Augg(ustorum) nn(ostrorum),/agente u(ice) p(raesidis),/marito suo,/libens soluit*; von Finály 1912: 531 (= *AE* 1913, 51 = *ILS* 9515) = *IDR* III/2, 220: *Deae Aechatae/pro salutae/Aeliae Saturninae, coniu/⁵gis suae, Aeren/nius Gemelli/nus, tribunus,/statum con/iugis redemit/ ex uisu et/u(otum) s(oluit) l(ibens) m(erito).*
58 *PFCR* 80.
59 *PIR*² C 185 (A. Stein); *CP* p. 1066; Piso 2013: 226–7, nr. 101.
60 Daicoviciu 1932: 83–4, nr. 1 (= *AE* 1930, 134) = *IDR* III/2, 331: *[I]nuicto/deo Serapidi,/Caesidius/Respectus,/proc(urator) Aug(usti) n(ostri),/et Apronilla,/eius.*
61 *PFCR* 361.
62 *PIR*² L 357 (L. Petersen); Piso 2013: 221–6, nr. 100.
63 Piso 1983: 246–7, nr. 15 (= *AE* 1983, 840): *Deae praesen/tissimae Cor<a>e/M(arcus) Lucceius Felix,/proc(urator) Aug(usti) n(ostri), et/Hostilia Fausti/na, eius.*
64 *PFCR* 467.
65 Piso 2013: 251–2, nr. 106.
66 Daicoviciu 1938: 392, Fig. 38 (= *AE* 1939, 5) = *IDR* III/2, 222: Διὶ Ὑψίστῳ/ἐπηκόῳ,/ Αἴλ(ιος) Ἀπολ<λ>ινά/ριος, ἐπίτροπος,/καὶ Μάξιμα,/εὐχαριστήριον.
67 See Ozcáriz Gil 2013: 42, 188–200, who notes that the two districts, *Asturia et Callaecia* as well as the *Citerior*, whose procurator originally sat in *Tarraco*, were merged during the Severan dynasty and that the high official managed the whole province from *Asturica Augusta* while moving periodically to the provincial capital. Furthermore, the role of *Asturica Augusta* was relegated to the background when the short-lived province of *Hispania Superior* was created, with its capital at *Lucus Augusti*. For more on this issue, see Alföldy 2000.

68 On the circumstances of the discovery, see García y Bellido 1968: 191–3; Diego Santos 1968: 91–2. On the original location of these texts, see Scheid 1998: 274. The existence of the *praetorium* can be deduced based on an allusion to the *Genius praetorii* by Q. Mamilius Capitolinus, *legatus Augusti per Asturiam et Callaeciam* and *dux legionis VII Geminae Piae Fidelis* (cf. *PIR*² M 121 (L. Petersen)) in *CIL* II, 2634 (p. 707) (= *ILS* 2299) = *ERPLeón* 82 = *ILAstorga* 12 = *CIMRM* I, 804 (now lost). Was this *praetorium* only intended for use by the senatorial legates or also by the procurators?
69 Navarro Caballero 2017: 663–4, nr. 437; *PFCR* 511.
70 *PIR*² O 176 K.-P. Johne; *SAIE* 56.
71 García y Bellido 1968: 206–7, nr. 8 (= *AE* 1968, 234) = *EyNAstorga* 6 = *IRPLeón* 10 = *ERPLeón* 36 = *ILAstorga* 6: *Fortunae Reduci sanctae/G(aius)* (!) *Otacilius Octauius/Saturninus, u(ir) e(gregius), proc(urator)/[A]ug(usti),/dicauit cum filia et/nepote*. For the chronology, see Alföldy 2000: 66–7.
72 Navarro Caballero 2017: 664, nr. 438; *PFCR* 716.
73 *PIR*² V 838 K. Wachtel and M. Heil; *SAIE* 57 (who call him P. Ul(pius) Maximus). García y Bellido 1968: 204–6, nr. 6 (= *AE* 1968, 233) = *EyNAstorga* 5 = *IRPLeón* 9 = *ERPLeón* 35 = *ILAstorga* 5: *Fortunae/Bonae Reduci,/Pul(lius?) Maximus,/proc(urator) Aug(usti), cum uxore/et filio*. For the chronology, see Alföldy 2000: 66.
74 *PIR*² I 869 L. Petersen; Navarro Caballero 2017: 662, nr. 435; *PFCR* 415.
75 *PIR*² C 306 A. Stein; *CP* 306; *SAIE* 61.
76 *PIR*² M 330 L. Petersen; Navarro Caballero 2017: 662–3, nr. 436; *PFCR* 465.
77 *PIR*² T 357 J. Heinrichs; *CP* 216; Dobson 1978: nr. 161; *SAIE* 54; Sablayrolles 1996: 567–8, nr. 50.
78 *CIL* II, 2642 = *EyNAstorga* 71 = *IRPLeón* 115 = *ERPLeón* 187 = *ILAstorga* 30: *Iustinae,/uxori/sanctissi/mae,/Calpurnius/Quadra/tus,/proc(urator) Aug(usti)* and *CIL* II, 2643 = *EyNAstorga* 48 = *IRPLeón* 121 = *ERPLeón* 203 = *ILAstorga* 29: *[D(is)] M(anibus)/Marriniae, M(arci) f(iliae),/Proculae,/coniugi sanctissimae/castissimae,/ Truttedius Clem[ens], proc(urator)/Asturiae et/Gallaeciae,/Dalmatiae et Hist[riae]*. For the chronology, see Alföldy 2000: 47, 63–4.
79 *PFCR* 528.
80 *PIR*² P 490 (L. Vidman).
81 *PIR*² P 493 (G. Winkler).
82 Plin., *Ep.* 6.16.4 and 21; *Ep.* 20 *passim*.
83 Reddé 1986: 193–5.
84 Haensch 1997: 154–6.
85 Zucca 2009: 573–4.
86 Faoro 2011: 60.
87 *PIR*² C 1541 (E. Groag).
88 Mastino and Zucca 2014.
89 Zucca 2009: 578. For the promotion by Trajan, see Mastino and Zucca 2012, 2014: 207–214.
90 Zucca 2009: 575–6.
91 Based on a list provided by Mastino and Zucca 2021: 423–9.
92 *PIR*² F 442 (A. Stein); *PFCR* 319.
93 *PIR*² F 288 (A. Stein).
94 *PIR*² F 429 (A. Stein); *PFCR* 313.
95 *CIL* X, 7859 = *CILSard* 815 = *EDR* 152994: *Nimphis sac[rum]/Flauia, T(iti) fili[a],/Tertulla, L(uci) [F]l[aui]/Honorati, pro[c(uratoris)]/et praef(ecti) prou(inciae), [uxor],/[e]t Honoratia[n(us) et Mar]/cellina, fil[i(i) eor(um)],/u(otum) s(oluerunt) l(ibentes) [m(erito)]*. On Honoratus, see *PIR*² F 289 A. Stein; *CP* p. 1045; Faoro 2011: 320, nr. 30 (end of second and beginning of the third century).
96 Mastino and Zucca 2021: 429–440 = *EDR* 181204: *Nymphis [– –?]/Valeria Modesta, M. Valeri Optati,/proc(uratoris) Aug(usti) praef(ecti)/prouinc(iae) Sard(iniae),/lib(erta), d(ono) d(edit) uel d(e)d(icauit)*.

97 Haensch 1997: 155–6; Faoro 2011: 176–7; Ibba 2014; Mastino and Zucca 2021: 440.
98 Faoro 2011: 176–8; Ibba 2014.
99 Zucca 1992 (= *AE* 1992, 892) = *CILSard* 902 = Spanu and Zucca 2006 (= *AE* 2005, 688) = *EDR* 170111: *[– – D]omini n(ostri) [M(arci) Au]reli [Antonini]/ [– –] propter compendium itiner[is]/ [– –] commeantiu[m] Aurelius/[Sebastenus?, proc(urator) Aug(usti) pra[ef(ectus) p]rou(inciae) Sard(iniae), praetorium/ [– –]SO pecunia publica/ [– –]E ciuitatis Forotraianensium/[re]stituit dedicauitque.*
100 Zucca 1992: 613–5.
101 Faoro 2011: 315–6, nr. 23 (Aurelius) and 359, nr. 33 (M. Aurelius Sebastenus); Mastino and Zucca 2021: 440. *PIR*² A 1604 (A. Stein); *SCP* p. 147.
102 Zucca 1992: 600–3, 612, 618–624; Spanu and Zucca 2006.
103 See Zucca 1992: 613, 625, who does not exclude the fact that the *praetorium* served as the administrative headquarters for the imperial domains; Spanu and Zucca 2006: 681–2.
104 Navarro Caballero 2017: 499–501, nr. 199; *PFCR* 4.
105 Cafaro 2021: 424, nr. 248.
106 Navarro Caballero 2017: 503–5, nr. 204; *PFCR* 183. Cf. Sillières 1978: 468–473, nr. II (= *AE* 1978, 400) = *CIL* II²/5, 782: *Caruiliae, P(ubli) f(iliae), Censonill(ae) Magni/Rufi, proc(uratoris) Aug(usti) XX her(editatium) per Hisp(aniam)/Baet(icam) et Lusitan(iam), item proc(uratoris) Aug(usti)/per Baet(icam) ad kal(endarium) Vegetian(um), item pr[o]c(uratoris)/Augusti prou(inciae) Baet(icae) ad ducena (milia) (scil. uxori), Ac[il(ia) Plec(usa)],/amicae op[timae, d(onum) d(edit)].*
107 *PIR*² M 98 (L. Petersen); *CP* 236; *PME* M 13; *SAIE* 13.
108 Atencia Páez 1993: 125–127 (= *AE* 1994, 922b = *HEp* 1995, 575) = *CIL* II²/5, 781: *[P(ublio) Magnio, Q(uinti)] f(ilio), Quir(ina), Rufo/[Magonia]no, tr(ibuno) mil(itum) IIII,/ [proc(uratori) Aug(usti) X]X her(editatium) per Hisp(aniam) Baet(icam)/[et Lusitan(iam) i]tem proc(uratori) Aug(usti)/[per Baetic(am)] ad kal(endarium) Veget(ianum)/[item proc(uratori) A]ug(usti) prou(inciae) Baet(icae) ad/[ducen(a), Acil(ia) P]lec(usa), amico optim[o]/[et bene] de provincia/[semper me]rito, d(onum) d(edit).*
109 *CIL* II²/5, 780: *P(ublio) Magnio, Q(uinti) f(ilio), Quir(ina), Rufo/Magoniano, tr(ibuno) mil(itum) IIII,/proc(uratori) Aug(usti) XX her(editatium) per Hisp(aniam) Baet(icam)/et Lusitan(iam) item proc(uratori) Aug(usti)/per Baetic(am) ad kal(endarium) Veget(ianum)/item proc(uratori) Aug(usti) prou(inciae) Baet(icae) ad/ducen(a), Acili(a) Plec(usa), amico optimo/et bene de prouincia/semper merito, d(onum) d(edit).*
110 Haensch 1997: 184–5.
111 Haensch 1997: 178–184.
112 *EE* VIII, 311 (p. 524) = *IRLugo* 32: *D(is) M(anibus)/Philtates,/ornatricis/[[C [– –]]]/ [[Cạttunillae]],/[[c(larissimae) f(eminae)]],/domo August(is)/Taurinis,/conserui/eius.* See also Alföldy 2000: 49, n. 88; Alföldy 2001 (= *AE* 2001, 1213 = *HEp* 2001, 320); Navarro Caballero 2017: 730, nr. 548.
113 See Alföldy 2000 and 2001.
114 See Ozcáriz Gil 2013: 75–95.
115 On the town planning of *Lucus Augusti*, see Dopico Caínzos 2017; Carreño Gascón 2018.
116 *PIR*² B 36 (A. Stein); *CP* 173; Dobson 1978: nr. 133.
117 Haensch 1997: 112.
118 *PIR*² S 499 (M. Heil); *PFCR* 589.
119 *PIR*² B 37 (A. Stein); *PFCR* 146.
120 *CIL* IX, 4964 (= *ILS* 1363) = *EDR* 092731: *D(is) [M(anibus)]/Sex(to) Baio [Pudenti],/ proc(uratori) Aug(usti) [– –]/item [– –] Norici, Raetiae/Vindelic[iae, Maur]etaniae Caesar(iensis), et/Septi[miae? – –]e, M(arci) filiae,/Baia P[udentilla?, par]entib(us) dulciss(imis).*
121 *CIL* VIII, 21007: *[Dis] Manibus Ba[iae]/Ygiae, lib(ertae) Bai Puden/tis, proc(uratoris) Aug(usti), Verecun/dus, lib(ertus) eiusdem, con/ⁿiugi karissim<a>e fecit;/uixit an(nis) XXII.*

References

Albana, M. 2017: '*Ne quem magistratum, cui provincia obvenisset, uxor comitaretur* (Tac. Ann. 3, 33, 4): presenze femminili al seguito di magistrati e militari nelle province', *Studia Europaea Gnesnensia* 16, 127–153.

Alessio, S. 2006: '"*Praetorium*" e "*palatium*" come residenze di imperatori e governatori', *Latomus* 65, 679–689.

Alföldy, G. 1969: *Die Personennamen in der römischen Provinz Dalmatia. Beiträge zur Namensforschung. Neue Folge 4*, Heidelberg.

Alföldy, G. 2000: *Provincia Hispania Superior. Schriften der philosophisch-historischen Klasse der Heidelberger Akademie der Wissenschaften 19*, Heidelberg.

Alföldy, G. 2001: 'Eine *clarissima femina* in *Lucus Augusti*', *Zeitschrift für Papyrologie und Epigraphik* 136, 233–238.

Álvarez Melero, A. 2018: *Matronae equestres. La parenté féminine des chevaliers romains originaires des provinces occidentales sous le Haut-Empire romain (Ier-IIIe siècles)*. Institut historique belge de Rome. Études 4, Bruxelles-Roma.

Atencia Páez, R. 1993: '*Proc. Aug. ad "Fal. Veget"*. Sobre un epígrafe gemelo de *CIL*, II, 2029 (P. Magnius Rufus Magonianus)', *Estudios dedicados a Alberto Balil in memoriam*, 113–132.

Baier, C. 2013: '*Attolitur monte Pione*. Neue Untersuchungen im Stadtviertel oberhalb des Theaters von Ephesos', *Jahreshefte des Österreichischen Archäologischen Institutes in Wien* 82, 23–68.

Baier, C. 2017: 'A P(a)lace of Remembrance? Reflections on the Historical Depth of a Monumental Domus in Ephesos', in E. Mortensen and B. Poulsen (eds), *Cityscapes and Monuments of Western Asia Minor: Memories and Identities*, Oxford-Philadelphia, 122–136.

Baier, C. 2021: 'Capitals in the Making. A Palace in Ephesos and Its Possible Historical Implications', in M. Raycheva and M. Steskal (eds), *Roman Provincial Capitals under Transition. Proceedings of the International Conference Held in Plovdiv 04.-07. November 2019*, Wien, 33–60.

Barrett, A. 2002: *Livia. First Lady of Imperial Rome*, New Haven, CT.

Cafaro, A. 2021: *Governare l'impero. La 'praefectura fabrum' fra legami personali e azione politica (II sec. a.C. – III sec. d.C.)*. Alte Geschichte 262, Stuttgart.

Cagnat, R. 1907: '*Praetorium*', *Dictionnaire des antiquités grecques et romaines d'après les textes et les monuments contenant l'explication des termes qui se rapportent aux mœurs, aux institutions, à la religion, aux arts, aux sciences, au costume, au mobilier, à la guerre, à la marine, aux métiers, au monnaies, poids et mesures, etc. et en général à la vie publique et privée des anciens. Tome quatrième. Première partie (N-Q)*, Paris, 640–642.

Campanile, M. D. 1994: *I sacerdoti del Koinon d'Asia (I sec. a.C.-III sec. d.C.). Contributo allo studio della romanizzazione delle élites provinciali nell'Oriente greco*. Biblioteca di studi antichi/Studi ellenistici 74/7, Pisa.

Carreño Gascón, M. C. 2018: 'El foro romano de *Lucus Augusti*: primicias de su descubrimiento', in A. Ruiz Gutiérrez and C. Cortés Bárcena (eds), *Memoriae civitatum: arqueología y epigrafía de la ciudad romana. Estudios en homenaje a José Manuel Iglesias Gil*. Heri 5, Santander, 431–459.

Christol, M., Drew-Bear, T., and Taşlıalan, M. 2005: 'Appius Alexander, serviteur de l'État romain et philosophe', *Anatolia Antiqua* 13, 271–284.

Christol, M., and Pont, A.-V. 2017: 'Autour des *Appii* d'Asie: réseaux familiaux, ascension sociale, carrières et cités au cours du IIIe siècle', *Journal des Savants* 51–92.

Corsi, C. 2000: *Le strutture di servizio del cursus publicus in Italia: ricerche topografiche ed evidenze archeologiche* (BAR International Series 875), Oxford.

Coşkun, A. 2009: 'Das Edikt des Sex. Sotidius Strabo Libuscidianus und die Fasten der Statthalter Galatiens in augusteischer und tiberianischer Zeit', *Gephyra* 6, 159–164.

Daicoviciu, C. 1932: 'Contribuţii la syncretismul religios in *Sarmizegetusa*', *Universitatea „Regele Ferdinand I" din Cluj. Anuarul pe anii 1928–1932*, 81–88.

Daicoviciu, C. 1938: '*Sarmizegetusa* (*Ulpia Traiana*) in lumina săpăturilor', *Anuarul comisiunii monumentelor istorice. Secţia pentru Transilvania* 4 (1932–1938), 355–413.

Diego Santos, F. 1968: 'Ocho lápidas votivas de Astorga sobre epigrafía romana', *Archivum Ovetense* 18, 91–106.

Dobson, B. 1978: *Die Primipilares. Entwicklung und Bedeutung, Laufbahnen und Persönlichkeiten eines römischen Offiziersranges*, Köln-Bonn.

Dopico Caínzos, M. D. 2017: '*Lucus Augusti*: perspectivas para su investigación', *Estudios Humanísticos* 16, 55–81.

Egger, R. 1966: *Das Praetorium als Amtssitz und Quartier römischer Spitzenfunktionäre. Österreichische Akademie der Wissenschaften. Philosophisch-Historische Klasse. Sitzungsberichte 250*, 4, Wien.

Engelmann, H., and Knibbe, D. 1978: 'Aus ephesischen Skizzenbüchern', *Jahreshefte des Österreichischen Archäologischen Institutes in Wien* 52, 19–61.

Faoro, D. 2011: *Praefectus, procurator, praeses. Genesi delle cariche presidiali equestri nell'alto Impero romano* (Studi Udinesi sul mondo antico 8), Firenze.

Fertl, E. 2019: '. . . führten sie jetzt, der Fesseln ledig, zu Hause, auf dem Forum, ja schon im Heere das Regiment. "Römische Amtsträgerehefrauen und ihre politische, gesellschaftliche und religiös-kultische Rolle in den Provinzen', *Kultur und Bildung* 2, 16–23.

García y Bellido, A. 1968: 'Lápidas votivas a deidades exóticas halladas recientemente en Astorga y León', *Boletín de la Real Academia de la Historia* 163, 191–209.

Haensch, R. 1997: *Capita provinciarum. Statthaltersitze und Provinzialverwaltung in der römischen Kaiserzeit* (Kölner Forschungen 7), Mainz.

Herrmann, P., and Malay, H. 2003: 'Statue Bases of the Mid Third Century A.D. from Smyrna', *Epigraphica Anatolica* 36, 1–11.

Ibba, A. 2014: '*Itinera praesidis in prouincia Sardiniae*: una proposta di ricostruzione', in S. Demougin and M. Navarro Caballero (eds), *Se déplacer dans l'Empire romain. Approches épigraphiques. XVIIIe rencontre franco-italienne d'épigraphie du monde romain, Bordeaux 7–8 octobre 2011* (Scripta Antiqua 59), Bordeaux, 31–53.

Kany, R. 1995: 'Die Frau des Pilatus und ihr Name. Ein Kapitel aus der Geschichte neutestamentlicher Wissenschaft', *Zeitschrift für die Neutestamentliche Wissenschaft und die Kunde der älteren Kirche* 86, 104–110.

Keil, J. 1923: '7. Inschriften', in E. Reisch (ed.), *Forschungen in Ephesos*. III, Wien, 91–168.

Keil, J. 1951: 'Die Inschriften', in J. Keil (ed.), *Forschungen in Ephesos*. IV/3. *Die Johanneskirche*, Wien, 275–295.

Kirbihler, F. 2008: 'Les grands-prêtres d'Éphèse: aspects instutionnels et sociaux de l'asiarchie', in A. Rizakis and F. Camia (eds), *Civic Elites in the Eastern Part of the Roman Empire. Proceedings of the International Workshop held at Athens. Scuola archeologica italiana d'Atene, 19 december 2005* (Tripodes 6), Athens, 107–149.

Kirbihler, F. 2019: 'Les prêtresses d'Artémis à Éphèse (Ier siècle av. J.-C. – IIIe siècle apr. J.-C.) ou comment faire du neuf en prétendant restaurer un état ancien ?', in S. Lalanne (ed.), *Femmes grecques de l'Orient romain. Dialogues d'Histoire Ancienne – Supplément 18*, Besançon, 21–79.

Kolb, A. 2000: *Transport und Nachrichtentransfer im Römischen Reich*, Berlin.

Le Guennec, M.-A. 2019: *Aubergistes et clients. L'accueil mercantile dans l'Occident romain (IIIe siècle av. J.-C. – IVe siècle apr. J.-C.)*. Bibliothèque des Écoles françaises d'Athènes et de Rome 381, Roma.

Leveau, P. 2016: '*Praetoria* et *tabernae* en Gaule. Contribution à l'identification des établissements de bord de route', *Gallia* 73, 29–38.

Marshall, A. J. 1975: 'Roman Women and the Provinces', *Ancient Society* 6, 109–127.

Mastino, A., and Zucca, R. 2012: 'La *constitutio* del *Forum Traiani* in *Sardinia* nel 111 d.C.', *Rivista di topografia antica* 22, 31–50.

Mastino, A., and Zucca, R. 2014: '*L. Cossonius L. f. Stell(atina tribu) Gallus Vecilius Crispinus Mansuanius Marcellinus Numisius Sabinus pro consule provinciae Sardiniae* e la *constitutio* del *Forum Traiani*', *Gerión* 32, 199–223.

Mastino, A., and Zucca, R. 2021: '*M. Valerius Optatus, proc(urator) praef(ectus) provinc(iae) Sard(iniae)*. Un nuovo titulus di un governatore della *Sardinia* da *Forum Traiani*', in S. Antolini and S. M. Marengo (eds), *Pro merito laborum. Miscellanea epigrafica per Gianfranco Paci*, Tivoli, 417–440.

Merkelbach, R. 1977: 'Ephesische Parerga (4): Die Familie des Aurelius Daphnus', *Zeitschrift für Papyrologie und Epigraphik* 24, 185–186.

Miltner, F. 1960: 'XXIV. Vorläufiger Bericht über die Ausgrabungen in Ephesos', *Jahreshefte des Österreichischen Archäologischen Institutes in Wien (Beiblatt)* 45, 1–76.

Mitchell, S. 1976: 'Requisitioned Transport in the Roman Empire: A New Inscription from Pisidia', *Journal of Roman Studies* 66, 106–131.

Mitchell, S. 1986: 'Galatia Under Tiberius', *Chiron* 16, 17–33.

Mommsen, T. 1900: '*Praetorium*', *Hermes* 35, 437–442.

Navarro Caballero, M. 2017: *Perfectissima femina. Femmes de l'élite dans l'Hispanie romaine*. Scripta Antiqua 101, Bordeaux.

Ozcáriz Gil, P. 2013: *La administración de la provincia Hispania citerior durante el alto imperio romano: organización territorial, cargos administrativos y fiscalidad*. Col·lecció Instrumenta, 44, Barcelona.

Patrich, J. 2011: *Studies in the Archaeology and History of Caesarea Maritima. Ancient Judaism and Early Christianity* 77, Leiden-Boston, MA.

Piso, I. 1983: 'Inschriften von Prokuratoren aus Sarmizegetusa (I)', *Zeitschrift für Papyrologie und Epigraphik* 50, 233–251.

Piso, I. 1998: 'Inschriften von Prokuratoren aus Sarmizegetusa (II)', *Zeitschrift für Papyrologie und Epigraphik* 120, 253–271.

Piso, I. 2001: '*Colonia Ulpia Traiana Augusta Dacica Sarmizegetusa*. Brève présentation et état de la recherche', *Transylvanian Review* 10, 16–37.

Piso, I. 2005: *An der Nordgrenze des römischen Reiches. Ausgewählte Studien (1972–2003)*. Heidelberger althistorische Beiträge und epigraphische Studien 41, Stuttgart.

Piso, I. 2013: *Fasti provinciae Daciae II: die ritterlischen Amtsträger. Antiquitas. Reihe 1. Abhandlungen zur alten Geschichte 60*, Bonn.

Raepsaet-Charlier, M.-T. 1982: 'Épouses et familles de magistrats dans les provinces romaines aux deux premiers siècles de l'Empire', *Historia* 31, 56–69.

Raepsaet-Charlier, M.-T. 1999: '*Matronae equestres*. La parenté féminine de l'ordre équestre', in S. Demougin, H. Devijver, and M.-T. Raepsaet-Charlier (eds), *L'ordre équestre. Histoire d'une aristocratie (IIe siècle av. J.-C.-IIIe siècle ap. J.-C.). Actes du colloque international organisé par Ségolène Demougin, Hubert Devijver et Marie-Thérèse Raepsaet-Charlier (Bruxelles-Leuven, 5–7 octobre 1995). Collection de l'École française de Rome* 257, Roma, 215–236.

Raepsaet-Charlier, M.-T. 2016: *Clarissima femina. Études d'histoire sociale des femmes de l'élite à Rome. Scripta varia. Travaux rassemblés et édités par Anthony Álvarez Melero*, Bruxelles-Roma.

Reddé, M. 1986: *Mare nostrum. Les infrastructures, le dispositif et l'histoire de la marine militaire sous l'Empire romain* (Bibliothèque des Écoles françaises d'Athènes et de Rome 260), Roma.

Sablayrolles, R. 1996: *Libertinus miles. Les cohortes de vigiles* (Collection de l'École française de Rome 224), Roma.

Schäfer, F. F. 2014: *Praetoria. Paläste zum Wohnen und Verwalten in Köln und anderen römischen Provinzhauptstädten*, Mainz.

Scheid, J. 1998: 'La piété des procurateurs des Gaules et des Germanies', *Cahiers du Centre G. Glotz* 9, 265–275.

Sillières, P. 1978: 'Nouvelles inscriptions de *Singilia Barba* (El Castillón, Antequera, Málaga)', *Mélanges de la Casa de Velázquez* 14, 465–476.

Spanu, P. G., and Zucca, R. 2006: 'Il *cursus publicus* nella *Sardinia* tardoantica: l'esempio di Muru de Bangius', in G. Volpe and M. Turchiano (eds), *Paesaggi e insediamenti rurali in Italia meridionale fra tardoantico e altomedievo. Atti del Primo seminario sul Tardo-antico e l'Altomedievo in Italia meridionale (Foggia, 12–14 febbraio 2004)* (Insulae Diomedeae. Collana di ricerche storiche e archeologiche 4), Bari, 675–690.

van Bremen, R. 1996: *The Limits of Participation. Women and Civic Life in the Greek East in the Hellenistic and Roman Periods*, Amsterdam.

von Finály, G. 1912: 'Archäologische Funde im Jahre 1911. Ungarn', *Jahrbuch des Kaiser-lich Deutschen Archäologischen Instituts* 27, 526–546.

Wilkes, J. J. 1970: 'Equestrian Rank in Dalmatia under the Principate', *Adriatica praehistorica et antiqua. Miscellanea G. Novak dicata*, Zagreb, 529–551.

Zucca, R. 1992: 'Un'iscrizione monumentale dell'Oristanese', in A. Mastino (ed.), *L'Africa romana. Atti del IX convegno di studio su "L'Africa romana". Nuoro, 13–15 dicembre 1991, Vol. 2. Pubblicazioni del Dipartimento di storia dell'Università degli studi di Sassari 20*, Sassari, 595–636.

Zucca, R. 2009: 'L'urbanistica di *Forum Traiani*', in C. Marangio and G. Laudizi (eds), Παλαιὰ Φιλία. *Studi di topografia antica in onore di Giovanni Uggeri*, Galatina, 573–586.

Part IV
Displaying Authority Over the Public Space and Religious Space

11 From Honour to Dishonour – The Different Readings of *Columna Maenia*[1]

Anna-Maria Wilskman

I Introduction

Republican Rome was filled with monuments that triggered memories of the past and served as inspiration for the future deeds of ambitious individuals.[2] However, we do not enter common, shared spaces with equal experiences, and a monument in a public space can have a wide range of effects and meanings, which can vary greatly between different individuals and spatiotemporal contexts.[3] Rather than being a stable manifestation of a specific moment that lasts unchanged for eternity, a space, or a monument, is a construction that is always dependent on the actors and their relationships with it.[4] Furthermore, the "museum" or "collection" (and Rome can be seen as such)[5] can have contingent identities because of random events.[6]

Monuments played an important role in the rewriting and reimagining of Roman history, especially the monuments in the Forum.[7] Recently, Nicholas Purcell has investigated the multiple functions of the Forum in the eyes of historians and of Romans themselves: "The Romans, like us, could never step twice into the same public space".[8] In republican Rome, individuals could use space and building projects to bring something private into the place of the public.[9]

In this essay, I discuss the different layers of meanings and interpretations given to a specific monument. The case study is the well-researched column that was linked to the name Maenius and that was located close to the Comitium. Both ancient writers and modern scholars refer to it as *columna Maenia*. Friedrich Osann's *Commentatio de columna Maenia* (1844) was the first comprehensive study of the monument. Since then, the column has interested scholars due to the inconsistent information regarding its origin,[10] topography[11] and art history.[12] This work is based on research on these issues, especially that of Erik Welin (1953), Filippo Coarelli (1983, 1985) and Claudia Conese (2012), but I turn my focus more on the changing roles, relationships, activities and reception of the *columna Maenia*.

My discussion is rooted in both the ancient sources as well as modern studies and their interpretations. The first part of this chapter is devoted to the functions of the monument in the daily life of the Romans. The second part of the chapter is based on the first part, and it discusses how the reception by an individual affects our interpretation of common, public spaces and their monuments and how

DOI: 10.4324/b23090-15

This chapter has been made available under a CC BY-NC 4.0 license.

social memory affects the interpretation of such places. By re-evaluating the textual sources and taking into account the importance of social memory, I highlight how the public perception and memory of "Maenius" affected the column's evolution of becoming a place of dishonour rather than of honour. As we move from practical functions to more symbolic ones, we start to see how big a role "memory" plays in the understanding of the monument, its place and symbolism.

II Functions of the *Columna Maenia*

Instead of starting the discussion by giving a general history of the monument, I record the different functions of the monument that can be gathered from the ancient sources and the interpretations that scholars have drawn based on the sources. I choose this method because it makes it easier for us to understand how the monument functioned in the daily life of the Romans, who did not necessarily have all the information about the past that we have today (but who simultaneously had other information available).

The first time that the *columna Maenia* appears in extant ancient literature is in Cicero's speech *Divinatio in Q. Caecilium*, written around 70 B.C.[13]

> *vobis autem tanta inopia reorum est ut mihi causam praeripere conemini potius quam aliquos ad columnam Maeniam vestri ordinis reos reperiatis?*
> And are they so badly off for persons to accuse that they must try to snatch my own case out of my hands, instead of finding themselves victims of their own social standing in the neighbourhood of the Maenian Column?[14]

We see how the surroundings of the *columna Maenia* were linked to "reos", i.e., those who are "accused or arraigned, defendants, prisoners, criminals, culprits".[15] During Cicero's time, therefore, it appears that this area was a place to find people who were in trouble. We learn more from Cicero's speech in defence of Cluentius, written around 66 B.C. Here, Cicero refers to a certain Q. Manlius, who was known for taking bribes. Since Cicero mentions Manlius' office as a "*triumvir*", which in this context should be understood as *triumvir capitalis*, we learn that the column and the office were connected.[16] Cicero paints a picture of a man who now holds office in the same place where he had been accused many times. We return to the column as the working place of the *triumviri capitales* later.

In addition to mentioning the column as a place of accused people and as the judgement seat of the *triumviri capitales*, the column figures as an allusion to debt in Cicero, as well as a topographical mark. These mentions occur in his speech *pro Sestio*, written around 56 B.C. Here, Cicero refers to the future consul Aulus Gabinius, who as a young man, sought a haven from the office of the tribune of the plebs in 67 B.C. so that he could not be accused.[17] Even though the column is not mentioned by name, scholiasts and researchers alike understand this as a reference to the *columna Maenia* (see later). The topographical mention appears later in the speech, when Publius Sestius, who acted as the tribune of the plebs during the time to which Cicero is referring, arrived from the Maenian column to see the gladiator games held at the Forum. The audience was seated "right down from the Capitol, and all the barriers of the Forum", and they saw how Sestius arrived from the column and greeted him with applause and cheers.[18]

From these passages of Cicero, we can directly deduce that the Maenian column was: 1) A place where people were accused; 2) a place linked to Roman administration, namely the seat of the *triumviri capitales*; 3) in the view of the slope on the Capitol and the barriers at the Forum; 4) a place for debtors, but whether they were there to suffer punishment or to seek help for their problems from the *triumviri capitales*, we cannot say; and 5) close to *puteal* and usurers.

Cicero is not the only source of topographical information regarding the column in the Forum. I now turn to the information provided by other ancient authors. The most crucial passage about the location and *terminus ante quem* of the erection of the column comes from Pliny the Elder. According to him, the column served as an important vehicle for keeping time from "a few years after" the Twelve Tables (451–450 B.C.) until the first Punic War (264–241 B.C.): On clear days, the *apparitor* of the consuls, watching from the Curia, would announce the last hour of the day when the sun sloped from the *columna Maenia* to the *Carcer*.[19] This has led to the estimation that the column was located at the northeast end of the area that today is occupied by the Arch of Septimius Severus, at the feet of the *clivus Capitolinus*.[20] Thus, at one point in its history, the column had a very practical function.

Pliny the Elder records another functional purpose for the monument, namely that it served as a statue base. In his chapter on the bronze statuary, Pliny recalls how the habit of "erecting statues on columns is more ancient" than the practice of erecting two-horse chariots in honour of praetors who had ridden around the *circus*.[21] It should be noted that this passage has sometimes been interpreted to mean that the statue of Maenius was the same as the Maenian "column" and that the column simply means a high pedestal.[22] However, today it is commonly accepted that the equestrian statue and the column were two different monuments. In any case, this is the first time that we learn something about the origin of the column. Pliny links it clearly to C. Maenius, who defeated the Latins in the battle at the river Astura and celebrated his triumph over Antium, Lavinium and Velitrae in 338 B.C.[23] Pliny also mentions that the *rostra* (beaks of ships) taken from the victory were fixed to the orator's platform. We will return to the monuments linked to Maenius later.

Summing up our information derived from Pliny, we can say that the column was indeed located in the Forum in the 6) close vicinity of *curia* and *carcer*; that it was 7) a vehicle for time keeping until the second Punic war; 8) a statue base; and 9) a monument linked to C. Maenius (cos. 338 B.C.), defeater of the Latins.

The next time that the name Maenius is linked to a column comes from the grammarian Festus (late second century A.D.). He records how *maeniana* were named after Maenius the censor, who was the first to extend these spectator's seats over the [buildings'] columns with wooden beams. This censor of 318 B.C. is the same as the consul whom we met in Pliny's writings. The early fourth century writer Nonius also refers to Maenius together with *maeniana*, but he specifically mentions the *columna Maenia* as well ("Maeninana ab inventore eorum Maenio dicta sunt; unde et columna Maenia").[24] In contrast to Nonius, Festus refers to multiple columns (*in foro ultra **columnas** tigna proiecit*)[25] that had beams fixed to them but not to a specific *columna Maenia*. Nonius mentions the column as a side note and continues with a citation from Cicero that refers to *maeniana*. Later, in his encyclopaedia *Origines* (ca. A.D. 570–636), Isidorus describes how Maenius, the colleague of Crassus, set up *maeniana* in the Forum.[26]

The grammarians Festus and Nonius, and later Isidorus, provide us the information that there were elevated beams called *maeniana* that allowed spectators to see the games and that these platforms were associated with *censor* Maenius. Their relation to the actual *columna Maenia* that has figured in other sources is, however, uncertain.

We now move to the scholiasts of ancient writers. The majority of these references to *columna Maenia* come from commentators of Cicero's passages mentioned earlier, but we also learn something from Horace's commentators. Porphyry (third century) and Pseudo-Acro (late antiquity) both comment on Horace's Satire 1.3.21, where they give a new explanation for the column's origin. According to these scholiasts, a certain Maenius sold his house but kept one column so that he could watch the games. Porphyry includes the verse "Maenius columnam cum peteret" from the second century B.C. satirist Lucilius, and Pseudo-Acro mentions that the column that Maenius kept was called Maenia.[27] Similar information appears in Pseudo-Asconius' commentary on Cicero's *Divinatio in Caecilium* 16.50, where the author mentions the Maenius who sold his house but kept one column in order for him and his descendants to watch the games held at the Forum. This scholiast also mentions how the *triumviri capitales* punished thieves and slaves at the column.[28] This interpretation of the origin of the column is understandable in light of Livy's note that Cato the Elder purchased *atrium Maenium* and built a basilica and other houses in the area of the atrium.[29] *Scholia Bobiensia*, also a scholia on Cicero, seems to have recorded the origin of the monument as well, but the relevant passages have unfortunately not survived to our day intact. The information that the scholiast records is that creditors prosecuted debtors and that the column was near the Forum and adhered to the Comitium.[30]

The scholiasts therefore link the column directly to *maeniana* and give a suggestion about the origin of the column. Even though this interpretation about the origin has been taken into account in scholarship as a possible fact,[31] the common opinion is that it is a fabrication that occurred later and that the column was indeed originally an honorific monument.[32]

Finally, the last mention comes from Symmachus, who in his letter to Felix mentions a procurator at the *columna Maenia*.[33] This has been taken as proof that the column still existed during the time of Symmachus (ca. A.D. 340–402).[34]

Summing up the ancient writers' reports on the usage of the column:

i) a place for debtors and creditors (Cicero, scholiasts)
ii) a place from where a tribune of the plebs came (Cicero)
iii) a place that was in view of the games held at the Forum (Cicero)
iv) a place where "common people" or "lower or dubious people" congregate (Cicero)

v) a place where the *triumviri capitales* had their tribunal (Cicero, scholiasts)
 vi) a vehicle for time keeping (in the past) (Pliny)
 vii) a place for a statue (Pliny)
 viii) taken from an *atrium* (scholiasts)
 ix) the place of the first *maeniana* in order to see the games (scholiasts, maybe grammarians)
 x) a place where thieves and slaves were punished by the *triumviri capitales* (scholiasts)
 xi) a place where the procurator operated (Symmachus)

The sources clearly link the *columna Maenia* to the Roman administration and everyday life on the Forum and indicate the visual importance of the monument. Another "visual" aspect of the monument that some have suggested is that it blocked the view of the tribunes of the plebs to their *subsellia* (benches). Plutarch records that the tribunes of the plebs wanted to get rid of a column that was blocking their *subsellia* and that Cato the Younger gave his first public speech in the Forum while defending a column. His ancestor built the Basilica Porcia, and it is probable that the column in the passage refers to one of these instead of the *columna Maenia*.[35]

III The Monument and Its Symbolic Relations

But in Rome, monuments are not merely monuments, inanimate objects. They are symbols. In this section, I concentrate especially on the symbolic meanings of the *columna Maenia*, the relationship between the column and the *gens Maenia*, the relationship between the monument and its surroundings, and how this relationship paints different pictures of the same monument and place in the social memory.

The Maenii, Spectacles and the Money-Lenders

As mentioned earlier, it is generally agreed that the column was erected in honour of C. Maenius, consul of 338 B.C. and champion over the Latins. In 318, Maenius renovated the area of the Forum and Comitium as the censor. The reorganisation included new pavement in the Forum, an equestrian statue of Q. Marcius Tremulus in front of the Temple of Castor and Pollux, as well as changing the uses of the shops and porticoes of the Forum. The butchers moved to Forum Cuppidinis and Forum Piscatorium, and they were replaced by moneychangers "in order to make the Forum more dignified".[36] The second half of the fourth century is also the first occasion when we may perceive how the Forum became a venue for making a message and part of the Roman community and its public history.[37]

Even Maenius himself became more visible in the Forum. In addition to the column, he was honoured with an equestrian statue as was his fellow consul Furius Camillus. According to Livy, this was uncommon for that time.[38] Moreover, after Maenius' victory at the river Astura, some of the war ships from Antium were burned and their *rostra* were set up on the speaker's platform (*suggestum*) in the Forum, which then became known as the Rostra.[39] This manifested Rome's victory

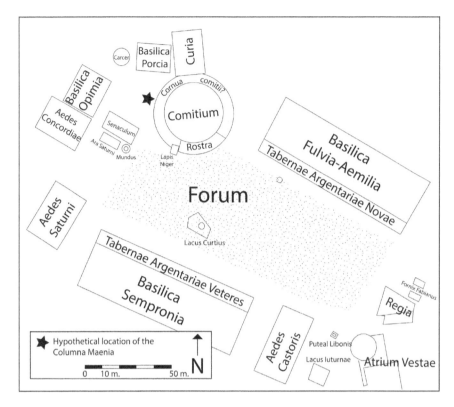

Figure 11.1 The estimated location of the *columna Maenia*. Based on the interpretation of Coarelli (1983).

Source: Author: Antonio Lopez Garcia.

over the Latins, but it was also a personal honour to Maenius' accomplishment as the victorious general. Equestrian statues, and especially Maenius' *rostra*, created a new honorific language and were the points of reference for all similar future monuments.[40] These monuments indicate that Maenius was instrumental in the building projects of this part of the Forum during his censorship in 318 B.C. and that he used the space to manifest his personal power.[41] This was no insignificant location but the heart of Rome itself, the place to enjoy spectacles of triumph, the highest honour a Roman could receive! It is no unimportant matter that Festus records Maenius as the originator of *maeniana*.[42] Maenius himself celebrated a triumph, and through his monuments and invention of elevated terraces, he was always associated with this important event also in the future. The ancient writers tend to associate the *maeniana* both with columns but also with balconies "beneath the Old Shops".[43]

However, as we learned from the scholiasts Porphyry, Pseudo-Acro and Pseudo-Asconius, the *maeninana* were also associated with a certain Maenius of the second century B.C. According to them, the column originally belonged to the *atrium*

Maenium. They recount that when this particular Maenius sold the building to M. Porcius Cato, he kept one column of the house for himself to set up a wooden platform to enjoy a splendid view of the gladiator games that were held at the Forum. It is possible that these later scholiasts have just confused the histories, but is it possible that there is truth in both of these stories? Perhaps C. Maenius, the consul of the fourth century, erected the column,[44] and he and his descendants used it to watch the games. Then, the later Maenius, of the second century, held the right to use one of the columns in front of the old location of the *atrium Maenium* to watch the spectacles. Cicero mentions this kind of right to use monuments and their surroundings when he records how the descendants of Servius Sulpicius used the surroundings of Sulpicius' statue to watch the games (Servius had died on a diplomatic mission).[45] It was only a right to use, not a right to own. Perhaps the same applied to the *columna Maenia*, i.e., the descendants of Maenius could use it but not own it. In any case, the significant aspects that these two histories of the column relate are honour and the power and prestige of Maenius and his family. It was a privilege to have this kind of column as an honorific monument in a highly visible place that is frequently visited by many, and it was a privilege to have "a private" enclosure to watch the games. What was also relevant was the name of the column, which kept the name of the Maenian family alive.

But it was not only honour and prestige that were associated with the name Maenius. In his *Epist.* 1.15., Horace paints a picture of a mean parasite who vigorously (*fortiter*) spent his parents' fortune.[46] In Horace's text, Maenius became a *scurra*, a figure we meet in Plautine comedy.[47] A similar characterisation continues in Horace's *Sat.* 1.3.21., where Maenius is speaking ill of one Novius. Porphyry says that those who wrote about Horatian characters say this Maenius was known in Rome for squandering and that he had lost his parents' property. Moreover, he had declared on the Capitol on 1 January that he wanted a loan of 400 000 sesterces. Someone asked him for a reason, and he said he already had a debt of 800 000 sesterces. After this, Porphyry records how this was the same man who sold his *domus* but kept one column in order to see the gladiator games and that the *columna Maenia* gets its name from him. Porphyry closes with a quotation from Lucilius: "Maenius columnam cum peteret".[48] Claudia Conese has translated the phrase as "went to the column",[49] while Coarelli interprets the phrase "recandosi alla colonna", with the gerund of "recarsi" ("to go"). However, this is not the only possible translation. *Peto* can mean "to seek, to direct one's course to, to go or repair to, to make for, to travel to a place", as well as "to demand, seek, require", or "to endeavor to obtain or pursue, to seek, to strive after". Other meanings are "to solicit for an office, to be a candidate for office".[50] So without context, the passage could mean that Maenius tried to get to the column, or that he pursued or sought after it (trying to keep it in his family's possession),[51] or even that he was running for office. Because the passage appears in Lucilius' satirical text, its actual meaning may very well, in my opinion, be ambiguous.

It is a pity that we do not have the original context of Lucilius' passage. He was Cato's contemporary, and it is possible that the satirist's Maenius is indeed someone who had financial difficulties. This is one probable meaning if Porphyry had the whole satire in his use. But even then, we should be mindful that Porphyry cites unnamed commentators as sources for identifying the notorious Maenius, and he himself adds to the story.[52] The commentators adapted and contextualised information based on their own historical memories.[53] As we noted from Cicero's passages, the column and its surroundings were clearly associated with debtors, creditors and the tribunal of the *triumviri capitales*, and the accentuation of this context could influence the reading that relates to the second century Maenius.

Spatial Interlinks

As the contestation across different accounts of Maenius' use of the monument demonstrates, the spatial and visual links between monuments and statues are anything but insignificant. Cultural objects could form new ideological meanings when placed next to each other.[54] In the case of the *columna Maenia*, its close connection to the statue of Marsyas created a symbolic place for both acquiring and getting out of debt and for plebeian *libertas*.[55] Before discussing this symbolic connection, it is good to survey briefly the topographical connections that link the column to administration.

As noted earlier, the column served as a working place for the *triumviri capitales*, whose duties included the supervision of prisoners.[56] The distance between the column and the *carcer*, as well as the *saxum Tarpeium* and *lautumiae* – places where detentions were served – was very efficient. The vicinity to the tribunal of the urban praetor and the plebeian tribunals was also very practical.[57] We learn of an additional connection between the Maenii and this theme from Livy, mainly that the *atrium Maenium* was *in lautumiis*.[58] The *lautumiae* were stone quarries that served also as prisons.[59] Richardson counts that the *lautumiae* were used as prisons only around thirty years until 180 B.C.[60] Platner and Ashby think that the *atrium Maenium* could have been an office or hall instead of a private house, but Richardson notes that at the time, there were probably already plenty of private houses near the Forum.[61] This confusion between the *atrium* and a private house (*domus*) is probably behind the misinterpretation of Porphyry and Pseudo-Asconius.[62] As Conese notes, following Coarelli and Welin, this term could refer to an atrium-shaped building that had public functions.[63]

It is interesting that the Maenii were also associated with the prison as their column became a place where people were convicted for crimes. The symbolic, or even practical, connection between the Maenii and usurers deepens when we turn our attention to the monuments in the vicinity of the column.

The most famous (and actually the only) visual presentation of the column is on a coin. The young moneyer L. Marcius Censorinus issued coins in 82 B.C., both with his colleagues and without them. On his personal coin (*RRC* 363/1), he chose to portray the statue of Marsyas, which stands in front of a column, and which is interpreted widely as the *columna Maenia* (Figure 11.2).[64] The close connection between the statue and the column might be the reason why the surroundings of the column became associated with debt and usury in the first place. The statue of Marsyas portrays the satyr as the minister of Pater Liber.[65] According to Torelli, the statue of Marsyas on the Roman Forum symbolized the freedom that the *plebs*

Figure 11.2 The *denarius* issued by L. Marcius Censorinus. Reverse: The statue of Marsyas with a wineskin on his shoulder. The column behind the statue is presumably the *columna Maenia*. Obverse: The head of Apollo.

Source: Image: Münzkabinett der Staatlichen Museen zu Berlin, 18217391. Photographs by Reinhard Saczewski. Public Domain Mark 1.0.

had acquired through offices and priesthoods.[66] The link to usury and debt comes from the dedicator of the monument. C. Marcius Rutilus Censorinus (cens. 294 and 265 B.C.) is thought to have erected the statue of Marsyas in the early third century.[67] His father, C. Marcius Rutilus, was the first consul (357 B.C.) of a plebeian *gens* and perhaps the originator behind the *lex Marcia* concerning usury.[68] The father and the son both practiced politics in favour of the *plebs*.[69] During this time, many plebeians were condemned to slavery because they were not able to pay their debts. Coarelli and Conese believe that there is a close semantic connection between the column and the Marsyas statue, a connection that is above all related to debtors, creditors, usurers and *libertas*.[70] The connection was so clear that the 'reader' of Horace's satire could place the characters to the area of the Forum and between the two monuments.[71] Conese also notes the important aspect that *gens Maenia* and *gens Marcia* were both plebeian families, and their presence through monuments and high offices during the fourth century patrician – plebeian conflict is significant.[72] Again, this highlights the honour bestowed to Maenius' family in a time when families competed to show their historical importance in the cityscape.[73]

How and when did the column evolve from a high symbol of honour to a means to allude to a person's misfortune and dishonour? I suggest that it was the practical location of the column and the activities that occurred near it, as well as the satirical portrayal of Horace's Maenius, that led to the accentuation of dishonour in the social memory of people perhaps already during Lucilius' time, but definitely in Horace's era and also among the later scholiasts. The money lenders operated near, not at, the column already in the time of Plautus. Mathias Hanses discusses the speech of choragus in Plautus' *Curculio* as a space "read" as a narrative.[74] He notes that when *Curculio* was performed in the late third or early second century, the Forum was turned "into a site for competitive messaging that would occasionally have seemed confused or even outright contradictory" and that the choragus "chooses which structures to highlight, which monuments to connect with one another, and what to say about them". The choragus also "tells his listeners what to remember, and conversely, what to forget".[75] The whole passage (Plaut. *Curc.* 462–86) is highly illustrative, but for us, line 480 is especially interesting: *sub veteribus, ibi sunt qui dant quique accipiunt fenore* ("Under the Old Shops, there are those who give and receive at interest").[76] As Hanses notes, the Old Shops were adorned with shields from the Samnite Wars, an example of the virtuous past, and the choragus suggests that *argentarii* dishonoured the Old Shops with their actions.[77] There might be many reasons why Plautus' choragus does not mention the *columna Maenia* in his speech. Perhaps this had to do with the orientation of the stage,[78] the rhythm of the passage[79] or just the plain reason of it being unnecessary. However, one reason for this could be that at this point, the column was not that connected to creditors and debtors yet. During Plautus' time, the column could still have been serving "only" in its original function as an honorific column.

What we do know about the column is that the *triumviri capitales* kept their office there during the time of Cicero. Cicero, Pseudo-Asconius and Symmachus are the only authors who refer to the column as standing in their own day – but even with the two latter authors as is with all others, the references are questionable. Pliny refers clearly to the past when speaking about the column's role in timekeeping. In his note about the statue on top of the column, he does not actually indicate whether the column is still standing – but he does mention right after that the column of Duillius is still at the Forum. Would it have been logical to mention that these columns (Duillius and Maenius') were both still in the Forum?[80] Possible explanations for the exclusion of this information are that the column did not exist anymore, that it had been moved away from the Forum, or that Pliny forgot it or just decided not to mention it. Nonius refers to the *columna Maenia* without a clear reference to time. Only Pseudo-Asconius uses the present tense, and Symmachus even uses the word *nunc*, "now". Pseudo-Asconius' text implies that the column still existed as a working place of the *triumviri capitales*, but this still leaves room for the interpretation that the "columna Maenia" was used as a term for the seat (similar to Cicero's reference to *ad columnam*) even if the column did not exist anymore. In Symmachus, the mention is not actually proof of the column's existence but rather a learned archaism that Symmachus uses when referring to ancient and outdated real estate rights.[81]

This leaves us with the notion that in Cicero's time, the column was used as a seat for the *triumviri capitales* and that it was utilised when pronouncing debts. In my opinion, however, we cannot say that it was the only place where the seat was located. The *triumviri capitales* were closely linked to the urban praetor, and the location of this seat changed many times.[82] Cosimo Cascione has listed office holders up until the mid-third century.[83] The spaces of the Forum were always fluctuating, with magistrates moving around with their tribunals, and it would be too much to assume that the *triumviri capitales* worked statically at the same place for centuries.

IV Conclusion

Objects can be socially powerful. With regard to honorific monuments, meaning and significance are incorporated in them at the moment of dedication. However, the meaning and significance can change as time goes by.[84] For ancient Romans, the *columna Maenia* was just another monument at the Forum, with a statue on top of it. Sometimes it was used for timekeeping, and sometimes it served as the first working place of a *triumvir capitalis*, a young man at the beginning of his career. Perhaps it was a good place to watch gladiator games held at the Forum, and sometimes it was a place for punishment.

Even though these are the practical functions of the column, people linked it to the name Maenius in different ways, and it is from these connections between the individual and the monument that people began to associate the column with debt as well. How did this happen? I offer this suggestion: Cicero is our only contemporaneous source with the *columna Maenia*, while Horace is the only one who describes the contemporary Maenius. Horace's commentators relate that this Maenius had a huge debt. Then other – later – commentators connect this Maenius to the sale of *atrium Maenium* to Cato the Elder, even though the passage in question does not mention a Maenius. One explanation for combining the second century B.C. Maenius to the other Maenius derives from a passage by Lucilius, who notes "Maenius columnam cum peteret". This, however, can mean a lot of things, especially when it comes from a satirist. Memorable aspects of the column are that 1) there was a structure called *columna Maenia*; 2) there was a Maenius who had financial difficulties; and 3) suspects were accused of crimes at the column. In addition to these, there were *maeniana* for watching the games, and sometimes these were associated with the column.

However, we do not know whether the column was actually linked to debt as a place where lists of names were announced, as *Scholia Bobiensia* claims. It might be that the scholiast is right, but this might also be a later invention that stems from the confusion of the different ways in which the name Maenius and the column were linked to each other. I find it possible that the reason for associating the *columna Maenia* with debt is because of Horace's *scurra* Maenius: The column became the symbol, or *topos*, of this kind of dishonour. This was then projected on the possible second century Maenius. Cicero's mention of Aulus Gabinius might be the reason why the commentators link it so readily to debt (*pro Sest.* 8.18.). However, when we look at the passage, we notice that it does not actually say that the creditors used to assemble at the column but that the debtor would seek harbour from the tribunate so that he would not be fastened (*ad columnam adhaeresceret*) to the column – perhaps this does not mean that his name would be written on the column, as the commentators say, but that he would be concretely tied to it as a shaming punishment. In any case, during the time of Cicero, the column had already transferred from a place of honour to one of dishonour, perhaps not because of a poor Maenius but because the place served as the seat of the *triumviri capitales*.

Furthermore, I find it possible that the column disappeared, or was moved, before the time of Pliny. Symmachus mentions the column, but it might be only an educated allusion, or a *topos*, to a former, ancient location where people suffered dishonour and to a place where the Roman magistrate officiated. We cannot say for sure that the *columna Maenia* was seen as an allusion to the seat of the *triumiviri capitales* in antiquity, but it would be beneficial if we acknowledge that it might have become so in modern times. Like the commentators and scholiasts, we as historians also create the past and decontextualise it. We are at the mercy of the memory of others who have utilised the social memory of their time in order to emphasise and clarify actions in a way that makes sense to them in the moment. My interpretation of the column and its histories follows how I have explained it earlier, and I have based my formulations of them on the aspects in the sources that I found relevant in this moment. New interpretations (or histories) might arise when looking from another perspective.

Notes

1 This research has received funding from the European Research Council (ERC) under the European Union's Horizon 2020 research and innovation programme (grant agreement No. 771874). I thank my colleagues Kaius Tuori, Samuli Simelius, Antonio Lopez Garcia and Vesa Heikkinen in the project Law, Governance and Space: Questioning the Foundations of the Republican Tradition, and especially Dr. Antonio Lopez Garcia for his great work on the current volume. I express my sincere gratitude also to Urpo Kantola for his comments on this chapter and to Dr. Zoë Jay for proofreading an earlier version of this chapter, as well as Dr. Miika Tucker for the final proof-reading and Lilian Kiander for double-checking the bibliography. All errors remain my own.
2 Varro, *Ling.* 6.49; Hanses 2020: 634. For Rome as a repository of memory, see Edwards 1996.
3 The reality that people view objects and monuments in different ways has long been acknowledged. See, for example, Bal and Bryson 1991. In the Roman context, see, for example, Elsner 1995; Elsner 1996; Stewart 2003: 14–15; Rutledge 2012: 4. For the importance of the viewer, whose interpretations of objects depended on class, ethnicity and gender, among other things, see Elsner 1995: 1–4; Rutledge 2012: 10.
4 Gale 2012: 5.
5 Rutledge 2012.
6 Hooper Greenhill 1992: 172; Rutledge 2012: 4 n. 6.
7 Purcell 2022: 179.
8 Purcell 2022: 180.
9 Russell 2016.
10 Coarelli 1985; Lehmann-Hartleben 1938.
11 Plattner and Ashby 1929; Coarelli 1983, 1985; Richardson 1992; Torelli 1993; Filippi 2017.
12 Welin 1953; Conese 2012.
13 Cic., *Div. In Caec.* 16.50.
14 Translated by L. H. G. Greenwood. Loeb Classical Library 221, 1928.
15 Lewis and Short: s.v. "reus" II. B.
16 Cic., *Cluent.* 38–39: *in eum invadunt et hominem ante pedes Q. Manli, qui tum erat triumvir, constituunt: [– –] Manlium plerique noratis: non ille honorem a pueritia, non studia virtutis, non ullum existimationis bonae fructum umquam cogitarat: ex petulanti atque improbo scurra in discordiis civitatis ad eam columnam, ad quam multorum saepe conviciis perductus erat, tum suffragiis populi pervenerat.*; Cascione 1999: 212–213, no. 10.

17 Cic., *pro Sest.* 8,18: *Alter unguentis affluens, calamistrata coma, despiciens conscios stuprorum ac veteres vexatores aetatulae suae, puteali et faeneratorum gregibus inflatus, a quibus compulsus olim, ne in Scyllaeo illo aeris alieni tamquam in fretu ad columnam adhaeresceret, in tribunatus portum perfugerat, contemnebat equites Romanos, minitabatur senatui, venditabat se operis atque ab iis se ereptum, ne de ambitu causam diceret, praedicabat ab isdemque se etiam invito senatu provinciam sperare dicebat; eamque nisi adeptus esset, se incolumem nullo modo fore arbitrabatur.*
Translation: Here is one of them. Dripping with unguents, with waved hair, looking down on the partners of his debaucheries and the greybeard abusers of his dainty youth, puffed up with rage against the Exchange and the herds of usurers, who had once driven him to take refuge in the harbour of a tribunate from the danger of being stuck up on the Column in a sea of debt as in those Straits of Scylla, he spoke with contempt of the Roman Knights, he threatened the Senate, he ingratiated himself with hired ruffians, and boasted that they had saved him from standing his trial on a charge of bribery, he said that he hoped they would also help him to a province, Senate or no Senate, and if he failed to get it he thought nothing could save him. Translated by R. Gardner. Loeb Classical Library 309.

18 Kaster 2006: 356. Cicero refers to this when he explains how the Senate (and Sestius) was working to get him back from exile. The Senate met at the Temple of Honos and Virtus. The gladiator games were organised by P. Cornelius Scipio in memory of Q. Metellus Pius.

19 *Tertius consensus fuit in horarum observatione, iam hic ratione accedens, quando et a quo in Graecia reperta, diximus secundo volumine. serius etiam hoc Romae contigit: xii tabulis ortus tantum et occasus nominantur, post aliquot annos adiectus est et meridies, accenso consulum id pronuntiante cum a curia inter Rostra et Graecostasim proxpexisset solem. a columna Maenia ad carcerem inclinato sidere supremam pronuntiavit, sed hoc serenis tantum diebus, usque ad primum Punicum bellum.*

20 Torelli 1993: s.v. "Columna Maenia"; Coarelli 1983: 141; Richardson 1992: s.v. "Columna Maenia".

21 Plin., *HN* 34.20–21: *Non vetus et bigarum celebratio in iis, qui praetura functi curru vecti essent per circum; antiquior columnarum, sicuti C. Maenio, qui devicerat priscos Latinos, quibus ex foedere tertias praedae populus Romanus praestabat, eodemque in consulatu in suggestu rostra devictis Antiatibus fixerat anno urbis ccccxvi, item C. Duillio, qui primus navalem triumphum egit de Poenis, quae est etiam nunc in foro, item L. Minucio praefecto annonae extra portam Trigeminam unciaria stipe conlata – nescio an primo honore tali a populo, antea enim a senatu erat, – praeclara res, ni frivolis coepisset initiis.* The *columna* Minucia is depicted in the *denarii* of C. Minucius Augurinus (*RRC* 242/1, 135 B.C.) and Ti. Minucius Augurinus (*RRC* 243/1, 134 B.C.). The two moneyers were presumably brothers. Crawford 1974: 273–274; Yarrow 2021: 44, 178.

22 Jex-Blake and Sellers 1968: 17.

23 Liv. 8.13.5 and 9.

24 Non. 1, p. 91 L. He continues, "*Cicero Academicorum lib. IV (21) (II, 70): 'iterim ille, cum aestuaret, veterum, ut Maenianorum, sic Academicorum umbram secutus est.'*"

25 Fest., p. 120 L.

26 Isid., *Orig.* XV 3.11.

27 Porphyr., ad Hor. *Sat.* 1.3.21; Psudacr. ad Hor., *Sat.* 1.3.21.

28 Pseudascon., *ad* Cic. *divin. in Caecil.* 16.50.

29 Liv. 39.44.7.

30 Schol. Bob., *pro Sest.* 8.18.; Schol. Bob., *pro Sest.* 58.124.

31 Lehmann-Hartleben 1938.

32 Coarelli 1985; Conese 2012.

33 Symm., *Ep.* 5.54.3.

34 Richardson 1992: s.v. "columna Maenia".

35 Kondratieff 2009: 352–353; cf. Lehmann-Hartleben 1938: 286.
36 Filippi 2017:158; Coarelli 1985: 143–146.
37 Purcell 2022: 181.
38 They were awarded with a triumph over the victory, and that equestrian statues of them were erected to the Forum. Cf. Liv. 8.13.
39 Liv. 8.14.
40 Purcell 2022: 181.
41 Coarelli 1985: 44.
42 Purcell 2022: 181.
43 Plin., *HN* 35.42.: *"maeniana", inquit Varro, "omnia operiebat serapionis tabula sub veteribus"*. Also, Filippi sees *maeniana* specifically at shops behind the porticoes. Filippi 2017: 158.
44 Conese 2012: 46.
45 Cic., *Phil.* 9.7.16.
46 Hor., *Ep.* 1.15.26–32.
47 Conese 2012: 48.
48 Porph., *ad* Hor *Sat*. 1.3.21.
49 Conese 2012: 44.
50 Lewis and Short: s.v. "peto".
51 Noted also by Torelli 1993: s.v. "columna Maenia".
52 Hillard and Beness 2012: note 2.
53 Hillard and Beness 2012: 826.
54 Rutledge 2012: 21; Gregory 1994: 84–85.
55 Conese 2012.
56 Cascione 1999: 161ff.
57 Cascione 1999: 80.
58 Liv. 39.44.7.
59 Liv. 32.26.17; 37.3.8. Richardson 1992: s.v. "Lautumiae".
60 Richardson 1992: s.v. "Lautumiae".
61 Platner and Ashby 1929: 131–132; Richardson 1992: s.v. "Atrium Maenium". See Chapter 6 by S. Simelius in this volume.
62 Conese 2012: 45.
63 Conese 2012: 45.
64 Coarelli 1985; Torelli 1993: s.v. "columna Maenia"; Conese 2012.
65 Conese 2012: 35–36.
66 Statues of Marsyas as the minister of Liber Pater were also erected on the *fora* of *oppidae*. In the Roman Forum, it became a symbol of the freedom that the *plebs* had progressively acquired through the conquest of offices and priesthoods. Torelli 1982: 105.
67 Conese 2012: 37; Torelli 1982.
68 Mentioned by Gaius in Inst. 4,23.: *lex Marcia adversus fenatores, ut si usuras exegissent, de his reddendis per manus iniectionem cum eis ageretur*. "Lex Marcia against money-lenders, whereby if they demand interest, the proceeding of the *manus iniectio* would be used against them to obtain a refund" Conese 2012; 39.
69 It is thought that C. Marcius Rutilus Censorinus served as a censor twice, in 294 and 265 B.C., – hence the cognomen Censorinus – and he continued his father's (C. Marcius Rutilus senior) politics in favour of the plebs and against debts.
70 Crawford does not agree. He sees the statue as only an allusion to the name Marcius, and the later use of Marsyas to symbolize a general claim to *libertas* is irrelevant according to him. Crawford 1974: 378. However, since we are now talking about the changes of places and their reception, I see that it is not irrelevant but is connected to the use of the space. Conese 2012: 36.
71 Conese 2012: 51.
72 Conese 2012: 47.

73 Hanses 2020: 635.
74 Hanses 2020.
75 Hanses 2020: 635.
76 Translation in Hanses 2020: 638.
77 Hanses 2020: 651.
78 For different options, see Hanses 2020: 639–642.
79 But if Plautus would have wanted to include the column to the speech, the meter would not have been an obstacle.
80 Noted in Lehmann-Hartleben 1938: 288.
81 Lehmann-Hartleben 1938: 285; Rivolta Tiberga 1992: 164.
82 Kondratieff 2009, 2010; Lopez Garcia forthcoming.
83 Cascione 1999.
84 Marshall describes these socially powerful objects as "inscribed" objects. Marshall 2008. The different meanings of an object and its relationships to people can be approached by the framework of "biography of objects". For the "biography of objects", see Kopytoff 1986; Gosden and Marshall 1999; for a clear synopsis for the anthropological and archaeological approach with this framework, see Joy 2009.

References

Bal, M., and Bryson, N. 1991: 'Semiotics and Art History', *The Art Bulletin (New York, N.Y.)* 73, 174–208.

Cascione, C. 1999: *Tresviri Capitales. Storia Di Una Magistratura Minore*. Pubblicazioni del dipartimento di diritto romano e storia della scienza romanistica dell'universita degli studi di Napoli 'Frederico II'.

Coarelli, F. 1983: *Il Foro Romano. 1, Periodo arcaico*, Roma.

Coarelli, F. 1985: *Il Foro Romano. 2, Periodo Repubblicano e Augusteo*, Roma.

Conese, C. 2012: 'Maenius absentem Novium cum carperet (Horace, Satires 1.3.21.): Characters, Places, Monuments', *Hermathena* 193, 33–54.

Crawford, M.H. 1974: *Roman Republican Coinage*, 2 vols, London.

Edwards, C. 1996: *Writing Rome: Textual Approaches to the City* (Roman Literature and Its Contexts), New York.

Elsner, J. 1995: *Art and the Roman Viewer: The Transformation of Art from the Pagan World to Christianity* (Cambridge Studies in New Art History and Criticism), Cambridge.

Elsner, J. (ed.) 1996: *Art and Text in Roman Culture* (Cambridge Studies in New Art History and Criticism), Cambridge, New York.

Filippi, D. 2017: 'Region VIII. Forum Romanum Magnum', in A. Carandini, P. Carafa, and A. C. Halavais (eds), *The Atlas of Ancient Rome: Biography and Portraits of the City*, Princeton, NJ, 143–206.

Gale, M. 2012: 'Editorial', *Hermathena* 2012, 5–9.

Gosden, C., and Marshall, Y. 1999: 'The Cultural Biography of Objects', *World Archaeology* 31, 169–178.

Gregory, A. P. 1994: '"Powerful Images": Responses to Portraits and the Political Uses of Images in Rome', *Journal of Roman Archaeology* 7, 80–99.

Hanses, M. 2020: 'Men among Monuments: Roman Topography and Roman Memory in Plautus' Curculio', *Classical Philology* 115, 630–658.

Hillard, T. W., and Beness, J. L. 2012: 'Late Antique Memories of Republican Political Polemic: Pseudo-Acro *ad* Hor. *Sat.* 2.1.67 and a *Dictum Macedonici*', *The Classical Quarterly* 62, 816–826.

Hooper Greenhill, E. 1992: *Museums and the Shaping of Knowledge*, London.
Jex-Blake, K., and Sellers, E. 1968: *The Elder Pliny's Chapters on the History of Art*, Chicago, IL.
Joy, J. 2009: 'Reinvigorating Object Biography: Reproducing the Drama of Object Lives', *World Archaeology* 41(4), 540–556.
Kaster, R. A. 2006: *Cicero: Speech on Behalf of Publius Sestius* (Clarendon Ancient History Series), Oxford.
Kondratieff, E. 2010: 'The Urban Praetor's Tribunal in the Roman Republic', in F. De Angelis (ed.), *Spaces of Justice in the Roman World*, Leiden, Boston, MA, 89–126.
Kondratieff, E. J. 2009: 'Reading Rome's Evolving Civic Landscape in Context: Tribunes of the Plebs and the Praetor's Tribunal', *Phoenix* 63, 322–360.
Kopytoff, I. 1986: 'The Cultural Biography of Things: Commoditization as Process', *The Social Life of Things*, 64–92.
Lehmann-Hartleben, K. 1938: 'Maenianum and Basilica', *American Journal of Philology* 59, 280–296.
Lopez Garcia, A. forthcoming: 'Fora Litibus Omnia Fervent: The Transfer of the Tribunals in Rome from the Forum to the Courtroom'.
Marshall, Y. 2008: 'The Social Lives of Lived and Inscribed Objects: A Lapita Perspective', *Journal of the Polynesian Society* 117, 59–101.
Osann, F. 1844: *Commentatio de Columna Maenia*, Hessen.
Platner, S. B., and Ashby, T. 1929: *A Topographical Dictionary of Ancient Rome*, London.
Purcell, N. 2022: 'Historians in the Forum', in D. Filippi (ed.), *Rethinking the Roman City. Studies in Roman Space and Urbanism*, London, New York, 177–212.
Richardson, L., Jr 1992: *A New Topographical Dictionary of Ancient Rome*, Baltimore, MD.
Rivolta Tiberga, P. 1992: *Commento storico al libro V dell'Epistolario di Q. Aurelio Simmaco: introduzione, commento storico, testo, traduzione, indici*. Biblioteca di studi antichi 67, Pisa.
Russell, A. 2016: *The Politics of Public Space in Republican Rome*, Cambridge.
Rutledge, S. H. 2012: *Ancient Rome as a Museum: Power, Identity, and the Culture of Collecting* (Oxford Studies in Ancient Culture and Representation), Oxford.
Stewart, P. 2003: *Statues in Roman Society: Representation and Response* (Oxford Studies in Ancient Culture and Representation), Oxford.
Torelli, M. 1982: *Typology & Structure of Roman Historical Reliefs*, Ann Arbor, MI.
Torelli, M. 1993: 'Columna Maenia' in E. Steinby (ed.), *Lexicon Topographicum Urbis*, 301–302.
Welin, E. 1953: *Studien zur Topographie des Forum Romanum*, Lund.
Yarrow, L. M. 2021: *The Roman Republic to 49 BCE. Using Coins as Sources* (Guides to the Coinage of the Ancient World), Cambridge.

12 A Measure of Economy? The Organisation of Public Games in the City of Rome and the Development of the Urban Cityscape

Jessica Bartz

I Introduction

During the republican period, entertainment structures such as theatres, amphitheatres, stadia, and circuses functioned as an important instrument for the formation of political opinion, as well as the expression of opinions about elected magistrates and senators by Roman citizens.[1] Therefore, in addition to common meeting places such as the Roman Forum or the Saepta, both temporary and permanent venues in Rome were an important platform for the communication between the political elite and the population.[2]

The reason why permanent theatres were absent in Rome, while such permanent buildings already existed in other Italian cities, is assumed to lie in a ban on such structures dating to the second century B.C.,[3] which is partly seen as a measure to prevent the political assembly of the population and thus counteract the excessive politicisation and democratisation of the people, as well as being a concrete visualisation of senatorial power.[4] Despite the fact that the judicial basis is very vague, the complex system of the organisation of the *ludi publici*[5] during the republican and the imperial period – with a focus on the diachronic shifts – has to be reviewed in detail in order to understand the reasons for the gradual adoption of the construction of permanent structures for these various games.

II The Organisation of Games Staged in Public

In the preface of the tenth book of his treatise on architecture, Vitruvius advises:

> *Nec solum id vitium in aedificiis, sed etiam in muneribus, quae a magistratibus foro gladiatorum scaenisque ludorum dantur, quibus nec mora neque expectatio conceditur, sed necessitas finito tempore perficere cogit, id est sedes spectaculorum velorumque inductiones et ea omnia, quae scaenicis moribus per machinationem ad spectationes populo comparantur. in his vero opus est prudentia diligens et ingenii doctissimi cogitata, quod nihil eorum perficitur sine machinatione studiorumque vario ac sollerti vigore.*

And this defect [of miscalculations] is found not only in building, but also in the public spectacles which are given by magistrates; whether of gladiators in the forum, or of plays with a theatrical setting. In these neither delay nor expectation is permitted, but necessity compels the performance to take place within a fixed time. There is the seating for the shows, and there are the awnings to be drawn, and all those other things which, in accordance with theatrical tradition, are provided for popular spectacles by means of machinery. Herein the requisites are careful foresight and the resources of a highly trained intelligence. For nothing of this sort is done without mechanical contrivance to which an alert and masterly attention has been applied.[6]

As Vitruvius points out, by organising games the Roman magistrates and aristocrats literally turn into event managers. From different ancient sources it becomes clear that parameters such as budgeting,[7] logistics,[8] marketing,[9] scheduling,[10] and security[11] – which are also key aspects of modern event management – were important factors in ancient Rome as well.

The organisation of public games as part of cultic festivals in honour of the Roman gods primarily lay in the hands of the elected magistrates who were responsible for their successful realisation[12] (*cura ludorum*),[13] which would as a side effect also promote their prospective political careers.[14] In addition to the official *ludi* listed in the cultic calendar, public games were also irregularly given in the context of triumphal processions,[15] as dedication games after finishing a building project,[16] or as honorary funeral games,[17] which were all organized and funded by aristocrats.[18] The growing total number of all types of public games increased the pressure on the available spaces. Areas such as the Circus Maximus, which housed chariot races, animal fights, and athletic games,[19] were also used for the publicly and privately funded games. The Roman Forum, on the other hand, was a particularly heavily used space where other functions had to be suspended in order to host games.[20]

Both sites, the Circus Maximus and the Roman Forum, were permanent venues for different kinds of games, for which they were also given various temporary configurations and were adapted to the needs of the different types of spectacles. In contrast, temporary theatres were erected for the scenic games, whose localisation is still uncertain.[21]

III The Emerge of Permanent Theatres: A Measure of Economy?

During the course of the republican period the official public games continuously became longer,[22] and in connection with this the financial burden[23] of the elected magistrates also grew, and the pressure on the spaces used for the games increased. From this perspective, it might be the case that practical and not only political considerations led to the disappearance of temporary entertainment structures and to the emergence of permanent venues.

Organisation of Public Games and Development of Cityscape 253

This assumption also seems to be reflected in ancient accounts. Reflecting on permanent theatres, the earlier temporarily erected monumental structures were evaluated by Tacitus as follows:

Sed et consultum parsimoniae, quod perpetua sedes theatro locata sit potius, quam immenso sumptu singulos per annos consurgeret ac destrueretur.

But, more than this, it had been a measure of economy when the theatre was housed in a permanent building instead of being reared and razed, year after year, at enormous expense.[24]

The ancient historian implied that erecting permanent theatres seemed more reasonable than the use of expensive, annually erected theatres. Indeed, the luxurious but also lavish decoration of the temporary theatres, connected with the increased prosperity that accompanied Roman military conquests, is repeatedly described. Concerning their outward appearance, Valerius Maximus notes:

Religionem ludorum crescentibus opibus secuta lautitia est. eius instinctu Q. Catulus, Campanam imitatus luxuriam, primus spectantium consessum velorum umbraculis texit. Cn. Pompeius ante omnes aquae per semitas decursu aestivum minuit fervorem. Claudius Pulcher scaenam varietate colorum adumbravit, vacuis ante pictura tabulis extentam. quam totam argento C. Antonius, auro Petreius, ebore Q. Catulus praetexuit. versatilem fecerunt Luculli, argentatis choragiis P. Lentulus Spinther adornavit. translatum, antea punicis indutum tunicis, M. Scaurus exquisito genere vestis cultum induxit.

As wealth increased, elegance followed religion in the games. At its prompting Q. Catulus [69 B.C.] was the first to cover the sitting spectators with a shady awning in imitation of Campanian luxury. Cn. Pompeius [55 B.C.] led the way in tempering summer heat with water flowing in channels. Claudius Pulcher [100/99 B.C.] applied a variety of colours to the stage, which previously had consisted of unpainted boards. C. Antonius [66 B.C.] lined the whole of it with silver, Petreius [60s B.C.] with gold, Q. Catulus [69 B.C.] with ivory. The Luculli [79 B.C.] made it revolving, P. Lentulus Spinther [60 B.C.] decorated it with silver properties. M. Scaurus [58 B.C.] brought on the parade, previously dressed in scarlet tunics, arrayed in specially chosen costume.[25]

The Scaurus theatre seems to be the culmination of the development of temporary theatres.[26] Built in 58 B.C. by the curule aedile, the magnificent theatre should have consisted of a three-storey stage decorated with 360 rows of columns made of marble, glass, and gilded wood with 3,000 bronze statues between them; the building is also said to have been able to accommodate more than 80,000 people.[27] However, what is usually not noted is the fact that Pliny does not regard this theatre as an example of the greatness of temporary theatres – but quite the opposite. Together with Curio's famous rotating double theatre of 52 B.C.,[28] Pliny uses these two structures to illustrate the comparable luxury and extravagance of the emperors of his days. However, it is very likely that the numbers provided in such sources are highly exaggerated and do not provide any reliable indication of the structures' actual size (and outward appearance), which one could then use to locate them somewhere in the urban context.

Nevertheless, it seems that it was not possible to erect theatres or similar structures everywhere in the urban public space during the late republican period, as prescriptions preserved on the Tabula Heracleensis indicate:

> *Quos lud[os] quisque ⟨urbei⟩ Romae p(ropius)ue u(rbei) R(omae) passus m(ille) faciet, quo minus ei eorum ludorum caussa scaenam pulpitum ceteraque quae ad eos ludos opus erunt in loco publico ponere statuere eisque diebus, quibus eos faciet, loco publico utei liceat, e(ius) h(ac) l(ege) n(ihilum) r(ogatur). vacat*
>
> Whatever games anyone shall hold within (the city of) Rome or nearer the city of Rome than one mile, to the effect that it may not be lawful for him for the sake of those games to set up or erect a stage and platform and whatever else shall be necessary for those games in public space and to use public space on those days on which he shall hold them (the games), nothing of it is proposed by this statute.[29]

The presumably Caesarean text implies that from the time these prescriptions came into effect the magistrates were allowed to erect structures for the *ludi* everywhere in the public space *(in loco publico)*. Unfortunately, the text does not provide any further information about the situation before the law came into force. However, there are some indications that these structures could not be erected everywhere throughout the city.[30] This is finally connected to the question of the temporal organisation of the usually used spaces, as well as the prestige associated with being allowed to use such spaces, like the Roman Forum, especially for private games.

IV The Location of Wooden Theatres, Italian Theatre-Temples, and the Theatre of Pompey

In the case of public games, however, the question of whether theatres could have been erected in a public space does not arise, since this was, after all, done in the context of cultic festivals for which a religious obligation to hold these games existed. Accordingly, spaces must have been available and architectures built for this purpose. However, it has not yet been clarified where exactly these structures were located in the city of Rome. Only a few ancient indications provide reliable hints for a possible location of the frequently used, but certainly temporary theatres:[31]

i) In 179 B.C. a *theatrum et proscaenium* was erected *ad Apollinis*, which is commonly assumed to be a spot near the temple of Apollo Medicus, later Apollo Sosianus.[32] This might be confirmed by an episode of 63 B.C., when Cicero was able to switch between the theatre and the temple of Bellona nearby.[33] Planned by Caesar and later realised under Augustus, the permanent Theatre of Marcellus was also erected in this area,[34] which indicates a possible functional continuity.

ii) For the year 56 B.C. Cicero explicitly described scenic games on the Palatine hill as part of the *ludi Megalenses*.[35] It has already been suggested that the temple podium and the steps of the temple may have been used as a kind of a *cavea*,[36] but it is not clear whether and to what extent an additional wooden theatre was constructed there.[37]

iii) Under Augustus in 17 B.C., a wooden theatre was erected *in campo secundum* or *ad Tiberim*, where the reintroduced *ludi Latini* were performed as part of the *ludi saeculares*.[38] The choice of location can be explained by religious motives, as the secular games have been connected to the nearby the altar of Dis and Proserpina at the *Tarentum*.[39]

iv) Another temporary wooden theatre on the Palatine hill is documented for the imperial period, when during the *ludi Augustales* in A.D. 41 the emperor Caligula was murdered in a wooden theatre there.[40]

Excepting that there is no evidence preserved for scenic games of the *ludi Romani* taking place on the Capitoline Hill, no example of a wooden theatre exists that indicates that such structures were not erected nearby the actual place of worship. Therefore, it seems that in Rome not only did a close sacred connection to the specific cult and scenic games exist,[41] but also a topographical relation. Analogous examples of a close connection between cult temples and entertainment structures are illustrated by various examples of so-called theatre-temples in Italy, which can be understood as permanent role models of the situation in Rome.[42]

The Theatre of Pompey also represents a comparable theatre-temple.[43] It is generally assumed that Pompey had a need to legalise his new complex. Tertullian notes that he secured his theatre by building a temple for Venus Victrix on top of it, and therefore the *cavea* did not represent seats for spectators, but rather functioned as a huge semi-circular staircase to the temple.[44] The cause for this behaviour is seen in the already mentioned *senatus consultum* from the mid-second century B.C., which – according to many scholars – banned stone theatres.[45] However, on the one hand the records do not lead to the conclusion that the ban specifically involved a building made of stone,[46] and on the other hand, following Valerius Maximus, no specific kind of architecture was forbidden by the senatorial decree:

atque etiam senatus consulto cautum est ne quis in urbe propiusve passus mille subsellia posuisse sedensve ludos spectare vellet, ut scilicet remissioni animorum standi virilitas propria Romanae gentis iuncta esset.

It was also laid down by senatorial decree that no one in Rome or within a mile thereof should set up benches or make to watch a show sitting down, no doubt to the intent that mental relaxation should go together with the virility of a standing posture proper to the Roman nation.[47]

The *subsellia* mentioned as being prospectively banned are simple small seats, not a fully elaborated structure. Furthermore, it is above all a prohibition of sitting, which was apparently understood as effeminate.[48] Even if the discussion about the meaning of the *senatus consultum* is difficult, because of the divergent ancient traditions and thoroughly controversial scholarly discussion, it does not seem to have had any sustainable influence,[49] as later theatres were continuously erected, especially during the first century B.C. But the lack of permanent theatres in Rome, which needs to be explained, cannot be argued to be a consequence of the *senatus consultum*.

To return to Tertullian's estimation of the Theatre of Pompey, the late antique and Christian author, who had a fundamentally negative attitude towards games, merely instrumentalised the episode of 154/1 B.C. around the supposed ban initiated by P. Scipio Nasica Corculum and the permanent structure erected by Pompey, so that the credibility of his statements must be treated with caution.[50] In general, any ancient criticism of Pompey's complex must be viewed in a differentiated manner.[51]

So, leaving aside subjective assessments of the ancient sources, one could ask: Was the Theatre of Pompey the right solution for the use of urban space regarding entertainment structures? Did this building effectively replace the expensive practice of raising up wooden theatres year after year? What is known about the functional role of this complex?

Apart from hosting games for Venus Victrix, the complex does not seem to have hosted any other important games.[52] It is known that when Caesar was murdered on the Ides of March in 44 B.C. near the Curia, gladiators came rushing from the theatre.[53] No specific cult festival is scheduled for this day, and gladiatorial combats were not part of any important cultic festival at this time,[54] which means that their presence must have been due to a more minor occasion.

After Marcus Titius executed Sextus Pompeius in Miletus, he returned to Rome, where he organised games in 35 or 34 B.C. in the theatre of the famous ancestor of Sextus Pompeius.[55] The audience, which still honoured Pompeius Magnus as well as his relatives, expelled Marcus Titius from the theatre. It is not known whether Marcus Titius later held a magistracy or received a triumph.[56]

Games of a rather minor character are suggested in an inscription (Figure 12.1) wherein the freedman Cornelius Surus as *magister scribarum poetarum* organised *ludi* or *munera "in theatro lapidio"*.[57]

It is very likely that this designation refers to the Theatre of Pompey, as the description of a 'stone theatre' is similar to several mentions in the *fasti* and inscriptions using *theatrum marmoreum/lapideum* as a synonym for the complex.[58] The focus on the building material seems to be a reflex to distinguish between the previously common wooden theatres and the newly built permanent structure.

[-Cor]nelius P(ubli) l(ibertus) Surus,/
[nome]nclator, mag(ister)/
[Capito]linus V a(nnis) VIIII,/
[mag(ister)? s]utorum, praeco/
[ab ae]rario, ex tribus/
[decuri]eis (:decuriis), mag(ister) scr(ibarum) poetar(um)/
[ludos] fecit in theatro lapidio (:lapideo),/
[ac]cens(us) co(n)s(ulis) et cens(oris)

Organisation of Public Games and Development of Cityscape 257

Figure 12.1 Funerary inscription of Cornelius Surus (*AE* 1959 147), 55–20 B.C., found in Rome at the Piazzale Labicano, now in Rome, Musei Capitolini, Tabularium, CE 6765.

Source: Image: Epigraphic Database Roma with the authorisation of Epigraphic Database Roma. © Roma – Sovraintendenza Capitolina ai Beni Culturali.

The first time that the Theatre of Pompey became part of an important official cultic festival was a rather unusual one, namely the *ludi saeculares* of 17 B.C., when the theatre was integrated into the venues for the scenic games.[59]

On the other hand, temporary theatres were still erected; for example, the already mentioned rotating double theatre of the senator C. Scribonius Curio, which was erected in 52 B.C.[60] It is also known that Curio was curule aedile the year before. Plutarch reports that he and Favonius erected separate theatres for the *ludi Romani*.[61] In 46 B.C. the Forum Iulium was inaugurated, an event which was combined with funeral games for Caesar's deceased daughter Iulia and his outstanding triumphal celebrations. These games were described in various written sources,[62] and none of them report that the Theatre of Pompey was used. The Theatre of Pompey thus did not seem to have functioned as the main venue for scenic games, at least not from the beginning of its existence. Wooden theatres still seemed to be the norm until the early Augustan period,[63] but the advantages of stone theatres were indeed established over time,[64] as more political factors formed the background for a shift away from temporary theatres.

V The Rising Imperial System and the Transformation of the Roman *Ludi*

After the assassination of Caesar, the sources reporting public games are very rare. This is reflected in the fragmentary list of known curule and plebeian aediles as well as the *praetores urbani*. Except for an inscribed column naming the aediles of 44 B.C.,[65] only sporadic anecdotes prove that magistrates were responsible for games. For example, Critonius, the aedile of the plebs, gave the *ludi Cereales* and forbade the display of a gilded throne and garland for Caesar in 44 B.C.[66] In 37 B.C., M. Oppius, son of the proscribed M. Oppius, did not have enough money for holding the office of curule aedile, which is why he refused the election.[67] In 36 B.C., due to a lack of appropriate candidates, no aediles were elected.[68] Only the close follower of Augustus, M. Vipsanius Agrippa, was able to present himself as an organiser of games, in 40 B.C. as *praetor urbanus* and later in 33 B.C. as an aedile.[69]

On a coin of L. Regulus the obverse shows a portrait and on the reverse one of the very rare depictions of republican *venationes* can be seen (Figure 12.2).[70] The interpretation of the image is not easy. On the one hand it can be assumed that Regulus, in addition to his office as a moneyer, also functioned as an aedile or praetor,[71] and drew attention to his achievements as an organiser of games; however, the image can also be interpreted prospectively, in the sense that Regulus is promising that he would organise games if he was elected to a future office.[72] Alternatively, games by someone else could have been depicted.[73] The coin image exemplifies the difficulties in properly understanding the organisation of games outside of the network connected to Augustus.

To sum up: on the one hand, the state of knowledge regarding public games for the period between 44 and 33 B.C. is very thin. This may be due to the fact that the games were no longer as sensational as they had been in the previous decades. Furthermore, the available information suggests that due to the proscriptions that took place during the time of the second triumvirate there was no longer a financially strong aristocracy in Rome that could afford to host splendid games. In addition, considering the high costs on the one hand and the developing principate system on the other, official magistracies were increasingly unattractive for ambitious

Figure 12.2 Coin depicting head of L. Regulus (praetor) (obverse) and animal hunting scene (reverse). Institute of Classical Archaeology of the Eberhard Karls University of Tübingen, ID1479.

Source: Photographs by Stefan Krmnicek.

politicians. It therefore makes sense that in one of Horace's *Satirae* a father recommends the following to his sons:

> *praeterea, ne vos titillet gloria, iure*
> 180 *iurando obstringam ambo: uter aedilis fueritve*
> *vestrum praetor, is intestabilis et sacer esto.*
> *in cicere atque faba bona tu perdasque lupinis,*
> *latus ut in circo spatiere aut1 aeneus ut stes,*
> *nudus agris, nudus nummis, insane, paternis?*
> 185 *scilicet ut plausus, quos fert Agrippa, feras tu,*
> *astuta ingenuum volpes imitata leonem.*

Further, that ambition may not tickle your fancy, I shall bind you both by an oath: whichever of you becomes aedile or praetor, let him be outlawed and accursed. Would you waste your wealth on vetches, beans, and lupines, that you may play the swell and strut in the Circus, or be set up in bronze, though stripped of the lands, stripped, madman, of the money your father left: to the end, oh yes, that you may win the applause which Agrippa wins – a cunning fox mimicking the noble lion?[74]

But it was not only due to the barriers to private investments that the old republican system had collapsed. Cassius Dio reports in 28 B.C. that the *aerarium* was empty, which is why Augustus had to step in to finance the mandatory religious games:

> Ὁ δ' οὖν Καῖσαρ ἔς τε τὰς θεωρίας ἐκ τῶν ἰδίων δῆθεν ἀνήλισκε, καὶ ἐπειδὴ χρημάτων τῷ δημοσίῳ ἐδέησεν, ἐδανείσατό τινα καὶ ἔδωκεν αὐτῷ, πρός τε τὴν διοίκησίν σφων δύο κατ' ἔτος ἐκ τῶν ἐστρατηγηκότων αἱρεῖσθαι ἐκέλευσε. . . . πρὸς δὲ δὴ τούτοις τὸν ἀστυνόμον αὐτὸς ἀπέδειξεν· ὃ καὶ αὖθις πολλάκις ἐποίησε.

> Now Caesar allowed it to be understood that he was spending his private means upon these festivals, and when money was needed for the public treasury, he borrowed some and supplied the want. . . . In addition to all this, Caesar himself appointed the praetor urbanus, as, indeed, he often did subsequently.[75]

As stated before, it seemed to have become incredibly difficult to find financially strong politicians who could afford the magistracies. Augustus, who now also contributed to the public funds, took the right to appoint the *praetor urbanus* without any election. After 22 B.C., as Cassius Dio again points out, the organisation of the public games was also strongly reformed and regulated by the princeps:

> καὶ τοῖς μὲν στρατηγοῖς τὰς πανηγύρεις πάσας προσέταξεν, ἔκ τε τοῦ δημοσίου δίδοσθαί τι αὐτοῖς κελεύσας, καὶ προσαπειπὼν μήτε ἐς ἐκείνας οἴκοθέν τινα πλεῖον τοῦ ἑτέρου ἀναλίσκειν μήθ' ὁπλομαχίαν μήτ' ἄλλως εἰ μὴ ἡ βουλὴ ψηφίσαιτο, μήτ' αὖ πλεονάκις ἢ δὶς ἐν ἑκάστῳ ἔτει, μήτε

πλειόνων εἴκοσι καὶ ἑκατὸν ἀνδρῶν ποιεῖν· τοῖς δ' ἀγορανόμοις τοῖς κουρουλίοις τὴν τῶν ἐμπιμπραμένων1 κατάσβεσιν ἐνεχείρισεν, ἑξακοσίους σφίσι βοηθοὺς δούλους δούς.

He committed the charge of all the festivals to the praetors, commanding that an appropriation should be given them from the public treasury, and also forbidding any one of them to spend more than another from his own means on these festivals, or to give a gladiatorial combat unless the senate decreed it, or, in fact, oftener than twice in each year or with more than one hundred and twenty men. To the curule aediles he entrusted the putting out of fires, for which purpose he granted them six hundred slaves as assistants.[76]

The old system with competing magistrates and immeasurably high expenses could no longer be sustained, and with his new regulations Augustus addressed the criticism that republican aristocrats had wasted money in doing so. From now on, only the praetors would be organisers of public games, and the intense competition of upcoming aristocrats finally came to an end.[77]

It is important to note, however, that the imperial family seems to have been excluded from these regulations, so that Augustus' games and those of his family always overshadowed those of the magistrates. In addition, Augustus had managed to connect all kinds of public and formerly private games to himself and his family. For example, following Caesar's assassination for the first time,[78] and especially during the time of the Principate, gladiatorial combats were no longer exclusively staged at public funerals, but also at triumphal processions, as part of games following dedications, and as part of public religious festivals.[79] This gave them the character of state-regulated and public events.[80] These various new regulations had the aim of concentrating or monopolising the games by the princeps, and also the later Iulian-Claudian emperors.[81]

VI Conclusion

The following aspects must be considered to answer the question of why it took so long to build a permanent theatre in Rome:

i) Permanent entertainment venues had already existed since the time of the Etruscan kings.[82] The Circus Maximus was a highly multifunctional space, where not only chariot races took place, but also *venationes* and athletic contests. Only if the planned event were of such a huge size that it could not be held in the Circus Maximus would separate buildings have been erected.[83] On the other hand, an official permission seems to have been needed to use certain spaces, such as the Forum Romanum.[84]

ii) It is very likely that scenic performances took place in the vicinity of the corresponding temple. Because of its historical development the city of Rome had a huge number of important religious centres for which no permanent stone theatre was viable. This led to a multitude of temporary 'theatre-temple-complexes' in the city of Rome.

iii) As mentioned in the ancient sources, erecting a huge temporary theatre was costly. However, it has to be taken into account that building a permanent theatre did not only entail the costs of the construction materials. As Tacitus notes for the Theatre of Pompey:
At Pompei theatrum igne fortuito haustum Caesar exstructurum pollicitus est, eo quod nemo e familia restaurando sufficeret, manente tamen nomine Pompei.

On the other hand, the rebuilding of the Theatre of Pompey, destroyed by a casual fire, was undertaken by the Caesar [Augustus], on the ground that no member of the family was equal to the task of restoration: the name of Pompey was, however, to remain.[85]

The first stone theatre did not belong to the public infrastructure, which is why no magistrate had been made responsible for its care and maintenance in the early Augustan period. Permanent complexes meant a significant and lasting financial burden.[86] For temporary buildings, on the other hand, no long-term financial planning and maintenance were necessary, as such structures could have been erected for a specific event and for a relatively short period of use. It is therefore not surprising that the first permanent entertainment structures could only be maintained if they were collectively overseen[87] or were supported by a very rich benefactor, which in the city of Rome could only be the princeps.

iv) Permanent entertainment structures that were privately financed were primarily built on privately owned land.[88] Thus, the cityscape of Rome is partly a conglomerate of constructed complexes that have been transferred from the private to the public sphere.

The shift away from temporary to permanent entertainment structures is a rather gradual and experimental process, which worked particularly well especially during the imperial period. The emperor Augustus became the only conceivable benefactor of such buildings and the games taking place in them, who without any competitors guaranteed a stable environment for religious affairs after a period of civil war and economic decline. The fact that multiple stone theatres, which today shape our idea of the Roman cityscape, were erected in the city is somewhat the result of a development that reacted to previous problems and was not possible until the establishment of the new political system.

Notes

1 Various behaviours were used for the expression of opinions towards magistrates, who were sometimes cheered – or jeered (cf. Cic., *Sest*. 124; Plut., *Vit. Cic*. 13.3–4; Val. Max. 2.10.8), sometimes even pelted with stones – or since 56 B.C. with fruit – when the Roman population was unsatisfied with them (cf. Macrob., *Sat*. 2.6.1). Cf. also Heil 2011: 29–33.

2 Cf. Cic., *Sest*. 106. See Heil 2011: 32. The political use of theatres is also documented for Athens. E.g. Cic., *Flacc*. 16 refers to a criticism of the seating at political events in Greek theatres. Cf. Heil 2011: 27–8.

3 Bernstein 1998: 295; Heil 2011: 23; Russell 2016: 169–171; Thuillier 1999: 176. Some of these scholars suggest that in 154/1 B.C. a *senatus consultum* banned permanent entertainment structures. See note 46.
4 Cf. Beacham 1991: 16, 66; Rumpf 1950: 44–5; Thuillier 1999: 176. Against this interpretation Bernstein 1998: 296.
5 According to Bernstein 1998: 14–5 the composite term '*ludi publici*' refers to games that were financed from the state treasury, the *aerarium*, organised by elected magistrates, and to a certain extent also co-financed by them, as well as listed as annually recurring festivals in the public festival calendar. However, despite this quite accurate definition, this conceptual composition was hardly used in antiquity. Only Cicero uses both terms together (Cic., *Cael*. 3.1.1; Cic., *Leg*. 2.22, 2.38); in another usage *publicus* is omitted in some text-critical editions (Cic., *Clu*. 27). Perhaps, these games could also be defined as *ludi magistri*, which is also attested once in Cicero (Cic., *Pis*. 8).
6 Vitr. 10.*praef*. 3 (transl. by F. Gardener).
7 The magistrates and aristocrats had to handle a specific budget consisting of public and private money. Cf. Bernstein 1998: 73–6, 143–7, 300–1. Expenditures from private money in particular were a financial burden that also created dependencies: See Asc., *in Scaur*. 18 for the debts of the aedile M. Aemilius Scaurus in 58 B.C. or App. *B Civ*. 2.1.1, Plut., *Vit. Caes*. 5.4–5 and Sall., *Catil*. 49.3 for the debts that Caesar accrued due to giving games during his term as aedile in 65 B.C. Some aristocrats even had to borrow money to realise spectacular games (e.g. Caesar loaned a large amount of money to Scribonius Curio, cf. App., *BC* 2.26; Dio 40.60.2–3; Plut., *Vit. Ant*. 5.2; Plut., *Vit. Caes*. 29.3; Suet., *Iul*. 29.1; Vell. Pat. 2.48.4). Concerning the indebtedness of benefactors cf. Baltrusch 1989: 108–9; Bernstein 1998: 301, 305 and 327. The under-investment or even lack of investment in giving games could also have a negative impact on one's political career. See Cic., *Off*. 2.57–9 reflecting on the right level ("*mediocritas . . . optima*") of investments for public games.
8 Cicero e.g. helped aediles to import wild animals from the province of Cilicia, which he administered as proconsul (Cic., *Att*. 5.21.5, 6.1.21; Cic., *Fam*. 8.2.2, 8.4.5, 8.6.5, 8.8.10, 8.9.3). The acquisition of actors for the scenic games is described at Plut., *Vit. Brut*. 21.1–6. During Caesar's games in 46 B.C. additional tents had to be erected for visitors throughout the city (Suet., *Iul*. 39.4).
9 Several dipinti from Pompeii announced future games which were to be held in the amphitheatre: *AE* 1915 61b; *AE* 1928 113; *AE* 1990 177b; *CIL* IV 1180; *CIL* IV 1185; *CIL* IV 1190; *CIL* IV 3883; *CIL* IV 7994. They mentioned not only the type of games but also the comforts to be expected, such as *sparsiones* and *vela*.
10 A good example of such strictly scheduled events is testified by the Acta Augusti (*CIL* VI 877) listing all the events during the *ludi saeculares* in 17 B.C. Cf. mainly Schnegg-Köhler 2002 and Schnegg 2020, but also Sear 2006: 56–7; Wiseman 2015: 154–6.
11 Suet., *Iul*. 39.4 describes the opulent games of Caesar in 46 B.C., at which spectators – including senators – had been crushed to death by the overcrowding.
12 Livy often judges the appropriate fulfilment of the realisation of the games with phrases like *magnus/magnificus apparatus* (cf. Liv. 25.2.8, 27.6.19, 31.4.6, 31.50.3, 33.42.8, 38.35.6, etc.). Games frequently had to be repeated (*instauratio*), as Livy reports on several occasions (cf. Liv. 23.30.16, 25.2.8–10, 27.6.19, 31.50.3). Sometimes those repetitions were made necessary due to prodigies, sometimes due to catastrophes or other interruptions of the festive activities, or sometimes due to celebrations of victorious battles, all of which could lead to an extension of games. In more detail see Morgan 1990: 20; Taylor 1937: 294–5; Thuillier 1999: 41–4.
13 For further reading see Beacham 1991: 2; Bernstein 1998: esp. 59–63, 76–8.
14 Cic., *Mur*. 38; Plin., *HN* 36.120. Cf. further Beacham 1991: 16, 25; Beck 2005: 84–8.
15 One of the most impressive games took place during the quadruple triumph of C. Julius Caesar in 46 B.C. See App., *BC* 2.101–2; Dio 43.19.1–43.24.4; Plin., *HN* 19.6.23; Plut., *Vit. Caes*. 55.1,2; Suet., *Iul*. 39.1–4; Vell. Pat. 2.56.1–2. The triumph celebrations were

combined with the inauguration of the Temple of Venus Genetrix and the Forum Iulium, as well as the funeral games for his deceased daughter Julia.

16 Like in 69 B.C. by Q. Lutatius Catulus, after finishing the temple of Jupiter Optimus Maximus (Plin., *HN* 19.23; Val. Max. 2.4.6–7), in 55 B.C. by Pompeius Magnus, for the dedication of his theatre complex (Cic., *Pis*. 65; Tert., *De spect*. 10), or in 46 B.C. by C. Julius Caesar after finishing the temple of Venus Genetrix and his Forum Iulium (cf. note 15). See also Bernstein 1998: 39–41, 302.

17 The earliest known example is the funeral games for Decimus Junius Brutus Pera in 264 B.C. (cf. Liv. 23.30.15). Mainly gladiatorial combats were performed during public funeral games, which were never part of the official *ludi* during the republican period. Only for the second century B.C. scenic games are attested as part of *ludi funebris* (see Liv. 41.28.11 for 174 B.C. and the *didascalia* of Ter., *Ad*. and Ter., *Hec*. as well as Ter., *Hec. prol*. 28–42 for 160 B.C.; cf. Taylor 1937: 301; Wiseman 2015: 60). The most important architectural setting for these *munera* was the Roman Forum. According to Vitruvius, Roman *fora* have to be designed in such a way that they could also be used for gladiatorial combats. Cf. Vitr. 5.1.1–2. See esp. Wesch-Klein 1993: 41–52, further Welch 2007: 30–8.

18 A conceivable subsumption, such as *ludi privati* (e.g. suggested by Beacham 1991: 22), seems rather inappropriate, as those games also took place in public spaces and had to some extent been legitimised by the Roman senate. In general, such games were gifts to the people and understood as *munera*.

19 Whether scenic games actually took place on a larger scale inside the Circus Maximus (or the Circus Flaminius) is difficult to judge but is repeatedly cited in research. Cf. for example Bernstein 1998: 184; Bieber 1961: 167. Bernstein bases this assumption on Liv. 7.3.1–2. Although scenic performances are mentioned as taking place in the Circus Maximus during the *ludi Romani* of 364 B.C. they consisted, as Liv. 7.2.3–5 also points out, mainly of musical and dance performances and not of dramatic theatre performances comparable to the third/second century B.C. Similarly, Hanson 1959: 12; Nielsen 2007: 242–3. For the general development of scenic games in Rome cf. Beacham 1991: 13–26; Bieber 1961: 141–160.

20 For example, no court trials could take place during public games in Rome. Cf. Cic., *Verr*. 1.10.31 for the year 70 B.C.

21 For the most important analyses on the development of temporary theatrical structures, see Beacham 1991: 56–70.

22 Whereas during the third century B.C. *ludi scaenici* took place over 12 days, in the early imperial period they were performed over a total of 43 days a year. Cf. Beacham 1991: 22; Morgan 1990: 17–8, 26–7; Taylor 1937: 284–5. Therefore, as during the Augustan period the total amount of festival days continuously increased, Varro laments that instead of supplying their fields, the landowners preferred to import products because they were always so busy at the circus and the theatre (Varro, *Rust*. 2.3). Cf. also Morgan 1990: 30–4 on some assumptions regarding the increasing amount of festival days during the second century B.C.

23 See note 7.

24 Tac., *Ann*. 14.21 (transl. by J. Jackson). Cf. Heil 2011: 24–5.

25 Val. Max. 2.4.6–7 (transl. by D. R. Shackleton Bailey). For a chronological orientation, the dates Valerius Maximus is referring to have been added, who interestingly does not distinguish between the earlier wooden and the first stone theatres.

26 See above all Plin. *HN* 36.24, 36.50, 36.113–5; further Asc. *in Scaur*. 18 and 27 is actually referring to Cicero, but certainly taking his information from Pliny. In general, Pliny's given information is very likely exaggerated, because he was concerned with supplying negative examples for the decline in morals of the aristocrats, as seen in their organising lavish games. This might explain why, for example, contemporary witnesses such as Cicero did not pay any further attention to a special construction of Scaurus and saw his games as equivalent to the ones of the other aediles (cf. Cic., *Off*. 2.57) or Val.

Max. 2.4.6 only mentions costumes and no further architecture, which is astonishing as he is also comparing the luxury decoration of the theatres from the first century B.C. For the display of wild animals during the games of Scaurus see also Amm. Marc. 22.15.24.
27 See Bieber 1961: 168 and Rumpf 1950: 47–8, who correctly assume that the number of spectators for the theatre of Scaurus is exaggerated, also compared to the later built permanent theatres. Cf. also Bartz 2020: 14–5; Heil 2011: 22; Sear 2006: 57–67 for further estimating the capacity of permanent theatres in Rome. It does not seem plausible that wooden theatres had a much larger capacity than the first permanent stone theatres, especially if they were probably erected in the same places (cf. the argumentation for the probable location of wooden theatres below).
28 Plin., *HN* 36.116-7, 36.120. Cf. Heil 2011: 26–7; Sear 2006: 56. Even though various scholars see a connection between Curio's debts to Caesar (cf. note 7) and his games, the ancient sources do not mention the games or even the rotating double theatre, but only emphasise Curio's extravagance (like Plut., *Vit. Ant.* 2.3; 5.1). In Val. Max. 9.1.6 bad investments in his youth are mentioned, and his debts are placed at 60 million sesterces. The omission of the extravagant double theatre in other ancient sources, e.g. at Val. Max. 2.4.6, seems at least surprising in view of its apparent exceptionality, as well as the lavish character of Curio repeatedly mentioned. Cicero e.g. warned the young Curio not to win the favour of the people through excessive expenditure at giving games, but rather to find other ways (Cic. *Fam.* 2.3). He also mentions a theatre of Curio, surprisingly without elaborating on any notable feature (Cic. *Fam.* 2.8.1). Plut. *Cato min.* 46.4 describes a theatre erected by Curio as well and also seems to be unaware of the extravagance identified by Pliny.
29 *CIL* I 593 (vv. 77–9, transl. by Nicolet and Crawford 1996: 375).
30 E.g. the rotating double theatre built by Curio in 52 B.C. was intended for his father's funeral games. However, it was erected in the area of his father's tomb (cf. Plin., *HN* 36.120) and not in the Forum, as one would assume for such games. It was probably not that the topography of the Forum did not meet the requirements for such a construction, but rather the fact that his father was simply not granted a public burial by the Roman senate. Caesar constructed his *naumachia* on privately owned land called 'Codeta' during his games in 46 B.C. (cf. Fest. 38 M. s.v. *Codeta*; Suet., *Iul.* 39.4, 44.1).
31 Several sources indicate that the theatres were erected and dismantled annually: descriptions such as the passages of Val. Max. 2.4.6–7 and Tac., *Ann.* 14.20–21 hand down that such structures were repeatedly erected. See also Dio 37.58.4 who describes the collapse of a wooden theatre in 60 B.C. built especially for a not further mentioned festival ("καί τι καὶ θέατρον πρὸς πανήγυρίν τινα ἐκ θυρῶν ᾠκοδομημένον ἀνετράπη"). Joseph., *AJ* 19.90 mentions an annually erected theatre for the imperial *ludi Platini* on the Palatine hill. An unusually long period of use of one month was noted for the theatre of the Scaurus (Plin., *HN* 36.5), which is nevertheless called a *temporarium theatrum* (Plin., *HN* 34.36). Cf. also Serv., *Georg.* 3.24.
32 Liv. 40.51.3. See further Bernstein 1998: 294; Rumpf 1950: 42–3; Sear 2006: 54–5. There are many researchers who associate a permanent structure with this reference. For a different perspective cf. Rumpf 1950: 42–3; Sear 2006: 54–5.
33 Plut., *Vit. Cic.* 13.2–4. Since 67 B.C. the first 14 rows of each theatre were reserved for knights by a much-discussed law of the plebeian tribune L. Roscius Otho (cf. Dio 36.42.1; Cic., *Mur.* 40; Cic., *Phil.* 2.44; Liv., *Per.* 99; Plin., *HN* 7.117; Plut., *Vit. Cic.* 13.2–4; Vell. Pat. 2.32.3 etc.), tumults broke out when L. Roscius Otho, in the role of the *praetor* (*urbanus*?), showed himself in a theatre during the *ludi Apollinares* of 63 B.C. Cicero rushed over and led the spectators into the temple of Bellona to exhort them to order. This change of localisation only makes sense if both structures were directly next to each other. See also Heil 2011: 28–9; Nielsen 2007: 248.
34 Dio 43.49.2–3; Suet., *Iul.*, 44.1. Cf. Hanson 1959: 18–22, followed by Bieber 1961: 168; Sear 2006: 54.
35 Cic., *Har. Resp.* 24.

36 Cf. Pensabene 2002: 85–7. Further, Hanson 1959: 14–5; Heil 2011: 21; Nielsen 2002: 172–5, 2007: 244–245, 2016: 86; Wiseman 2015: 55–6.
37 In the 80s B.C. the aedile placed a crown, previously displayed on a stage (*scena*), on the cult statue of Magna Mater, which was placed in front of the temple and attended the games. See Varro, *Sat. Men.* 150B (= Non. 171 L). The episode has only survived in fragmentary references, and hardly allows an estimate of the topographical proximity of the mentioned stage and the temple.
38 *CIL* VI 877 (ll. 90–102. 115–8. 134–7. 155–8). Cf. Schnegg 2020: 140–1, 144, 192, 212–4; Schnegg-Köhler 2002: 179. 186–7. 195 and further Nielsen 2002: 176, 2007: 245–246.
39 For the localisation of the *Tarentum* cf. Schnegg 2020: 200–210; Schnegg-Köhler 2002: 186–196. The first *ludi saeculares*, which were established on the basis of a prophecy from the Sibylline books, seem to be closely related to the *ludi Tarentini* (Fest. 329 M. s.v. *spondere*; L Liv., *Per.* 49). Cf. esp. Weinstock 1932, but also Bernstein 1998: 136–142; Nielsen 2007: 246–7.
40 Joseph., *AJ* 19.88–106; Suet., *Calig.* 56.2, 58.1–3. For this episode cf. Nielsen 2002: 179–178, 2007: 249.
41 Cf. Morgan 1990: 19–20.
42 For a detailed analysis see Hanson 1959: esp. 59–80.
43 Hanson 1959: 43–58. See also Bieber 1961: 181; Russell 2016: 173–6.
44 Tert., *Apol.* 6; Tert., *De spect.* 10. See Beacham 1991: 65–7; Bernstein 1998: 330–1; Sear 2006: 57.
45 Ancient records of the *senatus consultum* of 154 or 151 B.C. are: App., *BC* 1.4.28; Aug., *De civ. D.* 1.31; Liv., *Per.* 48.25; Oros. 4.21.4; Val. Max. 2.4.2; Vell. Pat. 1.15.3. This episode is also taken up frequently in research. Particularly important for critical reflection are the contributions of: North 1992; Sordi 1988; Tan 2016. The various interpretations of this episode reflected in the ancient sources, as well as the diverse scientific interpretations, cannot be discussed in detail here.
46 Oros. 4.21.4 is the only author who mentions a stone theatre. The other authors only mention a theatre, from which the materiality cannot be deduced. On the mention, cf. also Sordi 1988: 331–2.
47 Val. Max. 2.4.2 (transl. by D. R. Shackleton Bailey). His mention that the material was auctioned off maybe gives an indication that wood was used for the construction. Free-standing stone theatres are a phenomenon of the first century B.C.; permanent stone theatres of the second century B.C. were instead mostly built into hillsides, so not much material for the grandstands would be expected. Only the *scaenae* had to be constructed separately, but they played no role in the *senatus consultum* as the actual scenic games were not banned. A construction made of *opus caementicium* could not be auctioned off, despite the fact that they could be constructed in the second century B.C. For a different view on the auctioned material see Rumpf 1950: 41–2.
48 For a similar estimation of the performative aspect of standing while watching games cf. Tac., *Ann.* 14.20.
49 Indeed Liv., *Per.* 48.25 mentions that the spectators only stood for a while when watching the games: "*populusque aliquamdiu stans ludos spectavit*".
50 Cf. again Tert., *De spect.* 10 where several inaccuracies can be observed. E.g. he blames the censors who repeatedly tore down theatres, but according to other sources the censors had built the theatre. Tertullian describes the construction of the theatre as well as the temple as one event, but in fact the theatre may have been inaugurated earlier in 55 B.C., while the temple was finished in 52 B.C. Cf. Gell., *NA* 10.1.6–7 with reference to the year 52 B.C., when Pompeius was consul for the third time. Other sources on the opening ceremony of the theatre in 55 B.C., however, do not mention a temple (cf. Dio 39.38.1–3; Cic., *Fam.* 7.1.3; Plut., *Vit. Pomp.* 52.4). Only Plin., *HN* 8.7.20 mentions the dedication of the temple of Venus Victrix during the second consulate of Pompey. Cf. mainly Phillips 2001: 209, 212–6, but also Bieber 1961: 181; Russell 2016: 164–6; Sear 1993: 687.

51 Even the contemporary witness Cicero, who considered financial investments in infrastructure and the common good to be more sensible, hardly dared to criticise Pompey's complex (Cic., *Off.* 2.60). A criticism of Pompey's theatre-complex is quoted in Tac., *Ann.* 14.20, which is actually cited to criticise Nero's new games. Cf. Heil 2011: 23–4.
52 The *ludi* for Venus Victrix are mentioned in several *fasti*. Cf. some examples in note 58.
53 App., *BC* 2.115, 2.118, 3.132; Dio 44.16.2; Nic. Dam. in FGrH F 130.23 and 25; Nic. Dam. M 101 XXV, 92. M 101 XXVIa, 98. Appian and Nicolae of Damascus mention games (θέαι) with fighting gladiators inside the theatre, but Cassius Dio says only that the gladiators waited in the porticos. Nic. Dam. in FGrH F 130, 26a describes, however, that gladiators were again posted there on the day of Caesar's funeral to protect the senators, so that Cassius Dio could have been confused and perhaps refers to this event. Cf. Russell 2016: 169.
54 Gladiatorial combats no longer related to a public funeral event were given after Caesar's assassination. This trend started with a decree by the Roman senate that a festival be held in Caesar's honour every four years, for which a day was reserved for gladiatorial combat (cf. Dio 44.6.2), and increased during the Principate. See below, esp. note 79.
55 Vell. Pat. 2.79.6.
56 Possibly he was *pontifex maximus* in 34 B.C. (cf. *CIL* IX 5853).
57 *AE* 1959 147. For the inscription cf. Jory 1968 and Panciera 1986: esp. 38–9 with some doubts regarding the attribution of the theatre to the complex of Pompey. In my opinion her doubts are not substantiated and are based on an inaccurate analysis of the sources mentioning the materiality of the theatre (for some sources see note 58).
58 See the early Augustan *fasti fratrum Arvalium CIL* IX 2295 (cf. Rüpke 2011: 16–8) mentioning games for Venus Victrix "*[in theatre]o marmoreo*". It is striking that Pompey is not mentioned as the benefactor of the building, whereas in the same *fasti* the *theatrum Marcelli* is explicitly named after its benefactor. A similar phenomenon can also be seen in the *fasti Amiterni* (*CIL* IX 4192, dated to the Tiberian period) and in the *fasti Allifani* (*CIL* IX 2319, dated to A.D. 17–40. Note that the part mentioning the stone theatre has been reconstructed.). In the Acta Augusti recording the *ludi saeculares* of Augustus in 17 B.C., however, this is reversed: here the Theatre of Pompey is explicitly mentioned, whereas the Theatre of Marcellus, which was probably being referred to although not yet inaugurated, is addressed as "*theatrum in Circo Flaminio*" (see *CIL* VI 877 [ll. 157–8. 161], cf. Schnegg 2020: 67. 160–1; Schnegg-Köhler 2002: 150–2). Some ancient authors also repeatedly refer to the building as a stone theatre: Vitr. 3.3.2 ("*ad theatrum lapideum*"); Ov., *Am.* 2.7.3 ("*marmorei . . . theatri*"); Ov., *Ars. am.* 1.103 ("*marmoreo . . . theatro*").
59 *CIL* VI 877 (ll. 157–8. 161), cf. Schnegg 2020: 160; Schnegg-Köhler 2002: 150–2.
60 Plin., *HN* 36.120. Maybe also Cic., *Fam.* 8.2.1 refers to the same theatre.
61 Plut., *Vit. Cat. Min.* 46.4.
62 Cf. note 15.
63 Also, for Vitr. 5.5.7 as well as 10.*praef.* 3 temporary theatres were quite common.
64 A disadvantage of stone structures was that they absorbed an incredible amount of heat in the summer, so that the use of the hot stone seats cannot have been particularly pleasant. For example, in order to cool down the Theatre of Pompey before an event, running water was directed over the seats. Cicero describes this measure in a letter to M. Marius on the day of the opening of the theatre in 55 B.C., which he attended (Cic., *Fam.* 7.1, besides cf. Val. Max. 2.4.6).
65 *CIL* VI 1324. The column marked the dedication of the site by the curule aediles A. Terentius Varro Murena and L. Trebellius in 44 B.C. (?).
66 App., *BC* 3.28. Further Cic., *Att.* 15.3.2; Plut., *Vit. Ant.* 16.2.
67 App., *BC* 4.41; Dio 48.53.4–5. Therefore, the actors performed for free and the Roman citizens threw money into the orchestra to make the games possible.
68 Dio 49.16.2.

69 For the *ludi circenses* of 40 B.C. see Dio 48.20.2. Contrary to the normal *cursus honorum* Agrippa held his aedilship in 33 B.C. after his consulship (cf. Frontin., *Aq.* 1.98). Relating to the constructing efforts of Agrippa see Dio 49.43.1–5; Frontin., *Aq.* 1.9; Plin., *HN* 36.104, 36.121 and *CIL* VI 31270. Cf. also Purcell 2006: 788–9. The ancient sources do not specify the games given, which is why it remains unclear whether he was a plebeian or a curule aedile.
70 *RRC* 494/30: Coin of L. Livineius Regulus, 42 B.C. minted in Rome. For the coin cf. Böhm 1997: 142–3 cat. 55.4; Woytek 2003: 462–6.
71 This is known from Aemilius Scaurus, who was also moneyer (*RRC* 422/1) and aedile in 58 B.C. For an understanding of his coinage cf. Bartz 2020: 15–6. Nothing else, including any further magistracies, is known about the historical person of L. Livineius Regulus, who was *quattuorvir* together with P. Clodius, C. Varus, and L. Longus. Only two mentions in Cicero's letters confirm his existence: Cic., *Att.* 3.1.1 and Cic., *Fam.* 13.60.
72 Such promises of future events are not, to my knowledge, attested in republican coinage.
73 This connection would be very subtle, as there exists no explicit reference to the presumptive benefactor of the games.
74 Hor., *Sat.* 2.3.179–186 (transl. by H. Rushton).
75 Dio 53.2.1–2 (transl. by E. Cary and H. B. Foster).
76 Dio 54.2.4 (transl. by E. Cary and H. B. Foster).
77 Cf. Baltrusch 1988: 336 note 74; Bartz 2020: 18–20.
78 Dio 44.6.2.
79 For gladiatorial combats in the context of a *pompa triumphalis* see Dio 51.7.2 (for Mark Antony); 53.1.4–6 (28 B.C.); included in dedication games see Dio 51.22.4–9; 51.23.1 (29 B.C.); 54.19.5 (16 B.C.); 55.10.6–8 (2 B.C.); Vell. Pat. 2.100.2 (2 B.C.); as part of religious festivals see Dio 47.40.6 (42 B.C.); Ov., *Fast.* 3.809–14.
80 First published by Baltrusch 1988: esp. 336–7. However, the transition is fluid and difficult to define chronologically. See e.g. Welch 2007: 78 and 289 note 16, who argues that the *Lex Ursonensis* (parts 70–1) proves that gladiatorial combats were part of the state festivals since the Caesarean period. Despite the fact that the charter only refers to a municipium and not to Rome itself (cf. Baltrusch 1988: 333), the problem here is the correct translation and understanding of *munus*, which could of course mean 'gladiatorial combats', but could also be understood in a more comprehensive way, such as 'a show offered to the people', which might have included *venationes* as well. Furthermore, the text of the *Lex Ursonensis* was copied and updated in the Flavian period, so that the original republican text remains uncertain in some details. For both aspects cf. Crawford 1996: 395. On the basis of the epigraphical evidence, *gladiatores* seems to be the official term for the organisation of gladiatorial combats from the late republican period until ca. A.D. 100, after which the term *munus* is mainly used in inscriptions (cf. Fora 1996: 100).
81 Also, only the imperial family was able to hold public funeral games. See Dio 54.28.3–5 (for Agrippa), 55.2.2 (for Drusus), 56.34.4 (for Augustus), 56.42.1–3 (for Augustus), 57.22.4a (for Drusus); Serv., *Aen.* 6.861 (for Marcellus); Suet., *Aug.* 8.1 (for Augustus' grandmother Iulia), 100.3 (for Augustus); Suet., *Cal.* 10.1 (for Livia); Suet., *Tib.* 6.4–7.1 (for Augustus); Tac., *Ann.* 3.5 (for Augustus). Cf. Baltrusch 1988: 336; Wesch-Klein 1993: 15–9, 26–33. Public funerals for individuals outside the imperial house required the permission of the emperor (already under Augustus, cf. Dio 54.12.2; later by Tiberius, cf. Dio 58.19.5). Similar strategies to those used in order to monopolise the opportunities for giving games were also used to limit triumphal processions. Cf. Itgenshorst 2008: esp. 29–39.
82 Explanations that understand the postulated ban on stone theatres in Rome as a measure to regulate a possible politicisation of the population (cf. note 3) therefore seem somehow implausible.
83 E.g. a temporary stadium was erected on the Campus Martius (Suet., *Iul.* 39.3).

84 For an analysis of the topographic and political character see most recently Russell 2016: esp. 43–76.
85 Tac., *Ann.* 3.72 (transl. by C. H. Moore and J. Jackson). Cf. also Suet., *Aug.* 31.9; *RG Div. Aug.* 20. The later emperors were also responsible for maintenance and renovation: Suet., *Calig.* 21; Suet. *Claud.* 21; Suet., *Tib.* 47.1.
86 The permanent structures, for example, had continuously to be cleared of vegetation (Juv. 3.173).
87 That is why later they were sometimes donated to the citizens of a city. Cf. the dedicatory inscriptions of the amphitheatre of Pompeii *CIL* X 852: "*et coloneis locum in perpetuom deder(unt)*". See Welch 2007: 76–7.
88 For the planned, but not realised, theatre of Caesar see Dio 43.49.2–3 and Suet. *Iul.* 44.1 (cf. Bernstein 1998: 332; Wiseman 2015: 273 note 155). The Theatre of Pompey was also built on private land (see Plut. *Vit. Pomp.* 40.5. Cf. further Russell 2016: 160–2 for Pompey's estates on the Campus Martius.). Cf. *AE* 1937 64 and *AE* 1938 110 for the amphitheatre of Lucera, which was built on "*loco privato*".

References

Baltrusch, E. 1988: 'Die Verstaatlichung der Gladiatorenspiele', *Hermes* 116, 324–337.
Baltrusch, E. 1989: *Regimen morum. Die Reglementierung des Privatlebens der Senatoren und Ritter in der römischen Republik und frühen Kaiserzeit*, Munich.
Bartz, J. 2020: 'Eine Stadt als Bühne der Selbstinszenierung. Augustus'(im)mobile Bespielung Roms', in J. Bartz, M. Müller, and R. F. Sporleder (eds), *Augustus immortalis. Aktuelle Forschungen zum Princeps im interdisziplinären Diskurs. Beiträge des interdisziplinären Symposions an der Humboldt-Universität zu Berlin, Berlin, Oktober 25–27, 2019*, 13–21. https://doi.org/10.18452/22226.
Beacham, R. C. 1991: *The Roman Theatre and Its Audience*, London.
Beck, H. 2005: 'Züge in die Ewigkeit. Prozessionen durch das republikanische Rom', *Göttinger Forum für Altertumswissenschaft* 8, 73–104.
Bernstein, F. 1998: *Ludi publici. Untersuchungen zur Entstehung und Entwicklung der öffentlichen Spiele im republikanischen Rom*, Stuttgart.
Bieber, M. 1961: *The History of the Greek and Roman Theater*, Princeton, NJ.
Böhm, S. 1997: *Die Münzen der Römischen Republik und ihre Bildquellen*, Mainz.
Crawford, M. H. 1996: 'Lex Coloniae Genetivae', in M. H. Crawford (ed.), *Roman Statutes*, London, 393–454.
Fora, M. 1996: *Epigrafia anfiteatrale dell'Occidente romano*, vol. 4. Regio Italiae I.: Latium, Rome.
Hanson, J. A. 1959: *Roman Theater-Temples*, Princeton.
Heil, A. 2011: 'Literarische Kommunikation in der späten römischen Republik. Versuch einer Topographie', in A. Haltenhoff, A. Heil, F.-H. Mutschler (eds), *O tempora, o mores! Römische Werte und römische Literatur in den letzten Jahrzehnten der Republik*, Berlin and Boston, MA, 5–50.
Itgenshorst, T. 2008: 'Der Princeps triumphiert nicht. Vom Verschwinden des Siegesrituals in augusteischer Zeit', in H. Kasser, D. Pausch and I. Petrovic (eds), *Triplici Invectus Triumpho. Der Römische Triumph in Augusteischer Zeit*, Stuttgart, 27–53.
Jory, E. J. 1968: 'P. Cornelius P. L. Surus. An Epigraphical Note', *Bulletin of the Institute of Classical Studies* 15, 125–126.
Morgan, M. G. 1990: 'Politics, Religion and the Games in Rome, 200–150 B.C.', *Philologus* 134.1, 14–36.
Nicolet, C. L., and Crawford, M. H. 1996: 'Tabvla Heracleensis', in M. H. Crawford (ed.), *Roman Statutes*, London, 355–391.

Nielsen, I. 2002: *Cultic Theatres and Ritual Drama. A Study in Regional Development and Religious Interchange between East and West in Antiquity*, Aarhus.
Nielsen, I. 2007: 'Cultic Theatres and Ritual Drama in Ancient Rome', in A. Leone, D. Palombi, S. Walker, and E. M. Steinby (eds), *Res Bene Gestae. Ricerche di storia urbana su Roma antica in onore di Eva Margareta Steinby*, Rome, 239–255.
Nielsen, I. 2016: 'Kultische Theater in Italien und in den Westlichen Provinzen. Ein Vergleich', in T. Hufschmid (ed.), *Theaterbauten als Teil monumentaler Heiligtümer in den nordwestlichen Provinzen des Imperium Romanum. Architektur – Organisation – Nutzung*. Internationales Kolloquium in Augusta Raurica, September 18–21, 2013, 81–94.
North, J. A. 1992: 'Deconstructing Stone Theatres', in A. Cameron (ed.), *Apodosis. Essays presented to Dr W. W. Cruickshank to mark his Eightieth Birthday*, London, 75–83.
Panciera, S. 1986: 'Ancora sull'iscrizione di Cornelius Surus magister scribarum poetarum', *Bullettino Della Commissione Archeologica Comunale Di Roma* 91(1), 35–44.
Pensabene, P. 2002: 'Venticinque Anni di Ricerche sul Palatino. I Santuari e il Sistema Sostruttivo dell'area Sud Ovest', *Archeologia Classica* 53, 65–136.
Phillips, D. A. 2001: 'Tertullian on the Opening of Pompey's Theater in Rome', *Syllecta Classica* 12, 208–220. https://doi.org/10.1353/syl.2001.0004.
Purcell, N. 2006: 'Rome and Its Development Under Augustus and His Successors', in A. K. Bowman, E. Champlin, and A. W. Lintott (eds), *The Cambridge Ancient History, Vol. 10. The Augustan Empire, 43 B.C. – A.D. 69* (5th ed.), Cambridge, 782–811.
Rumpf, A. 1950: 'Die Entstehung des römischen Theaters', *Mitteilungen des Deutschen Archäologischen Instituts* 3, 40–50.
Rüpke, J. 2011: *The Roman Calendar from Numa to Constantine. Time, History, and the Fasti*, West Sussex.
Russell, A. 2016: *The Politics of Public Space in Republican Rome*, Cambridge.
Schnegg, B. 2020: *Die Inschriften zu den Ludi saeculares. Acta ludorum saecularium*. Berlin and Boston, MA.
Schnegg-Köhler, B. 2002: *Die augusteischen Säkularspiele*, Munich.
Sear, F. B. 1993: 'The Scaenae Frons of the Theater of Pompey', *American Journal of Archaeology* 97(4), 687–701.
Sear, F. B. 2006: *Roman Theatres. An Architectural Study* (Oxford Monographs in Classical Archaeology), Oxford.
Sordi, M. 1988: 'La Decadenza della Repubblica e il Teatro del 154 a. C.', *Invigilata Lucernis* 10, 324–341.
Tan, J. K. 2016: 'The Ambitions of Scipio Nasica and the Destruction of the Stone Theatre', *Antichthon. Journal of the Australian Society for Classical Studies* 50, 70–79.
Taylor, L. R. 1937: 'The Opportunities for Dramatic Performances in the Time of Plautus and Terence', *TransactAmPhilAss* 68, 284–304.
Thuillier, J.-P. 1999: *Sport im antiken Rom*, Darmstadt.
Weinstock, St. 1932: 'Ludi Tarentini und Ludi Saeculares', *Glotta. Zeitschrift für griechische und lateinische Sprache* 21(1/2), 40–52.
Welch, K. E. 2007: *The Roman Amphitheatre: From Its Origins to the Colosseum*, Cambridge.
Wesch-Klein, G. 1993: *Funus Publicum. Eine Studie zur öffentlichen Beisetzung und Gewährung von Ehrengräbern in Rom und den Westprovinzen*, Stuttgart.
Wiseman, T. P. 2015: *The Roman Audience. Classical Literature as Social History*, Oxford.
Woytek, B. 2003: *Arma et Nummi. Forschungen zur römischen Finanzgeschichte und Münzprägung der Jahre 49 bis 42 v. Chr.*, Vienna.

13 The Administration of the Imperial Property Under Constantine in the Light of His Donations to the Church of Rome

Paolo Liverani

I Introduction

This chapter analyzes a pair of issues related to the Constantinian building of the Christian basilicas. The *Liber Pontificalis* lists a series of records, each one concerning the building and endowment of a basilica of Rome at the expense of the emperor. The pattern follows an extremely regular scheme, recording the furniture and liturgical vessels according to fixed headings and distinguishing between *instrumentum* and *ornamentum*. Secondly, the list enumerates estates and *domus* of the endowment. This order reveals some of the administrative principles and traditions of the imperial chancellery. A further series of imperial letters and administrative documents informs us about the building of the basilicas, and the general lines of the administrative procedures, with a clear division among the political and financial responsibility, the architectural project, the administration, and the involvement of the final users of the building – mostly the bishop and the Christian community. In this chapter, I will analyse a pair of issues related to the Constantinian donations to the Christian community of Rome and the building of new cult places: the basilicas. The evidence outlines some administrative practices, and, in some cases, we have the opportunity to get a peek inside the archive of the imperial chancellery.

II The Donations to the Christian Community

We can begin from a very peculiar source, the *Liber Pontificalis* or *Book of the Popes*, which is extremely helpful in order to understand some administrative mechanisms of the imperial patrimony in the age of Constantine and, more generally speaking, in the fourth and fifth century. First of all, it is important to describe some features of this text, since its nature is very different from the literary sources generally used by historians or archaeologists. The *Liber* consists of a series of biographies of the Roman bishops from St. Peter to the end of the Middle Ages. Its first section – the one that interests us most – was drawn up in the sixth century, according to Louis Duchesne[1] just after the pontificate of Pope Felix IV, who died in 530. This date has been accepted by most scholars.[2]

The text is known through three versions, with slight but sometimes significant differences among them: for this reason, the manuscripts transmitting the *Liber* fall

Imperial Property Under Constantine and His Donations to Church of Rome 271

into three classes or families. Furthermore, we have two epitomes: the *Cononiana* and the *Feliciana*, perhaps deriving from a recension earlier than the three versions that have come down to us. The situation is quite complex and requires a careful knowledge of the various issues connected with the tradition of the text and some methodological cautions.

In recent times the value of this source has been questioned but not always with good reasons. It is evident that the first pontifical biographies, those prior to Constantine and the Edict of Milan, were reconstructed by the sixth-century ecclesiastical compiler on the basis of fragmented reports and traditions, sometimes of doubtful value. Furthermore, in subsequent lives many aspects of the narrative may have been elaborated in support of the position of the Roman bishop and the papal chancellery, with a version of the events that cannot be uncritically accepted. On the other hand, these lives contain invaluable information, mainly concerning buildings, donations, or other administrative details.

One of the most interesting sections is the so-called Constantinian *libellus*, isolated by Duchesne in his fundamental study for the modern edition of the *Liber*.[3] It consists of a series of records, each one concerning the building and endowment of a basilica of Rome at the expense of the emperor. This list of basilicas with their donations constitutes an insertion into the life of Pope Sylvester.[4] A first element stands out even at a superficial reading: the *libellus* lists not only basilicas of Rome, but also of other cities which are dioceses in their own right over which the pope had no jurisdiction. They are Ostia, Albanum, Capua and Naples, where the *libellus* even mentions interventions on the aqueduct and the forum, something clearly outside the competence of a fourth-century bishop. The only explanation is to consider it as a document from the imperial chancellery, mechanically inserted into Sylvester's life with very few adaptations.

Elsewhere, I analyzed in detail the *libellus* with a view to establishing its degree of reliability.[5] I will summarize here the main results in order to develop on this basis some more general observations concerning the subject of this chapter. The most important feature is the rigorous structure according to which information is organized. This scheme allows us to detect a series of minor interpolations by the sixth-century compiler. Usually, they are narrative insertions at the beginning of each record causing some recognizable alterations of the textual order, which is easy to reestablish after their deletion.

The various records are very different in length according to the importance of each basilica and its endowment, but the pattern is always the same. At the beginning the name of the basilica appears after an introductory formula with few variations: *eodem tempore fecit Constantinus Augustus*. Then, the record lists the precious furniture and liturgical vessels donated by the emperor. Finally, there is the patrimony which provides the income for the maintenance of the basilica and its clergy, coming from the imperial properties.

More in detail: the furniture and vessels are organized according to a series of headings. Only the Lateran Basilica, by far the richest by endowment, has the entire series of six headings. The other basilicas present from five headings to one, but always in the same order. The first heading includes the gifts of exceptional nature, like the *fastigium* in the Lateran Basilica or the spiral columns decorated with vine scrolls in St. Peter's. The second heading concerns the lighting, listing the various precious lights (*fara*), crowns (*coronae*), chandeliers (*fara canthara*) and candlestick chandeliers (*cantara cirostata*). The third section lists the liturgical vessels. The last three headings are included under the label *ornamentum in basilica*[6]: they concern respectively a second series of lights of the same types of the second heading, some few other vessels and finally the censers.

An obvious question is why the headings of the lights and vessels were doubled: an answer could be the difference of status between the two occurrences. This hypothesis finds support if we pay attention to the definition of *ornamentum*, which is a technical term. According to the bishop Optatus of Milevis an inventory of the *ornamenta* of the churches of Carthage existed in the age of Maxentius,[7] and the emperor Constans "had sent *ornamenta* to the house of God".[8] For the first three headings, in contrast, we do not have a common label, but we can consider the juridical definitions of the furnishings of the pagan temples. For these, Macrobius clarifies that:

> In sacred precincts some things are classed as implements and sacred furnishings, other things as *ornamenta*: things classed as implements are regarded as by way of being *instrumenta*, that is to say, they are the things which are always used in the offering of sacrifices. . . . But shields, crowns, and similar votive offerings are classed as *ornamenta*, for these are not dedicated at the same time as the temple is consecrated.[9]

This distinction is considered to date back to the lex Papiria, mentioned by Cicero.[10] If we consider this as the legal framework of Constantine and his chancellery, it seems likely that the first three headings are included in the *instrumentum* and the last three in the *ornamentum*. The *instrumentum* was functionally connected to the cult and, in principle, inalienable; the *ornamentum*, in contrast, consisted of the gifts and ex-votos arrived to the cult place in a moment after the consecration and, in case of need, it could be sold to respond to emergencies.[11] Something similar is attested in a Greek papyrus of the fifth or sixth century, with the inventory of a church in the Egyptian village of Ibion[12] defined as ἀναγρ[α]φ(ὴ) τῶν ἁγί(ων) κ[ει]μηλ(ίων) καὶ ἑτέρων σκευῶν, that is "inventory of the holy treasures and other utensils", but already Eusebius of Caesarea knows the same terminology, speaking about "the sacred utensils and treasures of the Church".[13]

If we accept this classification, then the lights and vessels of the *instrumentum* were liturgical furniture, those of the *ornamentum*, in contrast, were part of the decoration or at any rate not strictly connected with the cult. This detail has an interesting corollary for the censers listed in the last heading. These elements were considered by some scholars as an anachronism and thus as index of later interpolation because in the Christian worship the incense is attested only starting from the late fourth century. The incense, indeed – as I tried to demonstrate elsewhere – was already in use among the Christians in the early fourth century but only for funerary rites and in any case the *Liber Pontificalis* mentions *aromata* and not specifically incense, that is, a variety of aromas used for hygienic or honorary purposes.[14] The position of the censers in the list confirms this interpretation: they were part of the *ornamenta* and thus they were not intended for worship, otherwise they should have been listed in the *instrumentum*.

After lights and vessels, the last section of the records is devoted to the list of landed properties donated to each basilica. In cases where some of them were located outside Italy – the endowments of the Lateran baptistery, St. Peter's and St. Paul outside the Walls – they are listed according to the province and the city to whose territory each estate belonged. For every donation the list specifies the amount of annual income.

This same rigorous pattern, listing first the furniture and liturgical vessels according to the various headings and then the estates and *domus* of the endowment, occurs in subsequent papal lives in the records of the foundation of other basilicas until Leo III in the mid-fifth century. It is worthwhile noting here that the pattern is the same for both imperial and papal foundations. This means that it depends on administrative principles and traditions common to the imperial and papal chancellery, but we can also trace it in other cases. The best one is the so-called *Charta Cornutiana*, a list of Flavius Valila's donations in 471 to a church in the territory of Tibur (now Tivoli), near Rome.[15] Other interesting comparisons are the brief inventory with a list of vessels and lights of the church of Cirta in Numidia, preserved in a trial transcript from Diocletian's persecution,[16] and a couple of later church inventories preserved in Egyptian papyri.[17]

How should we consider these records from a formal point of view? Several years ago, Ludwig Voelkl analyzed the problem observing that when Constantine declared the Christian cult to be a *religio licita*, the emperor needed to elaborate a juridical frame for his relation to the new divinity.[18] He could do nothing but adopt the conceptual tools that the previous juridical tradition made available to him. In other words, the individual entries with the donations to the basilicas would be derived from foundation charters, the Christian equivalent of the *leges templorum*, of which they would retain the fundamental elements. Among them there were the donor, the divinity to whom the goods were destined and sometimes the procedure that gave rise to the donation. I think this intuition is correct, and we can explore further some implications. Let us begin with the procedure. The origin of the foundations is specified for some of them: St. Peter's was built *ex rogatu Silvestri*, that is, "at request of Pope Sylvester"[19]; Saint Agnes outside the Walls *ex rogatu Constantiae filiae suae*, "at request of her daughter Constantia".[20] Later, in the fifth century, the *fastigium* of the Lateran Basilica robbed by the Vandals was restored by Valentinian III *ex rogatu Xysti*, "at request of Pope Xystus III".[21] St. Paul outside the Walls was built *ex suggestione Silvestri*, "at the petition of Pope Sylvester",[22] and the basilica along Via Ardeatina, recently discovered, was founded *ex suggestione Marci*, "at the petition of Pope Marcus".[23] These formulae preserve the terminology of the imperial chancellery and refer to the practice of the petition, a fundamental institution in the imperial system, that Constantine solicited and encouraged especially in relation to the financing of churches, as Noel Lenski has cogently shown.[24]

Constantine was very generous in endowing the new basilicas with imperial properties from his own *res privata*. Marco Maiuro observed that some of these properties maintain a trace of their original provenance.[25] They were *fundi fiscales*, that is assets accumulated by the *res privata* by donation, confiscation or by claiming a vacant inheritance.

There are several examples: Constantine gave to the Lateran Baptistry the estate received as a gift by Festus, chief of the imperial bedchamber;[26] to St. Peter's the emperor gave three estates received as gifts from otherwise unknown people: Ambrosius, Hybromius, Agapius, two more whose original owner is missing and finally Euthymius' escheated estate.[27] To the Basilica of the Holy Cross in Jerusalem Constantine donated the property received from a certain Herculius,[28] to St Lawrence outside the Walls the estate of a religious woman, Cyriaces, confiscated during the last persecution.[29] Among all the provenances, the donations are particularly interesting. Probably we could add to this list also the important donation of Gallicanus,[30] which otherwise is difficult to justify as apparently it would have been donated directly to the basilica of Ostia: why an imperial document had to mention a private donation? If we hypothesize that the first passage with the gift to the emperor went lost in the textual transmission, the case is much more normal.[31]

In any case, the main question is: why did the *libellus* need to maintain the memory of the original owners? I can imagine only one explanation, depending once again on the juridical frame adopted by the emperor. When the ownership of estates, buildings, things or people had been transferred and consecrated to one of the deities recognized by the *res publica*, they were regulated by the *ius sacrum*, the divine law. In this case the transfer could only take place by virtue of the *potestas* or *imperium* of a magistrate or a legitimate representative of the *res publica*.[32] The emperor intervened in his double capacity as representative of the *res publica* and as *pontifex maximus*, the only one who could guarantee the correctness of an act of sacred law. On the other hand, the gifts of a private individual to the divinity fell within the *ius privatum*, the private law. Consequently, when a private party wanted to contribute to the endowment of a sacred place by making sure that his gift was inalienable, he first had to donate it to the emperor, who would then have it consecrated. In this way, the would-be donor could obtain a double advantage: the first was political from his association with the emperor, the second spiritual for his gift to the divinity.[33]

III The Construction of the Basilicas

Let us now address the second point of this chapter: the construction of the basilicas by the emperor. In this case it is useful to compare and integrate the evidence relating to the Constantinian basilicas with that relating to imperial constructions of a later age. It is well known that Constantine promoted the building of several churches: we have just examined the case of Rome, the best documented, but there are other examples in the various provinces of the Empire where the sources help us to understand, at least in its broadest outlines, the organization of the work and division of the responsibility. We can examine in more detail three cases documented by imperial letters included by Eusebius of Caesarea in his *Ecclesiastical History*.[34]

The first letter was addressed to the bishop Macarius of Jerusalem for the building of the Basilica of the Holy Sepulchre.[35] What strikes us in reading it is the lack of any indication about the architectural structure and design: the emperor is exclusively concerned that the building shows through its grandeur and richness its importance and the imperial level of its patron. He, instead, gives some precise administrative instructions: the construction of the structural part is entrusted to the praetorian prefect of the East, Dracilianus, and to the governor of the province, while the supply of marbles and columns and of the gold for the coffered ceiling decoration is the responsibility of the central administration, based on the indications requested of Macarius himself. Theophanes, in his Chronicle,[36] informs us about the name of the architect, a certain Zenobius. It is debated whether or not the architect was sent to Macarius by Constantine, but either way it is clear that the project of the basilica was carried out as a collaboration between Zenobius and Macarius, the only one who really knew the needs of the Christian community of Jerusalem and its liturgy.

The second letter is much briefer: it is addressed to the same Macarius and to the other bishops of Palestine in relation to the Oak of Mamre,[37] where, according to the Bible, Abraham entertained the three angels. Eutropia, emperor's mother-in-law, had informed Constantine that the place was occupied by an ancient pagan sanctuary. The letter gives instructions for the "reclamation" of pagan cults and the erection of a church. The person in charge of the construction this time is the Comes Acacius, while the bishops of Palestine and Phoenicia are in charge of drawing up the project of a basilica "worthy of the Catholic and apostolic Church", and also expressive of imperial magnificence.

The third case concerns the basilica of Constantina in Numidia, where the Donatists had taken possession of the Catholic church of the city.[38] The bishop had complained to the emperor, who gives him a domus from the imperial property to resolve the dispute and orders that the local governor build a new basilica in its place at the expense of the *fiscus*. Here, too, it seems that he should do the work on the basis of the bishop's instructions.

In the two latter cases we find once again that the emperor's initiative was undertaken as an answer to the petition respectively of Eutropia and the local bishop. Furthermore, there is a clear subdivision of the competences: the funding and the political responsibility of the building falls to the emperor, while the execution is assigned to the bishop assisted by an architect, the management of the construction is entrusted to the civil authority of the region.

Confirmations of this scheme can be found in sources relating to later basilicas. One of the better documented is the second basilica of St. Paul outside the Walls in Rome.[39] The first one – built by Constantine – was a small church, not large enough to accommodate the crowds of pilgrims visiting the apostle's tomb. Furthermore, the difference in dimension and wealth between St. Paul's and St. Peter's, the basilicas of the apostles considered the pillars of the Church of Rome, created a disturbing asymmetry. For these reasons the emperors Valentinian II, Theodosius and Arcadius decided to renovate the building according to the model of St. Peter's. The project implied important works, including the reorganization of the streets around the church.

The imperial instructions to the Urban Prefect Sallustius are extremely detailed and give us a good idea of the procedure undertaken before the beginning of construction[40]: first of all, he had to send to the emperors a preliminary report about the state of the area, then to make contact with the bishop of Rome, the clergy and the Christian community in order to have a precise idea of their needs. Subsequently, the prefect needed the authorization from the senate for the reorganization of the streets, and finally he had to send to the court the *synopsis operis construendi* for final approval. *Synopsis* is a rare and technical term: we find it only in an inscription from the city of Constantina,[41] with the meaning of "inventory", and it is used by Ulpianus in the Digest for the inventory of the property of a minor.[42] In our context, it likely means the project's bill of analytical costs.

We cannot generalize this procedure in a mechanical way, because it is only documented for the city of Rome, where there was a strong organization and where both civil and ecclesiastical administrations had a long tradition and very specialized competencies. We cannot be sure that the situation was similarly routinized in all the provinces and cities. In any event, it is clear that the pattern we have already seen for the Constantinian basilicas was basically the same: the political input and the funds came from the emperor, the project was executed with the involvement of the bishop and the Christian community but likely with the technical assistance by architects of the *Praefectura Urbis*.[43] Some years ago, a new examination of the inscription[44] on the base of a column of the basilica allowed us to recognize the names of the two senators directing the construction: the administrative director was Flavius Filippus and the architect Flavius Anastasius.

An even more specialized division between technical and administrative direction is documented for a later building, the basilica of Mary the Theotokos in Jerusalem, the so-called *Nea*, dedicated by the emperor Justinian.[45] Considering only the essentials of a long story, the church was decreed and paid by the emperor at the request of the holy monk Saba, after an earlier project by the bishop Elias was halted for political reasons. The technical direction was entrusted by Constantinople to the architect Theodorus, and the funds were made available by the imperial tax collectors for Palestine; on the administrative side Jerusalem's Patriarch had the overall supervision, and Barachos, bishop of the city of Bakatha, was the manager.

I pass over here a few other cases such as the building of the *basilica nova* – or *basilica Piniani* – together with the *pons novus* – or *pons Theodosii* – in Rome, because their stories are very complicated and cannot reflect the normal situation.[46] I am thinking of the Eudoxian basilica at Gaza in the early fifth century,[47] because the situation of the sources is not completely clear, or the building of the city of Dara along the Persian boundary decreed by the emperor Anastasius,[48] because it is late and difficult to compare with the other examples.

IV Conclusion

We can synthesize in a schematic table (Table 13.1) the various examples just discussed: even if we cannot know the technical administrative details, the general framework and the distribution of the tasks are clear and seem not to be subject to significant changes from the Constantinian age to the fifth and maybe even

Table 13.1 Christian basilicas under imperial patronage, synthetic view

Basilica	Project	Years	Funds	Administration	Sources
Jerusalem, Holy Sepulchre	-Bishop Macarius, -Architect Zenobius	326	provincial + imperial	-Dracilianus PPO -Provincial governor	Eus., *VC* 3.31; Theophan., *Chronogr.* a. 5825
Mamre	Bishops of Palestine and Phoenicia	326	provincial + imperial	*Acacius comes*	Eus., *VC* 3.52–53
Cirta	Bishop of Cirta	330 ca.	*fiscus*	*Consularis Numidiae*	*CSEL* XXVI app. X, p. 215
Rome, St. Paul	-Bishop, -Architect *Flavius Anastasius*	386	imperial	*Flavius Philippus vc administrante*	*CSEL* XXXV, 46–47, n. 3; *ICUR* II, 4778
Jerusalem, St. Mary the Theotokos (Nea)	Architect Theodorus	530	imperial tax collectors for Palestine	-Peter, Jerusalem's Patriarch, -Barachos, bishop of the city of Bakatha	Proc., *Aed.* 5.6; Cyr. Skythop., *Vita Sabae* 72–73

the sixth century. Of course, the political and financial responsibility was always reserved for the emperor, but the execution of the project could rely on a well-articulated system involving, since the beginning, the final users of the building – in most of our cases the bishop and the Christian community – in order to define the fundamental needs to which the architect had to respond. The project did not arrive directly from the court because the technical and logistical constraints could be evaluated only on site and, contrary to many archaeological interpretations of imperial architecture, the influence of imperial choices was quite indirect. To put it simply, the emperor was interested only in obtaining a building worthy of his name and imperial majesty. The local representative of the emperor – governor, tax collector, urban prefect – was in charge of providing the funds, the work force and the materials, except for the marble and precious metals, which arrived directly from the imperial administration. The administration and the technical directions were divided between two or more officials to avoid misuse of the funds. The building scandal of the *basilica nova* and the *pons novus* in Rome in the late fourth century, documented in detail by Quintus Aurelius Symmachus in his official reports and letters, clearly demonstrated the risks of a unified direction which – as far as we know – was never again proposed in the administrative imperial practice.[49]

Concerning the first part of this chapter, it is now clear that some practices of the imperial chancellery were widely shared, as we find archival traces of them both in public and private administrations, with well-structured inventories for asset management and reporting, with categories grouping the furnishing of a foundation according to the value and function of the various items. These accounting techniques must have been developed over centuries: even without going back to the inventories of Hellenistic temples, we have a number of inventories of the imperial age from pagan shrines with some similarities.[50] Obviously, while the technique was common, regardless of the pagan or Christian orientation of the communities, what is peculiar to the Christians is the classification of the furnishing according to their liturgical functions. These practices were well studied for classical and Hellenistic Greece but much less so for the imperial period – when the documentation is thinner – and the late-antique period. Now is the time to reconsider this history from a long-term perspective.

Notes

1 Duchesne 1886.
2 *Status quaestionis* in Capo 2009: 3–58; more recently Geertman 2009; Verardi 2016, 2020; Simperl 2020; McKitterick 2020.
3 Duchesne 1886: clii-cliv n. 84.
4 *LP* 34.9–33.
5 Liverani 2019.
6 *LP* 34.11.
7 Optat. 1.17.
8 Optat. 3.3.
9 Macrob., *Sat*. 3.11.6: *In fanis alia vasorum sunt et sacrae supellectilis, alia ornamentorum. Quae vasorum sunt instrumenti instar habent, quibus semper sacrificia conficiuntur . . . Ornamenta vero sunt clipei, coronae et cuiuscemodi donaria. Neque enim dedicantur eo tempore quo delubra sacrantur.*
10 Cic., *Dom*. 50.128; Paoli 1946–47: 166–170; Cavallero 2018: 234–240.
11 De Marini Avonzo 2008: 115–6; Ramon 2016: 299–307.
12 *P.Grenf*. 2.111.
13 Eus., *m. P.* 12: ὅσα τε τῶν ἱερῶν σκευῶν τῶν ἐκκλεσιαστικῶν ἕνεκα κειμελίων . . . ἀνατετλήκασι.
14 Liverani 2019: 186–190, 195–6.
15 Duchesne 1886, cxlvi – cxlvii, nr. 81; Geertman 2011.
16 *Gesta apud Zenophilum*, in Ziwsa 1893: 187.
17 *P.Grenf*. 2.111 (Hunt and Edgar 1932: 432–435 nr. 192); P.Batav. 25.13 (Van Minnen 1991: 40–77).
18 Voelkl 1964.
19 *LP* 34.16.
20 *LP* 34.23
21 *LP* 46.4.
22 *LP* 34.21.
23 *LP* 35.3.
24 Lenski 2016: 15, 180–2, 187, 281–2.
25 Maiuro 2007: 243–252.
26 *LP* 34.14.
27 *LP* 34.19.
28 *LP* 34.22.
29 *LP* 34.25.
30 *LP* 34.29.
31 Liverani 2019: 180–1.
32 Voelkl 1964; Cavallero 2018.
33 Voelkl 1964; Liverani 2019: 180.
34 Krautheimer 1993; Liverani 2003a, 2011; Brandenburg 2004; Guidobaldi 2016 accepted this approach changing his original opinion (Guidobaldi 2001: 20).
35 Eus., *VC* 3.31.
36 Thphn., *Chron*. a. 5825, ed. De Boor 1883: 33.

37 Eus., *VC* 3.52–53.
38 Ziwsa 1893: app. X, 215.
39 After the fundamental study by Krautheimer and Frazer 1977, cf. Liverani 1989; Filippi and De Blaauw 2000; Brandenburg 2002; Filippi 2004; Brandenburg 2005–2006; Filippi 2005–2006, 2006, 2008; Liverani 2012; Camerlenghi 2018.
40 Guenther 1895: 46–47 nr. 3.
41 *CIL* VIII 6981–6982 add. pp. 965, 1847.
42 *Dig.* 27.9.5.11 (Ulp.): *In primis igitur quotiens desideratur ab eo, ut remittat distrahi, requirere debet eum, qui se instruat de fortunis pupilli, nec nimium tutoribus vel curatoribus credere, qui nonnumquam lucri sui gratia adseverare praetori solent necesse esse distrahi possessiones vel obligari. requirat ergo necessarios pupilli vel parentes vel libertos aliquos fideles vel quem alium, qui notitiam rerum pupillarium habet, aut, si nemo inveniatur aut suspecti sint qui inveniuntur, iubere debet edi rationes itemque synopsin bonorum pupillarium, advocatumque pupillo dare, qui instruere possit praetoris religionem, an adsentire venditioni vel obligationi debeat.*
43 See above chapter 7 by A. Lopez Garcia.
44 *ICUR* II, 4778 c; *ILCV* 1857; Filippi 2000; *AE* 1959, 64 = 2000, 187; Liverani 2003b.
45 Proc., *Aed.* 5.6; Cyr. Skythop., *Vita Sabae* 72–73.
46 Liverani 2003b. For the identification of the *pons novus* cf. Liverani 2020: 23–24.
47 Marc. Diac., *Vita Porphyrii.*
48 Ps.-Zach., *HE* 7.6; Marc. Comes, a. 518, *MGH, AA* XI, 100.
49 Martinez-Fazio 1972; Vera 1978; Liverani 2003b.
50 Liverani 2015.

References

Brandenburg, H. 2002: 'Beobachtungen zur architektonischen Ausstattung der Basilica von S. Paolo fuori le Mura in Rom', *Vivarium. Festschrift für Christian Gnilka, Jahrbuch für Antike und Christentum Ergänzungsband* 30, 83–107.

Brandenburg, H. 2004: 'Prachtentfaltung und Monumentalität als Bauaufgaben frühchristlicher Kirchenbaukunst', in J. Gebauer, E. Grabow, F. Jünger, and D. Metzler (eds), *Bildergeschichte. Festschrift Klaus Stähler*, Möhnesee, 59–76.

Brandenburg, H. 2005–2006: 'Die Architektur der Basilika San Paolo fuori le mura. Das Apostelgrab als Zentrum der Liturgie und des Märtyrerkultes', *Mitteilungen des Deutschen Archäologischen Instituts, Römische Abteilung* 112, 237–275.

Camerlenghi, N., 2018: *St. Paul's Outside the Walls. A Roman Basilica, from Antiquity to the Modern era*, Cambridge.

Capo, L. 2009: *Il Liber Pontificalis, i Longobardi e la nascita del dominio territoriale della chiesa romana*, Spoleto.

Cavallero, F. G. 2018: '*Ius publicum dedicandi* (e *consecrandi*): il diritto di dedica a Roma', *Mélanges de l'Ecole française de Rome. Antiquité* 130, 219–249.

De Boor, C. 1883: *Theophanis Chronographia*, Leipzig.

De Marini Avonzo, F. 2008: 'La delimitazione territoriale nel mondo romano. Significato religioso ed effetti giuridici', *Rivista di Diritto Romano* 8, 108–130.

Duchesne, L. 1886: *Le Liber Pontificalis. Texte, introduction et commentaire*, I, Rome.

Filippi, G. 2000: *Iscrizione relativa alla dedicazione della basilica teodosiana*, in A. Donati (ed.), *Pietro e Paolo. La storia, il culto, la memoria nei primi secoli* (Exhibition catalogue – Rome), Milan, 228–229 nr. 101.

Filippi, G. 2004: 'La tomba di S. Paolo e le fasi della Basilica tra il IV e il VII secolo. Primi risultati di indagini archeologiche e ricerche d'archivio', *Bollettino dei Monumenti, Musei e Gallerie Pontificie* 24, 187–224.

Filippi, G. 2005–2006: 'Die Ergebnisse der neuen Ausgrabungen am Grab des Apostels Paulus. Reliquienkult und Eucharistie im Presbyterium der Paulsbasilika', *Mitteilungen des Deutschen Archäologischen Instituts, Römische Abteilung* 112, 277–292.

Filippi, G. 2006: 'Nuovi documenti sui lavori del 1838 nella vecchia Confessione', *Bollettino dei Monumenti, Musei e Gallerie Pontificie* 25, 87–95.

Filippi, G. 2008: 'La tomba di S. Paolo. I dati archeologici del 2006 e il taccuino Moreschi del 1850', *Bollettino dei Monumenti, Musei e Gallerie Pontificie* 28, 321–348.

Filippi, G., and de Blaauw, S. 2000: 'San Paolo fuori le mura: la disposizione liturgica fino a Gregorio Magno', *Mededelingen van het Nederlands Instituut te Rome* 59, 5–25.

Geertman, H. 2009: 'La Genesi del *Liber pontificalis* romano: un processo di organizzazione della memoria', in F. Bougard, and M. Sot (eds), *Liber, gesta, histoire: écrire l'histoire des papes et des évêques, de l'Antiquité au XXIe siècle*, Paris, 37–107.

Geertman, H. 2011: 'L'arredo della *Ecclesia Cornutianensis*. Annotazioni intorno alla donazione di Flavius Valila (471)', in O. Brandt and P. Pergola (eds), *Marmoribus Vestita. Miscellanea in onore di Federico Guidobaldi I*, Vatican City, 599–611.

Guenther, O. 1895: *Collectio Avellana; Pars I: Prolegomena. Epistulae I-CIV, Corpus scriptorum ecclesiasticorum Latinorum* 35.1, Pragae, Vindobonae and Lipsiae.

Guidobaldi, F. 2001: 'Architettura come codice di trasmissione dell'immagine dell'imperatore dai Severi a Costanzo II', in J. R. Brandt, O. Steen (eds), *Imperial Art as Christian Art – Christian Art as Imperial Art. Expression and Meaning in Art and Architecture from Constantine to Justinian, Acta ad archaeologiam et artium historiam pertinentia* 15, Rome, 13–26.

Guidobaldi, F. 2016: 'La formulazione progettuale della basilica cristiana come ulteriore espressione dell'innovazione costantiniana nel campo dell'architettura', in O. Brandt and V. Fiocchi Nicolai (eds), *Costantino e i Costantinidi: l'innovazione costantiniana, le sue radici e i suoi sviluppi* (Acta XVI Congressus Internationalis Archaeologiae Christianae, Romae 22–28.9.2013), Vatican City, 461–492.

Hunt, A. S., and Edgar, C. C. 1932: *Select Papyri* I, London and New York.

Krautheimer, R. 1993: 'The Ecclesiastical Building Policy of Constantine', in G. Bonamente and F. Fusco (eds), *Costantino il Grande, dall'antichità all'umanesimo* (Atti del Colloquio – Macerata 18–20.12.1990, II), Macerata, 509–552.

Krautheimer, R., and Frazer, A. 1977: 'S. Paolo fuori le mura', in R. Krautheimer, S. Corbett and A. Frazer (eds), *Corpus Basilicarum Christianarum Romae* 5, Vatican City, 93–164.

Lenski, N. 2016: *Constantine and the Cities. Imperial Authority and Civic Politics*, Philadelphia, PA.

Liverani, P. 1989: 'S. Paolo fuori le mura e l'*iter vetus*', *Bollettino dei Monumenti, Musei e Gallerie Pontificie* 9(1), 79–84.

Liverani, P. 2003a: 'Progetto architettonico e percezione comune in età tardoantica', *Bulletin antieke beschaving. Annual Papers on Classical Archaeology* 78, 205–219.

Liverani, P. 2003b: 'Basilica di S. Paolo, *basilica nova, basilica Piniani*', *Boreas. Münstersche Beiträge zur Archäologie* 26, 73–81.

Liverani, P. 2011: 'I Vescovi nell'edilizia pubblica', in R. Lizzi Testa and P. Brown (eds), *Pagans and Christians in the Roman Empire: The Breaking of a Dialogue (IVth-VIth Century A.D.), Proceedings of the International Conference at the Monastery of Bose (October 2008)*, Münster, 529–539.

Liverani, P. 2012: 'La cronologia della seconda S. Paolo f.l.m.', in H. Brandenburg and F. Guidobaldi (eds), *Atti della giornata di studi "Scavi e scoperte recenti nelle chiese di Roma"* (Pontificio Istituto di Archeologia Cristiana 13 marzo 2008), Vatican City, 107–123.

Liverani, P. 2015: *The Culture of Collecting in Roma: Between Politics and Administration*, in M. Wellington Gahtan and D. Pegazzano (eds), *Museum Archetypes and Collecting in the Ancient World*, Leiden and Boston, MA, 72–77.
Liverani, P. 2019: 'Osservazioni sul *libellus* delle donazioni costantiniane nel *Liber Pontificalis*', *Athenaeum. Studi di letteratura e storia dell'antichità* 107(1), 169–217.
Liverani, P. 2020: 'Il Tevere, i ponti e l'Annona', in M. T. D'Alessio and C. M. Marchetti (eds), *RAC in Rome. Atti della 12ª Roman Archaeology Conference (2016), le sessioni di Roma*, Rome, 19–27.
Maiuro, M. 2007: 'Archivi, amministrazione del patrimonio e proprietà imperiali nel *Liber Pontificalis*. La redazione del *libellus* imperiale copiato nella *vita Sylvestri*', in D. Pupillo (ed.), *Le proprietà imperiali nell'Italia romana. Economia, produzione, amministrazione*, Florence, 235–258.
Martinez-Fazio, L. M. 1972: *La segunda basilica de S. Pablo extramuros. Estudios sobre su fundación*, Rome.
McKitterick, R. 2020: *Rome and the Invention of the Papacy: The "Liber Pontificalis"*, Cambridge.
Paoli, J. 1946–1947: 'Le "Ius Papirianum" et la Loi Papiria'. *Revue historique de droit français et étranger* 24, 157–200.
Ramon, A. 2016: 'L'appartenenza e la gestione delle *res sacrae* in età classica', in L. Garofalo (ed.), *I beni di interesse pubblico nell'esperienza giuridica romana* I, Naples, 249–316.
Simperl, M. 2020: 'Beobachtungen und Überlegungen zur frühen Redaktionsgeschichte des *Liber pontificalis*', in K. Herbers and M. Simperl (eds), *Das Buch der Päpste* – Liber Pontificalis, *Ein Schlüsseldokument europäischer Geschichte*, RömQSchr Supplementband 67, Freiburg, Basel and Wien, 52–76.
Van Minnen, P. 1991: 'Inventory of Church Property', in F. A. J. Hoogendijk and P. van Minnen (eds), *Papyri, Ostraca, Parchments and Waxed Tablets in the Leiden Papyrological Institute (P.L. Bat. 25)*, Leide.
Vera, D. 1978: 'Lo scandalo edilizio di Cyriades e Auxentius e i titolari della *praefectura urbis* dal 383 al 387. Opere pubbliche e corruzione in Roma alla fine del IV secolo d. C.', *Studia et documenta historiae et iuris* 44, 45–94.
Verardi, A. A. 2016: *La memoria legittimante: il Liber Pontificalis e la chiesa di Roma nel secolo VI*, Rome.
Verardi, A. A. 2020: 'Ricostruire dalle fondamenta: L'origine poligenetica del *Liber pontificalis* romano e le sue implicazioni storiche ed ecclesiologiche', in K. Herbers and M. Simperl (eds), *Das Buch der Päpste* – Liber Pontificalis, *Ein Schlüsseldokument europäischer Geschichte*, Römische Quartalschrift für christliche Altertumskunde und Kirchengeschichte, Supplementband 67, Freiburg, Basel and Wien, 37–50.
Voelkl, L. 1964: *Die Kirchenstiftungen des Kaisers Konstantin im Lichte des römischen Sakralrechts* (Arbeitsgemeinschaft für Forschung des Landes Nordrhein-Westfalen, Geisteswissenschaften. Heft 117), Cologne and Opladen.
Ziwsa, C. 1893: *S. Optati Milevitani libri vii. Accedunt decem monumenta vetera ad donatistarum Historiam pertinentia*, Corpus scriptorum ecclesiasticorum Latinorum 26, Pragae, Vindobonae and Lipsiae.

14 Topography of Power in the Conflict of the Basilicas Between Valentinian II and Ambrose of Milan in A.D. 385/6

Jasmin Lukkari

I Introduction

In this chapter, I examine the so-called conflict of the basilicas between Valentinian II and Ambrose of Milan from 385 to 386 from the point of view of the topography of power. The conflict has traditionally been seen as a part of the longer Arian-Nicene controversy of the fourth century, but fundamentally, it was about Ambrose's attempts to consolidate episcopal authority over the ecclesiastical hierarchy of the era, when the line between imperial and episcopal authority was blurred. Both the general topography of ancient Milan and the literary sources on the conflict have been eagerly studied by archaeologists, historians and theologians.[1] However, very few scholars have focused on the spatial aspects of this power struggle that emerge from Ambrose's writings. Indeed, the city of Milan functioned as the symbolic battleground between the emperor and the bishop. R. Krautheimer touches on this subject in his study of the Christian topography of Milan in the political context of the late fourth century, and H. O. Maier goes even further in his essay on the uses of private spaces for Arian services during and before the conflict.[2] This subject could benefit from an examination of both the topography and literary narrative of the conflict in light of new theoretical and methodological approaches to the concept of space. I suggest some ways in which these new approaches could be applied in this context. I argue that Ambrose did not only attempt to control the basilicas that were involved in the conflict. Through his narrative, he also attempted to redefine the meaning of sacred space in the Christian context and in relation to imperial authority, which he strived to distance and separate from episcopal authority. One way to assert this kind of dominance was to take control of the urban space.[3] Thus, by restricting the emperor's access to basilicas and his movements between them, Ambrose asserted the dominance of the Church over sacred spaces while founding even more basilicas around the city and one right next to the imperial palaces.

Ambrose's narrative of the conflict includes several important locations: the basilica Nova in the episcopal complex in the centre of Milan, the basilica Portiana and the basilica Martyrum outside the walls, the imperial palaces and the spaces between these locations. The primary literary sources for this conflict are Ambrose's letters, which he published as part of a larger collection of letters organized into ten books. Even though these letters are addressed to different individuals – for example, to emperor Valentinian II or his own sister Marcellina – they were clearly written with a wider audience in mind.[4] In fact, the letters are rhetorically and narratively elaborate, and one of them – the so-called *Sermo contra Auxentium* – is not a letter at all but a speech to his congregation. Thus, these letters provide a certain kind of historical narrative of the conflict: the narrative that Ambrose wanted to leave for posterity. This unilateral nature of the sources that publicize Ambrose's own interpretation of events has to be kept in mind when studying any aspect of this conflict.

II The City and the Imperial Court

Ambrose's episcopate in Milan coincided with the period when the emperors in the West constantly resided in Milan. In 286, Maximian, Diocletian's co-emperor, had established an imperial residence at Milan, which was a strategically advantageous location owing to the threat posed by the German tribes in the north. Subsequent Western emperors intermittently held their court there – and more permanently during the last half of the fourth century – until the year 402, when Emperor Honorius moved the court to Ravenna to escape the increasing Visigoth threat.[5] The imperial court of Milan resided and operated in the western part of the city, limited by the *cardo* and *decumanus* as well as the forum towards the east and the city gates towards the west.[6] At the time when the imperial residence was established in Milan, a circus was built in connection to the district of the imperial palaces, as was common in other cities of imperial residence, and the circus functioned as a defensive structure integrated into the city wall and the two gates on each side.[7] The imperial court comprised a large number of people, including administrative staff, imperial officials, scholars and servants of the court. Among the officials whose headquarters were in Milan was the praetorian prefect – the most powerful functionary after the emperor – in charge of the civil administration of the prefecture of Italy, one of the Empire's four large prefectures in the fourth century. The republican era city wall was amply extended by Maximian towards the east either due to the sudden growth of population or to the necessary relocation of habitants of the western part of the city to make space for the huge imperial court.[8] Soon after the Edict of Milan in 313 by Constantine I, the construction of the episcopal complex begun to the east of the forum, that is, to the opposite side of the city from the imperial palaces.[9] By the end of fourth century, the episcopal complex comprised four basilicas, including the basilica Nova and a domus of the bishop.[10] With the extended city walls, the episcopal complex was situated in the middle of the city (nowadays the piazza del Duomo). E. Arslan notes that this choice of location was certainly deliberate, and it accentuates the bipolarity of the urban plan of Milan with its imperial western part and its civic and episcopal eastern part.[11] In Milan, the urban space of the city centre was not charged with the tensions caused by the particularly strong presence of ancient cults as it was in Rome, which allowed the redefinition of such central spaces for Christian building projects more easily.

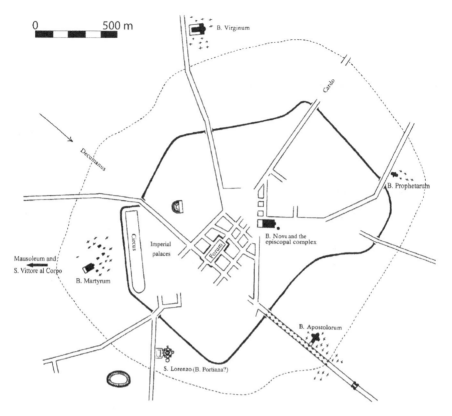

Figure 14.1 Map of late fourth-century Milan with here discussed places (after Villa 1956: 7; Lewis 1969: 91).

Source: Edited by Jasmin Lukkari.

During the fourth century, leaders of the Church made efforts to define an identity of their own for their organization, separate from the ancient cults, and to assert authority that was independent from imperial governance.[12] The new 'Arian' interpretation of the nature of the Trinity and of Christ, which had gained popularity all around the Empire and within the imperial family, was declared heretical in the First Council of Nicaea in 325.[13] This did not end the controversy, however. Emperor Constantius II convened a synod in Milan in 355, in the newly built basilica Nova in the episcopal complex, and he supported the election of the Arian theologian Auxentius as the bishop of Milan.[14] After this, the synod meetings were moved from the episcopal complex to the imperial palace 'probably so as to exclude the vociferous Nicene faction among the congregation', who were subsequently banished by the emperor.[15] Thus, the strife between imperial and episcopal powers began over the Arian controversy, and the dividing lines of the battleground were drawn between the episcopal complex in the east and the imperial palace district in the west. The status quo remained as such until the Arian bishop Auxentius died in 374 and a new bishop was needed. At this time, Ambrose (Aurelius Ambrosius) was working in Milan as the governor of the province of Liguria and Aemilia.[16] According to the famous account, the Arian and Nicene factions clashed over the choice of the next bishop, and Ambrose, in his capacity as a high public official responsible for maintaining order, went to the meeting to prevent it from escalating into violence.[17] His intervention and capacity to mediate between the two factions impressed the whole assembly so much that they suddenly decided to declare Ambrose the new bishop. Ambrose reputedly did not want to become the bishop and tried to escape, but Emperor Valentinian I succeeded in convincing him to accept the position. Ambrose was then baptized and consecrated as the new bishop of Milan.[18] Despite his earlier conciliatory attitude toward the strife between the Arian and Nicene creeds, as the bishop, Ambrose strongly supported the Nicene creed, and his influence has been argued to have been essential for the final victory of the Nicene creed. Gratian, the follower of Valentinian I, settled on supporting the Nicene faction, but his younger brother and co-ruler Valentinian II was under the influence of his mother Justina and many court officials who still professed an Arian interpretation of Christianity. This resulted in conflict for Ambrose when, during Gratian's military campaign against the usurper Magnus Maximus in Gaul and after Gratian's ensuing death in 383, the teenage Valentinian II remained the only emperor in Milan.[19]

III The Conflict Between Imperial and Episcopal Authority

In 385, Valentinian II requested from Ambrose that a church – the basilica Portiana – should be given to him so that he could attend a service there with his imperial entourage. The service was probably an important religious occasion such as Easter. Ambrose refused, not wanting to grant such privileges to Arians, which marked the beginning – or perhaps the escalation of long-standing disagreement – which marked the beginning of the basilica conflict.[20] The sources blame the 13-year-old emperor's pro-Arian mother Justina for initiating this conflict with the bishop during these trying times when the emperor's authority was constantly threatened by the ambitious Maximus, the killer of Valentinian II's brother and usurper of the title of emperor in Britannia and Gallia. However, N. B. McLynn argues that Justina's influence should not be exaggerated and that the influence of the emperor's court should be remembered.[21] For the current purpose of examining spatial aspects of the battle of the basilicas, it will suffice to summarize the main events of the conflict without delving deep into their chronology and other details, which are complicated on their own.[22] The conflict took several dramatic turns between the initial request of Valentinian II in 385 and the end of the conflict with the emperor's submission in 386. At the beginning, after Ambrose refused to consign the basilica Portiana, requested by the emperor, imperial troops surrounded the church with the purpose of pressuring Ambrose to leave the city while he stubbornly held services inside. Since besieging the church and threatening the bishop in other ways did not have the desired effect, the next year, right before Easter, the emperor requested both the basilica Portiana and the basilica Nova for his use. Ambrose again refused to even negotiate, and an entire week of heavy pressure and threats from the court ensued, involving armed men sent to besiege the basilicas. Ambrose's resistance obviously provoked the emperor: 'They ... say: "Ought not the emperor be given one basilica to attend in state, and does Ambrose want to have more power than the emperor, that he refuses him the opportunity of appearing in state?"'[23] Ambrose's purpose was to teach the emperor through this topographical power play that the emperor should not have authority over Church property or theological matters. Ambrose risked a lot with this open defiance, but in the end, the emperor gave up his claims without violence.

The basilica Nova was a part of the episcopal complex in the centre of Milan, whereas it is unclear which church the basilica Portiana was. The two most probable options seem to be either the basilica that is now dedicated to San Lorenzo, which is right outside the Porta Ticinensis, or the basilica of San Vittore al Corpo, which is farther away to the west.[24] In either case, the basilica Portiana was situated outside the walls and near the imperial palace district. R. Krautheimer, who argues in favour of S. Lorenzo, writes that using basilicas in the suburbs in this manner 'was apparently fourth-century practice for dissident religious minority groups'. He bases this claim on a comparison between this strife in Milan and similar ones in Rome and Constantinople.[25] However, it would not make sense for the emperor to admit his own heresy in this manner, as defined by Theodosius I's law of 381. It is more probable that the basilica Portiana was simply considered a sort of 'palace church' since both candidates – S. Lorenzo and S. Vittore al Corpo – are close to the palace district and housed imperial mausoleums. Still, McLynn notes that '[d]istinctions between different types of building were probably often blurred, and especially so in an imperial capital, where an emperor required a setting appropriate for the expression of his own Christian identity'.[26] In fact, for the nobility, celebrating religious events in public had always been an important opportunity to be seen and thus reassert their status in society, and this applied to the imperial family as well. Carlos Machado argues that in Rome '[i]t was this "public quality" of everyday Christianity that made active engagement with the community and the Church a relevant component in aristocratic social strategies while displaying (and redefining) their own social hierarchies'.[27] For this very reason, a celebration in the relative privacy of the imperial palace would not have been satisfactory for emperors.[28] During this era, the Christian emperors had significant freedom of action regarding matters of the Church, and this freedom had not yet been seriously contested. With the conflict of the basilicas, Milan became an early battleground of this contest. The emperor's claim to the basilica Portiana is a good illustration of the unclear boundaries and the grey areas between imperial and ecclesiastical authorities during the fourth century. While the episcopal complex clearly was the bishop's domain and the palaces the emperor's, suburban basilicas like Portiana became contested spaces more easily in this context.

It is notable that in his writings, Ambrose avoided discussing the legal point of view of the conflict.[29] Instead, he uses various rhetorical devices and metaphors to turn the debate into a question of episcopal authority. Indeed, for Ambrose, this was not only about Milan and about him and Valentinian II: for him, this conflict seemed to be about defining the identity of the new Christian Italy and the Church that was still struggling to find internal concord in these early years. Ambrose later wrote to his sister Marcellina and described the moment of greatest tension toward the end of the long conflict, when the emperor had sent armed men to the basilica Nova to remove him and his supporters:

> Yes, I was terrified when I learned that military men had been sent to seize the basilica of the Church, for I feared that their appropriation of the basilica would be accompanied by carnage, which would result in the ruin of the city as a whole. I kept praying that I might not survive the cremation of so great a city, perhaps of all Italy. I shrank from the odium of being the cause of bloodshed. I offered my own throat. Some tribunes of the Goths were standing close by. I assailed them saying: 'Was it for this that the Roman Empire admitted you, that you should offer yourselves as agents for the promotion of civil strife? To where will you emigrate if this region is destroyed?'[30]

Here, apart from expressing his willingness to become a martyr, Ambrose compares the destiny of the Milanese Christians to those of all Italy.[31] Also, he likened himself to an athlete or a champion who would do combat for them all against violence and 'barbarians'.[32] By barbarians, Ambrose meant the Goths who featured prominently in Valentinian II's army, and apparently many of them professed an Arian creed.[33] Ambrose thus used the discourse of Otherness as a rhetorical tool to win the favour of the people: on the narrative level, the basilica Portiana symbolically functioned as the first line of defence between the heretic barbarians, the Others, and the orthodox Romans of Italy.

In the opening of his *Sermo Contra Auxentium de basilicis tradendis*, reputedly delivered during a service in the church while the emperor's soldiers menacingly surrounded it, Ambrose defines his position as the defender of the citadel of episcopal authority and likens the basilica to the *Ecclesia* as an institution:

> The desire to desert the Church could not possibly occur to me, since I feared the Lord of the universe more than the emperor of this world; that if force was used to drag me away me from the Church, my body might be forcibly moved, but my mind could not be.[34]

However, the conflict did not limit itself to the basilica Portiana. During the second year of the conflict in 386, Valentinian II requested the basilica Nova in the heart of the episcopal complex as well for his Easter celebrations. This was a direct attack on the bishop's territory, but Ambrose once again refused to leave or surrender either basilica despite the persuasion of the praetorian prefect himself and, eventually, the appearance of armed soldiers who surrounded the basilicas.[35] The siege of the basilicas continued for days, and Ambrose's messages seemed to have no effect on the emperor. Recapitulating one of these messages in a letter to his sister, Ambrose likens the churches to a private domus and draws a clear line between laic and sacred spaces from the Christian point of view:

> 'No law entitles you to violate the house of a private individual, do you think that you may seize the house of God?' The argument put forward is

that everything is permitted to the emperor, that the world is his. I reply: 'Do not make trouble for yourself, emperor, by thinking that you have any sort of imperial right over things that are God's. Do not exalt yourself. If you wish to rule for any length of time, be subject to God. It is written: *What is God's to God, what is Caesar's to Caesar* [*Matt.* 22.21]. Palaces belong to the emperor, churches to the bishop. The jurisdiction entrusted to you is over public buildings, not over sacred ones.[36]

For centuries, the emperors had represented themselves as divinities, and even after their adoption of Christianity during the fourth century, they had involved themselves in matters of the Church. Roman religion and politics had always been inseparable, and the spaces of politics had themselves been sacred.[37] It is therefore no wonder that attempts to redefine sacred space as separate from imperial jurisdiction caused polemic in this context, further aggravated by the Arian controversy.[38] Ambrose was determined to put an end to this awkward overlapping of imperial and episcopal authorities, and the urban space of Milan functioned as a concrete instrument to advance this mission of consolidating episcopal authority.[39]

IV The Basilicas and the Palace

In his *Sermo Contra Auxentium*, Ambrose further emphasized the importance of distinguishing sacred space from non-sacred space from the Christian point of view:

> I would gladly go to the emperor's palace, if it was compatible with my Episcopal duty to fight my case in the palace rather than in the church. But in the consistory it is usual for Christ to be present not as the accused but as the judge.[40]

Again and again, Ambrose stresses that the palace was the emperor's domain, whereas churches belonged to God. Nevertheless, Ambrose did go to the palace at the very beginning of the strife when the emperor had invited him there to request to use a church for his services. Referring to this, Ambrose explained in his *Sermo contra Auxentium* that he had felt out of place and powerless inside the imposing palace in front of the high officials of the consistory.[41] From a rhetorical point of view, this description of Ambrose's overwhelming experience of the imperial palace serves to emphasize his message about keeping the sacred and laic realties separate: a bishop did not have power in the imperial palace, and the emperor did not have power in a church. According to Ambrose, a multitude of his supporters had stormed the palace conveniently at the right moment to interrupt the awkward meeting. Curiously, Ambrose's earlier extensive political experience did not seem to have helped him feel at ease inside the consistory, but obviously remembering his past as a civil servant would not have helped his argumentation in this oration. The next year, in early 386, Ambrose was invited to the palace again to continue the discussion with Auxentius, an Arian ex-bishop of Durostorum residing in Milan.[42] This time, Ambrose outright refused to go, repeating in a letter to the emperor that he was 'unable to fight [his] case within the palace, whose secrets I neither know, nor wish to know'.[43] During this time, the tension between the imperial court and Ambrose was conspicuous and it did not help that the bishop passed right next to the imperial palaces on daily basis:

> Have I not been in the habit of going out every day, going to visit people, or going to martyrs' tombs? Have I not gone close to the imperial residence, both going and coming back? And yet nobody grabbed hold of me, even though they had it in mind to drive me out, as they revealed later, saying what they wanted [me to]: 'Leave the city and go wherever you wish to'.[44]

Another reason for this provocative daily walk past the palaces was probably to inspect the ongoing construction works of the basilica Martyrum (now called the basilica di Sant'Ambrogio) just outside the western city wall and thus very close to the imperial palace district.[45] During his episcopate, Ambrose had three other basilicas built around the city outside the walls: the basilica Apostolorum (now S. Nazaro in Brolo), the basilica Virginum (now S. Simpliciano) and the basilica Prophetarum (later S. Dionigi or S. Salvatore and then demolished).[46] In Rome too, bishops had taken control of the establishment of Christian topography by the second half of the fourth century, and in Milan this task fell conveniently to Ambrose.[47] Arslan suggests that this building program at every side of the city was aimed at symbolically attenuating the stark division of the city into the section of the imperial palaces and the civic section: all men were to be equal and unified in faith in front of the Christian God.[48] Maier argues in more detail that Ambrose's building program was, in fact, planned from the beginning as part of his campaign to assert episcopal authority.[49] Maier writes:

> Ambrose was thus arguing for the existence of a sacred space which was outside imperial control, a distinction he had been aggressively promoting as a builder and consecrator of churches, and one which had great implications for the status of the Arian community in Milan.[50]

Thus, by quickly building the four basilicas around the city, he increased the sacred space in his control and under his protection even further.

If Ambrose's building program is to be interpreted as a sort of topographical power play, then the basilica Martyrum close to the imperial palaces certainly was the most important part of this play. Ambrose had begun the construction works of the basilica Martyrum during the preceding years and had the intention to reserve a burial place for himself under the altar.[51] Krautheimer suggests that Ambrose's claim to that place of honour could be 'an implicit riposte to Constantine's first burial place under or near the altar in the chancel area of the church of the Holy Apostles in Constantinople'.[52] Constantine's son later moved his burial place because it was appropriate for priests – not for the laity, which included the emperor. Thus, according to Krautheimer, Ambrose's choice of burial place could have been meant to symbolically remind the emperors that their place was, in fact, among the laity.

Also, of particular interest are the original wooden doors of the basilica, of which two panels depicting scenes of the story of David are extant today: these have been interpreted to symbolize Ambrose's struggles with the emperor during the years of the basilica's construction.[53]

While the emperor was not able to remove Ambrose from the churches or to restrict his movements in the city and between his basilicas, which were arising in every corner, Ambrose was able to limit the emperor's physical space of manoeuvre considerably. McLynn argues that by the end of the fourth century, it had become common for emperors to attend public services on special occasions such as Easter, and 'the emperor's presence at a service, and above all his procession to and from church, soon became an important part of the imperial ceremonial'.[54] Indeed, J. H. W. G. Liebeschuetz notes, regarding the repeated use of the verb *prodire*:

> It has often been assumed that the church was demanded for regular worship of the Arian community of Milan, but the actual wording of the texts suggests that the church would be required only for a particular service, or series of services, for which the emperor would leave his palace, and proceed through the streets of the city in formal procession.[55]

Therefore, Ambrose was not only restricting the emperor's access to the two basilicas, but he might also have disrupted the imperial ceremony by denying to the emperor the possibility to move around the city in solemn procession during important Christian events. In other words, Ambrose had confined the emperor to his palaces and claimed all sacred space – even that produced by ritual procession – only for those of the Nicene creed.

And it was not only Ambrose who attempted to defend these sacred spaces from the emperor. Several times in Ambrose's narrative, the people, that is, his congregation, seemed to have their own agency. For example, Ambrose mentioned in his *Sermo contra Auxentium* that at the beginning of the conflict, when Ambrose had been summoned to the imperial palace, the people had heard about the bishop's appointment at the palace and about the emperor's request. He claims that they 'surged forward so violently that their rush could not be checked as they threw themselves at the general who had come out with light-armed troops to disperse them; for they were ready to die for their faith in Christ'.[56] Only Ambrose was able to calm the crowd with a long speech and thus transform the awkward visit to the palace into a small personal victory. Ambrose described this as an improvised incident that he had nothing to do with. Be it as it may, it was important for Ambrose to make it look like the people had their own will and that they were, perhaps, guided directly by the Holy Spirit and not the bishop's command. Similarly, in a letter to his sister, Ambrose told her about the Easter conflict of 386 and how the people once again, upon hearing that the basilica Portiana was in danger of being seized by the emperor, acted spontaneously and flocked to the church while Ambrose stayed at the besieged basilica Nova.[57] The people continued to occupy the basilica Portiana even without Ambrose's presence.[58] In this way, Ambrose presented his followers as a self-willed group that defended God's property against heretics wherever Ambrose himself could not be present. By this, Ambrose wanted to show that he and his congregation had total control of the city's churches.

V Conclusion

All this was meant to teach to the emperor that 'the emperor is within the Church, not above it'.[59] Ambrose seemingly prevailed: after days of resistance and fear, Valentinian II and Justina gave up and renounced their claims to use the churches for Arian services. It seems that Ambrose had not only won this battle, but he had won the whole war, so to speak. The end of the conflict and the definitive victory for Ambrose came soon after in June 386 with the consecration ceremony of the newly completed basilica Martyrum, already popularly called the Ambrosian basilica. As mentioned earlier, Ambrose had reserved a burial place for himself under the altar already during the construction of the basilica – an unprecedented deed from a bishop – to make sure that, if he should meet a violent death as he constantly expected during the conflict, he would already have a burial place worthy of a martyr. However, at the moment of its consecration, the congregation requested that the basilica should also have relics under the altar.[60] In a letter to his sister – which is, however, for the most part composed as if it were a sermon to the imperial court – Ambrose wrote that he immediately set out to satisfy the people's wish and consequently found the burials of Saints Gervasius and Protasius in the nearby Hortus Philippi.[61] The very next day, with a huge number of people attending, the relics were carried in a procession to the Ambrosian basilica accompanied by hymns and even a miracle.[62] The emperor and the Arians of the imperial court, profoundly humiliated by Ambrose less than three months ago, could do nothing but observe with *invidia* this final triumph of Ambrose, which was validated by the overwhelming support of the people. Machado notes that '[o]ver the course of the fourth and fifth centuries, Roman bishops used the cult of martyrs and their relics as a way of asserting their spiritual authority over the city, its calendar, and spaces'.[63] Ambrose used this same tactic in Milan: he now had his own 'fortress' right next to the imperial palace and was protected by his two new 'bodyguards', Gervasius and Protasius.[64] At his basilica, in a sermon to the congregation, Ambrose invited the imperial family and the Arians to come to pay their respects to the martyrs, for the relics were to benefit everyone. As McLynn notes, with this Ambrose invited his opponents to his territory: the new basilica and the discovery of the martyrs offered him a 'positive platform from which to institute negotiations'.[65]

After this, Ambrose was not persecuted, and the emperors did not try to interfere with theological matters any longer.[66] Within a year, Valentinian II and Justina left Milan to flee from the usurper Maximus, and the next emperor to reside in the Milanese court was Theodosius I, who arrived from the East to repel the usurper. Theodosius I was a keen supporter of the Nicene creed like Ambrose, and according to the enthusiastic narrative of Sozomen, he reputedly held the bishop in great respect.[67] With his energetic building program and his rhetorically elaborate historical narrative, Ambrose has given to posterity the impression that he had conquered Milan for his God one building at a time, and despite riding 'to the storm he had created with majestic aplomb', he had emerged the victor.[68]

Notes

1 For an introduction to earlier studies on Ambrose, see Williams 1995: 1–10; Liebeschuetz 2010: 3–4. Williams (2017) has written a recent monograph on the 'Arian' conflict in Milan.
2 Krautheimer 1983; Maier 1994.
3 In Milan, Ambrose was the first bishop to do this with success, while in Rome this turn came about later (Salzman 2013).
4 Liebeschuetz 2004: 104–105.
5 For a summary of the history of Milan during the presence of the imperial residence, see David 1999: 10–16.
6 On the area in general, see Arslan 1982: 198–203; Piras 2012: 35–44; Caporusso et al. 2014: 168–175. The district of the imperial palaces was a polyfunctional complex comprising of several different structures reserved, for example, for administrative, military, residential and representative use. Ausonius described the palaces of Milan as *aurea palatia* or *Palatinae arces*, likening them to the imperial palaces of Rome in terms of splendour: Auson., *Ordo nob. urb.* 40, *praef.* 25. Cf. Aur. Vict., *Caes.* 39.45.
7 On the circus, see Arslan 1982: 198–203; Blockley and Provenzali 2013: 52–67; Caporusso et al. 2014: 158–167. The circus with its spectacles and competitions was a powerful symbol of imperial power and a place where emperors could appear in public. For accounts of the emperors Theodosius and Honorius following spectacles at the circus of Milan, see Soz., *HE* 7.29.
8 On the new city walls, see Blockley and Provenzali 2013: 37–41; Caporusso et al. 2014: 147–157, 312. Maximian built public baths in the new eastern extension of the city (Arslan 1982: 196–8; Caporusso et al. 2014: 176–186).
9 For the episcopal complex, see Mirabella Roberti 1984: 106–111; Lusuardi Siena 1996; Caporusso et al. 2014: 211–220.
10 Amb. *Ep.* 76 (Maur. 20) 9. The basilica Nova was later dedicated to S. Tecla. It now lies in ruins under the piazza del Duomo.
11 Arslan 1982: 202–204.
12 E.g., Brown 1992: 71–158.
13 There were different branches of Arianism, such as the *Homoians* and the so-called semi-Arians. It should be noted that the Arians did not call themselves 'Arians' – only their enemies did. For the purpose of this chapter, however, it will not be necessary to make distinctions between the different sects. For a concise summary, see Liebeschuetz 2010: 7–11. On the problems of using different labels for Arians in modern scholarship, see Gwynn 2010: 231–233; Williams 2018.
14 Socrat., *HE* 2.36. On Arian-Nicene conflicts in Milan more broadly, see Williams 1995, 2017.
15 Citation from Krautheimer 1983: 71. Later, Ambrose criticized Constantius II for having started the habit of discussing theological matters in the imperial palace, which was not a proper place for such discussions. See Amb., *Ep.* 75 (Maur. 21) 15.
16 He was originally from Augusta Trevorum (modern Trier), but he had studied in Rome and entered public service there before his appointment in Milan. On Ambrose's life before Milan, see McLynn 1994: 31–40; Liebeschuetz 2010: 5–7.
17 On Ambrose's election, see McLynn 1994: ch. 1; Liebeschuetz 2010: 7–11. On Ambrose's job as a governor, the 'terror of the public administration' (Amb., *De poen.* 2.67), see McLynn 1994: 5–6.
18 Even though his mother was a Christian, Ambrose did not have formal education in theology, and he had not yet been baptized.
19 On Ambrose under Gratian, see Liebeschuetz 2010: 11–14. For a detailed summary of the rule of Valentinian II and Ambrose's role in the events after Gratian's death, see McLynn 1994: 158–170.

20 For the spaces that Arians used in Milan before Ambrose's episcopate, see Maier 1994. However, M. S. Williams argues that the Arian controversy should not be given too much weight in this conflict, which was fundamentally between the Church and the state: Williams 2018.
21 McLynn 1994: 170–174.
22 The chronology of the events is unclear, and there are many valid theories. I have followed the chronology proposed by Liebeschuetz 2010: 129–135. For a different chronology, see McLynn 1994: 170–219; Williams 2017: ch. 5. The sources for the conflict are Amb., *Ep.* 76 (Maur. 20) 9, *Ep.* 75a (Maur. 21a); Soz., *HE* 7.13; Paul. Mil., *V. Ambr.* 12, 13, 20; August., *Conf.* 9.7.15; Rufinus, *HE* 2.15.16; Theodoret, *HE* 5.13; Socrat., *HE* 5.11.
23 Amb., *Ep.* 75a (Maur. 21a) 30: *Ergo non debet imperator unam basilicam accipere ad quam procedat, et plus vult Ambrosius posse quam imperator, ut imperatori prodeundi facultatem neget?*
24 Caporusso et al. 2014: 266, 282. For a detailed analysis on why the basilica of San Lorenzo could have been the basilica Portiana, see Krautheimer 1983: 81–92. Cf. Calderini et al. 1951; Kinney 1972; McLynn 1994: 176–179. N. B. McLynn (1994: 179) states: 'The specific identification of the Portian Basilica with San Lorenzo, although attractive, must remain hypothetical'. For the theory regarding the basilica of San Vittore al Corpo, see Mirabella Roberti 1967; Lewis 1973; Mirabella Roberti 1984: 137–156.
25 Krautheimer 1983: 91. Cf. Lenox-Conyngham 1982: 357.
26 McLynn 1994: 175. He also notes: 'The term "palace church", often applied to the buildings used for imperial devotions, is not a particularly happy one, suggesting as it does a homogeneity barely detectable in structures that range from modest chapels to cathedrals. Imperial ceremonial was too versatile and flexible to be captured in a single designation or architectural form'.
27 Machado 2019: 181.
28 H. O. Maier argues that during this time, the Arians were indeed confined to having their services in private spaces since they did not have a church in the city: Maier 1994. Cf. Williams 2017: 205.
29 For the legal point of view, see Lenox-Conyngham 1985.
30 Amb., *Ep.* 76 (Maur. 20) 9: *Horrebam quippe animo cum armatos ad basilicam ecclesiae occupandam missos cognoscerem, ne dum basilicam vindicant, aliqua strages fieret, quae in perniciem totius vergeret civitatis. Orabam ne tantae urbis vel totius Italiae busto superviverem. Detestabar invidiam fundendi cruoris, offerebam jugulum meum. Aderant Gothi tribuni, adoriebar eos, dicens: Propterea vos possessio Romana suscepit, ut perturbationis publicae vos praebeatis ministros? Quo transibitis, si haec deleta fuerint?* All translations of Ambrose's texts are from Liebeschuetz 2010.
31 Liebeschuetz 2010: 131–132.
32 Amb., *Ep.* 75a (Maur. 21a) 6. Cf. '*athleta Christi*' at *Ep.* 75a (Maur. 21a) 15.
33 Cf. Amb., *Ep.* 76 (Maur. 20) 12, 16, 20; McLynn 1994: 182–183. For the Goths in Valentinian's army, see Heather 1994., esp. 340–341. Ambrose also emphasizes the foreignness of his rival Auxentius, an ex-bishop of Durostorum and a namesake of Ambrose's predecessor in Milan: Amb. *Ep.* 75 (Maur. 21) 8, *Ep.* 76 (Maur. 20) 22. As an Arian, Auxentius had been expelled and had taken refuge in Valentinian II's court in Milan.
34 Amb., *Ep.* 75a (Maur. 21a) 1: *Deserendae Ecclesiae mihi voluntatem subesse non posse, quia plus dominum mundi quam saeculi huius imperatorem timerem, sane si me vis aliqua abduceret ab ecclesia, carnem meam exturbari posse non mentem.*
35 The conflict of the second year over the basilica Portiana and basilica Nova is described in detail at Amb., *Ep.* 76 (Maur. 20).
36 Amb., *Ep.* 76 (Maur. 20) 19: "*Domum privati nullo potes iure temerare, domum dei existimas auferendam?" Allegatur imperatori licere omnia, ipsius esse universa. Respondeo: "Noli te gravare, imperator, ut putes te in ea quae divina sunt imperiali aliquod ius*

habere. Noli te extollere sed si vis diutius imperare esto deo subditus. Scriptum est: Quae Dei Deo, quae Caesaris Caesari. Ad imperatorem palatia pertinent, ad sacerdotem ecclesiae. Publicorum tibi moenium ius commissum est, non sacrorum". Cf. Amb., *Ep.* 75a (Maur. 21a) 5, where Ambrose gives examples of private properties.
37 For definitions of sacred space in the Roman Republic, see Russell 2016: ch. 5.
38 P. Brown emphasizes that, in fact, the very notion of sacred was redefined during Late Antiquity: Brown 1996.
39 Cf. Maier 1994: 88.
40 Amb., *Ep.* 75a (Maur. 21a) 3: *Ad palatium imperatoris irem libenter, si hoc congrueret sacerdotis officio, ut in palatio magis certarem quam in ecclesia. Sed in consistorio non reus solet Christus esse sed iudex.*
41 Amb., *Ep.* 75a (Maur. 21a) 29.
42 On Auxentius, see earlier in this chapter. On this invitation, see McLynn 1994: 173; Liebeschuetz 2010: 131–132.
43 Amb. *Ep.* 75 (Maur. 21) 20: *et intra palatium certare non possum, qui palatii secreta nec quaero, nec novi.* Ambrose states that other (unnamed) bishops and the people, too, agreed that the palace was not a place for a bishop: *Ep.* 75 (Maur. 21) 17.
44 Amb., *Ep.* 75a (Maur. 21a) 15: *Ego ipse non cottidie vel visitandi gratia prodibam vel pergebam ad martyres? Non regiam palatii praetexebam eundo atque redeundo? Et tamen nemo me tenuit, cum exturbandi me haberent, ut prodiderunt postea, voluntatem, dicentes: "Exi de civitate et vade quo vis.".* Cf. Amb., *Ep.* 75 (Maur. 21) 18.
45 See the map above.
46 On Ambrose's building program from an archaeological perspective, see Lusuardi Siena et al. 2015.
47 Piétri 1976: 3–69; Krautheimer 1980: 3–31.
48 Arslan 1982: 204–206.
49 Maier 1994: 90–92.
50 Maier 1994: 88.
51 Amb., *Ep.* 77 (Maur. 22) 12–13. Maier sees this, too, as an intentional jab towards the Arians: Maier 1994: 92. On the basilica, see Bovini 1970: 220–250; Mirabella Roberti 1984: 120–124; Caporusso et al. 2014: 240–247.
52 Krautheimer 1983: 79.
53 Caporusso et al. 2014: 241.
54 McLynn 2004. C. Machado (2019: 126) observes similar behaviour among the Roman aristocracy of this time period: 'At a time of profound religious and political changes, members of the Roman aristocracy found new opportunities to engage in the city's festive life, turning the city space into a stage where their power was reaffirmed and celebrated'. On the transformation of the imperial ceremonial, including the *adventus*, in Late Antiquity, see MacCormack 1981.
55 Liebeschuetz 2010: 129. *Prodire* at: Amb. *Ep.* 75a (Maur. 21a) 30, *Ep.* 76 (Maur. 20) 11, 27.
56 Amb., *Ep.* 75a (Maur. 21a) 29: *Nonne meminerunt quod ubi me cognovit populus palatium petisse, ita irruit, ut vim ejus ferre non possent; quando comiti militari cum expeditis ad fugandam multitudinem egresso obtulerunt omnes se neci pro fide Christi?*
57 Amb., *Ep.* 76 (Maur. 20) 4–5.
58 Amb., *Ep.* 76 (Maur. 20) 20. Even the children participated, in a way: Ibidem 24.
59 Amb., *Ep.* 75a (Maur. 21a) 36: *Imperator enim intra ecclesiam non supra ecclesiam est.*
60 For a thorough analysis of this request, see McLynn 1994: 209–219.
61 For the whole event, see Amb., *Ep.* 77 (22 Maur). Cf. Dassmann 1975; Zangara 1981. Reputedly, the location had been revealed to him in a dream: Aug., *Conf.* 9.7.16.
62 Amb., *Ep.* 77 (22 Maur) 2.
63 Machado 2019: 181–182.
64 *Defensores* and *milites Christi* at Amb., *Ep.* 77 (22 Maur) 10.
65 McLynn 1994: 212–215, citation from page 212. On the importance of the cult of the Saints during this period, see Brown 2015: 1–49.

66 On the end of the conflict, see Aug., *Conf.* 9.7.16; Paul. Mil., *V. Amb.* 15.1; Paul. Nola, *Carm.* 19.328.
67 Soz., *HE* 7.25. For Ambrose and Theodosius I, see Liebeschuetz 2010: 17–21.
68 Citation from McLynn 1994: 217.

References

Arslan, E. A. 1982: 'Urbanistica di Milano Romana. Dall'insediamento Insubre alla capitale dell'Impero', in H. Temporini (ed.), *ANRW II 12.1*, Berlin and Boston, MA, 179–211.

Blockley, P., and Provenzali, A. 2013: 'La trasformazione dell'area all'epoca dell'imperatore Massimiano', in Comune di Milano – Civico Museo Archeologico (ed.), *Archeologia a Milano: L'area del Monastero Maggiore in Epoca Romana*, Milano, 37–68.

Bovini, G. 1970: *Antichità Cristiane di Milano*, Bologna.

Brown, P. 1992: *Power and Persuasion in Late Antiquity: Towards a Christian Empire*, Madison, WI.

Brown, P. 1996: *The Making of Late Antiquity*, Cambridge, MA.

Brown, P. 2015: *The Cult of the Saints: Its Rise and Function in Latin Christianity*, Chicago, IL.

Calderini, A., Chierici, G., and Cecchelli, C. 1951: *La Basilica di S. Lorenzo Maggiore in Milano*, Milano.

Caporusso, D., Donati, M. T., Masseroli, S., and Tibiletti, T. 2014: *Immagini Di Mediolanum: Archeologia e Storia di Milano dal V Secolo a.C. al V Secolo d.C.*, Milano.

Dassmann, E. 1975: 'Ambrosius und die Märtyrer', *Jahrbuch für Antike und Christentum* 18, 49–68.

David, M. 1999: '"... Palatinaeque arces...". Temi di architettura palaziale a Milano tra III e X secolo', in M. David (ed.), *'Ubi Palatio Dicitur': Residenze di Re e Imperatori in Lombardia*, Cinisello Balsamo, 9–46.

Gwynn, D. M. 2010: 'Archaeology and the "Arian Controversy" in the Fourth Century', in S. Bangert, L. Lavan, and D. M. Gwynn (eds), *Religious Diversity in Late Antiquity*, Leiden, 229–263.

Heather, P. J. 1994: *Goths and Romans: 332–489*, Oxford.

Kinney, D. 1972: 'The Evidence for the Dating of S. Lorenzo in Milan', *Journal of the Society of Architectural Historians* 31(1), 92–107.

Krautheimer, R. 1980: *Rome: Profile of a City, 312–1308*, Princeton, NJ.

Krautheimer, R. 1983: *Three Christian Capitals*, Berkeley, Los Angeles, CA and London.

Lenox-Conyngham, A. 1982: 'The Topography of the Basilica Conflict of A.D. 385/6 in Milan', *Historia: Zeitschrift für Alte Geschichte* 31(3), 353–363.

Lenox-Conyngham, A. 1985: 'Juristic and Religious Aspects of the Basilica Conflict of A. D. 386', *Studia Patristica* 18, 55–58.

Lewis, S. 1969: 'Function and Symbolic Form in the Basilica Apostolorum at Milan', *Journal of the Society of Architectural Historians* 28(2), 83–98.

Lewis, S. 1973: 'San Lorenzo Revisited: A Theodosian Palace Church at Milan', *Journal of the Society of Architectural Historians* 32(3), 197–222.

Liebeschuetz, J. H. W. G. 2004: 'The Collected Letters of Ambrose of Milan: Correspondence with Contemporaries and with the Future', in L. Ellis and F. Kidner (eds), *Travel, Communication, and Geography in Late Antiquity: Sacred and Profane*, Milton Park, Abingdon and Oxon, 95–107.

Liebeschuetz, J. H. W. G. 2010: *Political Letters and Speeches*, Liverpool.

Lusuardi Siena, S. 1996: 'Il complesso episcopale di Milano: riconsiderazione della testimonianza ambrosiana nella Epistola ad sororem', *Antiquité Tardive* 4, 124–132.

Lusuardi Siena, S., Neri, E., and Greppi, P. 2015: 'Le chiese di Ambrogio e Milano. Ambito topografico ed evoluzione costruttiva dal punto di vista archeologico', in P. Boucheron and S. Gioanni (eds), *La Memoria di Ambrogio di Milano: usi Politici di una autorità patristica in Italia (Secc. V-XVIII)*, Rome, 31–86.

MacCormack, S. 1981: *Art and Ceremony in Late Antiquity*, Berkeley, CA.

Machado, C. 2019: *Urban Space and Aristocratic Power in Late Antique Rome: AD 270–535*, Oxford and New York.

Maier, H. O. 1994: 'Private Space as the Social Context of Arianism in Ambrose's Milan', *The Journal of Theological Studies* 45(1), 72–93.

McLynn, N. B. 1994: *Ambrose of Milan: Church and Court in a Christian Capital*, Berkeley, CA.

McLynn, N. B. 2004: 'The Transformation of Imperial Church-going in the Fourth Century', in S. Swain and M. Edwards (eds), *Approaching Late Antiquity: The Transformation from Early to Late Empire*, Oxford, 235–270.

Mirabella Roberti, M. 1967: 'Il recinto fortificato Romani di San Vittore a Milano', *Castellum* 6, 95–110.

Mirabella Roberti, M. 1984: *Milano Romana*, Milano.

Piétri, C. 1976: *Roma christiana: Recherches sur l'Eglise de Rome, son organisation, sa politique, son idéologie de Miltiade à Sixte III (311–440)*. Bibliothèque des Écoles Francaises d'Athènes et de Rome 224, Rome.

Piras, F. 2012: 'L'edificio romano di via Brisa: un settore del palazzo imperiale di Milano', *Rivista Online Della Scuola Di Specializzazione in Archeologia Dell'Università Degli Studi Di Milano* 11, 35–83.

Russell, A. 2016: *The Politics of Public Space in Republican Rome*, Cambridge.

Salzman, M. 2013: 'Leo's Liturgical Topography: Contestations for Space in Fifth-Century Rome', *Journal of Roman Studies* 103, 208–232.

Villa, E. 1956: 'Come risolse S. Ambrogio il problema delle chiese alla periferia di Milano', *Ambrosius: Rivista di spiritualità ambrosiana* 32(1), 1–25.

Williams, D. H. 1995: *Ambrose of Milan and the End of the Nicene-Arian Conflicts*, Oxford and New York.

Williams, M. S. 2017: *The Politics of Heresy in Ambrose of Milan: Community and Consensus in Late Antique Christianity*, Cambridge.

Williams, M. S. 2018: 'No Arians in Milan? Ambrose on the Basilica Crisis of 385/6', *Historia: Zeitschrift für Alte Geschichte* 67(3), 346–365.

Zangara, V. 1981: 'L'inventio dei martiri Gervasio e Protasio', *Augustinianum* 21, 119–133.

Part V
Coda

15 Afterword

Space and Roman Administration[1]

Antonio Lopez Garcia

This volume opens a new chapter in the historiography of Roman administration. It discusses key aspects of Roman institutional culture in a novel way, including the effects of governmental systems on physical space. Indeed, the studies presented in these chapters may well reveal a new direction for the field. The four parts of this book balance the dissection and comprehension of written sources with an exploration of built space in search of past human interactions – whether as individuals, groups, or institutions – with their cities and environs.

The lens offered by The Spatial Turn has recently spurred a paradigm shift in Roman studies. For obvious reasons, the use of the theoretical framework offered by The Spatial Turn has been our focus here, as it offers a comprehensive method of analyzing the available sources that emphasizes the importance of understanding space as a social and cultural product. This framework helps scholars to understand the ways in which the built environment was designed and used, as well as to recognize how public and private spaces shaped social and cultural practices – for example, to understand how different social groups interacted with each other or to shed light on the social and political hierarchies of the time. This approach is well suited to studying the spatial organization of many different aspects of the Roman world, and the study of Roman administration can certainly benefit from it.

Future research in the field of Roman administration must consider all of the elements that affected the development and performance of the tasks involved in the everyday life of Roman officials and their influence over the populace. Societies were spatially structured, and space is an element that future researchers should not disregard when analyzing the written sources, which often reflect only the personal – and biased – opinions of an ancient author about a political or administrative process, but do not portray the physical reality of that process, such as the space needed to carry out an official's assigned duties.

One of the main reasons that we wrote this volume was to offer an alternative to the traditional debates about the topography of administration by examining key elements such as the distinction between public and private, the movement of the magistrates, the placement of the organs of the administration within the urban tissue, and the multifunctionality of public spaces, among many other aspects.

How did all of these elements affect the practice of governance within the urban and statal context? Why did public spaces have such particular shapes? How did administrative practices fit into the built fabric of the city? How did all of the institutional organs interact with people and space? These are just some of the questions that we have endeavoured to answer in the previous pages, but these are also some of the questions that researchers must address when examining future discoveries, or when re-evaluating past observations.

Future investigations of administrative space must insist on the necessity of defining the nature of those spaces in many different ways. For example, we perceive the administrative space as existing in tension between the public nature of the buildings or open spaces – as they were originally conceived – and the private nature of the individuals that compose the society that conceived of those spaces, used them, and sometimes abused them. In this volume, we see many practical examples of this "abuse" of administrative space. Well-known examples of these abusive practices include the use of the fora and the basilicas for private activities such as trading or banking, the penetration of the magistrates' families in the provincial seats, and the use of public piazzas for profitable recreational activities to gain the favour of the citizens. Such abuse of the space can be bidirectional, and sometimes it was the private space of a magistrate that suffered an invasion of public life; some administrative tasks such as office work, the collection of archival material, and the conducting of meetings and trials could take over the private spaces of public officials.

Additionally, we must recognize a key feature of public space: multifunctionality. When analyzing a public space, we must be aware of the multiple purposes that it could have served. These purposes could have been enacted simultaneously, and might also have changed over time. Only rarely do we find a monofunctional public space. When thinking about the public space for an administrative function, we can see many activities incorporated there, which could have been bureaucratic, political, judicial, defensive, etc. Oftentimes, those administrative functions intermingled with other types of functions that may have been non-administrative, such as entertainment or cult. All of these activities could also have been either public or private. Thus, the analysis of these features has been one of the keys to the realization of this volume.

In the four sections comprising this book, we addressed several aspects that are essential to understanding the general development of Roman administration, as well as some specific case studies that provide a new conception of administrative space. The first section, "*Theory and methodology*", is the result of applying a combination of theoretical approaches that examine the uses of space to an examination of the current state of the art. The two chapters included in this section create a general framework to understand the essential and practical needs of Roman administration and how the historical expansion of this model within the city of Rome took form. Instead of using the traditional approach offered by Roman topographers and legal scholarship – which sometimes abuse a naive interpretation of administrative spaces and neglect the study of the practical functions of such spaces – this section offers an approach that focuses on the practicalities of administration and proposes a series of key questions about the physical needs of the main activities and institutions.

The second section, "*The space of the magistrate and politics*", offers three different case studies that examine administrative and political processes involving the Roman people and high-ranking officials. Although voting processes have been studied from several perspectives, previous studies often lack an examination of the practical needs of such a complex activity, which included managing large crowds in the forum. Similarly, the everyday work of magistrates has also been neglected in previous studies, which often focused on the most ceremonial aspects of their duties, ignoring their integration within the urban space and their interaction with the populace. For example, the locations of magistrates such as the aediles within the city were key to the effective implementation of their official duties. Movement through various spaces was also a significant part of magistrate's routines, and here we find a case study that examines the footprint of this movement in both the written sources and the archaeological record, to rebuild the quotidian path of officials inside a Roman city. Archaeological sources can provide clues about how people moved through space and interacted with their environment, but the fragmentary nature of surviving Roman cities might add extra difficulty to interpreting movement within the cityscape. The cautious approach followed in this stimulating study, which combines written and archaeological sources with spatial analysis, sheds some light on a challenging topic that will become a key methodology to understanding the everyday life of Roman magistrates.

"*The space of the institutions*" is the third part of this volume. The chapters included in this section dissect several aspects of known institutional organs of Roman administration, such as the Urban Prefecture and its hierarchy of institutions, and the relations of the institutions with semi-administrative associations such as *collegia* and *scholae*. Public institutions took control of the cityscape of Rome through several organs that administered all of the aspects of Roman public life, leaving an enormous footprint in many areas of the city. However, some duties of public administration were in the hands of professional associations. The power of the guilds was so significant for the common people that they became an essential part of the governance of Rome, and thus they gained the favour of the rulers as an essential part of the city administration.

However, the city of Rome is not the only focus of this volume; two case studies about the key spaces of provincial administration complete the third section. On the one hand, the role of civic archives in the implementation of Roman hegemony in the Eastern provinces illustrates the significant function of these administrative buildings to display the authority of Rome. On the other hand, we have the main administrative organ of Rome in the provinces: the *praetoria*. These essential organs of provincial administration were not only places of authority, but – as demonstrated here – also places for the families of the officials. Both classical authors and epigraphy confirm that archival/librarian buildings and *praetoria* were an essential part of magistrates' private lives. In this section we can clearly see how blurry, flexible, and permeable the border between private and public spaces was for the Romans.

In the fourth section of this volume, "*Displaying authority over the public space and religious space*", we offer four contributions that assess how the authorities displayed their power in two types of spaces: piazzas and religious spaces. The visual exhibition of power was a fundamental element of obtaining the favour of the population. It was a way to establish legitimacy and reinforce authority that could be manifested in many different ways but did not always work out as originally planned. The results depended much on the context and the specific strategies used by the administrators. For example, architectural projects were one of the most common ways to project power and shape the public's perceptions of those in power. Art and imagery were also powerful tools that permeated public space in Roman times to promote official ideology and reinforce the power of the state and the authority of some specific individuals. However, this authority was not only displayed in public spaces by the addition of permanent material elements to the cityscape. Ephemeral acts such as public ceremonies were also a powerful tool for projecting power, shaping public perception, and promoting social cohesion. Nevertheless, some of these elements were subject to contestation and resistance by marginalized groups, or by religious authorities seeking to challenge the dominant power structures of the time. One of the aims of the fourth section is the examination, through four case studies, of a variety of physical elements – such as the monumentalization of the Roman Forum and the Christian basilicas – and also ephemeral acts – such as the use of public space for entertainment activities and the attempts by the Roman authority to abuse religious spaces. The soft border between the Roman rulers and their use of public space became very penetrable over time. In contrast, the relationship between the administration and the official religion is a key question to understanding one of the firmest borders faced by public rulers. Indeed, the limited influence of Roman authorities over religious spaces – especially in the late imperial era – shows how Roman law could sometimes be very strict in matters of space.

Note

1 This work is part of the project "Law, Governance and Space: Questioning the Foundations of the Republican Tradition". This research has received funding from the European Research Council (ERC) under the European Union's Horizon 2020 research and innovation programme (grant agreement No 771874). This research has also received funding from the Next Generation framework of the European Commission through the programme "María Zambrano" for the attraction of international talent, which I hold through the University of Granada.

Index

Acacius 275–277
Achaia 170, 211
Acilia Plecusa 222
Adriatic 218
Aedes Iuturnae 166
Aelianus, Q. Axius 220–226
Aemilia Paulina Asiatica 41
Aemilius Paullus 83
Aerarium 14, 27–29, 53–56, 62, 74–79, 82–89, 123–124, 131, 141–142, 151, 174, 246–247, 261–262, 307, 325
Agapius 338
Agora 51, 129, 141, 205
Agrippa 126, 131, 185, 258, 323, 324–327
Akmoneia 248
Albanum 334
Albinus, Lucceius 238
Alesia 185–195, 227, 228, 229, 236'
Alexander, Appius 219, 282
Alexandria 264
Altars: Altar of Dis and Proserpina 317; Altar of Domitius Ahenobarbus 61; Altar of the Scribes 61, 76, 103, 119, 125
Ambrose of Milan 7, 349, 366–367
Ammianus Marcellinus 32, 201, 313
Anastasius 342, 344
Antequera 277, 284
Antioch 160
Antium 291, 294
Aphrodisias 203,
Apollinaris, Aelius 220
Apollo 30–33, 122, 140–142, 244, 316
Appian 266
Apronilla 270
Apuleius 106
Aquae Hypsitanae 221
Aquaeductium 174

Aquincum 181, 195–196
Arcadius 275
arcarii Caesariani 54, 55, 68
Archive of Juno Moneta 32
Argiletum 194
Aristotle 42, 198
Arızlı 204, 209
Arles 195, 217
Artemis 243–244, 119, 282
Asclepiades 248, 249
Asconius 134–140, 220, 236, 292–300
Asia Minor 1, 9, 241, 247–249, 256–261, 281
Asinius Pollio 32
Astura 291–294
Asturica Augusta 271–273
Athens 30, 193, 243, 282, 300
Atria: *Atrium Libertatis* 27–32, 41, 76–77, 82–87, 246, 201; *Atrium Maenium* 292–297, 301
Attalus III 251
Atticilla, Iulia 219, 225, 135, 149, 247, 309, 323–324, 358
Attis 219, 226
Auditoria of Hadrian 20, 163, 165
Augusta Taurinorum 277
Augusta Trevorum 353
Aulus Gabinius 289, 302
Aulus Gellius 31, 32, 132, 108
Aurelian 151
Aurelian Steps 18
Aurelian Wall 16, 21
Aurelius Artemidorus 187
Aurelius Victor 18
Ausonius 351
Auxentius 347–360
Aventine 22, 28, 42–43, 100, 118, 153, 184, 226

304 *Index*

Baetica 276, 277
Baia Prudentilla 223
Bakatha 342
balneum 275
Barachos 342
Basilicas (Ancient): *Basilica Antoniarum Duarum* 193; *Basilica Argentaria* 183; *Basilica Fulvia-Aemilia* 18; *Basilica Hilariana* 224, 226, 227, 237; *Basilica Iulia* 18, 31, 158, 162,; Basilica of Maxentius 20, 161, 163; Basilica of Ostia 339; *Basilica Opimia* 18; *Basilica Paulli* 159, 167; *Basilica Piniani* 342, 346; *Basilica Porcia* 18, 118, 293; *Basilica Portiana* 350, 354, 355, 356, 358, 363, 350, 354, 355, 356, 358, 363; *Basilica Sempronia* 18; *Basilica Ulpia* 18, 25–26, 54, 162, 217, 230–231
Bassus, Titus Pomponius 42
Baths of Trajan 159–160, 167
Bellicius, Valerius 160–163, 171–172
Bithynia 218
bouleuterion 205
Brigetio 223
Britannia 38–89, 354
Brolo 362
Brutus, Decimus Junius 263
Building of Eumachia 182, 192

Caelian hill 153, 154, 160, 166, 182
Caesarea Maritima 216, 224, 231
Caesidius Respectus 220
Caius Cracchus 83–86, 93
Caligula 255
Calpurnius Quadratus 220
Campidano 222
Campus Agrippae 33, 151, 166
Campus Martius 32, 63, 86, 153–154, 201, 268
cancelli, cancellus 53, 163
Cape Miseno 220
Capitoline 22–26, 32, 43, 75, 101, 164–166, 255
Capua 271
Caracalla 24, 31, 157, 220–223
Carbo, C. Papirius 86
Carinae 150, 171, 175
Carthage 103, 118, 119, 272
Carvilia Censonilla 222, 223
Casa del Medico 131, 142
Casa della Rissa nell'Anfiteatro 131

Caseggiato dei Triclini 182–185, 188
Cassius Dio 61, 155, 259, 266
castellum aquarum 154
Castra Praetoria 151, 166
Castricius, L. 203
Catilina, Lucius Sergius 91
Cato 24, 64, 73, 84, 92, 214, 238–245, 264
Cattunilla 223, 228
Catulus, Q. Lutatius 105, 263
Cauponae 178
Censorinus, L. Marcius 243, 249
Christian basilicas and churches: St. Agnes outside the walls (Rome) 274; St. Ambrogio, *Basilica Martyrum* (Milan) 350, 360–363; St. Bartolomeo (Rome) 44, 155, 166; Saints Cosmas and Damian (Rome) 25, 170; St. Dionigi, St. Salvatore, *Basilica Prophetarum* (Milan) 289; Saints Gervasius and Protasius (Milan) 291; Holy Apostles (Constantinople) 289; Holy Cross in Jerusalem (Rome) 338; Holy Sepulchre (Jerusalem) 340; St. Lawrence outside the walls (Rome) 275; St. Maria Antiqua (Rome) 154, 166; St. Mary the Theotokos (Jerusalem) 342; St. Nazaro in Brolo, *Basilica Apostolorum* (Milan) 289; St. Paul outside the walls (Rome) 274–277; St. Peter (Rome) 272–276; St. Pietro in Vincoli (Rome) 160–167, 182; St. Simpliciano, *Basilica Virginum* (Milan) 289; St. Tecla, *Basilica Nova* (Milan) 292; St. Vittore al Corpo (Milan) 355
Cilicia 205, 262
Circus: Circus Flaminius 113, 119, 163, 167, 263; Circus Maximus 30–36, 100–105, 163–167, 253–263
Cirta 274, 277
Città Dipinta, La 159, 160
Claudius 29, 43, 109, 169, 179–180, 191–192, 253
Clemens, Sex. Truttedius 220
Clodius 23, 88, 92, 96–109, 117, 119, 267
Cluentius 236
Codeta 264
Coelius, Q. 29
Collegium Silvani 184
Colosseum 31, 62, 270
Colossus of Memnon 224

Columna Maenia 7, 235–250
Column of Duillius 244
Column of Trajan 26
Comitium 16, 50, 61–66, 79, 82–97, 125, 235–239
Commodus 171
Constantia 274
Constantina 276
Constantine 7, 153, 169, 180, 269–289
Corduba 222
Cossonius, L. 221, 231
Crassus, Gaius Licinius 47, 82, 83, 84, 95, 238
Crassus, P. Licinius 41
Crispus, Gaius Sallustius 276
Critonius 107, 115, 258
Crypta Balbi 166–168
Cubicula 67
curae, curatores 150–156; *cura annonae* 60, 69; *cura aquarum, procuratores aquarum, curator aquarum et Minuciae* 51, 60, 65–69, 71–75, 154, 173; *curatores* or *praefecti frumenti dandi* 156; *cura ludorum* 252; *curator operis theatri* 155; *curatores regionum* 155; *cura riparum et alvei Tiberis* 154–155; *cura sacrarum et operum publicorum* 43, 154; *curator statuarum* 155; *curatories viarum* 155; *procurator monetae* 56
Cures Sabini 223
Curia Athletarum 171, 181–182, 191, 193
Curia Iulia 54, 69, 83, 163–167, 172, 256
Curia Hostilia 79, 95, 237
Curio, Gaius Scribonius 91, 253, 257, 262–264
Cybele 118, 179, 184
Cyriaces 275
Cyril Scythopolis 280

Dacia Apulensis 219
Dalmatia 225, 227, 229, 232
Daphnus, M. Aurelius 219
Dara 276
Decianus, C. Appuleius 203
Decimus Junius Brutus Pera 263
Deiotarus 58
Demeter 205
Desidiena Cincia 219
Desidienus Aemilianus 225
Diaconus, Marcus 280
Dianysius of Halicarnassus 42

Diocletian 31, 45, 155–157, 220, 274, 283
Domesticus, Marcus Ulpius 182
Domitian 24, 224
Domitius Ulpianus 26, 54, 158–159, 217, 276
domus Cilonis 158, 159
Domus of Aemilia Paulina Asiatica 41
Domus of L. Marius Vegetinus 42, 46
Domus of M. Aemilius Scaurus' father 20
Domus of Nummii 42, 46
Domus of P. Vergilius Maro 41
Domus of Q. Marcius Rex 42, 47
Domus of T. Pomponius Bassus 42
Domus of Volusius Saturninus 19, 46
Domus Pescenniana 41, 46
Domus Tiberiana 25–26
Dorylaion 203
Dracilianus 276
Drusus 36–39, 108, 267
Durostorum 288, 293
Dyme 211, 214

Echion 104
Egypt 54, 114, 191, 208, 214–216
Elias 276
Ephesus 182, 209, 219, 229
Esquiline 32, 99, 150, 182
Eumenes II 204
Eusebius of Caesarea 272, 275
Euthymius 275
Eutropia 276
excubitorium 153, 165

Faberius 41, 47
Fabius Cilo 158
Fabius Felix Passifilus Paulinus 163, 175
Falerii Novii 122
Fannius 107, 115
Favonius 257
Festus 95, 211, 238, 275, 241, 275
Fidus, Cornelius 218, 225
Firmianus, Lactantius Caecilius 68
Flaccus, L. Valerius 202, 209
Flavia Marcellina 221
Flavian 159, 160, 167, 222, 267
Flavia T. f. Tertulla 222–223
Flavius, Cn. 108
Flavius Valila 274
Flavola, Terentia 29
Forma Urbis 25, 62, 141, 159, 170
Fora: *Forum Cuppidinis* 239; *Forum Esquilinum* 33; *Forum Iulium* 257, 263,; Forum of Augustus

28–29, 62, 162, 170–172; Forum of Trajan 25–26, 29, 54, 153, 162, 167, 175; *Forum Piscatorium* 240; Roman Forum, *Forum Romanum* 5, 7, 16–21, 26–33, 46, 74–97, 154, 162, 174, 177, 243, 248–254, 260–263, 303; *Forum Suarium* 151, 156, 166, 170; *Forum Vespasiani* 62, 171; Imperial Fora 17, 18, 26, 32, 62, 162, 173; *Templum Pacis* 25, 62, 70, 159, 170, 173; Triangular Forum (Pompeii) 126
Francesco da Sangallo 161
Frontinus 54, 55, 65, 71, 73, 74, 177, 195
Fronto, Manius Acilius 222
Fulgentius 163, 171
Fulvius, C. 29
Fundilius, L. 99, 100, 112
Funisulana Vettula 224
Furius Camillus 240

Galatia 204, 217, 231
Galba 41, 218
Galenos, Klaudios 43
Gallicanus 275
Gallus Vecilius 221, 231
Ganymedes 104–112
Gaul 97, 196, 231, 232, 285
Gaza 276
Graecostasis 61
Granius Licinianus 42
Gratian 285, 292
Grattius Faliscus 114

Hadrian 157, 162–170, 187–190
Heraclides 203
Herculaneum 74, 75, 118, 143, 182–187, 192
Hercules 29
Herculius 275
Herennius Gemellinus 220, 226
Herod's Palace 216
Hilarus, Manius Poblicius 184, 192
Hispalis 222
Hispania 191, 195, 223, 226, 229
Honoratus, L. Flavius 221
Honoratus, Maurus Servius 221, 227
Honoratianus, Flavius 221
Honorius 283, 292
Horace 40, 43, 114, 117, 171, 238, 241–250, 259, 267
Horreum 220
Hortalus, Q. Hortensius 20

horti 20
Hortus Philippi 291
Hostilia Faustina 220
House of Caecilius Iucundus 56
House of the Faun 55
Hybromius 275
Hypata 106

Isidorus 42, 238, 248
Isola Tiberina 28, 44
Iulius Caesar, L. 192
Iustina 220, 227

Jerusalem 25, 216, 275, 276, 276, 277
Jesus 216
Josephus 42, 43, 264, 265
Judea 216
Julia 62, 263
Julius Caesar 17, 22, 29, 41, 87, 101, 128–129, 147–179, 185, 188, 190, 262–263, 288, 294
Justina 285, 291
Justinian 276, 281
Juvenal 113, 173

Karales 221, 222
Kos 199, 209

Lacus Curtius 28
Lacus Iuturnae 65, 71, 166–177, 193
Lamia, L. Aelius 29, 36, 37, 38, 39
Large Palaestra 126, 128, 140
Largo Argentina 29, 65, 72, 154, 166, 175
Largo G. Agnesi 161, 167
Lateran Basilica 272–275
Lavinium 237
Lentulus Sura 110
Lepidus, M. Aemilius 43
Leto 199
Leukothea 187
Libraries: *Bibliotheca ad Apollinis* 30; *Bibliotheca Ulpia* 32–33; Library of Hadrian 170; Library of Timgad 160
Ligarius 58
Liguria 285
Livia 17, 37, 217, 229, 267
Livineius Regulus, L. 267
Livius Drusus, M. 108
Livy 23, 63, 70–71, 80, 92, 100–101, 201, 238–242, 262
Lollianus 29

Index   307

Lollius Palicanus, L. 107
Longus, L. 267
Lucan 42
Lucceius Felix, M. 220, 226
Lucilius, Gaius 238, 241, 242, 244, 245
Lucius 106, 192
Lucullus 26
Lucus Augusti 223, 226, 228, 229, 230
Lugdunum 190
Lycia 207
Lydus, Johannes 158
Lysanias of Temnos 203
Lysias 212

Macarius of Jerusalem 276, 277
Macedonia 205
Macrobius 87, 140, 211, 262, 272, 278
Maecenas, Gaius Cilnius 150
Maenius, Gaius 235–246
Magonianus, Publius Magnius Rufus 222, 229
Mamertime Prison, *carcer* 65, 163–166, 237–247
Manius Manilius 126, 184, 192
Marcellina 221, 283, 287
Marcian 188
Marius, C. 85, 86, 93, 96, 102, 105
Mark Antony 123, 267
Marrinia M. f. Procula 220, 227
Martialis, Marcus Valerius 25, 43, 70, 124, 140, 159, 162, 170, 172
Matthew 216, 288
Mauretania Caesariensis 218
Maxentius 169
Maxima 220
Maximian 283, 292
Maximus, Valerius 95, 253, 255, 264
Menaechmus 106
Messalla, Vipstanus 123
Metellus Dalmaticus 83
Metellus Pius, Q. 247
Milan 7, 72, 119, 144, 174, 272, 280–296
Miletus 206, 256
Milvian Bridge 155
Misenum 184, 192, 220
Mithridates V Euergetes 204
Monime, Iulia 184
Monte Arci 222
Mount Peion 219
Mucius, Q. 123
Murena, A. Terentius Varro 266
Muru de Bangius 221, 232
Musei Capitolini 257

Naples 118, 142, 144, 181, 194, 272, 282
Nero 56, 108, 151, 166, 266
Nerva 29, 81, 88–93, 220
Nerva, P. 81
Nicolaus of Damascus 266
Nicomedes 203
Nonius 238, 244
Noricum 223
Novaria 106
Numidia 274, 276, 277
nymphaeum 201

Oak of Mamre 276, 277
officia publica 53
Ogulnius, Cn. 101
Ogulnius, Q. 101
Opimius, L. 86
Oppius, M. 258
Optatus of Milevis 272
Optatus, M. Valerius 221, 231
Oratorio dei Quaranta Martiri 154, 166
Oropos 212
Ostia 9, 142, 143, 144, 155, 182–188, 191–196, 271, 274
Otacilia 220
Othoca 220
Ovid 23, 24, 40, 43, 87, 166, 217, 218, 225
Ovidia 217, 218
Ovile 87, 91

Palatine 17, 19, 24–33, 40, 55, 58, 108, 110, 116, 163, 255, 264
Palestine 275, 276–277
Pannonia 181, 191
Pantheon 17, 32
Paros 199, 200, 214
Paulinus of Milan 293, 295
Pedanius Secundus 68
Pedianus, Quintus Asconius 191
Pergamon 203, 210, 215
Pesaro 179
Petreius 253
Petronius 100, 104, 105, 109, 114, 118
Philip the Arab 219, 225
Philo 224
Philtate 223, 228
Phoenicia 275
Phyrygia 204, 213, 215
Piazza del Duomo 283, 292
Piazza della Madonna di Loreto 163, 165
Piazza SS. Apostoli 166
Piazzale Labicano 257
Pica, P. Numicius 44

Piccolo Aventino 159
Pirro Ligorio 161
Piscina Publica 31, 45
Pisidia 208, 213, 231
Piso Frugi, M. Calpurnius 29
Piso, L. Calpurnius 29, 92, 108, 115, 151, 219, 226
Placidius, Ulpius 68
Plancus, L. Munatius 108
Platorinus, C. Sulpicius 107
Plautus 113, 117, 244, 249, 250, 269
Plinia 220
Pliny the Elder 45, 110, 220, 237
Pliny the Younger 56, 220
Plutarch 42, 64, 82–85, 95–96, 105, 113, 239, 257
plutei Traiani 57
Pollio, M. Barbatus 28
Polybius, C. Iulius 102, 104, 114, 214
Pomerium 23, 31, 60
Pompeii 5, 9, 43, 48, 57, 73, 75, 109–144, 154, 182, 192, 262, 268
Pompeius, Auctus 124
Pompeius, Sextus 256
Pompey the Great, *Pompeius Magnus* 106, 155, 252–257, 261–269
Pomponius 42, 46, 69
Pons Theodosii 276
Pontes 79–89, 92, 93
Pontius Pilate 216–218
Pontus 204
Pope Felix IV 270
Pope Leo III 273
Pope Marcus 273
Pope Sylvester 273
Pope Xystus III 273
Porphyry 40, 238–242, 248, 280
Porta di San Sebastiano 24
Porta Fontinalis 26
Porta Naevia 153, 166
Porta Ticinensis 286
Porta Vesuvio 118, 129, 137, 143
Porta Viminale 153, 166
Portico of Caecilius Metellus 83
Portico of Octavia, *porticus Octaviae* 24–26, 32
Portico of the Danaids 24
Porticus Minucia 65, 76, 114
Porticus Minucia Frumentaria 76, 114, 169
Porticus Minucia Vetus 114
praetoris officio 53
praetorium 67, 71, 74, 158, 218–231
Priene 206, 212

principia 67, 74
Prisca, Mulvia 110, 111, 112
Priscus, C. Vestorius 5, 99–119, 143
Provincia Asia 197, 205, 210
Prudens, Sextus Baius 223
Publicola, Valerius 64
Pulcher, Publius Clodius 119
Pullius Maximus 220, 227
Puteal Libonis 16
Pyramid of Cestius 28
Pythias 106
Python 199

quadriporticus 126, 140
Quintilian 17, 124
Quirinal Hill 23

Ravenna 283
Regia 63, 294
regiones 33, 132, 151; *II regio* 153, 166; *III regio* 150; *V regio* 153, 166; *VI regio* 143, 166; *VII regio* 152, 166; *VIII regio* 153; *XIV regio* 153, 166
Rhaetia 223
Romana, Aelia 202, 226
Roscius Otho, L. 264
Rostra 79, 80, 83, 88–96, 105–107, 168, 237, 240, 247
Rufinus, Tyrannius 293
Rufus, M. Holconius 138
Rullus, Publius Servilius 201
Rutilus Censorinus, C. Marcius 243, 249

Saba 276, 277
sacrarium 114
saepta 91, 251
Safinius 104, 105, 108, 109, 114
Sagalassos 217
Sallustius 276
Salona 225
San Lorenzo 286
Sardinia 221, 230, 231, 232
Sarmizegetusa 219, 230, 231
Saturnina, Aelia 220
Saturninus, C. Otacilius Octavius 220
scaena 102, 253–254, 265, 269
Scaurus, M. Aemilius 20, 109, 110, 116, 253, 262, 264, 267
scholae 6, 144, 176–195, 302; Schola of Fabri 186; Schola of the Dendrophori 182, 184; *Schola Xanthi* 189

Scipio, P. Cornelius 247
Scipio Aemilianus 83
Scipio Nasica Corculum, P. 256
scrinia 62, 160, 161, 167
Scutarius 124
Scylla 247
Sebastenus, M. Aurelius 222, 228
secretaria, secretarium 18, 53, 62, 63, 68, 160–167, 172, 175; *Secretarium Circi* 163, 167; *Secretarium Tellurense* 62
Sejanus 29, 151
Seneca 17, 216, 218, 223, 224
Septimia 223, 228
Septimus Severus 151, 155–158, 170, 220, 237
Servilius Caepio, Q. 115
Severus Alexander 22, 153
Severus, A. Caecina 217
Sibidounda 208–210
Sidonius Apollinaris 26
Silus, C. Albucius 106
Silvanus 184–185
Singilia Barba 222–223, 232
Smyrna 203, 219, 230
Socrates 292, 293
Sotidius Strabo Libuscidianus, Sex. 23, 217
Spinther, Publius Cornelius Lentulus 110, 116, 253
stationes 2, 9, 45, 53–56, 65–68, 72, 76, 153–156, 166–177, 187–195; *Statio alvei Tiberis* 155; *Statio Aquarum* 65, 72, 154, 173, 177, 189, 193
Subura 17, 159
Suetonius 24–25, 41–43, 70–71, 106–115, 124, 140, 155, 158, 166–171, 190–192, 218, 224–225
Sulla 26, 42, 47, 60, 201, 212
Sulpicius, Servius 29, 107, 241
Surdinus, L. 28
Surus, Cornelius 256, 257, 269
Symmachus, Quintus Aurelius 62, 159, 163, 172, 239–246, 277
Synnada 204

Tabularium 13, 22–24, 63–67, 70–76, 201, 211, 257
Tabularium Castrense 63
Tacitus 16–17, 43, 58, 62, 123–124, 150, 155, 217, 251–253, 261
Tarentum 255, 265

Tarraco 187, 194, 226
Temples (Ancient): Temple of Apollo 24, 26, 199, 254; Temple of Apollo Medicus 102; Temple of Apollo Sosianus 254; Temple of Bellona 254, 265; Temple of Castor and Pollux 79, 80–89, 90–98, 239; Temple of Ceres 22–26, 100–105, 114, 156, 167, 211; Temple of Concordia 29; Temple of Diana 65; Temple of Divus Augustus 25; Temple of Hestia 199; Temple of Honos and Virtus 247; Temple of Jerusalem 25; Temple of Juno Moneta 22; Temple of Jupiter Optimus Maximus 101, 102, 114, 263; Temple of Magna Mater 83, 102; Temple of Mars Avenger 124; Temple of Minerva 184, 187, 192; Temple of Saturn 22–24, 64; Temple of Tellus 99–100, 113, 161, 171; Temple of the Nymphs 22–23, 43, 221; Temple of Venus and Rome 161, 165; Temple of Venus Genetrix 263; Temple of Venus Victrix 266
Tertullian 255–256, 265–269
Tettius, C. 224
Theatre of Marcellus 255, 265
Theatri Pompeiani 169
Theodoret of Cyrrhus 293
Theodorus 276, 277
Theodosius 387, 275, 291, 295
Theophanes 275
Thermarum Traianorum 171
Thracia 171
Tiberius 29, 52, 62, 151–157, 216–218, 225, 231, 267
Tiberius Graccus 85
Tibur, Tivoli 117, 193, 231, 273
Titius, C. 211
Titius, Marcus 256
Tlos 207, 208, 210
Tomis 217
Trajan 25–32, 44, 54, 153–171, 175, 179, 182, 191–193, 220, 227
Trastevere 153, 155, 166
Trebellius, L. 266
tribunalia 62, 106, 163–164, 167
Trimalchio 104
Tryphon 207
Turris Libisonis 221–222
Tusculum 110

310 *Index*

Ulubrae 113
Urban Prefecture, *Praefectura Urbana, Urbanae Sedis* 1, 6–8, 60, 72, 116, 150–168, 173
Uselis 221

Valentinian I 285
Valentinian II 275, 282–296
Valentinian III 273
Valeria Modesta 221, 222, 224, 227
Varro, Marcus Terentius 23, 63, 69–73, 83, 99, 108, 113–118, 171, 246–248, 263–267
Velia 31, 160, 175, 183–188, 194
Velitrae 237
Velleius Paterculus 114, 115, 262–267
Veranius, Q. 207, 208, 210
Verecundus 223
Vespasian 25, 58, 62, 71, 124, 159, 171
vestibulum, vestibula 55, 123
Vesuvius 120, 125, 138
Via Anicia 155
Via Appia 184–185, 194
Via Ardeatina 273
Via Consolare 134
Via Conte Verde 153, 166
Via degli Annibaldi 160
Via del Cardello 161, 167
Via del Vesuvio 137
Via dell'Abbondanza 137, 139, 144
Via della Fortuna 137, 139
Via della Polveriera 161, 167, 171
Via della Terme 137
Via delle Sette Sale 171
Via delle Terme 185

Via di Nola 137, 139
Via Eudossiana 161
Via Lata 40
Viale Ipponio 165
Via Marco Aurelio 160
Via Mediana 132, 137, 139
Via Principe Eugenio 153
Via Sacra 25
Via San Bartolomeo dei Vaccinari 155, 166
Via Stabiana 132, 136–139
Via Venere Felice 131
Vicolo Cenci 155, 166
Vicolo dei Vettii 137
Vicolo del Centenario 132
Vicolo del Farmacista 135
Vicolo delle Nozze d'Argento 138
Vicolo di Lucrezio Frontone 133
Vicolo di Mercurio 134
Vicolo di Modesto 134
vicus, vici 33, 62, 150–153
Villa di Giulia Felice 126–129, 144
Villa Publica 63, 67, 71
villae rusticae 16
Viminal Hill 166
Virgil 41, 46
Vitellius 151, 218
Vitruvius 49–55, 68, 113–123, 140, 252, 262–266
Vopiscus, C. Iulius Caesar Strabo 115

Ygia 223, 228

Zenobius 275, 277
Zonaras, Johannes 113–114